PENGUIN REFERENCE BOOKS

THE PENGUIN DICTIONARY OF THE THIRD REICH

James Taylor is a pseudonym for Donald James who is a graduate in history of Pembroke College, Cambridge. He is one of the founders of the Dictionary & Reference Group, among whose titles are *A Dictionary of World War One*, *A Dictionary of the Second World War* and *The Green Book*. His television work (as Donald James) includes acting as script consultant on the ten part IBP documentary *Russia's War*. He is the author of several novels and his work has been translated into more than a dozen languages.

Warren Shaw graduated from Trinity College, Dublin, as the remaining leaders of the Third Reich were brought to trial at Nuremberg. A period of teaching preceded his appointment to the government service, where he represented Britain as a senior officer with the British Council in Africa and Latin America. Subsequently he specialized in Central European affairs. In 1985 his services in Germany were recognized by the award of the OBE. Warren Shaw died in London shortly after the first edition of this book was completed.

THE PENGUIN DICTIONARY OF
THE THIRD REICH

James Taylor and Warren Shaw

PENGUIN BOOKS

PENGUIN BOOKS

Published by the Penguin Group
Penguin Books Ltd, 27 Wrights Lane, London w8 5tz, England
Penguin Putnam Inc., 375 Hudson Street, New York, New York 10014, USA
Penguin Books Australia Ltd, Ringwood, Victoria, Australia
Penguin Books Canada Ltd, 10 Alcorn Avenue, Toronto, Ontario, Canada m4v 3b2
Penguin Books (NZ) Ltd, 182–190 Wairau Road, Auckland 10, New Zealand

Penguin Books Ltd, Registered Offices: Harmondsworth, Middlesex, England

First published by Grafton Books as *A Dictionary of the Third Reich* 1987
Revised edition published in Penguin Books under the present title 1997
1 3 5 7 9 10 8 6 4 2

Set in 9/10.5pt Monotype Bembo
Typeset by Rowland Phototypesetting Ltd, Bury St Edmunds, Suffolk
Printed in England by Clays Ltd, St Ives plc

CONTENTS

The authors wish to thank David O'Leary, Marie-France Ariès and Tim Greenhous for their invaluable contribution to the research and compilation of this dictionary.

PREFACE

Every such work as *The Penguin Dictionary of the Third Reich* is an attempt to walk the tightrope between the fullest possible and the most accessible description of the period. Our aim has been to provide a basic source of information for these vastly important and often misrepresented years, enabling students to orient themselves rapidly or the general reader to browse through the entries following a theme by use of the cross-references. The chronologies, too, have been designed for this dual purpose.

In writing the dictionary we have not felt bound by the narrow limits of the Third Reich itself. To make the rise of Nazism comprehensible we have considered it necessary to delve freely in the Weimar past, without some understanding of which the Nazi phenomenon would seem an even more horrific and extraordinary occurrence than it was. Similarly we have placed limits on the biographical entries and balanced the subject entries as we thought most useful.

The dominant figure of the founder of the Third Reich presented special problems: clearly only the most unwieldy entry on Adolf Hitler could have any claim to be complete. At the same time it would be impossibly repetitious of the rest of the book. We have therefore chosen to provide a more general discussion of Hitler in the entry under his name leaving the reader to pursue specific interests through related entries in the text.

Three institutions must be particularly mentioned for the help they have provided: the Goethe Institute in London, the former DDR State Library in Berlin and, of course, the Imperial War Museum. Acknowledgement must also be made to the contributions by David O'Leary, Marie-France Ariès and (in this edition) Tim Greenhous.

Sadly, Warren Shaw died before the preparation of this edition began, but his belief in the importance of making available an accessible historical dictionary of this period for students and the general reader never wavered. He continued to believe the Third Reich to be a period uniquely worthy of study.

Finally it is worth underlining the extent to which the world of film and television is today taking over the Third Reich, exploiting its colour and drama but blurring the edge of those lessons to be learnt from the Nazi past. If this book has in any way contributed to righting this imbalance it will have fulfilled its object.

JAMES TAYLOR, London, 1997

CHRONOLOGY

1933–9

1933

January   'The Hour of the Birth of the Third Reich': Von Papen and
Hitler agree on a coalition with Hitler as its head. Chancellor von
Schleicher fails to win breakaway groups from the Nazis (e.g.
Strasser) and is unable to keep control over the Reichstag parties.
He resigns and President Hindenburg is persuaded to give Hitler
the Chancellorship, which is celebrated by Nazi parades in Berlin.

February   Thirty-three Decrees published including the banning of rival
political meetings or publications, the dissolution of the Prussian
parliament. Raids on Communist Party offices. On 27 February,
the Reichstag Fire. Hitler given emergency powers by presidential
decree.

March   Thousands rounded up and put into camps by police and the
'auxiliary police', the SA. Dachau concentration camp opened.
Reichstag elections, with 89 per cent of the electorate voting,
give the Nazis only 43.9 per cent of the vote with a further 8 per
cent for their allies DNVP. This gives them a small overall
majority. The communist vote falls slightly and the SPD not at
all. SA troops in all states force state government resignations;
Bavarian state government suppressed. Von Epp appointed new
Nazi Governor with Himmler as Bavarian Police President.

Hitler speaks on *Gleichschaltung* (the co-ordination of the political
will). Decrees on amnesty for all Nazis who committed offences
during 'the struggle'; punitive measures against malicious gossip,
setting up of special ('people's') courts. Enabling Law (*Ermächtigungsgesetz*) passed, giving special powers to the Chancellor
(Hitler) for four years. Lex van der Lubbe passed, giving retrospective sanction to execution for arson. First Co-ordination Law of
States and Reich.

Göbbels appointed Minister for Propaganda, Schirach made head
of reformed Hitler Jugend and Himmler made police president
of Munich.

April   Official boycott of Jewish shops and professional men.

Second Co-ordination Law appointing State Governors.

All but Nazi-controlled publications effectively suppressed.

Law on the Reconstruction of the Professional Civil Services, making no distinction between Reich, State or civil service cadres and giving transferability between each. All unqualified, disloyal or Jewish staff to be dismissed (in the event, 90 per cent of the civil service remained).

Himmler made Commander of the Bavarian Political Police.

May   All Labour Unions dissolved. Seizure of assets of Communist Party (KPD). German Labour Front formed. Göbbels organizes nationally 'Burning of the Books'.

June   Reich Cabinet revised, including Darré as Minister of Food; First Law for the Reduction of Unemployment; Law on Payments Abroad; Law on Betraying the German Economy; Law on the Formation of the German Peasantry.

Decrees dissolving political parties:

SPD	22 June
DNVP	27 June
State party	28 June
DVP	4 July
Bavarian Party	4 July
Centre Party	5 July

Theodor Eicke becomes Commandant of Dachau.

July   Concordat between the Third Reich and the Vatican; Law Against the Establishment of Parties, making Nazi Party only legal party; Law to Confiscate Property Detrimental to Interests of People and State; Reich Regulations for the Corporate Reorganization of Agriculture.

August to September: Fifth Nuremberg Rally.
September First Winterhilfe Campaign; Law on Reich Food Costs; Reich Chamber of Culture established.

October   Reich Entailed Farm Law, stabilizing the ownership of small farms. All journalists registered and licensed to write.

Hitler takes Germany out of the League of Nations.

November National referendum: 95 per cent approve Nazi policy. *Kraft durch Freude*, 'Strength through Joy' movement founded.

Cardinal Faulhaber speaks out against Nazi anti-Christianity. Old Freikorps units given a ceremonial dismissal parade.

December Law to Secure Unity of Party and Reich. End of Reichstag Fire trial. Only van der Lubbe is found guilty.

1934

March   Ex-Chancellor Brüning leaves Germany, for safety, settling in the USA.

April   Himmler becomes Inspector of the Prussian Gestapo and Heydrich heads Gestapo.

June   SD made sole intelligence service of the party.

The 'Röhm Purge', following von Papen's Marburg speech. A shot fired at Hitler wounds Himmler and is supposed to have been fired by the SA escort. The League of German Officers disowns Röhm and expels him; the Abwehr claims to have secret SA orders to stage a *coup d'état*; the army commander cancels all leave. Himmler informs senior SS and SD officers of an impending SA revolt. Göring makes a speech against monarchists. Sepp Dietrich, commanding the SS Guard in Berlin, goes to army HQ and is given extra weapons and transport. The rumour spreads that the SA plan to kill the army old guard. Hitler travels from Berlin to Essen to attend the wedding of the local Gauleiter, Terboven.

The *Völkischer Beobachter* prints an article by Blomberg pledging loyalty to Hitler and asking for curbs on the SA; Hitler visits Labour Camps and goes on to Bad Godesberg near Bonn, on the Rhine, where he is joined by Göbbels; Göring mobilizes his Berlin police and SS units; the SA in Munich are ordered out aimlessly on the streets by anonymous notes, and the Gauleiter tells Hitler of this as proof of the SA's dissidence.

Hitler flies at dawn to Munich with Göbbels, his press chief Dietrich and Lutze of the SA; he orders Schmidt and Schneidhuber (the leading SA officers) to Stadelheim jail. The Gauleiter is given lists of SA men and others in Bavaria to arrest; Hitler drives to Bad Weissee where Röhm and other SA men are staying at a hotel. He orders them all to Stadelheim, some 200 of them, except for Heines, the SA commander of Silesia, who is found in bed with a male and shot immediately. Göbbels now sends a code-word 'Colibri' to Berlin for action: SA leaders in Berlin are taken to the army cadet school at Lichterfelde and shot straight away; murders of hundreds thought dangerous to the Nazis take place including ex-Chancellor von Schleicher. Hitler prepares announcements from the Brown House in Munich and flies back to Berlin. But for the fate of Röhm himself the Night of the Long Knives is over.

July   Hitler's order to kill Röhm in his cell is carried out by Eicke. A law is issued legitimizing all the killings. Hitler makes a speech in the Reichstag explaining and justifying the affair, claiming that only nineteen senior and forty-two other SA men had been shot, while thirteen had been shot resisting arrest and three had committed suicide. The SS formally separated from SA.

Austrian Chancellor Dollfuss killed in attempted Nazi coup.

August   Death of President Hindenburg. The office of President is abolished, Hitler supreme as Führer of the Third Reich and commander of the armed forces (OKH), imposing personal loyalty oath on all officers and men.

Theodor Eicke becomes Inspector of Concentration Camps; Feder leaves his official posts and retreats to Munich University; Fritsch becomes commander of the army. Cardinal Galen publishes a critique of Rosenberg.

October   All workers forced to join German Labour Front.

1935

January   The Saar plebiscite returns the Saar to Germany.

March   Treaty of Versailles disarmament clauses renounced by Hitler; universal conscription ordered.

April   Luftwaffe's existence declared.

September   Nuremberg laws on Jews promulgated. The Nazi swastika banner is made the national flag.

November   National Law of Citizenship: definition of Jew and *Mischling*, 'mixed race'. To be Aryan is a precondition for public appointments. First Decree of the Law for the Protection of German Blood and Honour; marriages between Aryan and Jew or *Mischling* forbidden.

1936

February   Gestapo given national status, with Heydrich as head.

March   Locarno Treaty renounced; German troops re-enter the Rhineland.

SS camp guards formed as Totenkopfverbände, of 3,000 men.

June   Himmler combines posts of Reichsführer SS with Chief of all German Police. Introduction of Labour Service.

July   Spanish Civil War begins.

August   Olympic Games, resulting in a quietening of anti-semitic campaigns. German triumphs somewhat marred by the gold medals of the black American Jesse Owens.

October   Göring initiates the Four-Year Plan.

November   Rome–Berlin Axis announced. Anti-Comintern Pact with Japan. German Condor Legion sent to Spain.

during 1936	Death of General von Seekt, founder of post-WWI German army. Abwehr spies jailed in USA.

1937

March	Pope Pius XI issues *Mit brennender Sorge*.
April	German planes bomb Guernica in Spain.
	Gördeler resigns as Mayor of Leipzig.
June	Secret orders from SS (Heydrich) ordering 'protective custody' (i.e. concentration camp) for those jailed for racial offences after release from jail.
August	Schacht resigns as Minister of Economics. He is replaced by Funk.
November	Anti-Comintern Pact joined by Italy.
during 1937	Enabling Law renewed. Confiscation of Jewish businesses without legal justification continues.

1938

January	Minister of War Blomberg dismissed after 'scandal'. Fritsch, Commander-in-Chief of the army, forced to resign on false charges of homosexuality.
February	Hitler becomes Minister of War and Commander-in-Chief (OKH) of the armed forces, with Keitel his Chief of Staff and Brauchitsch succeeding Fritsch.
	Ribbentrop is appointed Foreign Minister.
	Austrian Chancellor Schuschnigg called to Berchtesgaden and given ultimatum.
March	*Anschluss* in Austria. Seyss-Inquart becomes Reich Governor of 'Ostmark'. All laws of Germany, including racial laws, applied to Austria.
April	All Jewish wealth to be registered.
May	Condor Legion leaves Spain.
June	Destruction of Munich synagogue. Decree demands registration of all Jewish businesses.
July	Gördeler goes to London and fails to convince British of strength of anti-Hitler resistance.
	Chamberlain visits Hitler at Berchtesgaden to consult with him on Czechoslovakia.
August	Beck, Chief of General Staff, having sent Ewald von Kleist-Schmenzin to London to try and warn the British of Hitler's plans, submits paper on military position to Brauchitsch, who informs Hitler. Beck resigns.
	Destruction of Nuremberg synagogue. Decree requiring all Jews to carry the first name of either Israel or Sarah from 1939.

September	Chamberlain meets first with Hitler at Godesberg, then with Daladier and Mussolini at Munich where they agree the Sudetenland should go to Germany.
	Collapse of army generals' plot against Hitler.
October	Parts of Czechoslovakia occupied. Passports for Jews to be stamped 'J'. Expulsion of 17,000 former Polish Jews.
November	Vom Rath, of German Embassy in Paris, killed by Herschel Grynszpan; 'Crystal Night' pogrom, more than 20,000 Jews imprisoned. Decrees eliminate Jews from the economy and demand a collective fine of over 1 billion marks for the destruction provoked by Von Rath's murder. Expulsion of all Jews from schools. Roosevelt recalls US Ambassador.
December	Compulsory Aryanization of all Jewish shops and firms.

1939

March	Germany occupies Bohemia and Moravia as 'Protectorates'. Memel annexed, Danzig and the 'Polish Corridor' demanded. Spain signs the Anti-Comintern Pact.
April	Confiscation of all Jewish valuables. Law on Tenancies, foreseeing all Jews living together in 'Jewish houses'.
August	Soviet-German non-aggression pact; Anglo-Polish treaty of mutual assistance.
September	German armies invade Poland and annex Danzig.
	Britain and France declare war on Germany.
	Soviet Russia invades Poland.
	Jews forbidden to be out of doors after 8 p.m. in winter or 9 p.m. in summer. Confiscation of all radios from Jews.
October	German armies advance rapidly through Poland.
November	Bomb explodes in Bürgerbräukeller, Munich, shortly after Hitler leaves. Little military activity on the Western Front. Period of the '*Sitzkrieg*' or phoney war.

1940–45

1940

February	First deportation of Jews from Germany, mainly from Pomerania.
April	German invasion of Denmark and Norway.
May	German invasion of Netherlands, Belgium, Luxemburg and France.
June	'Fall of France' surrender signed at Compiègne, France divided into occupied and unoccupied ('Vichy') zones.
July	Rumania, attacked by Russia, becomes ally of Germany.

August	Battle of Britain begins. Luftwaffe attacks on British targets, developing later in the year into night attacks on London and other cities: the 'Blitz'.
	Russia completes occupation of the Baltic states.
September	Axis treaty joined by Japan.
October	Deportations of 'non-Germans' from Alsace-Lorraine, Saar and Baden.
November	Hungary, Rumania and Slovakia sign treaties with Germany.

1941

January	Germany signs trade and frontier pacts with Russia.
	Afrika Korps formed for Libyan campaign.
	Bulgaria occupied by Germany.
April	Invasion and occupation of Yugoslavia and Greece by Germany.
May	Rudolf Hess flies to Britain.
	British sink German battleship *Bismarck*.
June	'Barbarossa': German invasion of Russia.
July	Göring orders Heydrich to clear occupied lands of Jews.
	German troops in the Ukraine.
September	Yellow star compulsory for Jews in Germany.
	General deportation of German Jews starts.
	German troops take Kiev and begin siege of Leningrad.
November	German drive towards Moscow begins to falter.
December	Japan attacks Pearl Harbor and the Dutch and British Asian empires. Germany declares war on USA. German troops falter 50 kilometres from Moscow.

1942

January	'United Nations' conference in Washington: Britain, USA and Soviet Russia agree on no separate peace with Germany.
	Wannsee Conference on the 'Final Solution'
April	German Jews banned from public transport.
May	Rommel's Afrika Korps takes the offensive, driving the British out of Libya.
	British air-raids on German cities intensify.
	Heydrich assassinated in Czechoslovakia.
June	Mass gassings begin at Auschwitz.
July	Afrika Korps reaches El Alamein in Egypt.
	Germans take Sevastopol in the Crimea.
August	Rote Kapelle communist spy network in Germany uncovered by Abwehr.
	Canadian and British troops raid Dieppe in France.

	First US air-raids on European targets.
September	German troops enter Stalingrad.
October	British defeat Rommel at El Alamein.
November	Anglo-American landings in Morocco and Algeria; Afrika Korps starts retreat from Egypt and Libya to Tunisia.
	Germans occupy 'Vichy' France.
	Russian counter-attack at Stalingrad begins.
during 1942	Groups in Germany begin to plan for the removal of Hitler, especially associates of Gördeler among civilians and Beck and von Kluge in the army.

1943

February	Defeat of Germans in Stalingrad. Von Paulus surrenders.
	Execution of Hans and Sophie Scholl of the 'White Rose' resistance in Munich.
May	Germans and Italians surrender in North Africa.
July	Soviet victory at Kursk.
	Anglo-Americans take Sicily.
	Mussolini overthrown and imprisoned in Italy.
August	Russians recapture Orël and Kharkov.
September	Allies land on Italian mainland; Italy surrenders.
	'Solf tea-party' resistance group penetrated by Gestapo.
October	Italy declares war on Germany.
	Stauffenberg joins Reserve army staff and takes over planning for a 1944 anti-Hitler coup.
	Russians recapture Kiev.

1944

January	Siege of Leningrad lifted.
February	Abwehr staff defect to British in Turkey; Abwehr closed and absorbed into SD under Schellenberg; Canaris dismissed.
May	Sevastopol recaptured by the Soviets.
June	Allies capture Rome; 'D-Day' Anglo-American landings in Normandy, France. Germans begin V-1 (flying bomb) attacks on Britain.
July	Hitler moves to his East Prussian headquarters at Rastenburg. Stauffenberg tries to assassinate Hitler and fails, but coup signals sent out to Berlin and Paris. Coup plotters and large numbers of suspects, including Canaris and Oster, rounded up. Stauffenberg executed. Beck and others commit suicide.
	From July 1944 until April 1945 trials and executions of suspects continue.

August	Paris retaken by Allies. Russians enter Bucharest, Rumania. Von Kluge commits suicide.
September	Russians enter Yugoslavia.
October	Last gassings at Auschwitz.
	Russians enter Hungary.
	Rommel commits suicide.
November	Auschwitz crematoria blown up by SS.
December	Ardennes offensive.

1945

January	Russians liberate Auschwitz.
February	Bombing of Dresden.
March	US forces take Rhine bridge at Remagen.
	British cross Rhine to the north. Patton's 3rd Army approaches Frankfurt.
April	Vienna taken by Russians.
	Anglo-American forces drive east.
	British liberate Bergen-Belsen. Berlin entered by first Soviet forces.
May	Fall of the Third Reich.

A

Abetz, Otto (1903–58).   German ambassador to Vichy French government, 1940–44. A Karlsruhe art teacher who rose to become Ribbentrop's assistant, Abetz first arrived on the international scene when he attended the Munich conference of 1938. Appointed German ambassador to France in 1940, he advised the German military administration in Paris and was responsible for dealings with Unoccupied (Vichy) France. He was loyally supported by Pierre Laval who treated Abetz as the most important German in France, according him higher status even than the German Military Commander. Following the German occupation of southern France he became responsible for SD operations throughout France and initiated anti-Jewish drives. After the Liberation he was sentenced in Paris to twenty years' imprisonment for war crimes. Released in 1958, his death in that year in a motor accident was widely believed to be a revenge killing by former members of the French Resistance.

Abwehr.   The German military intelligence organization. In 1929 General von Schleicher combined all service intelligence units under his Ministry of Defence. After 1933 the *Abwehr* came into frequent conflict with the Nazi intelligence departments, the SD and the Gestapo. When he was appointed head of military intelligence in January 1935, Admiral Canaris succeeded in reaching an agreement with Heydrich on the limits of the *Abwehr* which, while acknowledging the SD's role in state security, retained for military intelligence a central part in espionage. The two organizations often ran in parallel: both had spy schools and both ran spies overseas.

   Abwehr stations in Germany were based on army districts. When war came, stations opened throughout occupied Europe and in tolerant neutral countries (especially Portugal, Spain, Sweden, Switzerland and Turkey). Agents in other countries were run from Germany, the Hamburg office covering Britain and the USA.

   As a military rather than a Nazi Party organization, the *Abwehr* attracted non-Nazis and opponents of the regime – in some cases with the encouragement of Canaris whose chief assistant, Hans Oster, devoted himself to using *Abwehr* contacts to promote a number of resistance activities until dismissed in 1943. *Abwehr* personnel are known to have been deeply involved in the preparations for the Rastenburg attempt on Hitler's life; but by now the organization's loyalty was seen to be compromised and its functions were being heavily eroded by the SS security organization, SD.

Finally in 1944 the publicized defection of two German agents to the British in Turkey, following the *Abwehr*'s failure to predict Anglo-American moves in north-west Europe, gave Himmler the chance to take over. In June 1944 Kaltenbrunner absorbed the *Abwehr* into his SS RUSHA department and the *Abwehr* was formally dissolved. ►Canaris, Admiral

Abwehr Polizei. Frontier police forces under Gestapo control.

Abwehr, USA. Before the entry of the US into the war, the *Abwehr* mainly relied on the information provided by the military attaché General von Boetticher and avoided compromising the pro-Nazi German-American Bund by recruiting agents from sympathizers. In New York, however, a Dr Griebl had established a spy ring and began to send useful information on aircraft production, but one of his new recruits acted so openly that they were uncovered by the FBI. Several were jailed in 1936, but Griebl escaped to Austria. *Abwehr* executive officer Major Ritter was sent from Hamburg in 1937 to contact a German national working on a new bomb-sight and successfully transmitted drawings to Germany. In 1939 the *Abwehr* recruited and trained a naturalized American, William G. Sebold, and sent him to America to work with a group of agents as their radio operator. In fact he was in contact with the FBI who arrested the complete network.

Adenauer, Konrad (1876–1967). Mayor of Cologne 1917–33, who developed the city and its urban amenities, particularly ensuring its surround of field and forest. He opened Germany's first Autobahn from Cologne to Bonn, in 1932. Before 1933 he had been considered for election as candidate for Chancellor but the German people's preference was for Hindenburg who would protect them from extremism.

After the Enabling Law of 1933 he was dismissed by the Nazis. In the following year he was arrested during the Röhm Purge but was later released to live in retirement. After the 1944 Bomb Plot he was again arrested and held in the Cologne detention centre, avoiding a concentration camp by shamming illness. In December the American army entered Cologne and Adenauer was immediately put in charge of the city's administration. A British military government official dismissed him in June 1945, but this did not end his career in politics. Moving to the national stage he became the first Chancellor of the new German Bundesrepublik.

Adler und Falke ('Eagle and Hawk').   An early Nazi youth group.

Adlertag (Eagle Day).   Code-name for the first day of the air offensive against Britain. It had long been recognized in German planning circles that for Operation Sealion, the projected invasion of Britain, to be successful the German navy would be required to guarantee the passage of the English Channel to the German army. This guarantee the navy was in no position to give unless Britain's Royal Navy had first been neutralized by the Luftwaffe. This, in turn, was clearly not possible until the Royal Air Force had been driven from the skies by Göring's Luftwaffe. *Adlertag* was launched on 8 August 1940, the first day of a struggle which became better known as the Battle of Britain. Although the fighter element of the two air forces was reasonably matched in quality of aircraft, pilot skills and numbers, Göring made a serious tactical error in his failure to continue attacks on RAF airfields in the south of England. After heavy losses on both sides the Luftwaffe's major effort was transferred to night bombing attacks on British cities and it became clear to Hitler (if not at that time to the beleaguered British people) that Operation Sealion would have to be abandoned.

Administrative Boundaries of the Third Reich and its allies. The following is a list of the additions to the Reich and its allies from 1935 to the high-water mark of German expansion in 1942:

1935:
Saar reoccupied after plebiscite
1936:
Rhineland military re-entry
1938:
'*Anschluss*' with Austria

Czechoslovakia: Sudetenland to Germany; territory to Hungary; territory to Poland
1939:
Albania annexed by Italy

Czechoslovakia: Bohemia and Moravia German 'Protectorates'; Ruthenia taken by Hungary; Slovakia made a separate state

Memel (Lithuania) annexed by Germany

Poland: Danzig and 'Corridor' to Germany; East Poland under Russian rule; German-speaking areas of Poland absorbed into Germany while the remainder forms 'Government-General', with its HQ at Krakow under Frank

Rumania: Bessarabia to Russia
1940:
Rumania: Transylvania to Hungary; Trans-Danube to Bulgaria

Denmark: occupied, king and government remain, with a German Ambassador until November 1942; thereafter Best as plenipotentiary (*Reichsvollmächtiger*)

Norway: Terboven as *Reichskommissar* and government by Quisling's '*Nasjonal Samling*' Party

Netherlands: (May) Seyss-Inquart as *Reichskommissar*

Belgium: Military Government under General von Falkenhausen with General Reeder as Chief of Civil Administration covering Belgium and an extensive area of Northern France

France: Alsace-Lorraine to Germany, Paris and north-central France
under German military rule; Southern area under Vichy government
until November 1942

Britain: Channel Islands (June), military government

1941:

Yugoslavia divided into Croatia, independent kingdom; Dalmatia
(annexed by Italy); Serbia; Montenegro; Banat region claimed by
Hungary

Reichskommissariat Ostland   includes Baltic areas

Reichskommissariat Ukraine   established following German advance
towards Moscow

1942:

France: German forces occupy southern France; Vichy government
retained

***Adolf Hitler Schulen* (Adolf Hitler Schools)**.   ►Education in the Third
Reich

***Adolf Hitler Spende* (Adolf Hitler Fund)**.   A foundation set up shortly after
the Nazis came to power with Martin Bormann as Treasurer. Collected by
more or less open extortion, especially from Jewish businessmen, the proceeds
were used for the benefit of 'the Party' in the widest sense: holidays and
handouts for SA and SS men or equally the setting up of the Ribbentrop
Bureau as a rival to the Foreign Ministry.

Adolf Légalité.   Term used to describe what was considered Hitler's regard
for the achievement of power by legal means. The term was used on two levels
– first by those Germans who believed in Hitler's sincere wish to act legally
and secondly by those members of the early revolutionary SA elements who
used the term with contempt.

Afrika Korps.   German army unit in North Africa, 1941–3. In 1940 the Italian
army, attacking the British in Egypt, had run into serious trouble; and after
losing 130,000 prisoners it had retreated to Benghazi and seemed likely to be
driven out of North Africa altogether. Seeing the danger of losing control of
the Mediterranean and the Middle East, Hitler issued Führer Directive No. 22
to create a special force and despatched the new 5th Light Division (later
renamed 21 Panzer) as the nucleus of an *Afrika Korps*, under the command of
General Erwin Rommel.

Rommel landed with the division at Tripoli and, finding the British unprepared, immediately launched an attack. Joined by three reinforced Italian army
corps and, later, by the German 15 Panzer Division and the specially equipped
90 Light Division, he moved on through Libya towards Egypt, bypassing
Tobruk, which was left in a state of siege. Early in 1942 the British Eighth
Army counter-attacked and moved back into Libya until Rommel in turn

gathered reinforcements and advanced again, this time to within sixty miles of the Nile Delta.

The *Afrika Korps* was now within days of taking the Suez Canal and dominating the Middle East. In this event it is probable that Turkey would have joined Germany at war and that Russia's southern flank would have been turned and Stalingrad taken. At this point the *Afrika Korps* consisted of three divisions with supporting units, with three Italian corps under command. While they had started in ignorance of conditions, frequently issued with the wrong clothing and lacking diesel-engined vehicles and desert equipment, the *Afrika Korps* was at least the equal of its British opponents. In addition Erwin Rommel's tactical brilliance had so far proved sufficient to maintain a balance in Germany's favour. But Rommel's lines of communication were by now seriously over-extended.

In September 1942 Rommel's summer offensive was halted and the tide finally turned. In November the British Eighth Army, reinforced and with a new commander, General Bernard Montgomery, attacked and forced Rommel into a long retreat. With the *Afrika Korps* as the Axis' effective rearguard the retreat continued across the desert past Tripoli and into Tunisia. Here the retreating Germans met the recently landed Americans at the Kasserine Pass and inflicted some 10,000 casualties on inexperienced US units. But Rommel's force was now clearly doomed, and despite some reinforcements the Afrika Korps with its surviving Italian allies, 150,000 in all, surrendered in May 1943. Only Rommel and a small staff escaped. ➤Appendix III

Agriculture in the Third Reich. When the Nazis came to power in 1933 the parlous state of the German farmer was everywhere apparent. In the press conditions were somewhat fancifully compared to those of the sixteenth-century Peasants' War or the catastrophic Thirty Years' War of the next century. Yet the problem was genuinely acute. In 1932–3 agricultural income had fallen a billion marks below 1924–5, the worst post-war year, debt had risen steeply and interest was taking overall some 14 per cent of farm income.

In 1933 Walter Darré, a genuinely informed agriculturalist though still a Nazi ideologue, took over the Ministry of Agriculture with the brief to draw up a new deal for the German farmer. His Reich Entailed Farm Law of September 1933 awarded all farms up to 125 hectares to the incumbent farmer, at the same time declaring the land to be a hereditary estate which could not be sold, mortgaged or divided. On the incumbent's death the farm would be passed to the eldest son. The only qualification required of the farmer was that he prove Aryan blood purity back to the year 1800.

Under a second law of the same month, Darré tackled the problem of farm prices. Thereafter a Reich Food Estate was to obtain stable and profitable prices for the farmer and to aim at making Germany self-sufficient in agricultural production. Within two years agricultural prices had risen 20 per cent and many German farmers had come to see the Nazi State as a powerful partner after years of neglect.

Certainly many younger farmers benefited by the new hereditary laws, doubling their average land acreage by 1939. At the same time the farm labourer who had suffered a cut in wages of one-fifth during the Depression, now under the Nazis had his income restored to 1929 level. It remained, however, low when compared to the wages of workers on the Autobahns or in the new rearmament industry.

Yet despite some success Nazi agricultural policy never achieved more than 80 per cent self-sufficiency of food and although the farmer saw himself lauded in the press and honoured on political platforms, from 1935 his economic position ceased to improve. By 1937 the price balance was again operating against agriculture with farm incomes having risen only 34 per cent since 1933 as against industrial wages and salary rises of nearly 50 per cent. This was a difference which would remain marked until well into the war when the Nazi rural labour force became dominated by an ideologically unlooked-for combination of women farm workers and foreign slave labourers which made any comparison with pre-war agricultural wages and incomes irrelevant.

Ahnenerbe.   The shortened form of the 'German Ancestral Heritage Society for the study of German Prehistory'. Founded in 1935, it was funded through Darré's Ministry and encouraged by Himmler. With Darré's influence within the Nazi Party in decline, Himmler integrated the *Ahnenerbe* in the SS (1937), putting it under the same administrative branch as the concentration camps.

Ahnenerbe studied prehistory with a mix of science and romanticism, always in order to prove racist hypotheses. All archaeological excavation came under its control from 1938 onwards. With good funding and its wide range of research areas, many first-rate university academics were attracted. There were some substantial successes: the excavation of a ninth-century Viking fortress, expeditions to Tibet and the Near East, and later the protection of prehistoric sites in southern (occupied) Russia. In WWII *Ahnenerbe*'s heritage studies were curtailed and new research projects came under its wing, some anthropological (measuring the skulls of Auschwitz victims or of executed Russian commissars to compare with Aryan heads), some medical (including both the sinister Dachau experiments of Rascher and Mengele's work in Auschwitz).

Ahnenerbe justifies study as an example of the stages through which Nazi/ SS organizations frequently developed. Established for one purpose (more or less legitimate research) it became tainted with illegalities (the medical experiments). In its final phase *Ahnenerbe* was a bureaucratic octopus snatching power undiscriminatingly, for instance, achieving by the war's end control of the totally unrelated V-2 programme run by Werner von Braun.

Ahnenpass.   Racial identity card.

Air Defence (*Luftschutz*).   Against the Allied air attacks on German industries and cities, two principal levels of defence were organized. Fighter defence, anti-aircraft guns and searchlights were controlled by Luftwaffe commanders in their various regions (*Luftgau*). Yet ground defence of cities and their population was effectively a Nazi Party affair, and seen by the people to be so. From 1942 all party *Gauleiters* were also 'Reich Defence Commissioners'. The police chief, always with SS rank up to major general, was the Air Defence Leader. Under him came both the police and the fire brigades. His office co-ordinated the mass of Nazi volunteer organizations: workers of the Labour Front (RAD), women (RADWJ), Hitler Youth and its junior branches, and the Party welfare organization (NSV). Each locality would be immediately cared for by the Party *Blockwart* (the local senior member). By law, from August 1940 cellars were bomb-proofed and escape passages made between neighbouring buildings. Roofs, especially of factories, were given fire-proofing treatment. In the cities thought to be most at risk large concrete air-raid bunkers were built for those without basement shelters. After a raid the army's engineer units (TENO) would carry out heavy rescue work, and stand-by convoys of vehicles from other cities, driven by the Party's NSKK, might be sent, bringing emergency food, blankets, tents and medical help. The city's Security and Rescue Service (SHD) would be at work clearing and rehousing, and a Missing Persons Bureau (VNZ) would collect information on casualties and take over the burial of the dead.

Even after the most terrible raids, this massive organizational build-up brought relief quickly and made daily life possible. In Dresden, after the raids of February 1945, electricity was restored to most parts in a few days, trams within four days and factories on the outskirts began working within a week.

The Allied air offensive on cities was planned to undermine morale, to shake the German people's faith in the Nazi regime and to smash industry and fuel supplies. In spite of the firestorm of Hamburg and the continued area bombing of the Ruhr, German air defence, with the organization and improvisation of industry under Speer, kept morale high, and production even increased through the latter part of the war. Only in the very last weeks was the system brought to the point of collapse.

Alarich (**Alaric**).   Code-name for the occupation of Italy by German forces in 1943.

Alfarth, Felix (1901–23).   One of the earliest Nazi martyrs, having died in the 1923 Beer Hall Putsch. Alfarth's name appeared at the top of the list of dedicatees in *Mein Kampf*.

Allgemeine-SS **(the General SS)**.   The general pool of SS men. ➤SS: Groupings and Organizations

Alpenfestung **(Southern or Alpine Redoubt)**.   The idea of an Alpine fortress in which Nazism would make its last stand probably belonged to Göbbels. Its principal importance is in the significance attached to it by General Eisenhower, although it is true that certain SS military preparations were made for a last stand in 1945.

Alpine Violet (*Alpenveilchen*).   Code-name for German aid to the Italian forces, which were meeting difficulties on the Albanian front (1941).

Alte Kämpfer **(Old Fighters)**.   The early members of the Nazi Party were always accorded a special place in the affections of Hitler and his *Table Talk* is full of references to the events and personalities of the old days. Very real benefits also flowed from recognition as an Old Fighter: sinecures in government and the Party and military-style pensions for those wounded in the early days of street-fighting.

Altmark.   The German supply ship which had supported the 'pocket battle-ship' *Graf Spee* in its raid on British shipping in the South Atlantic in 1939. In February 1940 the *Altmark* was bringing back to Germany 299 British prisoners from ships caught by the raider. For safety she was keeping close to the Norwegian coast. The *Altmark*'s captain told the Norwegian authorities that he had no prisoners and was therefore allowed to sail inside Norway's territorial waters. A British destroyer, however, followed the *Altmark* in and boarded her, releasing the prisoners. Hitler was infuriated by this and the incident served to add to his fear that the British would land troops in Norway.

Amann, Max (1891–1957).   Hitler's WWI Sergeant and literary agent. Joining the SA in 1921, his business training made him party treasurer and manager of the party paper, the *Völkischer Beobachter*. From 1925 on he was in the SA central office and rose in the publishing world through the Nazi Party. He arranged publication of Hitler's *Mein Kampf* and organized its royalty payments (which were Hitler's main source of personal income). With *Gleich-schaltung* of the press he became President of the Reich Association of Newspaper Publishers and President of the Reich Press Chamber, and in 1943 he bought out Hugenberg's press empire for the Party.

Tough and greedy, Max Amann made himself a millionaire, but post-war trials in 1949 jailed him and he died penniless.

Amnesty Decree.   An attempt by Hitler to reassure the German establishment after the Röhm Purge of 1934. A limited but highly publicized amnesty was granted, benefiting a few prisoners and leaving the vast majority in the new camps which were now springing up in every part of Germany.

Ancestry, SS Requirements.   ➤SS: Ritual and Romance

Anglo-German Naval Agreement.   On 21 May 1935 Hitler advanced specific proposals to settle the 'naval question' between Britain and Germany. In a speech markedly friendly in tone he recognized 'the vital importance' to

Great Britain and its empire of a dominant fleet. He proclaimed Germany had 'not the intention, or the necessity or need' to engage in naval rivalry with Britain; a fleet of no more than 35 per cent of the tonnage of the Royal Navy was all Germany wanted. The German object was to trap the British government into an agreement to flout the naval restrictions of the Versailles Treaty. The British government, with what now seems a mixture of arrogance and credulity, fell into the trap. Neither the League of Nations nor France and Italy were consulted. The vital restriction on submarine building was lifted. 5 battleships, 21 cruisers and 64 destroyers were to be allowed. The agreed levels were such that the German ship-building industry would need a decade to reach them. The practical effect of the agreement was therefore to remove every significant Versailles naval restriction and to encourage Nazi Germany to expand her fleet as rapidly as possible.

***Angriff, Der* ('Attack').**   Berlin-based Nazi newspaper founded by Göbbels.

***Angstbrosche* (Badge of Fear).**   When the Nazis came to power in 1933 there was a rush of applications for membership of the Nazi Party. Old Party members regarded these new adherents with contempt, seeing their applications as pure opportunism. The *Angstbrosche* was the name jeeringly given to the Party badge worn by these new members.

***Anschluss*.**   The movement in Germany and Austria for the union of the two countries in a Greater Germany. When the Allies had decreed the break-up of the Austrian Empire the union of Austria and Germany had been specifically forbidden by the Treaty of Versailles; however, agitation for *Anschluss* continued in both countries throughout the 1920s. By 1931, nationalist movements were sufficiently influential to mount proposals for a customs union between the two countries. Clearly this was intended as a first step towards political union and France strongly rejected the proposal. Submitted to the International Court of The Hague, the Zollverein was declared illegal by a narrow majority and the German and Austrian governments abandoned the proposal.

   Nazi parties in both Germany and Austria strongly supported the political union of the two German states. In 1934 Austrian Nazis murdered Chancellor Dollfuss in an attempted coup. Government forces, led by Kurt von Schuschnigg, defeated the Nazi forces; and when Mussolini mobilized troops on the Brenner Pass, Hitler was forced to withdraw active support for the putschists in Vienna. In the next two years some accommodation was reached, with Hitler's recognition of Austria's independence and the Viennese government's acceptance of the Nazis as a legal party. It is now abundantly clear that Hitler was biding his time. In February 1938 he insisted Austrian Chancellor Schuschnigg come to Berchtesgaden, where he demanded concessions for the Austrian Nazi Party. Ranting and threatening, Hitler had set the scene on Schuschnigg's arrival. At Berchtesgaden he was introduced to three generals who 'had arrived quite by chance'. They were Keitel (the chief of OKW), von Reichenau (commander of the German forces on the Bavarian-Austrian border) and Sperrle (Luftwaffe general for the border area). The point was not lost on Bundeskanzler Schuschnigg and his Under-Secretary for Foreign Affairs, Guido Schmidt: if they were not prepared to concede to the Führer's demands, preparations for a solution by force were already under way. After lunch Hitler's terms were presented. There was to be no discussion. The ban against the Austrian Nazi Party was to be lifted immediately. Dr Seyss-Inquart, a covert Nazi, was to be made Minister of the Interior, another Nazi, Glaise-Horstenau, was to be Minister for War. Finally Austria was to be absorbed into the German economic system.

The Austrian Federal Chancellor realized immediately that his agreement would mean the end of Austrian independence. Expecting to be arrested at any moment, Schuschnigg desperately played for time, reminding Hitler that under the Austrian constitution the signature of Federal President Miklas would be required. Schuschnigg himself signed and returned to Austria to present Hitler's terms to the President. On 16 February the Austrian government began to put Germany's terms into effect.

But Hitler had by no means achieved his full aims. In a speech to the Reichstag he now laid claim, on behalf of Germany, to the responsibility for 'all those Germans in Austria who were constantly afflicted by the severest sufferings' for their faith in Germany.

In Austria Hitler's speech was a signal for carefully orchestrated demonstrations: in Vienna, Nazis attacked Jewish buildings and Jews on the street; in Graz, 20,000 demonstrators tore down the Austrian flag in the town square and raised the swastika in its place. Seyss-Inquart, in control of the police, did nothing. Schuschnigg's government was collapsing. It was the crisis which Hitler had organized and which he fully intended to exploit.

But Schuschnigg had one more card to play. At some time in the last frantic ten days the French had suggested through their legation in Vienna that a plebiscite of the Austrian people could strengthen his hand against Hitler. A significant vote against *Anschluss* would make it impossible for Hitler to resort to force. On 9 March, therefore, in a speech at Innsbruck, Federal Chancellor Schuschnigg announced the plebiscite for Sunday, 13 March.

Now all depended on whether the German army could prepare an occupying force in three days. The day after the Innsbruck speech, mobilization orders went out to three *Wehrmacht* Corps. At 2 a.m. the next morning, the Operational Directive to occupy Austria was issued. But first Mussolini had to be placated. Prince Philip of Hesse was immediately despatched to Rome with a letter from Hitler, a tissue of half-truths and complete lies, explaining the impossibility of the Führer accepting the mockery of a so-called plebiscite.

Now as the pressure from Germany and from the Nazis in the Austrian government built up, Schuschnigg's courage failed. At 2 p.m. on Friday, 11 March, he telephoned Seyss-Inquart to tell him that he agreed to cancel the plebiscite. But this alone was no longer sufficient. In twenty-seven recorded telephone calls to Vienna, Göring increased the pressure: Schuschnigg must resign in favour of Seyss-Inquart. At the same time Kaltenbrunner (in 1943 to be appointed Himmler's head of the RSHA) led Austrian SS attacks on Social Democrats and Jews and outstanding anti-Nazi individuals. The violence was planned and the outcome predetermined in Berlin. On Göring's order, Seyss-Inquart appealed to Berlin for help in restoring order. At dawn German troops began to cross the Austrian frontier. In their train they brought Gestapo and SD agents. Schuschnigg himself preceded 76,000 of his fellow citizens into Dachau. As the terror continued, an Austrian camp was established at Mauthausen where the executions of at least 35,000 victims of the *Anschluss* took place.

Kaltenbrunner's energy earned him the post of Minister of State and commander of the SS in what was now named Ostmark; then Globocnik (who would later acquire in Poland an almost unparalleled reputation for brutality even for an SS leader) was named Gauleiter of Vienna. A wave of anti-semitism, throughout all Austria, followed the Nazi seizure of power. Led by the Gestapo officer Adolf Eichmann, the SS devised the practice by which the Jewish community could buy exit permits or appeal to the generosity of friends overseas. Those unable to pay – the vast majority – remained to face the increasingly deadly anti-semitism of the Third Reich.

As a final seal on force and illegality, Hitler revived the device of the plebiscite. He was of course now in a position to determine its course. The ballot on the union of Austria and Germany duly took place on 10 April 1938. By a total vote in favour of 99 per cent it was claimed that the people of the two countries had voted for *Anschluss* and the Nazi Party of the Führer, Adolf Hitler.

Anschluss **Ballot**. In April 1938 a plebiscite was held in Germany and Austria on the month-old union of the two countries. The vote is recorded as overwhelming affirmation of Hitler's march into Austria.

Anthropoids. Code-name for the Czech soldiers who, in the spring of 1942, were flown from London and parachuted into Czechoslovakia with the object of assassinating Reinhard Heydrich, the Protector of Bohemia. ►Heydrich, Reinhard

Anti-Comintern Pact. German treaties with Japan and Italy aimed at subversive activities of the 'Comintern', the Russian-controlled system of international Communist parties. In 1936 Ribbentrop signed an agreement with the Japanese to act in concert to stop the spread of communism. Secret protocols pledged assistance in economic and diplomatic terms if either were at war with communist Russia. Hitler contrived to justify the alliance with Japan on racial grounds: 'the blood of Japan contains virtues close to the pure Nordic'. The second signatory of the pact, Mussolini's Italy, was persuaded to sign in November 1937, being already allied to Germany in the 'Axis'. ►Axis

Anti-Semit.   The brand-name of a rolling tobacco introduced by Nazi propagandists in the early days of their struggle for publicity.

Anti-semitism.   Hatred or fear of the Jews was a major force in the development of Nazism, but it was not exclusive to the NSDAP nor was it by any means started by them. For centuries there had been religious anti-semitism in Europe, and peoples and governments had from age to age alternated between tolerance or even encouragement of Jewish communities and violent scapegoat attacks on them. The most notorious anti-semitic practices of the nineteenth century were the 'pogroms' which, often organized by Russian imperial authorities, destroyed whole communities. In the nineteenth century racial motives replaced religious anti-semitism, as theories of Aryan or Nordic superiority were developed by Houston Stewart Chamberlain and others.

The term 'anti-semitism' was first used by Wilhelm Marr (1819–1904). In Russia, anti-semitism was practised by the state; and ghettos (designated areas) were decreed for Jews in many towns. In Germany in the 1870s a number of financial scandals were associated with Jews, and Chancellor Bismarck used the resulting wave of anti-semitism to attack his liberal political enemies. Generally in Europe anti-semitism became linked with conservative and right-wing politics and with the church movements close to them. In France in the 1890s the case of Captain Dreyfus, falsely accused of treason, became a focus of the debate between anti-semitism and liberal feeling. In Austria there was a major political crisis when the Pope sent a message of encouragement to a political leader outstanding for his anti-semitism. And it was the city of Vienna which elected Karl Lüger (1844–1910) mayor with policies which outspokenly blamed the Jews for the ills of the city.

In Germany at the end of WWI the frustrations of defeat and economic collapse often resulted in acts of violence linked with anti-semitism. The 1919 murders of Rosa Luxemburg in Berlin and Kurt Eisner in Munich were more than acts against Bolsheviks, they were seen as conscious acts of violence against Jews. The murder of foreign minister Rathenau in 1922 can be similarly viewed. The racial anti-semitism of Hitler and his party absorbed the full spectrum of theories of 'race'. Their attacks were directed at any person believed to have any Jewish ancestry or even any form of relationship with Jews in or out of marriage. Analysis of Jewishness rarely went beyond superficial pseudo-scientific statements and was more often expressed in the violent images of Julius Streicher's newspaper.

Once in power in 1933 the Nazis applied their anti-semitic theory by separating all those accused of 'racial impurity' from public life, then from business activity and, finally, from life itself. The stages are marked clearly through the Nuremberg Laws, Crystal Night and the Final Solution.

The Nazi drive to wipe out the Jews, like many other Nazi programmes, was not carried out coherently, for many Jews had industrial skills that could not be replaced. Thus while one department of the SS was devoted to mass murder, another was concerned with preserving a skilled Jewish slave-labour force. Both departments came under the same branch: the SS WVHA. At the outset the Nazis had tried to drive the Jews out of German living space, and were briefly in collaboration with the Zionist movement. Eichmann studied this aspect seriously and even, in May 1938, tried to curb Streicher's excesses. There were fantasies like the Madagascar plan (to turn that vast island into a Jewish colony) and, late in the war, Himmler's attempts to trade Jewish lives for war materials. In 1941, however, the *Einsatzgruppen* embarked on the destruction of Jews behind the advancing army in eastern Poland and Russia, but the policy was not formalized until the Wannsee conference of January 1942, and even that proposed a 'final solution' without spelling out the slaughter that followed. The ambiguities remained.

➤Nuremberg Laws, Crystal Night and Final Solution

Anton.   The *Wehrmacht* code-word for the occupation of Vichy France. In the event, as a counter-measure to the Anglo-American landings in North Africa, Anton was ordered on 10 November 1942.

AO (*Auslandsorganisation* – Overseas Organization).   A Nazi Party department responsible for German communities overseas. In many countries substantial numbers of citizens of German descent joined organizations like the German-American Bund or the Argentine Nazi Party. In the structure of the AO, countries with substantial German communities were considered as separate *Gaue* (political divisions). Substantial funds were devoted to these overseas organizations which often proved an effective cover for German political interference. In the 1940 US presidential election, the AO was deeply involved in the transfer of funds to Roosevelt's (sometimes unwitting) opponents.

Appeasement.   A term of contempt when applied nowadays to the policies of British Prime Minister Neville Chamberlain and French leaders of the period, most notably Edouard Daladier. In the usage of the time, however, appeasement was meant, by appeasers, to suggest those reasonable steps which might be taken to prevent Hitler taking the law into his own hands.

Appeasement can be seen to have had its roots in the growing feeling in the early 1930s in Britain and, to a lesser extent, in France that the terms imposed on Germany by the Versailles Treaty had been impossibly harsh. The justice of Adolf Hitler's demand for a rearmed Germany and the restoration of 'German' territories was at first largely accepted by Chamberlain. By appeasing Hitler, by assenting to these essentially just demands, Chamberlain believed he could lay the basis for a lasting European peace.

But it rapidly became apparent that appeasement was to be a policy which would include *both* fascist dictators, and even Franco's Spain. By 1938 Chamberlain had recognized Mussolini's conquest of Ethiopia, accepted international intervention in the Spanish Civil War and tolerated the annexation of Austria. At Munich in 1938, with French Premier Daladier he agreed to Hitler's demands for the incorporation into the Reich of the German-speaking Czechoslovak Sudetenland. He had persuaded himself that this would be Hitler's last demand, and he returned to England claiming that he had achieved 'peace for our time'.

The policy of appeasement surprised Hitler, who had expected a confrontation over the Sudetenland, and dismayed his critics in Germany, who had hoped for outside support to overthrow the Nazi regime. When Hitler marched into Czechoslovakia in March 1939 it was clear to Chamberlain that appeasement had failed. But the British and French governments which had appeased Hitler remained in power. Even after they had declared war over Germany's invasion of Poland they continued to follow unaggressive military policies until the *Wehrmacht* turned to attack the west in 1940 and appeasement became irrelevant to the immediate future of Western Europe. ➤Munich Agreement

Arbeit Macht Frei (**'Work brings freedom'**).   Part of the deception process at Auschwitz, the slogan over one of the gates suggests that honest labour entitles a prisoner to consideration for a pardon. The slogan appeared on the rear gate of Dachau, and possibly in other camps too – though for what purpose other than as an expression of the savage and perverted humour of the SS it is impossible to say.

Architecture.   Architecture in the Third Reich was profoundly affected by Adolf Hitler's passion for the subject. According to Albert Speer (who became his official architect after the death of Paul Ludwig Troost), Hitler's taste, despite his admiration for the restrained neo-classicism of Troost, was for the neo-baroque. He declared that Charles Garnier's Paris Opera House had the 'most beautiful stairway in the world' and his sketchbooks from the 1920s are full of sketches of similar designs.

Albert Speer, a third-generation architect from Mannheim, came to dominate the architectural climate of the Third Reich, though many of his more grandiose buildings were never realized. His first commission was at the Zeppelin Field at Nuremberg, and on the same site his spectacular staging of the Nazi Party Rally in 1934 included the 'Cathedral of Light', produced by the skilful use of searchlights.

Within months of coming to power Hitler's architectural megalomania knew no bounds, and its ultimate expression was to be the complete rebuilding of Berlin, to be carried out on the same scale as that of Haussmann's designs for Paris. The Adolf Hitler Platz was to contain a new Chancellery, a high command for the armed forces, a new Reichstag and a gigantic hall based on the Pantheon in Rome with a dome over 800 feet in diameter. The plans also included an Arch of Triumph more than 400 feet high. Hitler, despite his constant insistence on a 'simple' way of life, had sketched a palace for himself on the same enormous scale as the other buildings. The only building actually constructed was the Chancellery, destroyed by the attacking Russian forces in 1945.

Several other architects of note were working during this period. Among the best known was Wilhelm Kreis whose *Totenburgen*, vast memorials to the military, were planned for all the conquered territories. On a smaller scale, Nazi taste in domestic architecture tended away from the clean lines of the Bauhaus and towards exaggerated and quaint versions of Bavarian and Tyrolean cottages and inns.

Little of the public building of the Third Reich remains, bombing, shelling and even ideological fervour having carried most Nazi architecture away. In addition it should be emphasized that the effective building period of the Third Reich was little more than six years. Construction, though not planning and drawing, virtually ceased with the outbreak of war. Thus while the other Nazi arts flourished throughout the full course of the period, major architectural projects with their lengthy planning, site preparation and building times were few. The architectural history of the period lies more in intention than execution.

Ardennes Offensive.   German counter-attack in north-western Europe in December 1944. By December 1944 the Anglo-American armies had advanced to the edge of Germany and General Patton was expected to capture the Saar before Christmas. General Eisenhower commanding the Allied armies knew that there were uncommitted Panzer reserves, but the evidence of exhaustion among German soldiers was such that he feared no counter-attack by their commander, von Rundstedt. Eisenhower's intelligence estimated that von Rundstedt was too good a general to throw his reserves away in an unlikely gamble. But earlier in September Hitler had outlined a plan to drive through the Ardennes to capture Antwerp. Rundstedt planned only to pinch out an American salient and restore the West Wall (or Siegfried Line, as the Allies knew it). Hitler, however, made him accept a completely detailed plan of attack, endorsed in the Führer's own handwriting 'NOT TO BE ALTERED'. By dawn, fourteen German infantry, three Panzer and two parachute divisions had moved up, the noise of their tanks covered by the roar of V-1 flying bombs blasting overhead towards Antwerp and Liège. The Ardennes offensive took the Americans by surprise and though some, like the US 7th Armoured Division at the road junction of St Vith, stood firm, the Germans broke through. One special unit, the 'Panzer Brigade 150' of under 3,000 men, led by Skorzeny, used captured jeeps, tanks and trucks, and with as many English-speaking Germans in American uniforms as possible, attempted to create confusion and panic. American intelligence soon found out about this operation and minimized the damage. Several Germans captured in American uniforms were shot. Further German advances were dependent on the capture of Allied fuel stocks. Failing to take the American dumps they needed, they were soon running out of petrol. Large forces were tied up, trying to take the American-held road junctions at Bastogne (which held out) and St Vith (which was taken only after a week's fighting). When the weather cleared, Anglo-American air forces, which had been grounded, struck at the lines of German reinforcements along the Ardennes mountain roads. The Allies now reorganized. The British General, Montgomery, took temporary command of all forces on the northern side of the attack (a source of friction between the Allied generals); Patton regrouped and in a lightning advance-to-contact moved his Third Army from the south to relieve Bastogne and take the Germans in the flank. The German commander's wish to pull out was overruled by Hitler. In January the Führer ordered more divisions into the attack, but they were forced back to where they had started. The last attack on the Western Front had failed. The greatest Russian offensive of the war began in the East in the same month. ➤Bastogne

Armed SS.　Fighting SS units. ➤SS: Waffen SS

Armistice, 1940.　➤Compiègne

Army High Command.　After President Hindenburg died in 1934 Hitler became head of the Armed Forces with Blomberg as commander-in-chief and Minister of War. There were separate commanders of the army, navy and, from 1935, of the air force.

1934–8:

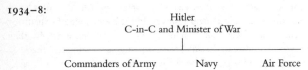

When Hitler forced Blomberg's resignation in 1938, he took over direct command of the Armed Forces, abolishing the Ministerial post. His new Chief of Staff, General Keitel, was now appointed to OKW (*Oberkommando der Wehrmacht*).

1938–41:

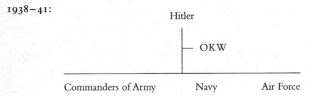

In 1941 he further altered the chain of command and increased his power. 1941–5:

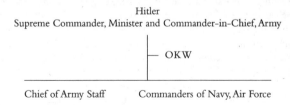

Hitler
Supreme Commander, Minister and Commander-in-Chief, Army

— OKW

Chief of Army Staff   Commanders of Navy, Air Force

Art in the Third Reich.   Despite his youthful failure in Vienna to be accepted as a student of the arts, Hitler had continued to consider himself an artist and his post-war entry into German politics did nothing to liberalize or even extend the rigid, mostly uninformed views which eventually came to form the basic artistic tenets of the Third Reich.

Apparently unaware how close his preferences were to Soviet socialist realism, Hitler demanded naturalism in style and idealism in subject. The heroic element (also present, though in a different form, in Soviet art) was to be provided by the myths of the Germanic past.

In 1933 Alfred Rosenberg, author of *The Myth of the Twentieth Century*, became the leader of the new Reich Chamber of Culture. Art movements which had developed in recent years were now suspect, and 'expressionism', 'surrealism' or other non-objective styles were banned and the painters forced into exile. Among the seven sub-chambers of the new Reich Chamber of Culture, Fine Art remained one of the most ideologically important. *Gleichschaltung* was of course to apply here too and over 40,000 artists and graphic designers were approved for membership of the Reich Chamber of Visual Art. Failure to maintain Nazi artistic and political standards meant expulsion and a Gestapo-enforced withdrawal of the artist's right to paint.

In July 1937 a House of German Art was opened in Munich and at the same time an exhibition of *Entartete Kunst* ('Degenerate Art'), was held. Included were works by Klee, Nolde, Beckmann and Kokoschka, a selection of the 6,500 'degenerate' paintings which had been purged from the nation's museums by a commission of the Reich Chamber of Visual Art.

Speaking at the opening of an art exhibition in 1938, Hitler said: 'Power and Beauty are the calls of today. Clarity and logic dominate our cultural struggle. Artists of this age must identify themselves with the age.' Nazi painting was not to occupy itself with studies of the artist's own personal concerns, nor was it to experiment with the medium. Nazi painting was clear, direct and heroic. Above all it was expected to express a view of German society. In this view there was no room for pessimism or complexity. It was the German world according to Dr Göbbels, considered to be most effectively displayed by the prosaic political works of such painters as Hermann Otto Heyer.

The Third Reich also demanded the heroic, pure, monumental style for sculpture. Arno Breker (b. 1900) had worked in the Bauhaus, but adapted his style to become Hitler's favourite sculptor. His massive bronze statues of naked men holding pagan swords stood outside the Reich Chancellery in Berlin. The Third Reich's other technically competent sculptor of gigantic statues was the Viennese, Josef Thorek, for whom Albert Speer designed an enormous studio. These and other sculptors were kept busy making busts of the Third Reich's leaders. In the tradition of Nazi art, commissioned through the Reich Chamber of Culture for the Ministry of Propaganda, they created objects worthy of reverence rather than analytical studies. The standing of an artist could be judged by the importance of the person or object he was commissioned to represent: lesser artists were left to sculpt the many eagles which were placed over the entrances to SS barracks, schools or air-raid shelters.

Artaman League.   Young nationalist organization founded in the early 1920s. Its roots were to be found in the Blood and Soil (*Blut und Boden*) preoccupations of many German youths of the period. Distaste for the cities, where Jews and capitalists abounded, was linked to a desire to defend the nation's soil against the depredations of Polish farmers on the eastern borders of Germany. Among the then known members of the league was Heinrich Himmler until, like many other members, he drifted away to join the burgeoning Nazi Party.

Aryan Clause (*Arierparagraph*).   A law of June 1933, which excluded Jews from taking part in cultural activities such as film-making or the theatre. Although the clause also applied to Christians of Jewish ancestry in the Protestant Churches and was denounced by the Confessional Church (►Churches in the Third Reich), outside Germany it received more publicity in its application to arts and entertainment. Many hundreds of actors and actresses, directors, producers and technicians left Germany for France, Britain and the United States. As they rose in the entertainment industry of their adopted lands, not unnaturally they favoured anti-Nazi subjects, adding to the vast body of anti-Nazi publicity outside the Third Reich.

Atlantic, Battle of the.   The Atlantic struggle between Allied convoys and U-boats in which 2,700 Allied ships were sunk, 30,000 sailors drowned, and 600 U-boats, 32,000 sailors and several capital ships were lost by Germany.

In September 1939 when Britain declared war on Germany, there were 2 German battleships and 21 submarines ('U-boats') on station in the Atlantic. For the first months of the war this force harried shipping bound for England. Although the force was not large enough to affect supplies seriously, the U-boats succeeded in sinking a British battleship and an aircraft carrier. Against these successes, one of the German battleships, the *Graf Spee*, after sinking a number of British ships in the South Atlantic, was forced to shelter at Montevideo and scuttle herself in December 1939. From the beginning of 1940 Germany sent out 9 converted armed merchant cruisers into the Atlantic, sinking 137 ships. But their own lives were short: 7 of the 9 were sunk and 2 reached safe ports, where they were forced to remain throughout the war.

The full attack against Britain's Atlantic supply routes began, however, when the German submarine commander, Admiral Dönitz, sent out his small force again in June 1940 and succeeded in sinking 63 ships in one month. Tactics now developed rapidly. The British countered the U-boat attacks by collecting ships in protected convoys; in response, Dönitz ordered his U-boats to gather in packs for their attacks. Convoys approaching Britain now began to lose as many as one-third of their ships. Admiral Raeder used this evidence to demonstrate to Hitler that his navy was more effective than Göring's Luftwaffe and deserved priority for submarine production. But the navy's own 'Z-Plan' had concentrated on battleships, and there was little current provision for U-boats. By February 1941 Dönitz still had only 21 ocean-going U-boats.

German battleships remained a threat to Atlantic convoys and when the *Bismarck* sailed into the North Atlantic in May 1941, the British navy devoted extensive forces to sink it. The *Tirpitz* was a threat to the convoys taking supplies by sea north of Norway to Russia until it too was finally sunk at anchor in a Norwegian fjord. The battleship *Scharnhorst* was the last of the surviving large German warships, and was not destroyed until the end of December 1943.

Yet despite these successes for the Allies the major danger remained the growing U-boat force which Germany could now dispose in the North Atlantic.

Even before the USA came into the war, her navy had collaborated with the British in escorting Atlantic convoys and had made her first attack on a U-boat in April 1941. The US had declared a 'security zone' in which it would attack suspicious targets along its own coasts and in the Caribbean area. In July 1941 the US navy included the area of Iceland in the zone, and when the USS *Greer* was attacked in September, the American fleet threatened full hostile action.

In mid-1941 U-boat production began to increase, so that by November there were 22 submarines in action but nearly 200 more were approaching completion. Allied shipping losses increased from a 1940 average of 100,000 tons per month first to 400,000 and then to 700,000 in the mid-year. Off the American coasts alone between January and July 1942, 460 ships (2,300,000 tons) were sunk.

From July 1942 Dönitz concentrated his growing U-boat packs on the North Atlantic convoys. At any one time there were 30 or 40 U-boats at sea. To counter them, convoys were given more light warships to protect them and long-range air patrols – the biggest danger to U-boats – were increased. Although the Anglo-American force of 300 ships sailed undamaged from Britain to land troops in North Africa in November 1942, in the Atlantic 800,000 tons of shipping were lost – the worst month of the war. By the end of 1942, Dönitz had 212 U-boats operational, mostly in the Atlantic. In January 1943, disappointed by the performance of his surface fleet, Hitler dismissed Raeder as commander of the navy and put Dönitz in his place. From now on German naval activity would be almost exclusively a U-boat campaign in the Atlantic.

In the months February to May 1943, the Battle of the Atlantic reached its height. Each day there were some 40 U-boats in place, with another 70 going to or from the battle. In this period 91 U-boats were lost but 83 new submarines joined the battle. In March two Allied convoys of 80 ships were followed by 41 U-boats in three packs. When the U-boats attacked, the convoy lost 21 ships for the destruction of one U-boat. It was a rate of attrition which, clearly, Britain and America could not continue to bear.

But the Allies were now intercepting all U-boat radio signals and increasing the range and frequency of air cover. As important were the new tactics devised by Britain's Admiral Sir Max Horton. The surface ships were now to go onto the attack. Hunter groups of destroyers were to follow convoys waiting for a U-boat attack. While this was fought off by the convoy's own escort, the hunter groups would position themselves to continue a relentless search for the U-boats long after the convoy had passed. In May another convoy was attacked by 41 U-boats, but fog blinded the Germans while radar continued to identify them to the British. Dönitz called off the attack when 6 U-boats were sunk and several others damaged. It was the beginning of the end. By early summer Dönitz was reporting to Hitler: 'We are facing the greatest crisis in submarine warfare since the enemy, by means of new location devices, is causing us heavy losses.' Those losses had been such that on 23 May 1943 Dönitz withdrew his U-boats from the North Atlantic until new technical advances were available. In a dramatic three-month period the battlefield had been left to the Anglo-Americans.

In September 1944 the U-boats returned to the Atlantic with *Schnorkel* (underwater breathing) devices and new long-range acoustic torpedoes. But with their radar, their new submarine hunter groups and the long-range Liberator bombers from the US, the Allies were now in a markedly superior position. The Battle of the Atlantic had been won.

Atlantis.   German armed cruiser. One of a number of sea raiders which achieved considerable success in their attacks on British shipping in the early part of the war.

Atomic Bomb Research.   Although German nuclear physicists had been early leaders in research, Nazi Germany made no real progress towards the creation of an atomic bomb. It was a German scientist who had discovered atomic fission and Germans had first published the theory of the chain-reacting pile. When the Anglo-American atomic bomb was being developed during WWII, it was feared that the Germans were conducting parallel research. A 'heavy water' plant was attacked and destroyed in Norway by a Norwegian resistance group in the hope that this would delay German production. But it was not until November 1944 that the Allies were sure that German research had not progressed beyond a comparatively primitive stage, and that atomic physicists had not been given any significant priority for their work. Once again, Hitler's production planning relied on conventional weaponry, while Himmler tried to divert the scientists to projects that he favoured ideologically. Furthermore, the early purging from the universities of suspected intellectuals and Jews had seriously weakened the research teams, many members of which had chosen to emigrate to the USA.

Attila.   Earlier code-name for German occupation of unoccupied France. ►Anton.

Auf Gut Deutsch **('Plain Speaking')**.   A newspaper published by Dietrich Eckart in Munich after WWI. ►Eckart, Dietrich.

Auschwitz (Oswiecim).   The largest and most notorious of *Vernichtungslager*, extermination camps. Auschwitz, some 150 miles from Warsaw, was first built as a concentration camp for Poles in May 1940 and was placed under the command of Rudolf Höss, who had been promoted from Sachsenhausen. In October a second camp, Birkenau, was added, first for 100,000 Russian prisoners and then for Jews to be used as slave labour.

In June 1941, under direct orders from Himmler, Auschwitz was greatly extended. 'Bathhouses', disguised gas chambers, were added and *Leichenkeller* (corpse cellars) were built to house the dead before the bodies were burned in the now effective crematoria. Commandant Höss has testified that at that time Belzek, Treblinka and Wolzek were being adapted to the purposes of mass extermination. Thus six months before the Wannsee conference (January 1942) the first practical steps in the organization of the Final Solution had already taken place.

There is no doubt that from the beginning Auschwitz was assigned a leading role. Commandant Höss was determined not to disappoint his superiors. Visiting Treblinka he was unimpressed by their killing method using carbon monoxide gas from truck or tank engines: he found the process too lengthy and too uncertain in outcome. Not without pride he claimed to have been responsible for the introduction of the considerably more efficient Zyklon-B gas system at Auschwitz. In the new gas chambers 2,000 people at a time could be accommodated, against 200 at Treblinka.

In his evidence at his post-war trial Höss then explained the process of selection by which some prisoners were diverted to work in the factory area which developed as part of the vast Auschwitz-Birkenau complex. Here IG Farben and companies like Krupp's worked their labourers until they collapsed. At the initial selection process a young and fit prisoner might win, by his or her appearance, another few months' lease of life. The others were directed to the column whose fate was to be immediate gassing. 'Children of tender years,' Höss said, 'were inevitably exterminated since by reason of their youth they were unable to work.'

From time to time riots occurred, but Höss intimated that they were suppressed without difficulty. Secrecy was a more intractable problem. People in the Polish communities around Auschwitz certainly knew what was happening, Höss conceded, 'since the foul and nauseating stench of the continuous burning of bodies permeated the whole area'.

Great efforts were made, however, to disguise from the incoming Jews the nature of their fate. At Birkenau the railway track – in fact in every sense the end of the line – appeared to run on at least as far as the next bend. Prisoners were informed that they were to be disinfected in the vast 'bathhouses', and some were even issued with printed postcards: 'We have work and are well treated. We await your arrival,' to be sent back to relatives or friends at home.

The numbers murdered were colossal. Frequently no count was made. The transports arriving from all over Europe from 1942 onwards carried 6,000–7,000 people at a time, sometimes more than once a day. The hideous suffering of the victims on journeys in crowded cattle-cars was nothing compared to the horrors on arrival at Auschwitz. On the ramp, SS doctors, of whom Mengele was just one serving officer, made the selection. If it was still difficult to believe that the purpose of their journey was extermination, no adult Jew at this point doubted that at the best only brutal mistreatment awaited them.

After gassing, the bodies were cremated. At Auschwitz the numbers were, by 1944, in excess of 6,000 daily. In the summer of that year over 250,000 Hungarian Jews were murdered in six weeks. The charnel house could not handle the task. Victims who might by now be gassed or shot were thrown into ditches, covered with benzene and burnt in the open.

As the pace of murder became more frenetic even Commandant Höss, proud of his totals though he was, could no longer keep accurate count. His own figure fluctuated between 3,000,000 and 1,135,000 killed. Perhaps a million and a half human beings, mostly European Jews but also Russian prisoners of war and gypsies, died at Auschwitz.

Austrian Legion. A paramilitary Austrian Nazi organization which had pressed for union with Germany before being banned by Chancellor Dollfuss.

Autarky. The concept of self-sufficiency which spurred much German nationalism in the 1920s. Many Germans saw the nation ringed by hostile countries and therefore needing to keep itself in readiness for siege. Thus the less Germany bought abroad and the more it produced at home, the stronger would be its economic position. Industrialists who traded in the world market were suspected of betraying their country. Autarky was part of the radical thinking of early Nazis such as Feder. To Hitler it was more than a matter of excluding imports, it was a part of his dream of a racially pure living space for the German people.

Industry gave massive support to the autarky concept, as is evidenced by IG Farben's interest in manufacturing substitutes for imported petrol and rubber. Schacht, with more conventional economic theories, worried that autarky would prevent Germany's re-entry into international markets. But independent of Schacht's Ministry of Economics, Hitler set up an office to ensure the replacement of imported raw materials.

The army and Luftwaffe were also supporters of Hitler's autarky proposals, seeing the need for reliable fuel supplies. Thus, when in 1936 the Four-Year Economic Plan was introduced, there was broad support for this part of it. Hitler, despite his public claims, did not think of autarky as a protection of German living standards. He saw it rather as a means to serve his expansionist ambitions; by 1939 any broad social idea of autarky had gone and economic planning was directed towards war.

Autobahns. The express highways built in Germany and widely regarded as a major achievement of the Third Reich.

The first Autobahn (literally 'motor way') was opened between Cologne and Bonn in 1932 before the Nazis came to power. From 1928 the Weimar Republic's programme of public works included plans for national highways. The Nazis at first campaigned against the programme; once in power, they appointed the Munich engineer Fritz Todt Inspector General of German Roads and claimed the credit for the programme themselves.

At the beginning of WWI the German railway network had formed part of the General Staff's plans for mobilization and deployment for war. Similarly in the build-up to WWII the Autobahns had a role in moving troops and materials rapidly to the frontiers. They differed from other road systems in being designed for motor vehicles with a speed of at least 25 mph and having four 25-foot-wide lanes for each traffic direction.

In the 1930s the German Autobahn construction programme was unique in Europe. Over 30,000 workers were committed to the task, a figure which more than doubled in the later 1930s. The programme called for the construction of 7,000 miles of road, and though less than a quarter was completed by the outbreak of war the Autobahn programme nevertheless provided for Germany a substantial modern road network long before its European rivals.

Axis. Following his success with the Anti-Comintern Pact, signed first with Japan in 1936 and with Italy the next year, Hitler proposed a Berlin–Tokyo–Rome alliance, as a counter-balance to the colonial empires of Britain, France and the Netherlands. But Japan was reluctant to commit herself at this stage, and the treaty signed in May 1939 established only a Berlin–Rome axis. With the collapse of France and the Netherlands in 1940, however, French Indochina and the Dutch East Indies were left without their colonial masters. The Japanese government, anxious to seize the territories but alarmed at the prospect of US counter-action, sought the backing of Germany and Italy. A tripartite Axis pact was therefore signed in September 1940.

Further to this, in March 1941 Germany assured Japan that if she were at war with the USA, Germany would join in on her side. When, in December 1941, the US made a formal declaration of war against Japan following the attack on Pearl Harbor, Hitler honoured his assurance to Japan and declared war on the US. With hindsight this must be considered an act of quixotic folly. The result for Germany was calamitous.

Axmann, Artur (1913–1996). Succeeded Baldur von Schirach as leader of the Hitler Youth in 1940. He had joined the movement in 1928 and rose through its hierarchy. In 1941 he fought in Russia, losing an arm. He oversaw the increasing militarization of the Hitler Youth, putting them to work in urban air defence, at first as messengers and finally by 1943 as anti-aircraft gunners. He was fierce in defence of the Hitler Youth and demanded that the SS hunt down the deviant *Swingjugend* in January 1942. At the end of the war he put 1,000 of his Hitler Youth into the final defence of Berlin. As one of the last survivors of Hitler's bunker, he gave important evidence about the deaths of Hitler and Eva Braun and claimed that he had seen the body of Martin Bormann. In the last hours he abandoned his Hitler Youth and made his escape, being arrested only in November 1945 in Bavaria. He survived 'denazification' to become a prosperous businessman after the war.

B

Babi Yar.   A ravine near the city of Kiev in the Ukraine, where SS units massacred thousands of Jews in September 1941. A German engineer, Gräbner, has left a horrific description of the 'reprisal' action which killed over 30,000 Jews in two days.

Bach-Zelewski, Erich von dem (1899–1972).   SS General in charge of campaigns against partisan or resistance movements on the Eastern Front. A professional soldier from a Junker family, he joined the Nazi party in 1930, the SS in 1931, and was Reichstag deputy 1932–4. During WWII he was senior SS and police leader in the Central Army Group area in Russia (1941–2) and later suppressed the Warsaw rising of 1944. In 1951 he was sentenced to ten years special labour (in effect house arrest) but was rearrested in 1958 and charged with murders committed in 1941–2. As further evidence about his wartime activities emerged, he was again retried and sentenced (in 1962) to life for murders committed during the early years of the Third Reich.

Bäck, Leo (1873–1956).   A Jewish scholar and leader of the Jewish community in Berlin. In 1933 he refused to leave Germany, and stayed to be a member of the Jewish Council set up by the Nazis, to defend what rights German Jews had left. In 1943 he was sent to Theresienstadt concentration camp, where he became the leader of the Jewish elders; he was reported to have debated whether or not he should unsettle his fellow Jews by telling them about the extermination camps. In 1945 he defended the camp guards against lynching by the prisoners. After the war he left Germany and lived in London and New York.

Backe, Herbert (1896–1947).   An agricultural specialist who became Minister of Food in 1944. He was one of the ministers named by Hitler in his last testament. Brought to trial by the Allies, he hanged himself in Nuremberg Prison in 1947.

Bamberg Conference.   A meeting of senior Nazis on 14 February 1926 which aimed to resolve the schism between those Nazis (like Gregor Strasser) more socialist than nationalist, and the right wing of the party led by Hitler. His speech at the conference warned the Party against the seductive road of expropriation. He was jeered at as *Adolf Légalité* but he was undoubtedly more concerned at the danger of frightening off the financial support of German industrialists and landowners. In the bitter dispute at Bamberg, Göbbels moved to the right wing of the Party, anticipating the conference's endorsement of Hitler's viewpoint. The struggle between the two wings nevertheless continued until Hitler's final victory over the advocates of 'continuous revolution' during the Night of the Long Knives in 1934. ➤Nazi Party

Banse, Ewald (1883–1953). Writer and professor of military science in the Third Reich. His views were set out in his book, *Raum und Volk in Weltkrieg* (*Living Areas and Race in World War*): internationalism was degenerate and war inevitable and desirable as a means for people to solve national problems, the acquisition of *Lebensraum* and the unification of national living areas.

Barbarossa. Code-name for the German attack on Russia of 22 June 1941. Führer Directive No. 21, issued on 18 December 1940, ordered that full preparations for a *Blitzkrieg* campaign against the Soviet Union should be completed by 15 May 1941. The object of the operation was, first, the destruction of the Soviet army in western Russia by a series of envelopments, and subsequently the establishment of a defence line from Archangel to the Volga River. In the event, the invasion was delayed until 22 June 1941. Nineteen Panzer and fourteen motorized divisions spearheaded the German army. Even so, German armoured strength totalled no more than 3,550 tanks against (according to Stalin's own figures) 24,000 Soviet tanks, of which half were in western Russia. The attack was launched in three parallel surges between the Baltic Sea and the Carpathians; German forces comprised Leeb's Northern Army Group and Rundstedt's Southern Army Group. Although vast numbers of Soviet prisoners were captured and immense quantities of equipment destroyed in four attempts to encircle the Soviet army, the Germans were being led deeper and deeper into Russia. By the onset of the first winter of the campaign the Soviet armies, though badly mauled, had not been conclusively beaten. ➤Appendix V for chronology of Russian campaign.

Barbie, Klaus (1914–91). A middle-ranking Gestapo officer who became notorious, after the Germans occupied the southern part of France in 1942, as the 'Butcher of Lyons'. In 1987 he was the subject of a widely publicized trial in the city he had terrorized during the war. For crimes against humanity he was sentenced to life imprisonment.

Barth, Karl (1886–1968). Swiss-born Protestant theologian who was outspokenly anti-Nazi. In July 1933 he founded a magazine which defended the Lutheran faith and attacked the Nazi-sponsored 'German Christians'. Unlike the majority of academics, he refused to give an oath of allegiance to Hitler and was reported to have opened his lectures with a perfunctory 'Heil Hitler'. In 1935 he was dismissed from his professorship at Bonn University and went back to Basel, Switzerland.

Bastogne. French town defended by the Americans in the December 1944

Ardennes offensive. When the Germans advanced, Bastogne was staffed only by engineer and Corps Headquarters troops. The senior officer nevertheless decided, without higher orders, to hold the town. The 101st Airborne Division under Brigadier-General McAuliffe moved from Rheims, driving 100 miles at full speed through the night. They reached Bastogne before the Germans could mount a full assault, and entrenched. They could not prevent the encirclement of the town – a vital road junction – but performed so aggressively that they could not be bypassed. Three German divisions of 47 Panzer Corps surrounded them and called for surrender. McAuliffe's reply has become a classic: 'Nuts!' They held out for eight days. On Christmas Day they were attacked by two more divisions but fought them off, so that at noon the German commander asked for permission to call off his attack. The next day General Patton's 3rd Army broke through and relieved the defenders.

The stubborn defence of Bastogne was a rock on which the Ardennes offensive – the last in the west – broke.

Battle Committee for Berlin Students.   A group of nationalistic students responsible for the book-burning episode on 11 May 1933 when works by Mann, Erich Kästner, Emil Ludwig and Erich Maria Remarque among others were destroyed.

Battle League (*Deutscher Kampfbund*).   An alliance of armed patriotic groups in Bavaria, established by Röhm at a mass rally in Nuremberg in September 1923. Here Hitler stood beside the venerable and prestigious General Ludendorff as one of the three joint leaders. Its main aim was the overthrow of the republican government and the tearing up of the Treaty of Versailles; as such, it brought together most of the right-wing activists of Southern Germany. With the SA, the Battle League assembled in Munich and marched with Hitler and Ludendorff in what became the Beer Hall Putsch. Banned with other like groups, Röhm absorbed the members he wanted into the SA.

Battle of Britain.   The critical air battle fought over southern England in 1940 between the Luftwaffe and the RAF.

In June 1940, with his victorious armies on the Channel coast in some places little more than 20 miles from Britain, Hitler accepted Göring's assurance that the Luftwaffe could engage and defeat RAF Fighter Command and thus open the way for the seaborne invasion code-named Sealion.

In pilot training and the quality of the fighter aircraft engaged, the two sides were evenly matched. Both the British and Germans had developed and produced all-metal monoplane fighters with top speeds of over 300 mph, able to fight at heights above 20,000 feet. The German Messerschmitt BF109 and the British Spitfire and Hurricane fighter planes were closely matched in combat capability. The British advantage lay in their development of radar and radio communication between squadrons and ground stations. Of the 3,000 RAF pilots, one in five was from the Empire, Poland or Czechoslovakia, with a few volunteers from the USA. The fact that the RAF were fighting over England meant that pilots parachuting from damaged aircraft might be back in battle the same day. Luftwaffe pilots parachuting to safety were likely to find themselves prisoners of war.

The battle opened in July 1940 when the Luftwaffe attempted to provoke air battles over the channel between the RAF and the fighter escorts of bombers raiding British coastal shipping. In August the major Luftwaffe assault began with 1,500 planes, both fighters and bombers, attacking targets further inland. But the Germans had not developed long-range heavy bombers, and were using the same medium bombers as in the Spanish Civil War and Poland. Slow and lightly armed, the Heinkels and Dorniers had not met modern fighters before. The Luftwaffe attack concentrated on the RAF's airfields but failed to destroy the radar system. Bombers flown to northern Britain from Denmark and Norway were intercepted and suffered heavy casualties. However, the attack continued and by the beginning of September many of the RAF's southern airfields were out of action, its pilots near exhaustion, its reserves of planes dependent on levels of production from the factories which could not always be achieved. Closer to defeat than Göring appreciated, Britain's Fighter Command still maintained a vigorous response to Luftwaffe attacks, but senior RAF officers knew that there was now a clear limit to Fighter Command's ability to continue the battle.

At this point in mid-September – for reasons which are still unclear – Göring changed the location of his attacks from the airfields to London. Convinced that this switch of targets meant that an invasion was imminent, the British put every effort into the air war and the Luftwaffe, seeing RAF fighters still coming up to attack their formations, began to lose confidence in the possibility of victory.

Both sides exaggerated their claims, but post-war counts reveal the degree of attrition suffered by both Luftwaffe and RAF. In the three months from July to October, the Luftwaffe lost 2,848 planes and the RAF half that number, 1,446. Relieved of pressure on their airfields and factories, the RAF began to rebuild its strength. To Hitler it was evident that Göring had failed to destroy Fighter Command, and by the beginning of 1941 Sealion was abandoned as plans for the invasion of Russia took precedence in the Führer's mind. Partly to save face, Göring again changed Luftwaffe tactics to the night bombing of London and other cities. In British terms a great battle had been fought and won; they alone had survived the Third Reich's attacks and lived to fight on.

Bauhaus. The school and research institute founded by the architect Walter Gropius in Weimar in 1919. The Bauhaus was part of the modern movement in industrial design which had been strong in Germany from the beginning of the century. In 1925, by now associated with socialism, Gropius moved to

Dessau near Halle. Gropius' successor, the architect Mies van der Rohe, was accused by radical students of being a 'formalist', and the Thuringian State Minister of the Interior, the newly elected Nazi Frick, called the Bauhaus a communist cell and demanded its closure. It was moved for a second time to Berlin, but in April 1933 the SA raided its buildings, claiming that Communist Party leaflets were printed there. The Bauhaus was closed down amid staff protest. Some would have been prepared to stay in an attempt to adapt to the new order, but modernism had been labelled degenerate and non-Aryan. The most important leaders chose emigration: Gropius, Mies van der Rohe, Albers, Moholy-Nagy, Marcel Breuer and other great names of the modern movement. Most continued their work in the USA.

Bayerische Kurier. Party newspaper of Held's BVP, the Bavarian People's Party.

Beck, Ludwig (1880–1944). A leading figure in German army opposition to Hitler. A WWI general staff officer and regular army officer in the Weimar Republic, he became Adjutant General of the army in 1933. As Chief of the General Staff in 1935, Beck tried to defend the army against Hitler's takeover and opposed his war plans. In 1938 he sent von Kleist to London to obtain evidence that Britain would go to war if Germany invaded Czechoslovakia, but the British policy of appeasement at that time disappointed his hopes. He urged von Brauchitsch, the army Commander-in-Chief, to oppose Hitler's plans and to unite the senior officers of the army in protest. Although von Brauchitsch read Beck's paper on the danger of Germany's going to war to other generals, he refused to support it. Instead he sent the paper to Hitler, and Beck was forced to resign in August 1938. Ludwig Beck stayed in touch with others who opposed Hitler's war, such as Oster, Canaris, von Hassell and Gördeler. However by 1944 his health was failing and his only involvement in the 1944 Bomb Plot was as titular head. On the plot's failure he twice attempted unsuccessfully to shoot himself until dragged out and shot unceremoniously in the head by a sergeant.

Beer Hall. Also known as a beer cellar. Munich breweries often have large drinking halls, used not only by individual customers but by large groups, clubs or political organizations. During the Weimar period, beer cellars were frequently used for political meetings of every colour. Among those most used by the Nazis were: the Bürgerbräukeller, the Hofbräuhaus, the Eberlbräuhaus, the Loewenbräuhaus and the Loewenbräukeller. The Torbräukeller near the Isartor was the centre for SA recruitment and it was in the Sterneckerbräu that the Nazi Party was founded.

Beer Hall Putsch. Attempted Nazi coup. In November 1923 Hitler attempted a rash and improvised takeover of the Bavarian state. Kahr, the State Commissioner in Bavaria with full powers to defend the Bavarian State against rightist outbreaks, was to address a patriotic meeting in the Bürgerbräukeller in Munich. Hitler, with Göring and others, burst in on the meeting and fired a shot at the ceiling. In a moment of high theatre he declared a national revolution and the deposition of both the Bavarian and German Reich governments. 600 SA men had surrounded the building, and Hitler took Kahr and others to a back room and forced them to declare co-operation; Hitler would direct political affairs in the new regime and Ludendorff (who had just been told of the attempt) would command the army. As soon as he was free of SA intimidation, Kahr renounced the agreement and the Putsch should have collapsed. Ludendorff, however, now heavily committed, persuaded Hitler to go ahead. At about noon the next day, with some 2,000 followers the Nazi leaders marched towards the centre of Munich, Odeonsplatz, where State police blocked the street. The police fired and Hitler and Göring were injured (sixteen party members and three police were killed). There was some panic and Hitler was taken away by car to Hanfstängl's house. Two days later he was arrested. In February 1924, Hitler was tried for high treason, found guilty and sentenced to five years' imprisonment at Landsberg Prison. The Beer Hall Putsch was an inglorious, ill-planned affair, but the trial provided Hitler with his first opportunity to put his name before the German people.

Bell, Dr George (1883–1958). Bishop of Chichester, England. When Bell visited Stockholm in 1942, Hans Oster provided Bonhöffer with a passport to travel to meet the English bishop. In Sweden, Bell was informed of the Gördeler conspiracy and given a list of names. The bishop passed the list to Eden, the British Foreign Secretary, who saw no reason to support the conspiracy.

Bishop Bell is notable, too, for his House of Lords protest, in the midst of a world war, against the form of 'area bombing' used by the RAF against German cities.

Bello, Heinz (1920–44). A non-commissioned officer in the German army who was called up in 1939 and took part in the Russian campaign. In March 1944 he was arrested for what appears to have been a casual denunciation of National Socialism and sentenced to death by shooting.

Belsen (also known as Bergen-Belsen). A labour camp in north-west Germany. Intended principally for political prisoners, when Belsen was liberated by British troops in April 1945 the number of prisoners had swollen to many times its capacity. The savagery of the guards had resulted in the death of many prisoners but was nothing compared with the results of the murderous neglect by its camp commandant, Josef Kramer (➤Kramer, Josef). Thousands of emaciated bodies lay in heaps, more in uncovered pits. Prisoners stumbled around in an advanced state of starvation. Even as the camp was being cleaned up by SS men, a film was made which was shown in every cinema in Britain.

It is estimated that in a camp intended for fewer than 10,000 prisoners, some

70,000 had arrived from other camps, evacuated before one or other of the advancing Allied armies. Within the Belsen compound on the day it was finally overrun were 30,000 living prisoners, many on the point of death, and the bodies of over 30,000 more.

Belzec.   Concentration camp on the Lublin–Lvov railway line opened in March 1942. Its six gas chambers and crematoria could theoretically deal with 15,000 people a day. It is estimated that 600,000 people died there. ➤Concentration Camps

Bendlerstrasse.   Location of the German War Ministry in Berlin.

Beneš, Eduard (1884–1948).   Czech statesman and President. Pressurized by Hitler after the Munich Agreement, Beneš resigned the Czech presidency. Living in the West, he organized the National Committee after the German invasion of Czechoslovakia and resumed the presidency of the Czech government in exile, first in Paris and then in London. Early in the war all the Allied powers had accorded the government in exile full recognition. Czechs fought as a brigade in the British army and as highly valued pilots in the RAF. At the same time Beneš succeeded in persuading Britain and de Gaulle's Free French to recognize that the Munich Agreement would not be applied to Czechoslovakia's post-war frontiers. By 1942 Russia and by 1943 the United States had both given assurances of support. After addressing both US Houses of Congress, Beneš moved on to Canada where he was similarly received by Parliament in Ottawa.

In 1944 Russian forces reached the Czech borders, and shortly afterwards Beneš returned to set up a provisional government. On 16 May 1945 he entered Prague to an enthusiastic welcome. For three years at least Czechoslovakia would be free of interference from the great powers.

Berchtesgaden.   A small town in the Bavarian Alps where Hitler's early rented home, Haus Wachenfeld, was first bought by him and then enlarged into the Berghof. It was used partly as a retreat and partly as a conference centre where Schuschnigg, Lloyd George, Ciano, Halifax and Chamberlain were taken and to which the German military commanders were often called. At Berchtesgaden Hitler, on home ground, could dominate visitors.

Above the Berghof was the 'Eagle's Nest', a fantastic mountain house 6,000 feet up on a mountain above Berchtesgaden. It was reached by ten miles of hairpin-bend road cut into the mountainside, with a final elevator ride for the last 370 feet to spectacular mountain views. The Berghof was burnt by the SS in May 1945 and the Americans demolished the surrounding buildings when they occupied the area.

Berger, Gottlob (1895–1975).   Head of SS Headquarters Department and an expert on racial selection for the SS. He was responsible for raising pan-

European Waffen SS units, such as the Viking and Charlemagne divisions. In his vision of a united Europe the Waffen SS was to be the central institution of European Nazism.

From October 1944 he ran the SS prisoner-of-war administration, holding internationally famous prisoners, and in 1945 he left Berlin for Bavaria to use these prisoners as possible bargaining counters. In 1949 he was tried and sentenced for war crimes, including the suppression of risings in Slovakia in 1944.

Berlin, Battle of. The final cataclysmic battle of the Third Reich. Forced into a pocket less than ten miles long and three miles wide, a rag-bag German force of SS, *Wehrmacht*, ageing Home Guard and Hitler Youth struggled to hold back the conquering Soviet forces. Bombed and shelled to the end, Berlin finally surrendered on 2 May 1945. As the men abandoned their weapons and uniforms and concealed themselves, the women of the city faced the first waves of the Soviet occupying troops. A degree of looting was authorized at the highest command level: every Soviet soldier was to be allowed to send home a limited weight of goods. In the first week, rape became a fact of daily life for the women of Berlin.

Berlitzbürgertum. The property-owning bourgeoisie. The object of early Nazi propaganda attacks. After 1933 and especially after the Röhm Purge, the Party line was modified in the interest of national unity.

Bernadotte, Count Folke (1895–1948). The vice-president of the Swedish Red Cross, a nephew of the King of Sweden, who was approached by Himmler to try and bring about an end to the war. It was Göring who first suggested that Bernadotte might be of use when he comprehended that the failure of the Ardennes offensive in December 1944 meant the loss of the war. Urged by Schellenberg, Himmler arranged a meeting in February 1945 in Berlin, with the knowledge of Ribbentrop, the Foreign Minister, but not of Hitler. The transfer of concentration camp prisoners to the Red Cross was discussed, but could not be agreed. In April 1945 Himmler met him again, but Bernadotte reported that the Allies would not negotiate and would insist on unconditional surrender. When the news of the meetings reached Hitler, he declared Himmler dismissed from all posts for treason.

Bernadotte was killed by an Israeli terrorist group in 1948 while trying to arrange an armistice in Palestine.

Best, Werner (1903–1989). A Rhineland law student who was imprisoned by the French during their post-WWI occupation of the Ruhr for his outspoken nationalist views. He became a legal adviser to the Nazi Party and was the drafter of the Boxheim Papers (a plan for a Nazi Putsch whose disclosure caused some embarrassment to them in 1931). He became Police Commissioner of Hesse in 1933 and State Governor in July of that year. He strengthened his career by becoming Deputy to Heydrich and Chief Legal Adviser to the SS. He helped build the Gestapo and the SD, heading a section of the RUSHA, 1939–40. From 1940 to 1942 he led the SD in France and then moved to Denmark as German Commissioner.

In Denmark his rule was (by Nazi standards) lenient, and he seems to have tried to soften the effect of the Final Solution there. There is evidence that he connived at a warning given to the Danish Resistance which enabled them to effect the escape of almost all Denmark's Jews to Sweden. But he was, notwithstanding, found guilty of murder by a Danish court and condemned to death, a sentence which was later commuted to five years' imprisonment. After serving his sentence he returned to Germany where he was found guilty of mass murder in 1958. He was released from prison for reasons of ill-health in 1972.

Biddle, Francis (1886–1968).   Distinguished American laywer. US Solicitor General and, from 1941, Attorney General. Appointed by President Truman in 1945 US member of the International Military Tribunal which was to try major war criminals at Nuremberg. He later described and analysed the issues arising from Nuremberg in his autobiography, *In Brief Authority*.

Birkenau.   Part of the much larger Auschwitz camp, Birkenau had a railway siding disguised as a complete railway station. It began operations in 1941 as a hastily constructed extermination camp for Russian prisoners and continued in use as a sub-camp of Auschwitz.

Black Front.   ➤Strasser, Otto

Black Order.   General term for the SS (➤SS).

Black Reichswehr.   A highly secret and illegal reinforcement to the 100,000-man official army, which was the total military force the German republic was allowed under the Versailles Treaty. Started by General von Seeckt under the cover-name of *Arbeitskommandos* (Labour Commandos), the Black Reichswehr was dissolved by him after an attempted Putsch in Berlin by Black Reichswehr units under Major Buchrucker on the night of 30 September 1923.

Blaskowitz, Johannes von (1884–1946).   German general who commanded an army in the invasion of Poland and in Russia in 1942 and 1943. In 1945, commanding an Army Group in the Netherlands, he surrendered to advancing Canadian forces. He was brought to trial for war crimes but committed suicide before the verdict.

Bleicher, Hugo (b. 1899).   The most successful *Abwehr* operator in WWII. Though never gaining a rank higher than sergeant, Bleicher worked, first in The Hague and then in occupied France, with great independence and marked success. His destruction of Interallié, the first major resistance network established in France, led to further successes when he personally arrested Peter Churchill and the celebrated SOE agent, Odette. Specializing in the so-called double-cross system (he passed himself off as a French agent, Colonel Henri), Hugo Bleicher established his *own* resistance network, the Lisiana, and used it to obtain information and entrap French resisters. He was arrested in 1945, tried and imprisoned.

Blitzkrieg.   The strategy of the 'lightning war' (►Guderian). German military tactics grew from the last offensive of WWI in spring 1918 when shock troops were trained to break through the Allied trench lines. They were armed with light machine-guns, mortars, flame-throwers and small artillery weapons that soldiers could carry forward. Young officers such as Rommel fighting in the Alps made brilliant tactical use of these new units.

After WWI the *Freikorps* added to these tactics the use of armoured cars and street-fighting techniques as they put down rebellion against their government. Guderian, who created the Third Reich's armoured Panzer divisions for WWII, was Chief of Staff to a *Freikorps* division fighting with these methods in eastern Germany. The General Staff used this experience in planning the attacks on Poland in 1939 and on western Europe in 1940. By adding strategic planning, supply systems, the use of air power in support of the army and, above all, the element of political surprise, a new form of offensive was born for which Germany's enemies were unprepared: *Blitzkrieg*.

The name '*Blitzkrieg*' was said to be Hitler's invention, but it is quite likely to be a word coined by *Time* Magazine. It caught the imagination, and the German air attacks on London and other cities in 1940 were called 'the Blitz'.

***Blitzkrieg*: the campaign in France and the Low Countries**. ►Appendix I

Blockwart.   The Nazi Party's political watch-dog. A low-ranking but vitally important local Party man who provided information for the local office on the people of his neighbourhood (or city block). The *Blockwart* kept people up to the mark, making sure that they joined the right organizations, turned out for the right demonstrations, paid subscriptions to Party magazines or made contributions to charities – especially Winterhilfe – and behaved in the way the Party wanted. The *Blockwart* would organize beds in homes for visiting Nazi demonstrators, since they knew how many people were in each apartment or house and what spare beds they had. After air-raids the *Blockwart* would get people out to clear up rubble in the streets.

Next to the Gestapo, *Blockwarts* were the least popular members of the regime, for they also reported rumours of anti-Nazi remarks. Typically, after 1939 they were men exempt from military service due to age or former injury.

Blomberg, Werner von (1878–1946).   Field Marshal and Minister of Defence from 1933 to 1938. From 1927 to 1929 he had been Adjutant General of the army, his duties taking him to Russia, where he was impressed by the prestige of the army in a totalitarian state. He was appointed army commander in East Prussia until General von Schleicher, the Chancellor, made him military adviser to the Geneva disarmament conference, thus giving him *entrée* to the political world. In 1933 he was ready to support Hitler, seeing him as a strong man who would control a disordered Germany, and was appointed Minister of Defence since he had the support of the traditional officer corps.

When Röhm challenged Blomberg, asserting the SA's right to control national security, Hitler made them sign a compromise agreement which Blomberg saw as a victory for the army. He welcomed the destruction of the SA in the Röhm Purge in 1934 and the death of Hindenburg two months later. He set an example by taking an oath of loyalty to Hitler in person, thereby in effect delivering the army into Hitler's hands.

But when Blomberg opposed Hitler's march into the Rhineland and his plans for Czechoslovakia, in the belief that Germany was too weak for war, Hitler (with Göring's help) planned his resignation. In 1938 Blomberg had remarried. His new, young wife, Erna Grün, had a police record, having appeared in a pornographic photograph. Göring, who had encouraged the marriage, now, by producing the record, forced Blomberg's resignation. At the same time General von Fritsch, the Commander-in-Chief of the army, was framed in a scandal and made to resign. The army was thus weakened, allowing Hitler to restructure the top commands, himself assuming the role of Minister of Defence and taking supreme command. It was a calculated defeat for the army. Blomberg thereafter retired into obscurity and was never recalled to duty. He died in a Nuremberg jail in March 1946, awaiting trial as a war criminal.

Blondi.   Hitler's German shepherd dog which was put to death in the Bunker on the same day Hitler committed suicide.

Blood.   The imagery of blood to evoke some elemental feeling in a German audience was a technique pioneered by Hitler and adopted by most Nazi speakers.

Among their favoured usages were:

'Blood and Soil' (*Blut und Boden*). Sometimes abbreviated to '*Blubo*' the phrase expressed a primitive relationship of earth and German peasant which Nazi speakers dwelt on as part of the anti-urban, anti-industry, anti-capitalist animus which is a constantly recurring theme in both the Party and the SS.

'Blood Shame' (*Blutschande*). Racial intermarriage, especially between Aryans and Jews.

'Blood Order' (*Blutorden*). The most prestigious of Nazi Party decorations.

'Blood Banner' (*Blutfahne*). Another of those Nazi propaganda concepts which walk the fine line between the ridiculous and the genuinely effective. The banner was seen as the primary flag of the Nazi movement, supposedly made sacrosanct by the blood of the martyrs of the abortive 1923 Putsch. At Nuremberg rallies, new party banners were dedicated by Hitler touching the new colours with one hand while the other held the blood flag. The atmosphere of blood and heroic sacrifice in the ceremony is fully communicated by contemporary film.

Blood Purge.   Also known as the Night of the Long Knives. ►Röhm Purge

Bock, Field Marshal Fedor von (1880–1945).   Commander of the German troops entering Austria, von Bock stood in third place of seniority in the Wehrmacht in 1939. After a command in the Polish campaign, he was transferred to the Western Front and at the armistice was made a Field Marshal. After two important commands in the Russian campaign, he was dismissed by Hitler and died in retirement in an air-raid in 1945.

Boger Swing.   A device by which a prisoner to be tortured at Auschwitz could be suspended between two chairs by having a pole placed under his knees in a position which enabled the guards to beat him as he swung forward, head down. The device was invented by Wilhelm Boger, a guard at the camp, who was tried in the Frankfurt trial (1963–5) and sentenced to life imprisonment and an additional five years' hard labour.

Bonhöffer, Dietrich (1906–45).   Evangelical Protestant theologian who maintained constant opposition to Hitler and Nazism. His father, Karl, a psychiatrist, had planned in the 1930s to have Hitler certified and confined as mentally ill; his elder brother, Klaus, a lawyer, was also connected with resistance groups and shot in 1945. Dietrich Bonhöffer studied theology in New York from 1930 to 1933. Dismayed by the Nazi victory he became a pastor in London until 1935 when he returned to Germany to work with the non-Nazi Confessional Church. He met others of his social background who equally loathed the Third Reich, in particular General Beck, and Hans Oster and Admiral Canaris of the *Abwehr*. In 1939 he went to London and the USA to try to establish contacts for a resistance, meeting Bishop Bell in England. At the outbreak of war, he was banned from preaching by Gestapo order, but he continued to make contacts, including the Kreisau Circle. In 1942 he was provided with forged papers by Oster and met Bishop Bell in Sweden, as an emissary of Oster and Beck. But the Allies' suspicion and determination to accept only the unconditional surrender of Germany meant his visit had little effect. In April 1943 he was arrested with Dohnanyi, Josef Müller and others by the SD who were trying to uncover the plotters behind plans for assassination attempts on Hitler. Bonhöffer was held in Buchenwald and executed in Flossenbürg concentration camp in April 1945.

Book burning. Göbbels as Propaganda Minister encouraged students throughout the nation to take 'un-German' books from their libraries and burn them. SA and SS bands played in Berlin on the night of 11 May 1933 and a torchlight parade took place in the city centre where 20,000 books were destroyed. Works by Jews, socialists and liberals were included, among them: Thomas Mann, Einstein, Freud, Proust and H. G. Wells.

Boris III (1894–1943). King of Bulgaria. Although not a Nazi himself, Boris was unable to resist Hitler's pressure on him to align Bulgaria with the Axis cause. In December 1941 he consented to a Bulgarian declaration of war on Britain, a decision he afterwards considered his greatest mistake. Boris III died (possibly murdered) in Germany after a meeting with Hitler in which he opposed further Nazi demands on Bulgaria. He was succeeded by his son, Simeon II.

Bormann, Martin (1900–1945?). Senior Nazi Party figure and head of Hitler's secretariat. Bormann was born in Halberstadt to an ex-soldier who had become a civil servant. He did not complete his secondary education but joined the army in the ranks in WWI. After the war he served in the Rossbach *Freikorps* and later the *Frontbann*, the paramilitary force put together by Röhm after the banning of the SA in 1923. He was jailed with Höss (later to be commandant of the Auschwitz extermination camp) for the murder of a man they claimed to be a traitor in French-occupied Ruhr. After his release in 1925, he joined the Nazi Party in Thuringia and became the local Party press secretary, rising to become Party *Gauleiter* in Thuringia in 1928. He became known for his fund-raising abilities and in that year was made party treasurer and Hitler's intermediary to run the 'Adolf Hitler Fund' into which donations or extortions were paid. A rumour has it that he paid off the police inspector investigating the death of Hitler's niece Geli Raubal and then recruited him – 'Gestapo' Müller – into the Party.

Bormann stayed close to Hitler, but kept himself in the background and was rarely photographed. Hitler relied on him to deal with his money and property affairs, such as the rebuilding of the Berghof at Berchtesgaden. Among Hitler's entourage he ranked next to the Deputy Führer Rudolf Hess, as Hess's *Chief de Cabinet*. But Bormann remained his own man: even when Himmler made him an honorary SS Major General he avoided both the induction rituals and the uniform.

When Hess flew to Britain in 1941 (and it has been speculated that Bormann encouraged or facilitated the flight) Bormann was promoted to Party Minister in charge of Party Headquarters. Here he controlled access to Hitler, sometimes blocking access even to Göring, Göbbels, Himmler and Speer. He organized Party matters while Hitler was preoccupied with the conduct of the war. When the 'People's Army', the *Volkssturm* (a Party military organization), was decreed in October 1944, Bormann became its commander.

Even in Hitler's retreat to the Bunker, Bormann continued his climb to power. He witnessed Hitler's will and marriage, tried to order Göring's execution, saw Göbbels' death and sent Dönitz news of his succession as Führer. When Hitler was dead, he considered trying to treat with the Russians but, realizing this was hopeless, he ordered a mass breakout from the Bunker. He was never seen alive again, although persistent rumours have placed him in several countries, usually in South America. He was tried *in absentia* with the twenty-one other major war criminals at Nuremberg, found guilty and sentenced to death.

Bouhler, Philip (1899–1945), the Head of Chancery in Hitler's personal office. One of the *Alte Kämpfer* (the Old Guard), Bouhler worked on the *Völkischer Beobachter* in the early days of the Party and was business manager of the NSDAP from 1925 to 1934.

In 1933 he was given the Party rank of *Reichsleiter*, and in 1934 followed Himmler as Police President of Munich. At the same time he took over the post of Head of Chancery in Hitler's office. He became chairman of the censorship committee which issued lists of approved and condemned books. In September 1939 Hitler gave him and Dr Karl Brandt responsibility for the programme of euthanasia. He committed suicide in 1945 before US troops came to arrest him.

Boxheim Papers. In November 1931 a Nazi group in Hesse under Werner Best drew up plans to deal with the contingency of a communist revolution. The group wrote draft papers which were seized by the state and became known by the name of the house where the meetings were held: Boxheimer Hof. The plans contained a proclamation to be issued by the SA and emergency decrees which a provisional Nazi government would make, including the immediate execution of anyone resisting or failing to co-operate or found with weapons. Private property rights would be suspended, interest debts annulled, work made compulsory without reward, while people would be fed through public kitchens and issued with food ration cards. There would be courts martial under Nazi presidents. The discovery of the documents resulted in a public scandal and Hitler was forced to disavow the Boxheim Papers, assuring Rhineland industrialists that he would take power only by legal means.

Brand, Joel (1906–64). Representative of a Hungarian relief committee which, at the height of the extermination of Hungarian Jewry in 1944, was invited by Adolf Eichmann to negotiate a deal exchanging US trucks for Jewish lives. Unable to resolve the moral and practical complexities of the deal, Brand became, at the war's end, a specialist in hunting war criminals.

Brandenburgers. The special services units of the German army, the equivalent of the British commandos or US rangers. The *Abwehr*, the German army's counter-intelligence unit, had secretly sent teams into Poland before the German attack in September 1939 to prevent key bridges from being destroyed by the defenders. From these were developed in October special companies, trained to operate ahead of the army, behind enemy lines.

The men selected were often multi-lingual and were trained on an estate near Brandenburg, thus giving the units their name: the Brandenburg battalions. They were trained both to defend and to demolish bridges or fortifications. In 1940 they seized road and rail bridges in the Netherlands and Belgium ahead of the German army, on one occasion wearing Dutch military uniform. In October 1940 the Brandenburgers were increased to regimental size. The army had contingency plans for their use in the Balkans, against oilfields in Rumania and the Danube bridges. In 1942 the army used Brandenburger units to defend their rear against Russian partisan attack as they retreated from the Caucasus. Brandenburgers with a knowledge of the local language were often used in disguise. A Brandenburger unit was also used as a long-range desert patrol in North Africa.

Brandenburger success was not popular with the SS, and they ensured that full publicity was given to Skorzeny's exploit in rescuing Mussolini. SS support was also given to Skorzeny for his use of a specially selected and equipped brigade in the December 1944 Ardennes offensive.

Brandt, Karl (1904–48).   One of Hitler's doctors. He was introduced to the Führer in 1933 and soon gained Hitler's confidence. He was made an SS General and a Reich Commissioner for health, and in September 1939, with Bouhler, was named by Hitler to be responsible for the programme of euthanasia.

Brandt tried unsuccessfully to counter the influence of Hitler's other doctor, Morell, and to reduce the Führer's dependency on drugs, urging rest and exercise. In 1945 Hitler found that Brandt was arranging for his family's safety with the Americans and declared him sentenced to death. Though avoiding the sentence passed upon him by his own side, Brandt was tried by a US court for having approved medical 'experiments' by SS doctors in concentration camps, and hanged in 1948.

Brandt, Willy (1913–1992).   A young SPD socialist who left Germany in 1933, took Norwegian citizenship, and used this to make trips in and out of Germany, keeping contact with socialists. When Germany invaded Norway in 1940, he went to Sweden. He returned to post-war Germany, regained German nationality and re-entered politics, becoming Mayor of Berlin from 1957 to 1966 and Chancellor of the Federal Republic from 1969 until a spy scandal forced his resignation in 1974. He then became a leader in international understanding of the underdeveloped world.

Brauchitsch, Walter von (1881–1948).   Army Commander-in-Chief (OKH) after von Fritsch from 1938 to 1941.

An artillery officer in WWI who had risen to a divisional command by 1933, Brauchitsch was promoted to OKH on the basis of his reputation for a slavish loyalty to the established power. Although Generals Beck and Halder and other professional staff officers sought his support against Hitler's war policies, Brauchitsch refused to join them.

He was the Commander-in-Chief of the victorious German armies in the campaigns of 1939 to 1941 in Poland, Denmark, Norway, the Netherlands, Belgium, France and the Balkans. After the victory in France, he was promoted to Field Marshal.

But when in December 1941 the German armies failed to take Moscow, von Brauchitsch became Hitler's scapegoat and was dismissed. Thereafter he was a sick, ageing man of no influence. Even so, his exaggerated sense of loyalty made him speak out against the conspirators of the 1944 Bomb Plot.

Braun, Eva (1912−45).　Hitler's mistress from 1932 and, in the last days of their lives, his wife. A Bavarian girl from Simbach on the river Inn beside the Austrian border, she was of limited education, with a pretty face and a certain talent for dancing. She was an assistant in the studio of Heinrich Hoffmann the photographer where Hitler met her and, in the year after the death of his niece and probable lover, Geli Raubal, she became his mistress.

At first she was given a flat in Munich but later moved into the Berghof in Berchtesgaden. Hitler's chauffeur said, 'She was the unhappiest woman in Germany. She spent most of her life waiting for Hitler.' Never allowed to appear in public with him, she was confined to his private life. For company she sometimes invited her sisters Ilse and Gretl to Berchtesgaden. She seems never to have exploited her position, though others used her to further their careers: her brother-in-law, Hermann Fegelein, rose to be an SS Major General, before Hitler had him shot for 'desertion' in the last days of the war.

In April 1945 Eva Braun joined Hitler in the Berlin Bunker, where Hitler went through a marriage ceremony with her. The next day she killed herself by poison and her body, with that of Hitler, was burned in the garden above the bunker.

Braun, Werner von (1912−1977).　Technical director of rocket research at Peenemünde. A brilliant scientist, he had been employed by the army on rocket research since the age of twenty. He moved to Peenemünde in 1937 and designed a prototype V-2 rocket in 1938, but Hitler was not interested and took men and materials away from the project. Only in 1945 did the Führer sanction mass production.

Von Braun resisted the SS takeover of his now successful project and was briefly imprisoned in 1944. In March 1945 he evacuated his research group and surrendered with them to the US army. He continued his research work in the USA, and in 1955 he was granted US citizenship, becoming a leading figure in the moon rocket programme.

Braunau am Inn.   Town on the Austrian side of the German–Austrian border. The birthplace of Adolf Hitler.

Brecht, Bertolt (1898–1956).   The communist playwright who escaped from Germany immediately after the Reichstag Fire in February 1933, living first in Denmark and then (from 1941) in the USA. He was already famous for his *Threepenny Opera* (1928), but his major works were written in America during the war and with the Berliner Ensemble after the war.

***Brown Book* of the Reichstag Fire**.   An anti-Nazi account of the Reichstag fire in which the Nazis were accused of starting it for political advantage. A second *Brown Book* covered the Reichstag Fire trial. Georgi M. Dimitrov, the Bulgarian communist who out-duelled Göring at the trial, wrote the introduction. The books were brought into Germany from Prague at great risk inside bogus bookbindings (often of Schiller's *Wallenstein*) by young people who called themselves the *Vereinigte Kletterabteilung*, the United Scramblers. It is believed that at least twenty-four of this group were murdered by the Gestapo and a further eighty-nine imprisoned.

'Brown House'.   The Munich Nazi Party headquarters in Briennerstrasse, Munich. A palatial private house until rebuilt by Hitler's favourite architect, Paul Ludwig Troost, as the headquarters of the state within a state, it was opened on New Year's Day 1931. Funded by donations to the Party (particularly through Kirdorf and Thyssen), the Brown House was imposingly furnished, evidence of the Party's substantial position and a clear advance on the modest premises they had occupied in Schellingstrasse since 1925.

On the second floor were the offices of the Führer, his Party Deputy Hess, Göbbels, the Party propaganda chief, and Strasser, chief of its organization and the head of the SA (soon again to be Röhm). Hitler's office was designed by Troost for splendour rather than work, overlooking the Königsplatz, with large windows and dominated by heroic portraiture – a painting of Frederick the Great, a bust of Mussolini, a battle scene from Flanders in WWI. In the basement there was a restaurant, with the Führer's own corner beneath a painting of Dietrich Eckart.

Brownshirts.   ➤S.A.

Brüning, Heinrich (1885–1970).   Chancellor 1930–32. A Westphalian member of the Catholic Centre Party, Brüning was proposed as Chancellor in March 1930 as a moderate, stable parliamentarian. His skill lay in careful financial legislation but moderation did not help in the growing economic crisis. Unable to obtain majority support for his financial measures, Brüning appealed to President Hindenburg to assent to the use of Article 48 of the Constitution, which would enable him to dispense with majority approval. The Reichstag reacted strongly and in July 1930 Brüning dismissed the assembly. Brüning had hoped that new elections would support him but both the Nazis and the communists increased their votes at the expense of the centre parties. Brüning's rule would henceforth be by presidential decree.

In the two years of Brüning's Chancellorship Germany's economic and governmental crisis deepened. Ruling by the use of Article 48 Brüning was nevertheless under pressure from General Schleicher, whose intrigues involved plans for the inclusion of the Nazi Party in government.

Brüning's own solution to the crisis, a revival of the Hohenzollern monarchy in the person of one of the sons of the Crown Prince, was rejected by Hindenburg who refused his support for restoration of anyone but the Emperor Wilhelm II himself. The end came for Brüning on 30 May 1932 when Hindenburg curtly dismissed him from the Chancellorship.

The passage of Hitler's Enabling Law in March 1933 provided a postscript to Brüning's political career. In a final attempt to modify the provisions of the Enabling Act, Brüning held a meeting on 21 March with Hitler's Nationalist allies. His object was to insert a clause in the act guaranteeing civil and political liberties. But the Nationalists refused their co-operation and Monsignor Kaas, the new leader of the Centre Party, had already been bought off by Hitler's promises of a concordat with the Vatican and a letter guaranteeing civil liberties.

The letter never arrived. Indeed, it was never written. When the vote was taken the Centre Party, including Brüning, joined the majority to assent to the act.

Brüning was now at risk as the Chancellor who had tried to ban both the SA and the SS. He escaped to the USA in 1934 before the Röhm Purge – when he would undoubtedly, like von Schleicher, have been killed. In the United States he became a professor at Harvard University, returning to Cologne University 1952–5. He died in Vermont, USA.

Buch, Walter (1883–1949).   After WWI he was a member of several ex-servicemen's groups and joined the SA in 1922, becoming leader of the Nuremberg SA in 1923. In 1927 he was made chairman of the USCHLA, the Nazi Party disciplinary court. In this role he was with Hitler at the raid at Weissensee when Röhm was arrested, and thus took charge of the executions in the June 1934 Röhm Purge at Stadelheim prison. Thereafter he retained a senior position in the Nazi hierarchy, becoming Supreme Party Judge in November 1934.

Buchenwald.   One of the original concentration camps of the Third Reich. Located in the woods just outside Weimar, Buchenwald supplied prisoners on twelve-hour shifts to local manufacturing plants producing armaments. Liberated by troops of the US 80th Division in April 1945, the camp was found to contain 20,000 starving, overworked men and boys. Deaths recorded in the *Totenbuch* were averaging over 200 per day, some 6,000 per month from 'starvation, beatings, tortures and sickness'. Even so, Buchenwald was not an extermination camp, and many of its inmates, experienced in other camps of the Third Reich, declared it to contain more long-term survivors than most.

Days after the US forces reached the camp, Ed Murrow delivered a famous and moving commentary for CBS radio from within the wire at Buchenwald.

Buchrucker Putsch. ➤Black Reichswehr

Bund Deutscher Mädel. ➤Youth Organizations

Bund Oberland. A 1920s paramilitary organization originating in Munich. Under Dr Frederick Weber, a local veterinarian, the *Bund* marched in the 1923 Beer Hall Putsch.

Bürgerbräukeller Attempt. A bomb placed, in November 1939, in the beer cellar where Hitler was to speak in celebration of the 1923 Beer Hall Putsch. The bomb exploded after Hitler left and killed seven Nazi Party members. ➤Elser, Johann

Bürkel, Josef (1894–1944). An early member of the Nazi party in the Rhineland, Bürkel was made Reich Commissioner for the Saar when it was brought back into the Reich in 1935. He was appointed *Gauleiter* of Vienna when the Austrian *Globocnik* proved incompetent, and later Reich Commissioner for *Ostmark* (Austria). In this capacity he ensured that Austria fell into line with the Third Reich, through *Gleichschaltung*, and was responsible for anti-Jewish actions there.

C

Cabinet, January 1933. Hitler's first cabinet on taking over the chancellorship was apparently broadly based, with only three Nazis:

Adolf Hitler	Chancellor	NSDAP
von Papen	Vice-Chancellor	ex-Centre Party
Göring	without portfolio	NSDAP
Frick	Interior	NSDAP
Hugenberg	Economics/Agriculture	DNVP (Nationalist)
von Blomberg	Defence	no party
Seldte	Labour	Stahlhelm
von Neurath	Foreign Affairs	no party
Schwerin von Krosigk	Finance	no party
Gürtner	Justice	DNVP (Nationalist)
Eltz-Rühenach	Communications	no party

Some of these (von Neurath and von Krosigk) were carry-overs from the previous government of von Papen. Some (like Seldte), although apparently non-Nazi, held ministerial posts right to the end of the Third Reich in 1945. Some (like von Papen) were pushed into backwaters or (like Hugenberg) were dropped from government.

The function of the cabinet dwindled under Hitler. Although it continued to exist as a formality, its last meeting took place in February 1938.

Canaris, Admiral Wilhelm Franz (1887–1945). Head of the intelligence department of the Armed Forces High Command, 1934–44. As a WWI naval officer whose cruiser, *Dresden*, was scuttled after the Battle of the Falklands, Canaris made his way through the Argentine and finally back to Germany. His success in passing through British controls on a false passport drew the attention of intelligence officers to him after the war, and in 1934 he took the place of Conrad Patzig as head of German military intelligence, the *Abwehr*. A complex and divided personality, Canaris left little indication for future historians as to the precise motive for his rejection of Nazism. It has been suggested that (like much of the Junker resistance) as a German patriot he feared the possible consequences of Nazi ambitions without mustering serious moral objections to national policy. It is possible that this is a grossly unfair interpretation of his attitude. He most certainly took breathtaking risks to advance the cause of resistance to Hitler, and as Head of *Abwehr* gave protection to active anti-Nazis of the calibre of Hans Oster.

When, in 1944, Hitler signed a decree transferring the *Abwehr*'s powers to Kaltenbrunner of Himmler's SD, it was clear that Canaris's days were numbered. Nevertheless he seems to have covered his tracks sufficiently to have been accused only of incompetence rather than treachery. But the July 1944 attempt on Hitler's life dramatically changed the Führer's attitude to those whose loyalty might be considered uncommitted. Among many others with no direct connection with the Bomb Plot (although in the case of Canaris this can never be certain) the former *Abwehr* chief was arrested by his SD successors. He was tried on charges of treachery, found guilty and hanged at Flossenbürg in April 1945.

Canned Goods.   Code-name for the plan devised by Heydrich in which German criminals dressed in Polish uniforms, their bodies torn by gunshot wounds, should be carefully arranged near German defence posts, just within the German–Polish border. The international press was invited to examine these 'Polish soldiers' who had clearly been shot down while attempting another foray across the German border. The most important 'target' was the Gleiwitz radio station.

These apparent Polish incursions into German territory were used by Hitler as a significant part of his pretext for the invasion of Poland on 1 September 1939.

Chamberlain, Houston Stewart (1855–1927).   Author of *Foundations of the Nineteenth Century*, a book published in Germany in 1899 which achieved large and continuing sales. Its ideas influenced Hitler and formed the basis of Rosenberg's book *The Myth of the Twentieth Century*. Chamberlain was brought up in France, Austria and Germany, and became a naturalized German in 1916. He worshipped Wagner and the Wagnerians, and married Eva, the composer's daughter. He lived and died in Bayreuth, Wagner's town, where Hitler met him in 1923. His key to history lay in his Theory of Race and especially the dominant role and vital importance of the Germans. In 1924 Chamberlain wrote that Hitler was destined to lead Germany. Perhaps not surprisingly, Hitler was one of the few public figures at Chamberlain's funeral in 1927.

Chamberlain, Neville (1869–1940).   British Prime Minister from May 1937 whose policy of 'appeasement' allowed Hitler's move into Austria and into the Sudetenland of Czechoslovakia. Essentially Chamberlain believed that Germany had grievances from Versailles and that the concessions he made at Munich would satisfy Hitler's needs. He returned from Munich in September 1938 and in an announcement from Downing Street declared, 'I believe it is peace for our time.'

After Hitler occupied Czechoslovakia in 1939 Chamberlain abandoned appeasement and gave guarantees to Poland which led to the declaration of war by Britain against Germany in September 1939. He resigned in May 1940, to be replaced by Churchill, and died shortly after. ►Munich Agreement

Channel Islands.   The only part of Britain to suffer occupation by the Third Reich.

After the fall of France in June 1940, the British made no attempt to defend the Channel Islands and they were occupied by German troops. The Islands' legislatures continued to function under the control of a military commandant. In churches, prayers for the British royal family continued, but the Salvation Army and Freemasons were banned and all British soldiers caught on leave were taken off as prisoners. In 1942 the Islands were to become part of the German Atlantic Wall defences: restrictions were increased and 1,200 people who had not been born on the Islands were interned in Germany. Slave labour came into operation under the Todt Organization, building gun emplacements and fortifications. In August 1943, 1,000 French Jews were imprisoned in a work camp established on Alderney.

Between July 1940 and December 1943 the British mounted seven commando raids on the Islands, but the most surprising raid was in the other direction. In March 1945 a German force was daringly landed at American headquarters at Granville on the Cherbourg peninsula and over twenty Americans were seized and taken prisoner.

At the end of the war the heavily fortified Channel Islands had still not been reoccupied by Allied troops and the German garrison surrendered as part of the general surrender of German forces in the west.

Chelmno.   The first extermination camp in history. Based on a mansion in the woods forty miles north-west of Lodz, the camp was opened in December 1941 by Commandant Lange. Its function was to 'clear' the 100,000 Jews living in the newly created Wartheland, an area of Poland annexed to the Reich. The final figure is believed to be 150,000 deaths. ➤Concentration Camps

Churches in the Third Reich.   The twenty-fourth point of the Nazi Party programme promised religious freedom, except for religions which endangered the German race, the Party not binding itself to any creed, although fighting Jewish materialism.

Hitler saw Nazism as a religious faith itself, which distinguished it from the purely political Italian fascism. Although religion bored Hitler and he left Himmler and Rosenberg to concern themselves with mysticism, his Roman Catholic upbringing had taught him the power of the Church's machinery. He believed that in Germany the Protestant churches had no equivalent strength.

In 1933 the process of *Gleichschaltung* was applied to the Protestant Evangelical churches and in May the Lutherans were persuaded to elect a single Reich bishop (Ludwig Müller), while a Concordat was signed with the Vatican in July. Most of the twenty-eight Protestant sects soon accepted Nazi domination, but some ministers stood firm. Pastor Niemöller openly opposed Nazism and the *Reichsbischof*'s 'German Church' from July 1933. In May 1934, at a synod of Protestant leaders, Professor Karl Barth, supported by Niemöller, reaffirmed fundamental spiritual values, their group becoming known as the 'Confessional Church'. From this came many of those who opposed Hitler and were imprisoned (like Niemöller), went into exile (like Barth) or became active in the resistance (like Dietrich Bonhöffer). A Reich Minister for Church Affairs, Dr Kerrl, was appointed in July 1935 to continue the repression of the churches. When in 1936 the Confessional Church wrote to Hitler objecting to interference in religion and to anti-semitism, the Nazi state acted ruthlessly, with hundreds of pastors put into camps and the church's funds confiscated.

Many Nazis, such as Bormann, were fanatically hostile to the churches and accused Roman Catholic priests and religious superiors of offences against the state, especially currency trafficking. In 1937 the Vatican's disappointment with the Third Reich's failure to honour the Concordat was expressed in the Papal encyclical *Mit brennender Sorge*. The Nazi response was to increase the number of charges of corruption against priests. Pope Pius XI condemned the Nuremberg race laws in July 1938, and it is probable that he had an encyclical in draft against anti-semitism, but he died in 1939 without it being published. His successor, Pius XII, as Monsignor and later Cardinal Pacelli, had lived many years in Germany and had prepared the Concordat; he proposed in vain an international peace conference in May 1939, but felt it best not to speak out against Nazi evils. He did, however, praise Bishop Galen's successful stand against euthanasia in 1941.

One church group was singled out for total repression: the Jehovah's Witnesses whose refusal to do military service and whose belief in the imminent return of a Messiah (other than Hitler) brought every single member into the shadow of the concentration camp.

Churchill, Winston Spencer (1874–1965). British statesman and Prime Minister from 1940 to 1945. Known throughout the western world for his implacable resistance to Nazi Germany in the 1930s, Winston Churchill became Prime Minister in the very week the *Wehrmacht* began their triumphant race across France. His energy and his parliamentary oratory were an inspiration to Great Britain and her Commonwealth allies and a powerful reminder to the United States of the basic kinship of Anglo-American ideals. Making no attempt to disguise the extent of the Nazi danger or of the sacrifices which would be required of the British people ('I have nothing to offer but blood, toil, tears and sweat'), Churchill conducted the war with energy and eccentricity. When Hitler attacked the Soviet Union in 1941, few – and certainly not Stalin – imagined that the British Prime Minister would welcome Russia as an ally and promise all possible British aid. When a colleague remonstrated that half Churchill's life had been spent looking forward to the downfall of the Soviet Union he replied, 'If Hitler were to launch an attack on Hell itself I would contrive to make at least a favourable reference to the Devil in the House of Commons.' His reputation continued to grow even throughout the military disasters of 1941. In the United States, invited to address both Houses of Congress in 1943, he reminded them he was half American ('but for a quirk of fate I may have made it here on my own merit'). Beneath his genuine feeling for the USA there was the statesman's certainty that Britain's fate was increasingly dependent on American military strength. Until the peace, he dealt with both Russia and America with keen awareness of the relative decline of British power within the alliance.

For Adolf Hitler he was to prove the totally unrelenting enemy. If he did not create the anti-Nazi alliance, he nurtured it until the war's end.

Cicero.   Code-name for the spy located inside the British Embassy in Turkey.

Throughout the war both Britain and Germany maintained embassies in neutral Turkey. The German Ambassador, Franz von Papen, once briefly Chancellor of Germany, had been appointed in 1939 after demotion from cabinet posts and his anti-Nazi 'Marburg' speech in 1934. The British Ambassador was an experienced diplomat, Sir Hughe Knatchbull-Hugessen. The manservant to Sir Hughe was an Albanian, Elyeza Bazna (1905–71), who had been a driver or personal manservant to other embassies before he was employed at the British embassy in April 1943.

In October 1943, while Sir Hughe was bathing before dinner, Bazna found the keys to his safe, copied them and photographed a selection of papers. He took them to the German embassy. There he demanded and eventually received enormous sums of money in English banknotes. In later thefts he obtained copies of top-level Anglo-American-Russian conferences at Moscow, Casablanca, Cairo and Teheran.

The head of SS intelligence and security, RUSHA, Kaltenbrunner took a direct interest in the quality of information flowing from what was code-named 'Operation Cicero'. But by now it was too late. In early 1944 Cicero's flow of information was detected by the British (helped by the US agent Allen Dulles in Switzerland who had knowledge of information being sent to German intelligence) and Cicero was now unsuspectingly given false information to send. But he had collected a fortune: £300,000 in English banknotes. He still believed he could retire in comfort until his bank told him that most of them were SS forgeries.

Cinema in the Third Reich.   In 1933 the golden days of German cinema lay in the past. The great classics of the silent screen, Robert Wiene's *Cabinet of Dr Caligari*, Fritz Lang's *Metropolis* and G. W. Pabst's *Kameradschaft*, had given German cinema an international reputation. But they also attracted the attention of Hollywood, and many actors and directors had already been tempted to California.

The great German sound films of the period, von Sternberg's *Blue Angel*, Lang's *M* and Pabst's *Westfront 1918*, were all shot before the Nazis came to power. But even before January 1933 the Nazi Party had been in a position to make 'suggestions'. *Morgenrot* ('Dawn'), premiered before Hitler came to power, had already been made by the leading German film company, UFA, with a marked Nazi propaganda line.

Interest in the cinema was strong among leading Nazis, but with Josef Göbbels it was obsessive. He made himself personally responsible for approving every film made in the Third Reich and it was said that a day never passed without a screening. He quickly developed a shrewd appreciation of the potentialities of film as a leading propaganda weapon in his ministry. But his first task, as he saw it, was to clear all Jewish workers from the *Filmwelt*, the film industry.

On 1 April 1933 the six American film companies with branch offices in Berlin received a letter calling on them to dismiss anyone of Jewish extraction in their employ. The *Arierparagraph* (Aryan Clause) which banned Jews from any part of the film industry was not announced until June, but the industry was thrown into immediate disarray. Over the next two years a sizeable fraction of the most talented directors, writers and actors (not by any means all Jewish), left Germany (►Hollywood exiles). When Dacho, the official directors' and actors' association, challenged Göbbels, presenting him with a list of members they felt should be allowed to work in the industry because of their war record or service to the film business, he promptly disbanded the association.

Having removed Jews and 'ideological undesirables' from the German film industry, Göbbels now brought the imported product under control. In January 1934 the *Reichsfilmkammer* (Reich Union of German Moving-Picture Department) appointed a *Filmdramaturg* whose job was to inspect all scenarios of foreign films to ensure that topics which ran counter to the spirit of the time were suppressed. Early examples of films banned were MGM's *The Prize Fighter and the Lady* because it starred the Jewish boxer Max Baer, *The Kid*, *Roman Scandals* and *Tarzan and his Mate* for 'displaying incorrect attitudes'. This, in turn, did not help the cause of German film exports, which plunged from RM22 million in 1930 to RM4 million in 1936.

By 1937 the German film industry consisted of three large film producers: UFA and Tobis in Berlin, and the smaller Bavaria Company in Munich. Because of government interference, rising expenses and the virtual collapse of the export market, all the companies were in serious financial difficulties. In a complex series of moves, therefore, the companies were nationalized. A system of grading films was announced by Göbbels on 25 March 1937 which carried subsidies in decreasing order of value, starting with 'politically and artistically especially valuable' at the top and 'educationally valuable' at the bottom of the list. Despite Göbbels' exhortation to the film makers: 'The German film must fulfil its duty to the State, nation and culture. It must become a world leader', the public obstinately preferred American pictures, even the rather poor selection allowed in under the new quota rules.

Citizenship: Adolf Hitler. Born in the old Austrian Empire, Hitler was legally Austrian. When in Munich in 1914 he was called to serve in the Austrian army, he managed to get himself excused as unfit; he enthusiastically volunteered for the German army on the outbreak of war a few months later. After the war he continued to live as a German in Germany and did not return to Austria until 1938 when he had made it part of 'Greater Germany'.

But his Austrian citizenship continued and if the Bavarian government had not treated him so leniently he might have been deported after his imprisonment in Landsberg in 1924. He formally renounced Austrian citizenship in April 1925, but this did not make him a German, only a man without nationality.

In 1932 he stood for election to the presidency of the German Republic. It was urgent that he immediately became a German citizen. Frick, a minister in the State government of Thuringia, offered to make him an official in a local police force, but Hitler chose to be made Counsellor to the State of Brunswick legation in Berlin. Taking the post he swore loyalty to the Weimar Republic, thus finally becoming a German citizen only months before his election victory of 1933 made him leader of Germany.

Classless Society (*Volksgemeinschaft*). Classlessness rather than class warfare was a theme that ran through Nazi ideology and expressed itself most strongly in the classlessness of the SS. It is a markedly different reaction to class from that of the SA before the Röhm Purge, when class hatred had blossomed in the more familiar form of class warfare. When Hitler spoke of 'class madness' therefore, he was not fostering class hatred but rather looking back to that idealized period of classlessness which front-line soldiers experienced in the trenches.

Colditz. The best-known prisoner-of-war camp in Nazi Germany. A castle built in 1014, converted to a prison in 1800 and to a lunatic asylum in 1828, in 1933 it was one of the many temporary Nazi concentration camps. In 1939, captured Polish officers were sent there, to be followed by Belgian officers in 1940. Its reputed impregnability led to its being used as a special camp for prisoners of many nationalities who were regarded as of poor behaviour, usually those who had attempted escape from other camps. There were many attempts at escape from Colditz, and of about thirty successes, several became famous. In 1945 an attempt was to have been made with a secretly assembled home-made glider – but the war ended before it could be tested. In 1985 the GDR held a reunion of surviving prisoners. Unpleasant though it may have been to be a prisoner of war, the treatment of the officer prisoners at Colditz contrasted sharply with that of prisoners the Nazis deemed sub-human: Jews, Slavs and others.

Commando Order. During 1942 the British had launched a series of raids along the coasts of western Europe, culminating in the Dieppe raid of August.

Hitler issued an order in October that all captured commandos were to be executed. This was similar to the 1941 'Commissar Decree' on the treatment of captured Russian officers. Later in the war it was ordered that all airmen captured after air-raids on Germany were to be handed over to the SD, or left to be lynched by the German public; orders which came from Hitler, though they were drafted and issued by Keitel. Many military commanders who carried out these orders were tried and found guilty at Nuremberg.

Communist Party of Germany (KPD). The German Communist Party (KPD) was the strongest Communist party in the world outside the Soviet Union until its eradication by Hitler in 1933. In 1917 and 1918, food shortages and opposition to the war led to strikes and riots, creating political opportunities for revolutionary movements. Some split from the socialist SPD to form new radical groups, such as the Independent Social Democrats and the Spartakus League. With the collapse of both the Kaiser's government and the army in November 1918, the SPD formed the government, with Ebert as Chancellor. But throughout Germany local Marxist groups continued to call for radical action, taking over towns and cities, often with the help of 'soldiers' councils'. In January 1919 the Spartacists took power in Berlin but failed to win full support from the army which, with *Freikorps* help, quelled the rising and murdered its leaders, Karl Liebknecht and Rosa Luxemburg. In Bavaria in April 1919 a 'Soviet Republic' was proclaimed and, again, *Freikorps* units were sent to put a bloody end to the new government. In 1920 the Communist Party, itself only a minor group, held a congress; this was addressed by Zinoviev who had been sent from Russia as head of the Moscow-based international organization, the Comintern. Under his inspiration a new party was founded, the United Communist Party of Germany (VKPD). The Party soon became simply the German Communist Party, the KPD. At that time young people were much attracted to the idea of a radical 'national Bolshevism' in their rejection of liberal-capitalist values. The young Göbbels and Otto Strasser were typical of their age, but their German nationalism inclined them to reject the internationalist aspect of the KPD. Conservative forces were naturally nervous of the trend to 'Bolshevism', and it was this fear that gave Hitler anti-communist support for his 1923 Beer Hall Putsch in Munich.

During the 1920s the KPD, following the Moscow line, misread the Nazis as being part of the ruling bourgeoisie, an extreme element of capitalist pseudo-democracy. They saw the Socialist Party, the SPD, as the real enemy. Many times the KPD and the Nazis worked together, breaking up Social Democratic meetings with a combination of SA men and Red Commandos. Only later were Nazi tactics, especially in Berlin where Göbbels was the Party Gauleiter, aimed at discrediting the communists.

Among the leaders of the KPD was Ernst Thälmann who, as the KPD candidate for the presidential elections of 1932, won 13.2 per cent of the vote compared to Hitler's 30.1; chief of the Party in the Reichstag was Ernst Torgeler, who surrendered himself to the police after the Reichstag Fire in 1933. Both were sent to concentration camps. Others, such as Walther Ulbricht, escaped to Russia, returning in 1945 to lead the East German Democratic Republic.

Communist/Socialist resistance.   Despite the dissolution of their organizations, some form of Communist, Social Democrat and trade union resistance was maintained in the stunned aftermath of Hitler's electoral victory. For a time a flood of brochures and pamphlets came from secret printing presses. Frequently printed abroad and smuggled into Germany under innocent bindings – classics or cookery books – underground literature at first achieved widespread distribution.

But by 1935 the Gestapo was better organized to deal with the internal opposition. In that year waves of arrests were quickly followed by mass trials – 400 social democrats at one trial, 628 trade unionists at another. By 1936 many German communists and social democrats saw the Civil War in Spain as a more effective means of fighting fascism. The majority of German volunteers, among them Wilhelm Zaisser, Walther Ulbricht, Alfred Kantorowicz, Ludwig Renn and Willy Brandt, saw service in the Thälmann Brigade.

In Germany left-wing resistance continued on a much reduced scale and communist resistance was, of course, completely stifled for the period of the Russo-German Pact. For the latter part of the war communist and socialist resistance accepted that it could play no major role in the overthrow of the regime. Yet leaders like the former Communist deputy Dr Theodor Neubauer continued, until 1944, to maintain some sort of organization based on Jena. The more formidable Rote Kapelle group was principally devoted to espionage but none of these organizations was able, in the conditions of the Third Reich, to achieve the sort of mass support their ideology told them was necessary for success. In the event the most effective conspirators, and even they failed signally in July 1944, were the army officers whose role gave them access to Hitler and made assassination a possible alternative to revolution.

Compiègne.   Site of the signing of the 1918 armistice and, on Hitler's insistence, of the 1940 capitulation of France.

In November 1918 the Germans had signed the armistice documents which ended WWI seated in a railway dining-car in the forest of Compiègne behind the French lines on the Marne. In June 1940 Hitler was at his forward headquarters '*Wolfsschlucht*' when news came that the French government wanted to surrender. He gave precise orders for the staging of the armistice at Compiègne where the old railway carriage was to be taken from a museum and returned to its 1918 site. Hitler took the seat formerly occupied by the French Marshal Foch who had dictated the terms of the 1918 armistice to the Germans. Around him sat Göring, Hess, Ribbentrop, Keitel, Brauchitsch and Raeder. A preamble to the armistice document was read and Hitler left in triumph for the French delegation to sign.

General Jodl took over the dictation of the terms, which were not negotiable. The French army was to lay down its arms, the navy was to be immobilized, Paris and the north were to be occupied and an unoccupied zone in the south and east left under French government. The railway carriage was taken to Berlin where it was later destroyed in an air-raid.

Concentration Camps. The vast hutted camps for prisoners of the Third Reich used as prisons, as slave-labour reservoirs and as killing sites.

The Nazi Party Boxheim Papers, uncovered in a scandal of 1931, had foretold the creation of special camps to hold enemies of the state. As soon as Hitler took power in Germany in January 1933, SA men, acting as 'auxiliary police', began rounding up all possible enemies and putting them under guard in hurriedly constructed camps, first at Esterwegen and Dachau and soon at other sites. Many of these SA 'wild camps' were closed down after the first enthusiasm for arrests, and reorganization on the pattern of Eicke's Dachau administration followed. The first detainees were those accused of membership of KPD or SPD or their auxiliary organizations, freemasons and Jehovah's Witnesses. They were soon joined by thousands accused of associating with Jews – or indeed anyone regarded as 'undesirable' by Nazi officials.

The camps were at first officially described as 're-education' camps, but the SS soon adopted the term 'concentration' camps, the name taken from camps set up by the British during the Boer War (1899–1902) to 'concentrate' Boer farming families during war operations. At this period the three main camps under Eicke's Concentration Camp Directorate were Dachau, Buchenwald and Sachsenhausen. By now every type of opponent of the regime was subject to *Schutzhaft* (protective custody): Jews, trade unionists and communists were followed by gypsies, homosexuals, petty criminals, Protestants, Catholics and dissenters of all kinds. It was, not surprisingly, a period when many old scores were settled. Camp inmates were regimented and wore serial numbers and coloured patches to identify their categories: red for 'politicals', blue for the stateless or those who had tried to escape from the Third Reich, violet for religious fundamentalists, green for criminals, black for those declared anti-social, and pink for homosexuals.

The regular camps (which rapidly came to include Belsen and Gross-Rosen in Germany, Mauthausen in Austria and Theresienstadt in Czechoslovakia) were commanded by an SS officer of the rank of colonel or major and divided into military-style companies with a captain or lieutenant in effective control of the prisoners. Each camp block was under the charge of a senior prisoner. The original mix of political and criminal elements was expected to make the latter harass the former, but in time the politicals proved more reliable prisoners and were given most of the posts of responsibility. After 1939, as more camps opened, staffing needs were often filled by Baltic or Ukrainian Germans who, having themselves suffered as members of depressed communities, were now willing to persecute Russians, Poles and Jews.

The SS-WVHA, responsible for the commercial and industrial interests of the SS, took over the administration of the camps from the beginning of 1942; new camps were set up to be associated with the new war munition factories being built away from old sites to avoid air attack. The growth of SS-WVHA industries led to competition in the SS between the extermination and the cheap-labour schools of thought, and both styles of camp survived to the end of the war. The system grew as the industry grew, main camps having their satellite camps, often built by the industries themselves, for the supply of labour. In August 1941 there were 10 main camps with 25 satellites; in April 1942, 15 with 10; by April 1944 the total had risen to 20 main camps with 65 sub-camps; and by the end of 1944 there were 13 parent camps (the number having been reduced by Russian advances in the east) with about 500 sub-camps. The SS charged industrial companies four to eight marks per day for the use of prisoners working a full twelve-hour day. The average survival of a prisoner in a work camp was nine months, and in this time the SS could count on a net gain of 1,431 marks from each labourer.

Following the Wannsee conference which in January 1942 sought to make the extermination of the Jews a systematically organized operation, extermination camps were founded in the East. Belzec opened in March with a planned killing capacity of 15,000 a day, Sobibor in April handled its full 20,000 deaths per day by May, followed by Treblinka, where most Warsaw Jews were taken, and Majdanek, both with a 25,000-per-day capacity. The capacity of Auschwitz was increased seven times between 1942 and 1944. Other camps, like Bergen-Belsen and Natzweiler, caused death by neglect. Recent research suggests that, between 1933 and 1945, a total of 1,600,000 people were sent to concentration work camps, of whom over one million died. The extermination camps are estimated by some historians to have taken in 18 million, killing as many as 11 million. But it is important to emphasize that this is one area of the Third Reich where accurate figures are impossible to obtain. A figure of close to six million deaths seems most likely.

Women were at first detained in ordinary prisons but, as the numbers grew, a special camp was opened, in October 1933, at Moringen in Bavaria. A poor-house director was placed in charge and guards were recruited from the Nazi Women's Front. In March 1938 men were moved out of Lichtenburg in Saxony and it was converted into a women's camp. But the major women's camp was Ravensbrück in Mecklenburg, surrounded by forest and lake, and opened in May 1939 with 867 prisoners. By October 1944 the number had grown to 42,000 from twenty-three nations; in all about 133,000 women were sent to Ravensbrück and 92,700 died there.

After the war many Germans claimed ignorance of the camps' existence –

but certainly, outside Germany, evidence abounded. The British government published a White Paper on them in 1939 and a widely read Penguin book on international affairs (1939) listed Buchenwald, Dachau, Oranienburg and Papenburg. Reluctance outside Germany to believe in horror stories was probably due to British allegations of German atrocities during the 1914–18 war which were later proved to be untrue. Karl Wolff, Himmler's SS Chief of Staff, however, claimed that Himmler had never spoken to him about extermination camps. Most seem to have imagined that the camps simply provided labour for delinquents, and to have closed their minds to accounts of brutality.

The principal camps, most of which had numbers of satellite work camps, often associated with particular factories, were:

Esterwegen (opened March 1933). The earliest major camp. Converted to a special punishment camp, it was at first run by the Ministry of Justice.

Dachau near Munich (March 1933). The camp whose administration under Eicke became a model for all other camps. Its deceptive slogan over the gate read: 'Work Brings Freedom'. At the end of WWII it was used to house the '*Prominenten*', the prisoners Himmler hoped might be used for some sort of bargaining.

Oranienburg (1933) which became a satellite of Sachsenhausen.

Buchenwald, near Weimar (1933). In 1945 there were 47,500 detainees from thirty countries.

Gross-Rosen (1934). A Silesian camp.

Sachsenhausen (1934) used as the Gestapo interrogation centre when its Berlin centre, Columbia House, became overcrowded in 1936. Over 100,000 deaths took place in this camp and its satellites.

Mauthausen, near Linz, Austria (1938–9).

Flossenbürg, Bavaria (1938), where many Gestapo prisoners were taken as the war ended and were hanged or shot, Canaris, Oster and Bonhöffer among them.

Theresienstadt (Terezin), Bohemia, Czechoslovakia (1939). At first it was advertised as a special ghetto home for Jews, and international visitors were persuaded of this. It was later converted to an extermination camp.

Ravensbrück (opened in 1939) for women. Fifty miles north of Berlin where the specialist industry was a clothing factory, re-modelling furs.

Neuengamme, near Hamburg (1940).

Auschwitz (Oswiecim), Poland (1940). The most infamous of all camps where the commandant, Höss, developed his mass extermination techniques. Possible 1,500,000 victims.

Natzweiler in Alsace (1941), where prisoners were worked in the quarries.

Birkenau (Brzezinka), Poland (1941), ordered by Himmler specifically as a killing centre for Russian officers.

Chelmno, Poland (1941). The first extermination camp.

Belzec, Poland (1942). 600,000 deaths.

Sobibor, Poland (1942). Extermination camp claiming 250,000 victims.

Treblinka, Poland (1942), where 700,000 people died.

Lublin-Majdanek, Poland (1942). Site of 200,000 murders.

Bergen-Belsen, near Hanover, where some 50,000 died from disease and starvation.

➤Final Solution

Concordat. On coming to power, the Nazi government, through von Papen, negotiated with the Papal Secretary of State, Pacelli (later Pope Pius XII) an agreement (July 1933) which assured German citizens freedom to profess and practise religion, the right of the Church to administer itself, and a guarantee of its legal status, its property and its role in education. In return, the Church agreed that priests should take no part in politics. Thus the precarious balance was struck which was to last until the end of Nazism in 1945. Serious objections have, however, been raised against the Concordat; it has been suggested that the notorious silence of the Vatican during the days of the Holocaust was in part the result of the deal struck between Pacelli and the Nazi regime. Vatican apologists who have claimed that the future Pope's sole concern was to defend the existence of the Church in Germany have not always succeeded in convincing their own Catholic critics.

Condor Legion. ➤Spanish Civil War

Confessional Church. The church of Niemöller and Karl Barth, formed in 1934 in response to Nazi harassment. ➤Churches in the Third Reich

Constitutional Article 48. A clause in the German post-WWI Weimar Constitution which empowered a Chancellor, with the assent of the President, to rule without a majority in the Reichstag. ➤Brüning

Council for a Democratic Germany. Formed in the USA in 1943 to plan for a future liberal Germany, the Council included Thomas Mann the writer, Paul Tillich the theologian, the dramatist Karl Zuckmayer and other intellectual refugees from Nazi Germany. It was not successful in attracting anyone of left-wing political persuasion and was attacked by some Americans as being too soft on German guilt. Moreover, it failed to establish links with the opposition to Hitler in Germany and was never consulted on the future of Germany by the victorious Allies.

Coventry. A town of, at that time, 200,000, in the English Midland manufacturing belt which was attacked by the Luftwaffe on the night of 15 November 1940. A munitions and military motor-vehicle producer, Coventry was also the site of one of the great European cathedrals. The raid left much of the city destroyed and the cathedral a burning ruin. Casualties, at 1,000 people dead or severely injured, were perhaps lower than might have been expected in a raid of such severity.

Crystal Night. Night of a Nazi pogrom throughout much of Germany, 9/10 November 1938. Organized by Heydrich after the murder in Paris of a German official, Ernst vom Rath, by Herschel Grynszpan, a German Jewish refugee. Grynszpan intended to assassinate the German Ambassador to France in protest against the deportation of his parents to Poland along with 10,000 other Jews. But he killed, in error, vom Rath who was, ironically, totally opposed to Nazism. At a meeting of Party leaders on 9 November, Göbbels announced the assassination and advised that 'spontaneous' anti-Jewish riots should not be discouraged. During the night of 9/10 November Reinhard Heydrich sent urgent guidelines to all police headquarters for 'spontaneous' riots: surrounding buildings must not be damaged when burning synagogues; as many Jews as possible to be arrested; police should not interfere with demonstrations. On 11 November Heydrich reported to Göring details of the night of terror: 74 Jews killed or seriously injured, 20,000 arrested, 815 shops and 171 homes destroyed, 191 synagogues set on fire; total damage costing 25 million marks, of which over 5 million was for broken glass. Thus the term 'Crystal Night'. In protest, the US Ambassador to Germany was recalled on 14 November. Roosevelt's condemnatory speech followed on 15 November. To pay for this state-sanctioned destruction, Germany's Jews were collectively fined one billion marks and Jewish businesses and property were confiscated. Crystal Night is seen as an indication of Nazi confidence in their ability (in terms of international sanctions) to act against German Jews with impunity; as such, it marked the transition of Nazi anti-semitism from isolated attacks to the beginnings of a national policy which was to end in the Final Solution.

Czechoslovakia. ➤Munich Agreement

D

Dachau. A village a few miles from Munich, once celebrated as the home of a Bavarian artistic community. Now notorious as the site of Nazi Germany's first concentration camp. Established in 1933 with Theodor Eicke as commandant, Dachau was staffed by volunteer SS who formed the Death's Head units – a designation based on their skull-and-crossbones cap-badge. By the end of 1933 there were already some fifty camps in Germany manned by the SA, but many of these were closed when Eicke took overall command of the system and applied his Dachau regulations throughout. To the early Nazi public, Dachau was a school for good citizenship, its success to be judged from the fact that, at the November 1933 elections, 2,154 of the 2,242 inmates were declared to have voted for the Nazi government.

The camp, which has been substantially preserved as a museum, is laid out with a large SS administration block facing the Appel square where prisoners were paraded each morning. The huts, which contained rabbit-hutch sleeping arrangements and were totally unheated, were built on either side of a central concrete avenue. The hanging beam and the furnaces, built in 1942, are at the far end of the camp. Perhaps the most surprising detail for today's visitors (apart from the sinister irony of the main gate's inscription, '*Arbeit macht frei*' – 'Work Brings Freedom') is the closeness of the camp wall to the main road. By 1943 Dachau controlled a vast network of camps stretching into Austria. Despite its furnaces it was not itself an extermination camp, the administration instead using its sub-camps for that purpose. An unknown number of prisoners were nevertheless murdered in Dachau, many in the course of medical experiments by doctors like Sigmund Rascher. Among the eminent prisoners at Dachau were Austrian Chancellor Schuschnigg, Pastor Niemöller, former French Premier Léon Blum, Elser (who had attempted to kill Hitler), Halder and Schacht. The camp was finally liberated by American troops in April 1945. ►Concentration Camps

DAF (*Deutsche Arbeitsfront*). German Labour Front. ►Labour Front

Daladier, Edouard (1884–1970). French Premier from April 1938 who followed Neville Chamberlain's policy of 'appeasement' to Hitler and signed the 1938 Munich agreement, ceding the Sudetenland of Czechoslovakia to Germany. He resigned as Premier in March 1940. The French Vichy government interned him and in February 1942 put him on trial for betraying his country. He was deported to Germany and held there until the end of the war.

Daluege, Kurt (1897–1946). The Protector of Bohemia and Moravia after the assassination of Heydrich in 1942. Having joined the *Freikorps* shortly after WWI, he became an early Nazi, founding the first SA group in Berlin. He was a senior SS officer from 1928, a Nazi delegate to the Prussian Assembly from 1932, and a member of the Reichstag from 1933. In that year he was moved by Göring and Himmler into the Prussian Ministry of the Interior, taking over the Order Police ('Orpo'). As the Nazis, through the process of *Gleichschaltung*, absorbed the police of all the German states, Daluege became head of the all-German Orpo. As the second in command to Heydrich in Himmler's SS organization, he was appointed Protector in Czechoslovakia and initiated the massive reprisal murders and imprisonments that followed the assassination. He was hanged by the Czechs in October 1946.

Danzig (Gdansk). An ancient seaport on the Baltic at the mouth of the river Vistula. Historically it was one of the Germanic Free Ports of the Hanseatic League, but subject to the old Kingdom of Poland. The Treaty of Versailles, in re-creating the Polish state, tried to solve Danzig's anomalous position by making it a demilitarized Free City. A strip of land with a coastline was given to Poland to assure access to the sea, the so-called 'Polish Corridor'. German nationalists saw this as the loss of German Danzig and the Polish Corridor as cutting off East Prussia from Germany. In March 1939 Hitler demanded the return of Danzig and the Corridor, having ensured that a local Nazi Party was agitating for this at the same time. The Poles tried to negotiate. In September 1939 Hitler settled the issue by the invasion of Poland and the incorporation of Danzig and the Corridor into the Reich.

Darré, Richard Walter (1895–1953). An early Party member and friend of Hitler. After 1933, Darré's value as an ideologue faded and his impracticality lost him Hitler's confidence. His ideas on agriculture and selective breeding, however, inspired Himmler's fantasy of creating a 'master race' from the SS. Born in the Argentine and educated partly in England, he preached the agrarian philosophy of *Blut und Boden* ('Blood and Soil') and the protection of the peasantry as the 'life source of the Nordic race'. He organized Nazi farmworkers as the 'NS-Bauernschaft' in 1931 and became Minister of Food and Agriculture in June 1933. At the same time he was appointed by Himmler an honorary SS General in charge of the SS Race and Resettlement Bureau. His laws gave inheritance rights to tenants of farms of 7.5 to 125 hectares. Thus he satisfied the small farmer without alienating the great landowner. In 1933 the Reich Food Estate was set up by Darré to control the millions of German farms, large and small, and the hundreds of thousands of food-producing enterprises. This gave him an opportunity for corruption on an immense scale and he successfully enriched himself. But in 1942 he was found to be involved in large-scale black-market food deals and was dismissed from his ministry. Captured in 1945, he was sentenced to five years' imprisonment.

Dawes Plan. ➤Reparations

De Gaulle, Charles (1890–1970). Leader of the Free French Movement and President of the provisional government established in Paris in August 1944.

Appointed in 1940 Under-Secretary of State for War in the last government of the Third Republic, Brigadier-General de Gaulle refused to co-operate with the defeatism of Marshal Pétain and fled from France to make his famous BBC broadcast on 18 June 1940. Calling on all Frenchmen to continue the struggle against Hitler he elevated himself to leader of the Free French. Despite considerable reluctance by Great Britain to recognize him, and even more reluctance by the United States, de Gaulle maintained his claims (against those of Giraud) to be seen as leader of Fighting France. His remarkable achievement was consummated by the end of the war when he was recognized as President of France (though not invited to Potsdam) and as a leading co-belligerent of Russia, Great Britain and the United States.

Degrelle, Léon (b. 1906). A Belgian politician, founder of the fascist Rexist Party. Growing up in the 1920s, Degrelle had been influenced by the French extreme Nationalist, Charles Maurras, to the extent that he set about forming a similarly nationalistic party in Belgium. In 1930 the Rex Party came into existence, a movement which was heavily influenced by Italian fascism and the growing Nazi Party in Germany. Anti-semitic and anti-communist, the Rexist Party was substantially rejected by the Belgian people in pre-war elections. After the defeat of 1940, however, Degrelle was able to revive Rexism as a Quisling organization loyal to the ideals of the New Order.

In 1945 the Belgian government sought to bring Degrelle to trial, but by then he had escaped to Spain and, later, to the Argentine where he successfully avoided all attempts at extradition.

Denazification. Screening process adopted by the Allies in the western zones of Germany by which Germans were checked for their Nazi record and classified by their degree of involvement: 1. *Hauptschuldige* (offender); 2. *Belastete* (an activist, a militarist, involved in war crimes, a profiteer); 3. *Minderbelastete* (a lesser offender, e.g. one who joined the Party in youth and is not known to have committed crimes); 4. *Mitläufer* (fellow-traveller, one who joined the Nazis to keep a job, to demonstrate allegiance); 5. *Entlastete* (the innocent, proven anti-Nazi).

Deutsche Ausrüstungswerke (DAW). German Armaments Works. An armaments production company under SS direction, DAW was set up in 1939.

Deutscher Blick **(The German Glance)**. An exaggeratedly furtive glance over the shoulder, sometimes in both directions, which preceded the telling of an anti-Nazi joke or story. Perhaps originating from the working-class district of Wedding, Berlin, the *Blick* was sometimes used as a substitute for the 'Heil Hitler' greeting.

'*Deutschland, Deutschland über Alles*'.   A poem (1841) by Hoffmann von Fallersleben set to the music (1797) of Haydn and used as the German National Anthem since 1922. The words from the first verse suggest a Greater Germany: '. . . from the Maas to the Memel, from the Etsch to the Belt . . .'; these are rivers in France (the Meuse), in Lithuania, in Italy (the Adige) and the narrowest part of the Danish mainland. The second and third verses (which refer to deeds of nobility, brotherhood throughout the world and freedom) were not used in the Third Reich.

***Deutschland Erwache* ('Germany Awake')**.   A powerful Nazi slogan suggesting the emergence (under Hitler's guidance) from a period in which Germany had been exploited and despoiled. Probably derived from Richard Wagner, '*Deutschland Erwache*' became the title of an immensely popular song.

Diaries: *Speer's Diary*.   The last of the three major diaries by prominent Nazis, it was written after he was sentenced to imprisonment at Nuremberg. The diary contains a great deal of valuable historical material on the decline and fall of the Third Reich. The author is unique among former Nazi leaders in his willingness to admit his guilt.

Diaries: *The Hitler Diaries*.   In April 1983 *Stern* Magazine in Germany announced it had bought sixty volumes of hidden Hitler diaries for $3 million. *Stern* showed them to the British historian, Hugh Trevor-Roper (Lord Dacre), under strict security and he, though he saw only a part briefly, authenticated them. The background story to the diaries was based on the memoirs of an SS general who said that a plane which had flown Hitler's papers out of Berlin in April 1945 had been shot down soon after take-off and that peasants had hidden the boxes.

The first contents to be shown were plausible accounts of everyday well-known events. But authentication was immediately withdrawn and Lord Dacre reversed his opinion; German Federal archives showed the paper used for the diaries to be of post-war manufacture, the Nazi eagles on the covers to be the wrong way round, and other conclusive details.

The journalist who had arranged the sale and the forger were both sentenced in July 1985.

Diary of Anne Frank.   The surviving journal of a Dutch Jewish girl, Anne Frank (1929–45), gives a harrowing day-to-day account of the impact on individual lives of the anti-Jewish measures adopted in 1941. For twenty-five months her family hid in rooms over the Prinsengracht Canal in Amsterdam. In August 1944 the family was discovered during a search by German security police. The family was sent in the last shipment of Jews from Holland to Auschwitz, where Anne Frank's mother died. From there in the last weeks of the war Anne and her sister Margot were transferred to Belsen, where both died of typhus. Of the four members of the family only the father survived. Anne Frank's diary was found on the floor of the secret annexe where she and her family were concealed for over two years. It has since been published in many languages.

Dick Tracy (Operation Dick Tracy).   Undercover operation conducted by American and British intelligence. In May 1945, as German forces surrendered, Luftwaffe officers led an Anglo-American team in a race against time to a German air intelligence unit near Berlin. They loaded boxes of documents and aerial photography onto jeeps and returned to the Western Allies' lines, unknown to the Soviets. Operation Dick Tracy had succeeded. The entire Luftwaffe intelligence material on the Soviet Union, painstakingly gathered over four years of war, was in Anglo-American hands. At once experts in London and Washington set to, analyzing and reinterpreting the material. The operation was perhaps the first act of the Cold War, and was arguably the first indication of a German element in the western alliance.

Diels, Rudolf (1900–1957).   An official in the Prussian Ministry of the Interior who had specialized in political policework. On taking over the ministry in 1933, Göring appointed him to head the new branch of secret political police, which became the Gestapo. Caught in the power struggle between Göring and Himmler, Diels found it prudent to hide in Czechoslovakia for a period in 1933. He was dismissed from the Gestapo in April 1934, but found employment in local government in Cologne, and later in an administrative post in the Hermann Göring Works. Throughout the war Göring continued to act as his patron and protector, for Diels had married a cousin. While working in local government in Hanover he refused to round up Jews, but again escaped punishment with Göring's help. After the July 1944 Bomb Plot, he was taken into Gestapo custody but survived the Third Reich and was allowed to be re-employed in local government after the war.

Dieppe Raid.   The landing by Canadian troops on the coast of France in August 1942. As a 'reconnaissance in force' the raid showed that there could be no easy assault from the sea on a defended port: of the 5,000 Canadians who took part, 3,369 became casualties.

From 1941 Russia called on Britain for a 'second front' to attack Germany in the rear by a landing in France. The importance to Russia of a second front (or even of the credible threat of a second front) was that German divisions, and particularly Panzer divisions, would be engaged in the West and so could not be transferred to Russia.

Throughout the early summer of 1942, as the *Wehrmacht*'s penetration of

Russia increased in depth, Stalin's demand for a second front became more pressing. The crisis was reached in late July when Rostov fell, cutting the vital oil pipeline to the north. The German army was now clearly poised for an even more rapid advance into southern Russia.

No other explanation of the 'reconnaissance in force' at Dieppe, except as a strategic diversion, holds water; there was clearly no other intention because in midsummer 1942 there was no Allied capacity to exploit the landing. Yet tanks were part of the equipment put ashore and every appearance was made of securing a permanent beach-head.

General Zeitzler repulsed the raid with appalling losses to the Canadian troops. Two years later, the Canadian forces who had suffered so many casualties in 1942 had the satisfaction of liberating Dieppe in September 1944.

Dietrich, Josef ('Sepp') (1892 – 1966).   Commander of Hitler's SS body-guard and later of an SS Panzer army. An ex-sergeant major from WWI, Dietrich's earlier career was the typical Nazi combination of *Freikorps*, unemployment and spare-time bully-boy, for which (with his background and physique) he was well suited. In 1928 he became a full-time SS man and, though far from possessing blond Aryan looks, was often chosen as Hitler's personal guard, becoming head of the élite group '*Leibstandarte Adolf Hitler*', distinguished even within the SS for their appearance and arrogance. With the rank of SS Major General, he was detailed for special execution work, leading a squad in the Röhm Purge of 1934. He commanded the 1st SS Panzer Division, which had grown from the *Leibstandarte*, in 1940 and 1941 in France, Greece and the invasion of Russia. The Waffen SS were not taken very seriously as a fighting force at this time, but in the bitter battles of the Eastern Front the SS rapidly dissolved the disdain of the establishment generals. For this change of attitude to the Waffen SS, Dietrich could claim a large part of the credit. After the *Leibstandarte* was decimated in the battles of 1942 it was refitted and returned to the front at the beginning of the following year, fighting most effectively on the Donetz and at Kharkov.

When the Anglo-American forces landed in Normandy in June 1944, Dietrich commanded three divisions as 1st SS Panzer Corps – a senior com-mander without staff training or the military background of his fellow com-manders. Though without strategic genius, he was undoubtedly an adequate general officer on divisional level. His skills lay in inspiration and leadership. Coarse, broken-nosed, foul-mouthed, his style of leadership was well suited to the desperate soldiers he led. In late 1944, when Hitler scraped his reserves together and created a new 6th SS Panzer Army, he entrusted to Dietrich the task of defeating the Anglo-Americans in the Ardennes. When the offensive failed, his army was moved south to the defence of Vienna, but the advancing Russians routed his formation. Hitler in fury ordered the dismissal of Dietrich and the dishonouring of his *Leibstandarte* troops by removing their special armband. Dietrich now concentrated on saving the remnant of his formation from the Russians. It was widely known that he had ordered, as a reprisal for the torture of SS men by their Soviet captors, that no prisoners should be taken for three days during the Battle of Kharkov. In the event, he was able to surrender his units to American forces in May 1945. Called to account by an American court, Dietrich was sentenced to twenty-five years' imprisonment, of which he served less than ten. In 1957 he was again tried, this time by a German court, for murders committed during the Röhm Purge and sentenced to prison for eighteen months. Sepp Dietrich could certainly count himself lucky that he never stood trial on Soviet charges. He died, a free man, at Ludwigsburg on 21 April 1966.

Dietrich, Otto (1897–1952). The press chief of the Nazi Party from 1931 to 1945, and from 1937 Göbbels' state secretary in his Ministry of Propaganda. Dietrich devised the 'Editors Law' which made each newspaper editor responsible for any suspect anti-Nazi utterance in their paper. His boast in October 1941 that 'Soviet Russia is done with and the British dream of a war on two fronts is dead' at first convinced the world but soon proved so wrong that Nazi propaganda lost international credibility.

After the war, he was sentenced at Nuremberg to imprisonment but was released in 1950.

Dimitrov, Georgi (1882–1949). The Bulgarian head of a secret communist network in Germany. Arrested after the Reichstag Fire and tried with other accused, he defended himself so efficiently at the trial that he made Göring, the prosecutor, sound like the guilty party. Although he was acquitted, he was held in custody until international pressure had him released in February 1934. Thence he went to Russia, where he stayed until after WWII. In 1946 he became Prime Minister of Bulgaria.

Dirksen, Herbert von (1882–1955). A career diplomat who was German ambassador in Moscow 1928–33 and then in Tokyo until 1938, obtaining Japan's signature to the Anti-Comintern Pact. He was a traditional diplomat and despised the upstart Nazi foreign affairs leader, Ribbentrop, whom he succeeded as ambassador in London in 1938. With the outbreak of WWII in 1939, he returned to Germany and retired, holding himself aloof from all politics. He was declared not to be tainted by Nazism after the war.

Disarmament Conference. The 1919 Treaty of Versailles had envisaged a later general disarmament as well as that of Germany. This did not happen, confirming German nationalist understanding that Versailles had been viciously anti-German and not in reality a treaty for peace. Over the years there were a number of League of Nations meetings to consider disarmament, but not until February 1932 was a full conference on disarmament held, at Geneva, in Switzerland. In December the Allied powers which had imposed the Versailles

Treaty consented to the principle of German equality in armament, together with steps towards general disarmament. This plan was agreed in June 1933, when Hitler was already German Chancellor. But he objected that the Disarmament Conference had not given Germany immediate parity, and in October the German delegation left Geneva, thus achieving the break-up of the conference which he desired. Hitler proceeded to deal with the powers separately and to re-arm openly. ➤Anglo-German Naval Agreement; Versailles Treaty

Dodd, William E. (1869–1940). American historian, US Ambassador to Germany, 1933–8. Born in Clayton, North Carolina, Dodd was a graduate of the Virginia Polytechnic Institute and holder of a doctor's degree from the University of Leipzig. Fluent in German and well versed in German culture, Dodd was called from the University of Chicago to take up his appointment within months of the Nazis coming to power. Direct and candid in his manner, Dodd failed to influence Hitler or his government or to reduce the growing excesses of Nazi policy. But he did provide for Washington a clear American liberal view of the gathering European crisis, a view which undoubtedly helped shape Roosevelt's own attitudes to the growth of Nazi Germany. Ambassador Dodd's diary was published in London and New York in 1941.

Dohnanyi, Hans von (1902–1945). A lawyer in the Ministry of Justice and from 1933 assistant to the President of the Supreme Court. Appalled by the Nazi practice of justice – he was officially involved in major cases from the Reichstag Fire trial onwards – he assembled a dossier of Party misdeeds which he hoped would be used at a future trial of Hitler and senior Nazis. From 1934, after the Röhm Purge, he associated with many who were opposing Hitler, including his brother-in-law, Dietrich Bonhöffer, the theologian, and Gördeler, both leading figures in later anti-Hitler conspiracies. In 1938 he was ready to join in a denunciation of Hitler under Halder's leadership, but British appeasement at Munich removed the opportunity. In 1939, his success in clearing General von Fritsch of trumped-up charges of homosexuality did not endear him to the Nazis; he was then dismissed, on Bormann's insistence, from the Ministry of Justice. By the outbreak of war, however, through the influence of other anti-Nazis he had secured a place in the *Abwehr* (German Military Intelligence). In March 1943 he was linked with von Tresckow's attempt to assassinate Hitler and was arrested. He was released, but after the 1944 Bomb Plot he was rounded up with other suspects, taken to Sachsenhausen and later, probably, to Flossenbürg. He was not found alive at the end of the war.

Dollfuss, Engelbert (1892–1934). Austrian Chancellor murdered by the Nazis in 1934. Rising rapidly in Austrian politics through the Farmers' League and the Lower Austrian Agricultural Chamber, Dollfuss was appointed Federal Minister for Agriculture in 1931. In May 1932 he was appointed Foreign Minister and Austrian Federal Chancellor. Dollfuss saw the threat to Austria as coming from both right and left. Ruling without Parliament, he provoked an attack on workers' apartments in February 1934 in the belief (or with the excuse) that he was suppressing a Social Democratic uprising. On the Nazi right of Austrian politics, Dollfuss's fears were more justified. On the very first page of *Mein Kampf* Hitler had insisted that the union (*Anschluss*) of Germany and Austria was 'a task to be furthered by every possible means'. Since the Nazi electoral victory of 1933, Berlin had made clear that the Führer's preoccupation with *Anschluss* was unchanged. Austrian Nazis, with support from across the border, conducted a terrorist campaign against the state. Government buildings were destroyed, power stations blown up and the political colleagues of the Federal Chancellor beaten and even murdered. From Germany the Austrian Nazi, Alfred Frauenfeld, broadcast nightly inciting his comrades in Vienna to acts of violence. On 25 July 1934, 150 SS men dressed in Austrian army uniform broke into the Federal Chancellery. Dollfuss was found and shot in the throat. As he lay dying the Nazis refused him medical help. At the Vienna radio station other Austrian SS men seized control and broadcast the 'news' that Dollfuss had resigned.

At Bayreuth where Hitler was attending the annual Wagner Festival he received the reports from Vienna with excitement he could barely disguise.

But meanwhile events in Vienna were working against the Nazi Putsch. The Austrian government forces, led by Dr Kurt von Schuschnigg, recovered control of the radio station and Chancellery. Even more important, however, Mussolini immediately ordered four divisions to the Brenner Pass. With Italy opposed there was no question of *Anschluss* in 1934. Four years later it would be different, but by then the relative balance of power between Hitler and Mussolini would have moved decisively in the Führer's favour.

Dönitz, Karl (1891–1981). Commander of the German navy from 1943 and Führer of Nazi Germany for seven days in May 1945. Entering the Imperial Navy in 1910, Dönitz served first as a signals officer on cruisers. In 1916 he retrained in submarine warfare, becoming a U-boat commander the following year. He was captured and taken to Britain in October 1918; on his release in 1919 he returned to the German navy. In 1923 he was posted as adviser to the Navy Inspectorate's U-boat department. Since the Treaty of Versailles had forbidden Germany submarines, his department was officially concerned with defence *against* them; but the navy was already planning its future U-boats and Dönitz was seen as a rising star. In 1924 he moved to the Naval High Command in Berlin in a liaison post with the army, with a particular interest in stamping out any hint of radicalism left from the mutinies of 1918 and 1919. After further sea service in 1929 he returned to Berlin as a staff officer in 1930. During the first months of Hitler's Chancellorship, Dönitz was absent in the Far East. He returned to a Germany that met with his approval. In 1934 he was given command of the cruiser *Emden* which he took on a flag-showing world cruise.

When the Anglo-German Naval Treaty removed many of the restrictions of Versailles and permitted Germany's navy to expand, Dönitz took command of the new U-boat flotilla with the rank of Captain. He was of course by no means an inexperienced submarine officer and quickly set to training crews. While the navy commander, Raeder, had embarked on a big ship programme (▶Z-Plan), Dönitz vigorously promoted submarine warfare strategies, publishing a book on this subject in 1939. The work was much more than a naval textbook; it showed his exalted mood of Nazi militarism and his fanatical devotion to the brotherhood of the submarine crew. During this period Dönitz was campaigning for a crash U-boat building programme, believing that a force of 300 using his 'pack' tactics could block Britain's trade routes and force her collapse in a future war. Though the outbreak of war found the U-boat force considerably smaller than Dönitz had envisaged, it nevertheless gained initial success. When one of his submarines sank the British battleship *Royal Oak* at anchor in her Scottish base he was promoted to Rear-Admiral and Commander-in-Chief of U-boats. In 1940 he moved his command to Lorient on the French coast to be near his men, but he was forced to return to Paris in 1942 to avoid air attacks. His campaign was fraught with difficulty; from his headquarters the view was of a small and courageous force, desperately short of resources, pitched against the two biggest navies in the world. The U-boats were seen to be up against the British convoy system, enemy interception and deciphering of radio messages and the development of new submarine-detection devices. In September 1942 a long-range U-boat sank the liner *Laconia* in the south Atlantic with 2,500 passengers, most of them Italian prisoners of war, and its captain tried to rescue them. The U-boat was spotted by Allied aircraft and bombs were dropped near it. Dönitz issued an order forbidding future rescue attempts. It was this order which was brought as evidence against him at his Nuremberg trial.

When, in January 1943, Hitler ordered the abandonment of the German navy's shipbuilding programme and its concentration on U-boats, Admiral Raeder resigned and Dönitz was promoted to full Admiral and Commander-in-Chief of the navy. He moved to Berlin and issued energetic orders to stop the repair or building of big ships and to redeploy their crews elsewhere. This was the climax of the Battle of the Atlantic: a U-boat force pitted against shipping protected by every means the Allies could devise. March 1943 saw the zenith of Dönitz's fortunes: the Allies lost twenty-one ships against only one U-boat sunk. But by April further electronic devices for the detection of U-boats were introduced. By May 1943 any hope of destroying the Allies' Atlantic shipping was broken.

Still, Dönitz retained the Führer's confidence and Hitler nominated him – Göring, Himmler and his other commanders having failed him – by decree of April 1945 the next Führer in succession. Perhaps remarkably, Bormann honoured the bequest. After Hitler's suicide, a telegram was sent to Dönitz at his headquarters in Schleswig-Holstein, telling him that he was the successor, but not yet that Hitler was dead. The next day Dönitz was told of the death and he at once assumed the position of Führer. The new Führer appointed a cabinet of his choice (not the one willed on him by Hitler). It included one of the old aristocrats who had been in Hitler's first cabinet, Schwerin von Krosigk. Effectively the new cabinet dismissed the Nazis from government: Himmler, Ribbentrop and Thierach, the Minister of Justice, had no place. Göring was already banished and Göbbels dead; Speer, however, was retained and he at once broadcast to the nation his practical plans for keeping the nation fed and alive. At the same time Admiral Dönitz sent an offer of surrender to the British Field Marshal Montgomery.

For a fortnight the skeleton of Dönitz's government remained, the cabinet meeting and voting on plans they could not implement, until the Allies instructed him to surrender himself on board the Hamburg-America liner *Patria*. It is perhaps a measure of his naïvety that he was surprised to be included among the major Nazi war criminals to be put on trial at Nuremberg in 1946. The court found him guilty not of U-boat warfare in general but only of sinking neutral ships. For the *Laconia* order, he was merely 'censured'. But he was found guilty of the overall charges of planning a war of aggression (a verdict that has later been queried). He was sentenced to ten years' imprisonment and was released in 1956 at the end of that term.

Dresden.   Location of a devastating air-raid in February 1945: Dresden burned for several days and nights and the number killed has never been precisely known. In 1945 Dresden was thought to be the safest town in Germany, but with the January Russian offensive, refugees from the east were pouring in and, with the 26,000 Allied prisoners held there, the city was overcrowded and the parks used for camps. The Russians at the Allied conference in Yalta in February asked for air attacks on communication centres ahead of their advance. Dresden was selected.

13 February was Shrove Tuesday and many carnival parties were ending when the first attack by the RAF started. The Luftwaffe had few night-fighters deployed and the air-raid warnings were not given until too late. In two attacks that night, 786 RAF bombers dropped 2,647 tons of bombs. Fires raged throughout the centre of the city and the air-defence services were overwhelmed. On the morning of 14 February, 316 USAAF bombers struck again. The next day, Thursday 15 February another 211 USAAF planes came by day. There is little doubt that the object of the bombing was to create the firestorm phenomenon which had been accidentally achieved (with utterly devastating results) in the great Hamburg raid. Casualty estimates have since been a matter of argument. The Dresden police are quoted as having given a first estimate of 18,000 dead, with an expectation of a greater number to be found on later counts; but since then there have been estimates as high as 130,000.

The Russians at first gave a low figure in reaction to German propaganda, but later found it useful to give the highest numbers as proof of Anglo-American ruthlessness in destroying one of Europe's most beautiful and defenceless cities.

The casualties were certainly high, probably as many as 70,000. The effectiveness of the raids may also be questioned for, in spite of major dislocation, trains ran through Dresden on 15 February, two days after the first attack. ➤Strategic Air Offensive

Drexler, Anton (1884–1942).   Bavarian idealist and nationalist. Frustrated by his unfitness for military service in WWI, in March 1918 he set up a committee of independent workmen with an anti-semitic and anti-foreigner emphasis. This was formalized in January 1919 as the German Workers' Party, which Hitler joined, the seventh member of the Party committee. With Gottfried Feder and Hitler, Drexler drew up the 25-point programme which was adopted on 1 April 1920 when the Party's name was altered to the National Socialist German Workers' Party, the NSDAP. The balance between socialism and nationalism is well illustrated by the 25 Points, the new Party's platform. Point 1 demanded the union of all Germans in a Greater Germany; Point 2 demanded the abrogation of the Versailles Treaty; Point 4 denied office and the rights of citizenship to Jews (those who had entered the Reich after August 1914 were to be expelled); Point 11 demanded abolition of unearned income; Point 13, the nationalization of trusts; Point 17, the abolition of land rents; Point 18, the death penalty for usurers and profiteers.

In 1921 Hitler assumed the leadership of the Party and Drexler was inexorably reduced to a background figure. He died, forgotten, in Munich in 1942. ➤Nazi Party Programme: 25 Points

Duelling.   In November 1935 Himmler laid down that every SS man had the right and duty to defend himself by force of arms. Duelling was thus made legal for the SS under certain precisely recorded conditions: the challenge must be issued within four hours of the offence, Sundays and holidays excepted, and written communication by a second must be made by registered letter.

Dulles, Allen Welsh (1893–1969).   The head of American intelligence in Switzerland from November 1942. A lawyer who had worked for the American State Department in Europe, Dulles had been on the American delegation at the Versailles Conference. In Switzerland he met Hans Gisevius and, through him, had contact with the anti-Hitler conspirators linked with Oster and the Abwehr. Adam Trott zu Solz made his way to Dulles in January 1943 and again in April 1944 to try and get more support from Washington. But the US was bound with its allies not to treat separately and to demand only unconditional surrender.

As the tide of war turned against Germany, the SS, through Schellenberg and with Himmler's knowledge, arranged for a lawyer sympathetic to the plotters to go to Dulles, but the contact came to nothing when the Gestapo independently discovered it and Schellenberg was forced to disown the attempt. But Germans of several persuasions continued to believe the US might be more flexible than the British; General Beck even sent Dulles a plan depicting a wholesale German withdrawal before US troops in France, to enable the Americans to reach Berlin before the Russians. Yet despite the unlikely nature of many of the proposals put to him, Dulles remained an important station chief for US wartime intelligence. After the war he was promoted to direct American intelligence operations and became head of the CIA.

Dutch Resistance Organizations.   The *Orde Dienst* (Order Service) was established in Holland shortly after the German invasion in 1940. It spread rapidly and soon became a national movement. At the same time the Knokploegen, set up shortly after the founding of the Orde Dienst, specialized in sabotage and attacks on the German occupying forces.

E

Ebert, Friedrich (1871–1925). First President of the Weimar Republic. Succeeding Ferdinand Bebel as chairman of the Social Democratic Party in 1913, Ebert led the socialists throughout WWI and emerged in 1919 as Provisional President of the Weimar National Assembly, a position later amended to appoint him President for four years.

During his period of office he was responsible for an even-handed policy which suppressed both left-wing uprisings and the Kapp Putsch (1920) on the right. He remained, nevertheless, a particular object of hatred by all right-wing parties and was reviled by the Nazis long after his death in 1925.

Eckart, Dietrich (1868–1923). A nationalist poet who joined Drexler's German Workers' Party and began a friendship with the young Hitler. He was responsible for introducing Hitler to Ludendorff and for finding the funds to buy the *Völkischer Beobachter*. His 'Storm Song' ('Germany, awake! Break your chains!') was sung by the Nazis as they marched to the 1923 Beer Hall Putsch. But Eckart, an alcoholic, was already close to death and, briefly imprisoned with Hitler in Landsberg, was released to die in December of that year.

Edelweiss Pirates. Although from 1936 all youth organizations other than the Hitler Youth were banned by the state, from the early 1930s small groups of teenagers, often styled 'Edelweiss Piraten', would meet to hike through the countryside. Scraps of evidence available suggest that they often had contact with political dissidents, deserters or escapees from concentration camps; certainly they were subjected to raids from the authorities. The edelweiss flower seems for this reason to have been a symbol of youth resistance to the Nazis. In Cologne in November 1944, twelve of them were hanged publicly as an example to other youths. ►Youth Resistance to Nazism; White Rose

Editors Law. Press law introduced by Otto Dietrich by which each Third Reich editor was personally responsible for any statement in his newspaper which might be construed as anti-Nazi.

Education in the Third Reich. German education historically maintained a tradition of firm discipline and a belief in Germany's imperial role. The Nazis therefore made some additions to the system but had little need to institute sweeping changes. In fact 97 per cent of all teachers joined the *Nationalsozialistische Lehrerbund*, and 32 per cent belonged to the Party by 1936, twice as many as in the equivalent civil service association. To ensure their ideological soundness, all teachers had to attend a month-long training course organized by the Party. Apart from the dismissal of Jewish teachers (which was carried out within the first six months of the Nazi assumption of power) the only significant change was the regime's law against the overcrowding of German schools and universities, which led to a drop in university enrolments of 57 per cent between 1933 and 1939. In particular it froze the percentage of female entrants at 10 per cent. This was not the only discriminatory move against higher education for women. The proportion of girls gaining entrance to grammar school was reduced and the emphasis on domestic science often led to a dead-end academic qualification known as 'Pudding Matric'.

In the Nazi curriculum, considerable emphasis was placed on physical training and at one time it was even suggested that the deputy headmaster of every school should be a physical training master; the study of history was supplemented by special courses on the origins of the Party; biology, given equal importance, stressed the Mendelian theories of natural selection. Indeed fourteen-year-old school-leavers were handed a ten-point eugenic plan for life, stating: 'Health is a precondition of eternal beauty – choose not a playmate but a comrade for marriage – wish for as many children as possible'. At the same time, religious instruction was gradually eroded. In 1935 it ceased to be a subject for school-leaving examinations and attendance at school prayers was made optional.

Conflict between the school authorities and the Hitler Youth organization was perennial. Often schools had to be instructed to grant pupils leave to attend Hitler Youth functions. In some cases special crammers had to be found to help active members through their exams.

The most important additions to the system made by the Third Reich consisted of the establishment of Nazi élite schools, the *Nationalpolitische Erziehungsanstalten* (national political educational establishments), or Napolas for short. These were conceived as successors to the Prussian cadet academies and were intended to produce the next generation of high-ranking Party and army personnel. Selection for entry was based upon membership of the Hitler Youth, sponsorship by the Party, Aryan origins and physical expertise. The education laid great stress on the acquisition of sporting and mechanical skills, sailing, boxing, riding motorcycles and driving cars. In addition, every pupil had to gain work experience in industry and agriculture. In 1936 control of the Napolas was handed over to the SS, and by 1942 there were more than 40 throughout the Reich.

The Adolf Hitler Schools, founded at the same time, were intended as training grounds for future political leaders. Pupils were selected largely on the basis of leadership qualities and complete racial purity, and even looks. Initially, the Adolf Hitler Schools had a profound anti-academic bias. They stressed discipline above all else, even classes were replaced by squads – though during the war this emphasis was abandoned and a more conventional curriculum was established.

After leaving school at the age of eighteen it was normal for young people to spend three years in labour service or the *Wehrmacht*, and another four years taking a professional qualification. Some might then proceed to the *Ordensburgen* (Castles of the Order). These establishments, set in remote and romantic settings, were the Nazi equivalent of Sandhurst or West Point, but heavy with echoes of medieval chivalry. There were four such castles: Sonthofen, Crossinsee, Vogesland and Marienburg. Each specialized in a particular activity: riding and athletics at Crossinsee, and skiing and mountaineering at Sonthofen, for example. The students were known as Junkers and the Party paid for their education and supported their families. But again ideology ruled. Intellectual standards of the *Ordensburgen* proved to be inadequate and many of the graduates failed to live up to expectations; in many cases they failed even to receive a commission in the *Wehrmacht*.

It is an interesting comment on education in the Third Reich that despite much rhetoric (particularly from Robert Ley, Labour Front leader) the educational opportunities of the underprivileged in the Nazi state were no better than in the Weimar Republic. Workers in the late 1930s represented 45 per cent of the population but furnished only 3 per cent of the senior student body, exactly the same percentage as in the pre-Nazi period. ➤ Universities in the Third Reich

Ehrhardt, Hermann (1881 – 1971). An ex-navy *Freikorps* commander whose 'No. 2 Naval Brigade' used the swastika symbol. A leader in crushing the 1919 Munich socialist government, Ehrhardt led the 1920 Kapp Putsch in Berlin. He organized terrorist groups impartially against both liberals and communists. His 'Viking League' was used as auxiliary police in Bavaria under Kahr. Hitler undoubtedly saw him as a rival, and for this reason did not join with him nor use him for the 1923 Beer Hall Putsch, though many of the old Ehrhardt Brigade were among the first SA men. Ehrhardt himself remained listed as an undesirable but, despite surveillance by the SD, managed to escape to Austria during the Röhm Purge.

Eichmann, Adolf (1906–62). The SS officer, head of the 'Jewish Evacuation Department' of the Gestapo, who oversaw and planned the mass murders of millions of Jews. Born in Solingen and educated in part in Linz, Austria (where Hitler too had lived), Eichmann was a solitary, moody child. Dark-complexioned, he was taunted for being a Jew by his schoolfellows. After leaving school when inflation destroyed his parents' funds, he became a travelling salesman, an anti-semite and finally a member of the Austrian Nazi Party. He was active in the Party in 1932 until forced to move to Germany. At first he wrote for the anti-semitic paper *Der Stürmer* but was soon employed by the SD as an expert on Jewish affairs. In 1937 he visited Palestine to meet Arab leaders (but was ordered out by the British Mandate police). For a time his policy favoured the Zionists as a means of getting the Jews out of Europe, but this became impracticable as Palestine immigration quotas filled up.

In 1941, as chief of department IVA4b of the Gestapo, he received Himmler's direct order for *Aktion 14F13*, the killing of Jews and others in the wake of an attack on Russia. It was Eichmann who summoned, through Heydrich his superior, the Wannsee Conference in January 1942, with the object of co-ordinating the efforts of those ministries involved in the arrest, transportation and extermination of Jews. From that time he travelled through Europe to see it carried out. He himself took charge of one of the mass deportations of Jews (from Moravia) and elected to supervise the Auschwitz camp for some weeks to appreciate at first hand the problem of the operation. The five million or more deaths that resulted from the Final Solution were at his orders, although it is notable that he never achieved exalted rank. To others who questioned the inhumanity of it all, he said, 'Don't be sentimental. This is a Führer order.'

In February 1945 he vanished from Prague. Moving through Germany, he escaped Europe with a Vatican passport in the name of 'Ricardo Klement'. In 1961 Israeli agents tracked him down in Argentina and kidnapped him. He reappeared on trial in Israel, where he was condemned to death and hanged.

Eicke, Theodor (1892–1943). Inventor of the concentration camp terror system. Born in Alsace-Lorraine, which was at that time German-occupied, he became a policeman after WWI, but his hostility to the new French government made him unemployable by the state. He was taken on by IG Farben in 1923 as an anti-commercial-espionage officer. He joined the Nazis as an SA man in 1928, rising to command an SS regiment in Rhine-Palatinate. He was sentenced to two years in prison in 1932 for taking part in bomb attacks on political enemies; but he fled to Italy, returning as soon as Hitler came to power. In June 1933 he took command of the recently opened concentration camp at Dachau and established such a regime that in 1934 Himmler appointed him Inspector of Concentration Camps and head of the SS *Totenkopfverbände* (the 'Death's Head' camp guards). In the Röhm Purge of 1934 he shot Röhm in his cell after Röhm had refused to shoot himself. Eicke took command of the Waffen SS Totenkopf Division for the Polish invasion of 1939 and was succeeded as inspector of the camps by Richard Glücks. Like Sepp Dietrich, he rapidly revealed himself as a gifted leader (if not a strategically inspired commander). His unit fought in the punishing Demyansk Battle of 1942 and when he was shot down behind Russian lines a volunteer squad from his division broke through the Russian lines to recover his body.

Eilbek Comrades. An anti-Nazi underground organization formed in 1934 by the Social Democrat Walter Schmedemann. The group, based on Eilbek, a borough of Hamburg just east of the Aussen-Alster Lake, produced an underground newspaper, ran courier services to Czechoslovakia and Denmark, and even smuggled news of prisoners' welfare from Oranienburg concentration camp.

But Gestapo interrogation methods were successfully uncovering one anti-Nazi group after another. Over sixty Eilbekers were arrested in 1935–6, among them Schmedemann, and many were beaten to death in Gestapo interrogation cells at Fuhlsbüttel concentration camp. Schmedemann himself was discharged after lengthy interrogations and survived to become a minister in Land Hamburg after the war.

Einsatzgruppen. SS Special Action Groups. First organized by Himmler and Heydrich in 1939, they followed the German armies into Poland, murdering national leaders and rounding up Jews to confine them in ghettos. When the Germans began the Russian campaign in 1941, the *Einsatzgruppen* again followed the army, but this time they had orders to exterminate all Jews and Soviet political commissars. The SS commandos would enter towns and villages and order prominent Jews in the community to call together all Jews for 'resettlement' elsewhere. The practice was for the Jews to be transported, in manageable numbers, to a place of execution where they were shot and thrown into ditches. In Russia the *Einsatzgruppen* were split into four units of 3,000 men each whose mission was, technically, to ensure the security of their respective operational zones; this included prevention of resistance by civilians. In August 1942 Himmler ordered an *Einsatz* detachment to execute 100 inmates of Minsk prison, in order to view the method. He was much affected by the effects of the first volley from the firing squad, and, it was reported, became hysterical when these first shots failed to kill two Jewish women outright. An outcome of this incident was Himmler's order that women and children should henceforth be killed using gas vans which were commissioned from two companies in Berlin. The victims were killed within fifteen minutes by pumping the exhaust fumes back into the van. Exact figures are not available, but the SS statistician Dr Richard Korherr informed Himmler on 23 March 1943 that 633,300 Jews in Russia had been 'resettled' – the *Einsatzgruppen* term for extermination; 100,000 more were murdered in 1944/45; and these two figures together are thought to be fairly accurate. There are no separate figures for numbers of Soviet communists killed.

Einstein, Albert (1879–1955). The physicist who published the 'Special and General Theory of Relativity' in 1916. Born in Württemberg, he had attended a Swiss university and taken Swiss citizenship. He became a professor in Berlin in 1913 and was awarded a Nobel prize in 1921 for his work. In 1933 he was visiting California when the Nazis took power and he never returned to Germany. He stayed on to continue his work in the US and in August 1939 wrote to President Roosevelt telling him of the possibility of developing an atomic bomb. It is believed to be from this letter that the Manhattan Project developed. In Berlin, his property was seized and, because he was Jewish, all his books were publicly burned in May 1933.

Eisenhower, Dwight D. (1890–1969). US General who, as Supreme Commander of the Allied Expeditionary Force, was responsible for the planning and execution of the landings in Normandy in June 1944 and the advance into Germany which concluded the war on the Western Front.

Charged with controlling egoists with the force of personality of Montgomery and Patton, Eisenhower achieved great success in maintaining the unity of purpose of the Allied armies. He was perhaps at his most effective in the face of defeat. At both the Kasserine Pass and the Battle of the Bulge he acted with speed and determination more than sufficient to refute the charges against him that consensus was always his sole aim. Eisenhower died, after serving for two terms as President of the United States, in the Walter Reed Army Hospital, Washington on 28 March 1969.

Eisner, Kurt (1867–1919). A Munich theatre critic who, a few days before the armistice at the end of WWI and before the Berlin Spartacist uprisings, led a revolt and found himself the head of a revolutionary Bavarian government.

Enthusiastic but naïve, he spoke of a new world of light, beauty and reason; however, by admitting German guilt for starting the war and by being alien to Bavarian culture (Berlin-born of a Jewish family, but not, as rumoured, a Russian émigré) he aroused great hostility. Elections were held in February 1919 in which he lost heavily. On his way to the assembly to resign he was shot by the young Count Arco-Valley. Murders followed this murder and the people of Munich (always more socialist than Bavaria) joined in a general strike, closed the university (where the students had applauded Arco-Valley) and found themselves under a communist government.

Hitler, as a soldier in Munich, witnessed the rise and fall of Eisner and the following 'soviet' government.

El Alamein. A decisive battle in the desert struggle between Rommel's *Afrika Korps* and the British forces. In August 1942 General Bernard Law Montgomery was appointed to command the Eighth Army. A cautious and methodical commander, Montgomery built up his forces with the aid of massive quantities of US equipment until on 23 October 1942 he was able to attack the German defensive positions with every chance of success. The *Afrika Korps* withdrawal which began on 2 November would, in effect, continue until there was no longer a German military presence left in North Africa. ➤*Afrika Korps*

Elections. The first election in which the NSDAP participated took place in 1928 although four years earlier, with the Party outlawed and Hitler in prison, some members had stood as the National Socialist Freedom Party. In the first election of 1924 this grouping had won nearly two million votes and 32 of its 34 candidates (among them Strasser, Röhm and Ludendorff) entered the Reichstag. The second election of 1924, however, saw the National Socialist vote more than halved. In 1928 the Nazis, now fighting as the NSDAP, received 810,000 votes, returning just 12 of 491 members. From this trough they were delivered by the election of September 1930 when, greatly helped by the organizational abilities of Göbbels, the National Socialists won 6,371,000 votes, entitling them to 107 Reichstag seats. From this date the Nazi Party was able to claim it was one of the major parties in the German state.

The year 1932 saw four separate elections. The first two polls were for the presidency in which Hitler, though losing to Hindenburg, received 30.1 per cent of the total vote in the first election and 36.8 per cent in the second. The Party was more successful in the Reichstag elections of July 1932 when, travelling by aeroplane, Hitler appeared in the last two weeks of the campaign in almost fifty cities. In Berlin 120,000 people heard him in the Grünewald Stadium while 100,000 listened via loudspeakers outside. When the polls closed, 13,732,779 Germans had voted for him, giving the NSDAP 230 Reichstag members. Hitler immediately demanded the Chancellorship and the passage of an Enabling Act to run Germany by decree – in effect, a dictatorship – but he was turned down on both counts. The last of that year's elections was held on 6 November 1932 and resulted in a setback. In it the Party lost two million votes and was reduced to 196 seats, while the Communists gained 750,000 votes and now had 100 seats. Even in alliance with the Nationalists, the Nazis could not command an overall majority.

But the Nazi seats in the Reichstag were enough to gain Hitler the Chancellorship in a new coalition put together by von Papen. Exploiting his new power as Chancellor (he was sworn in by Hindenburg on 30 January 1933), Hitler was able to bring many of the resources of the state to the aid of the Nazi Party in the election called for 5 March 1933. In preparation for election day Göring, as Prussian Minister of the Interior, gave the SA a virtual free hand to suppress opponents' meetings. But it was the Decree for the Protection of the People and the State which Hindenburg assented to on the day following the Reichstag Fire which gave the Nazis the wide powers they sought to arrest Communist and Social Democratic opponents. Five days later, on 5 March, the final election of the Weimar Republic took place. The result was less than the overall majority for the Nazi Party that their leaders expected but nevertheless the German people, voting for Hitler, von Papen and Hugenberg had given the Nazi-led coalition a majority of 51.9 per cent. Alone the Nazi Party attracted 17,227,180 votes.

Two plebiscites took place under the Third Reich. The first, in November 1933, was held to confirm Hitler's decision to walk out of the Disarmament Conference in Geneva, and 95.1 per cent of the electorate was said to have approved Hitler's action. The final election in the Third Reich, also a plebiscite, was a result of the *Anschluss* (the annexation of Austria) and asked the electorate of Germany and Austria to approve the absorption of Austria into Greater Germany. At the same time the electorate were asked to approve a new Nazi list of candidates to the Reichstag. It was claimed that 99.08 per cent of Germans voted 'yes' to the annexation and 99.75 per cent in Austria; of all Germans 99.8 per cent were said to have approved the new Reichstag list.

It is difficult to envisage the crucial 1933 electoral success without the oratory, the personality and the presence of Adolf Hitler. But Nazi electoral victories during the Weimar period were increasingly the result of a formidable and highly colourful organization, carefully directed SA violence, financial support from parts of German industry and the seizure of new opportunities offered by the aeroplane and radio. At the same time the anti-semitic rhetoric, the denial of reparations claims, the 'Stab-in-the-back' theory all exercised a potent appeal over an electorate which increasingly felt Germany to be the victim of an international conspiracy to deny the nation its rightful place in the sun.

Eliminationist. The term used (notably in Daniel Goldhagen's *Hitler's Willing Executioners*, 1996) to describe the extreme position in German, and later Nazi, anti-semitism. There are in theory several eliminationist positions (e.g. forms of mass, forced emigration) which fall short of genocide. Nevertheless the suggestion is that the logic of elimination of Jews from the national life leads inexorably, when enabling conditions exist, to extermination.

The extent of the conscious acceptance of a powerful eliminationist element in German anti-semitism has been at the heart of the discussions of German national guilt since 1945. ➤Anti-semitism

Elser, Johann Georg (1903–45). A carpenter accused of an attempt to kill Hitler in November 1939. Elser was said to have placed a time-bomb in the Bürgerbräukeller where Hitler was to speak on the anniversary of the 1923 Beer Hall Putsch. The bomb exploded after Hitler had left, but seven people were killed and sixty-three wounded. Elser was arrested (he was said to be on his way to Switzerland) and sent as a special prisoner to Sachsenhausen and then to Dachau. The SD suspected he was part of a British plot. A fellow prisoner in Dachau, the British agent Payne-Best, said that Elser had been framed by the SS in a plot to arouse sympathy for Hitler, but Payne-Best knew Elser only after he had been severely beaten by the Dachau guards. Elser was shot by the SS in April 1945. It is unlikely that the complete story will ever be known.

Enabling Law (*Ermächtigungsgesetz*). The first law submitted to the Hitler-controlled Reichstag, on 23 March 1933, was a 'Law for removing the distress of People and Reich'. A sweeping measure to enable the new government to make laws without the approval of the Reichstag, it was passed with a two-thirds majority. The 441:84 vote in favour was undoubtedly achieved by the exclusion of the Communists and by the intimidating presence of SA men in the Kroll Opera House, where the Reichstag was sitting. The failure of the Centre Party to vote against the Enabling Law was crucial (➤Brüning). Five articles of the

Act destroyed what was left of the German constitution. Article 1 transferred legislation from the Reichstag to the government. Article 2 gave the administration full power to make constitutional changes. Article 3 transferred from President to Chancellor the right to draft laws. Article 4 provided that the terms of the Enabling Act applied to treaties with foreign states. Article 5 required renewal in four years. The Enabling Law (renewed in 1937, 1939 and 1942) was followed by the process of *Gleichschaltung*, which replaced parliamentary power by Nazi power. The Reichstag continued in existence as a constitutional fiction, meeting only a dozen times up to 1939. It passed only four laws, all without a vote, and the only speeches it heard were those of Adolf Hitler and the Nazi leadership.

Epp, Franz Xaver Ritter von (1868–1947).   General von Epp, with Röhm as his ADC, led the *Freikorps* units which recovered Munich from the Socialist government which had taken power in 1919. He had soldiered in China and South-West Africa before WWI, in which as a career officer in the Royal Bavarian Army he commanded the king's bodyguard regiment. Later, the Weimar government was to use him to put down the Communist rising in the Ruhr. Although he had raised 60,000 marks in 1921 to turn the *Völkischer Beobachter* into the Nazi newspaper, his loyalty to the state from whose service he had recently retired was sufficient to inhibit his taking part in the 1923 Beer Hall Putsch. After a short period without active command, in 1926 he assumed control of the SA in Bavaria and became a Nazi delegate to the Reichstag in 1928. In 1933 he dismissed the government of Bavaria on Hitler's orders and installed himself as State Governor, holding this post until 1945. Although he voiced objections to some legally irregular acts by Himmler and Heydrich, he survived as a figurehead. He died in an American internment camp in January 1947.

Ermächtigungsgesetz.   ➤Enabling Law

Escape Organizations.   Leading Nazis escaped from Germany at the end of the war using SS funds and helped by international businesses, churchmen or sometimes US and British intelligence agencies hoping to use their skills. The SS organizations were always shadowy and only known by rumour or the boasting of those who escaped; we hear of *die Spinne* (the Spider), *die Schleuse* (the Sluice), *Stille Hilfe* (silent help), *Kreis Rudel* (the Rudel circle, named after a post-war neo-Nazi), and the *Bruderschaftwerk* or *Kameradschaftwerk* (the brotherhood or friendship groups). Most notorious, although nobody can be sure it was the most effective, was the *Odessa* organization. The most commonly used escape routes from Germany led over the Brenner Pass to Innsbruck and into Italy, or through the Allgäu by Lake Constance through Switzerland to Italy.

Both in southern Germany and in Italy there was often help from churchmen, some of whom had been appointed to the Vatican during Nazi days. Bishop Alois Hudal, for example, as Rector of the German church in Rome, Santa Maria dell'Anima, undoubtedly helped to issue Vatican passports to war criminals. His stand as a Nazi supporter had been made in his published writings before the war. It is not known to what extent Pope Pius XII supported his views. Certainly, Hudal's promotion to bishop was the act of this Pope. The activities of Hudal and his supporters in the Vatican immediately after WWII only add to the gravity and nature of the question mark which many European Catholics feel hangs over the 'Silent Pope'. Prominent Nazis like Eichmann are known to have used the Vatican route. From Italy some Nazis fled to Spain and some to South America, others to the Middle East, to work in Egypt or Syria; some Latvian and Lithuanian fascists found their way to Australia.

Esser, Hermann (1900–1981).   Co-founder with Drexler of the German Workers' Party (which became the Nazi Party) and an early worshipper of Hitler. As a young ex-soldier, a radical and nationalist with considerable powers of public speaking, he was, like Hitler, employed by the army to combat the Marxist activities in Bavaria. A crude and rowdy thug, rivalling Streicher's reputation for lechery and Jew-baiting, his fluent, lurid writing was a hallmark of the early *Völkischer Beobachter*. He was the first to call Hitler 'Führer' publicly. During the Beer Hall Putsch either nerves or illness kept him from the march. Having spoken in place of Hitler at the beer hall, he left and fled to Austria as the police began to round up everybody who had taken part. While Hitler was in Landsberg prison, Esser and Streicher took over the substitute party that Rosenberg had been nominated to run, the 'Greater Germany People's Group'. In spite of this he succeeded in ingratiating himself with Hitler on his release. He rose in the Party to hold posts in Bavaria after 1933, but was removed from office in 1935, his disreputable behaviour and lack of administrative ability being glaringly obvious. He continued to hold a series of titular posts but never again ranked as a prominent Nazi, although Hitler called him from obscurity in February 1945 to read a Party manifesto to the faithful in Munich. In post-war denazification he was rated as only a minor figure though his property was confiscated and he suffered loss of civic rights.

Euthanasia Programme.   The Nazis were not the first advocates of euthanasia in post-1918 Germany. They took their cue from a book published in 1920 by Karl Binding and Alfred Hoche, *Permission for the Destruction of Life Unworthy of Life*. With Germany in deep economic recession as the 1930s opened, there were demands for the reduction of the cost of looking after the mentally ill. Before the Nazi accession to power, these demands had already crystallized into calls for sterilization.

In July 1933, a sterilization law was passed but the direction of Nazi policy became clear when in 1935 Hitler announced that, in the event of war, he would enforce euthanasia for certain categories of the mentally ill. A media campaign supported the new policy direction. In the cinema *I Accuse* showed the decline of people suffering from multiple sclerosis in an attempt to put the case for 'mercy killing'; the widely distributed *Victims of the Past* offered comparisons between an idyllic life lived in a mental hospital with the lot of ordinary people.

By 1939, economies in expenditure were being made in asylums, and doctors, such as Pfanmuller, actively propagated the idea of euthanasia. In August Hitler informally instructed Dr Conti, of the Interior Ministry, to organize a euthanasia programme and a prerogative agency was set up, under the overall charge of Dr P. Bouhler, to carry it out.

On 18 August 1939, the Reich Committee for the Scientific Registration of Serious Hereditary and Congenitally Based Diseases was set up. Registration of all malformed children was now compulsory. In September, a circular was sent out to all asylums and clinics in the Reich calling for registration of those suffering from illnesses which prevented their employment in asylums. Known as T-4, the euthanasia programme was run from an anonymous villa in the Tiergarten area of Berlin.

In September 1939, registration forms (*Meldebogen*) were sent out with the object of listing all those who had been hospitalized for more than five years. Completed forms were sent to referees who decided who should die. Those condemned had an A+ placed by their name. The referees were paid piece-work rates, at the rate of ten pfennigs per decision.

The powers of T-4 (and the associated agency KdF) were considerable. They could, in some circumstances, override the authority of the Gau. If doctors were tardy in filling in the forms, then assessors from Berlin came to do the job. Selection for extermination was arbitrary, though some evaded this through plea-bargaining. The refusal of some doctors to participate in the euthanasia programme was accepted, provided they did not speak out against it. Other doctors participated from motives of professional advancement.

The programme began in autumn 1939. Carbon monoxide gas was selected as the means of death and several asylums were equipped with chambers for this purpose, the first large-scale killings taking place in Pomerania and East Prussia.

Elaborate procedures were set up to allay suspicion. In order to make the tracing of patients by their families more difficult, patients were transferred to temporary centres before being moved to the killing asylums. These centres had their own registration departments, which sent letters of condolence to the families, together with faked death certificates issued without post mortem.

But news of the sudden deaths of handicapped children or relatives began to pass from family to family. By 1941 there was widespread realization in Germany that an extermination programme was in progress. It was probably this as much as the courageously worded denunciation in August 1941, by the Bishop of Münster, Clemens von Galen, that brought the main programme to a halt.

Between October 1939 and August 1941, T-4 killed over 70,000 people. But aspects of the programmes continued until 1945, the killing of children, of 'insubordinate' psychiatric patients and, it was strongly rumoured, in some cases, badly wounded soldiers.

When the Allies entered Germany in 1945, Bouhler committed suicide while senior T-4 officers Dr Karl Brandt and Dr Victor Brack were found guilty at Nuremberg two years later and hanged. Initially families of the victims of sterilization were denied compensation on the grounds that the eugenic legislation was legal and it was not until 1981 that compensation was authorized. ➤Galen, Clemens August Graf von

Expulsions.   The displacement of some 16 million Germans from their homes in central and eastern Europe, which began as the Soviet Armies entered East Prussia in the last months of the war and which continued, in chaos, misery and often death for the trekkers, beyond the Potsdam agreement and into the post-war period. Over two million Germans were believed to have perished on their journey west from cold, hunger and disease.

F

Faulhaber, Cardinal Michael von (1869–1952). Archbishop of Munich from 1917 and a cardinal of the Roman Catholic Church from 1921. A patriot who supported Germany's cause in WWI as a 'just war', and was awarded the Iron Cross, First Class, for bravery. He became, as a cardinal, the leader of the Catholics in Bavaria. Strong in his opposition to socialism or atheistic communism, when Hitler became Chancellor in 1933 he saw him as a shield against Marxism and urged the Pope to look on the new government with favour. The 1933 Concordat between the Catholic Church and the Nazi state (signed by von Papen for the Third Reich and Cardinal Pacelli, the future Pope Pius XII, for the Church) was at first welcomed by Faulhaber. But he soon saw that the agreement limiting the role of churchmen in politics could prevent the Church speaking out on moral issues in the new state. By November 1933, when he felt it his Christian duty to speak out against the Nazis' non-Christian teaching and their declared paganism, he did not hesitate. In 1937 he helped draft a papal encyclical *Mit brennender Sorge* ('In Deep Concern'), accusing Hitler of ill-faith. Hitler's response was to increase his attacks on the Church and the arrests of priests suspected of anti-Nazi crimes. While the cardinal had not spoken out against anti-semitism, the excesses of Crystal Night in 1938 angered him and he sent transport to the Munich Chief Rabbi to carry away religious articles from his synagogue to safety. With the advent of war in 1939, Hitler reduced his attacks on the Church, many of whose members had a degree of sympathy for his actions. Faulhaber kept himself apart from resistance activity although he was approached by Gördeler for support in the anti-Hitler movement. After the July 1944 Bomb Plot, when interrogated by the Gestapo he condemned the idea of assassination and gave his continued loyalty to the state.

Feder, Gottfried (1883–1941). A founder member of the Nazi Party who had originally joined Drexler's Workers' Party in 1919. In the following year he helped draw up the '25 Points', the Party programme which emphasized the evils of financiers with the slogan 'Break the interest slavery of international capitalism'. He represented a strand in early Nazi thinking not unlike the socialist radicalism of Strasser. Feder was a populist, rural-based anti-industrialist. Although he was one of the faithful who marched in the 1923 Beer Hall Putsch, it was realized by more sophisticated Nazis that Feder held views which would not help the Party on its way to power. Both Schacht and Funk warned

Hitler that his violent anti-capitalism appalled industrialists. Thus, in the Nazi government of 1933, the old Party member was given only a junior post. Dispirited, he resigned in the following year and lived on in obscurity, teaching in the university until his death in Munich in 1941.

Fegelein, Hermann (1906–45). A Waffen SS General who had risen from being a horse groom to a full SS cavalry officer, he married Gretl, the sister of Eva Braun. He had served initially at Hitler's HQ as Himmler's agent but in the intrigues of the last months he moved to become a supporter of Bormann. In April 1945 he tried to slip away from the Führer's Berlin Bunker but was found by SS men and, by Hitler's order, taken out and shot immediately. There is no record of a protest from Eva Braun.

Feindhörer. Those who listened to enemy broadcasts. Imprisonment in a concentration camp or even death was the punishment in the Third Reich during the time of the war for those caught listening to the BBC. The accusation might vary from defeatism to the capital charge of being a *Volksschädling* (antisocial vermin).

Felix. The German code-name for the seizure of Gibraltar, the Spanish Canary Islands and the Portuguese Cape Verde Islands. The plan was part of German Mediterranean strategy as it emerged in Führer Directive No. 18, issued by Hitler on 12 November 1940. The operation was never carried out.

Femegerichte. Secret courts which dealt out arbitrary death sentences to Germans who revealed the activities of the 'Black Reichswehr' to the Allied Control Commission after WWI. ➤Black Reichswehr

Field Marshal. The highest rank in the German army. Hitler liberally promoted to Field Marshal as the mood took him, in far greater numbers than would have been expected by the army. However, the promotion benefited few of them in the end.

In July 1940, after the triumph in France, he promoted von Brauchitsch (resigned 1941), Keitel (hanged 1946), von Manstein (relieved of his command 1944), von Rundstedt (dismissed 1944), von Reichenau (killed in an air-crash 1942), von Bock (killed in an air raid 1945), von Leeb (dismissed 1942), von Kluge (suicide 1944) and von Witzleben (executed after the 1944 Bomb Plot).

In June 1942 he promoted Rommel (suicide 1944); in January 1943 von Paulus (captured at Stalingrad), von Busch (dismissed 1944), von Kleist (captured and died in Russian captivity) and von Weich. In March 1944 he promoted Model (suicide 1945); and finally in 1945 Schörner, the tough disciplinarian who fled to the Americans, only to be handed back to the Russians.

Hitler also created Luftwaffe Field Marshals. In 1940, having made Göring a special 'Reichsmarschall', he promoted Kesselring, Milch and Sperrle, and in 1945 von Richthofen and von Greim.

Fietz, Helmut.　One of the few known by name (among what was certainly hundreds of thousands) of uneducated opponents of Nazism. Fietz was arrested in 1943 for climbing on a beer barrel in a Bavarian village square and comparing Hitler, to his disadvantage, with hogs and other barnyard animals.

Fifth Column.　Those traitors within a country who would give active help in an invasion. The term was originally used by a nationalist general in the Spanish Civil War who claimed he had four columns (of troops) converging on Madrid and a 'Fifth Column' (of waiting supporters) ready in the city.

Before 1939, Nazi parties in Austria and the Sudetenland had served as effective Fifth Columns for Berlin, but the term most infamously applies after the outbreak of war to men like Quisling in Norway and Léon Degrelle in Belgium. Typically Fifth Columnists were given immediate recognition by the German invaders and some titular position, but real power was retained by the German rulers: Abetz in France, Seyss-Inquart in the Netherlands, Terboven in Norway and Best in Denmark. The Fifth Column (of waiting supporters) was more effective in propaganda than in reality.

Final Solution (*Endlösung*).　The wholesale destruction of European Jewry attempted by the Third Reich between 1941 and 1945. Even Hitler, Himmler and those senior Nazis fully privy to the intention to murder millions of European Jews were unwilling to describe the process in clear terms. Confusion has understandably arisen through the use of cover-names. Even though there seems no doubt that 'Final Solution' meant genocide from its first employment in 1941/2, it is still uncertain whether 'resettlement', when used in the late 1930s, was equally a cover-term for murder.

The Nazi Party programme (the '25 Points') had emphasized a ruthless racism: 'Citizenship is to be determined by race; no Jew to be a German.' To the Nazis racism and anti-semitism were fundamental topics that did not need further discussion. In *Mein Kampf* Hitler had written of 'a race' which would 'destroy the weak to give place to the strong'.

In the first years of the Third Reich many Jews were allowed to leave Germany and Austria, often to the profit of officials who confiscated any wealth or property they possessed. But emigration to Palestine was limited after 1936. It became more difficult for refugees to find a country to accept them and the poorer Jews had no resources to pay their way to safety.

With the victories in Poland in 1939, and even more so from the inception of Barbarossa in the summer of 1941, the fog of war was used to cloak a new ruthlessness towards Jews. By early 1942, the *Einsatzgruppen* had already killed about 500,000 people in eastern Poland, the Ukraine and Russia. These mixed teams of SD, Gestapo, police and Waffen SS men had followed the armies from June 1941 and set to killing identifiable communist officials or Communist Party members, intellectuals, professionals and especially the Jews from captured cities. Their methods were crude: pits were scooped out near a town; lines of victims were machine-gunned to fall into the improvised graves, which were then hurriedly covered with earth.

It is now generally agreed that the conference which took place in January 1942 at an entirely unremarkable villa in the Berlin suburb of Wannsee was the key event in the initiation of the Final Solution. The briefing given by Heydrich (►Wannsee Conference) set in train the administrative processes of genocide. From this point the Final Solution, as a formal state policy, can be said to have begun.

Deportations to the east were carefully arranged so that the victims thought they were being sent to work – and, indeed, before being killed many were used as workers. Families were taken, divided, used and marched to their death, often thinking they were entering a bathhouse, leaving their clothes outside. Teams of concentration camp prisoners helped herd them in and then piled the corpses into the incinerators, until they too were ordered in to die. In Auschwitz the victims were sometimes lulled by a macabre band of Jewish prisoners playing classical music to the queue.

The men used as mass-executioners in eastern Europe were often selected from the limited background of the '*Volksdeutsch*', those Baltic or Polish Germans brought up in hatred of the people among whom they lived. But even they found the killing methods intolerable and the psychological strain on an executioner shooting large numbers in the back of the head was sometimes too great. The only time Himmler saw a mass shooting, in August 1942, he collapsed. The Einsatzgruppen experimented with modifications to cattle slaughterhouse methods. Later, mobile gas chambers were tried, but these failed to dispose of sufficient numbers and permanent extermination sites were built early in 1942. Four were constructed in the 'Government-General' of Poland: Belzec, Lublin, Sobibor and Treblinka, and two in part of former Poland, then in Greater Germany: Kulm (Chelmno), where the first poison-gas experiments had been made in December 1941, and Auschwitz.

The new extermination camps began working in 1942. Auschwitz was the largest and probably accounted for one and a half million deaths. Belzec opened in March, with a planned killing capacity of 15,000 a day. In April, Sobibor followed with murder facilities for 20,000 a day. Treblinka, where most Warsaw Jews were taken, and Lublin-Majdanek, both with a 25,000-per-day capacity, functioned from July and September respectively. The SS had estimated the need to kill 11 million Jews; perhaps over 5 million Jews were killed before the war ended. Apart from the detailed Korherr report of March 1943, there is no record of the slaughter and the numbers can only be roughly estimated.

By early 1945 the Final Solution was grinding to a halt and SS local headquarters were making the last hopeless attempts to destroy the abundant evidence of their guilt. It was of course impossible, because the evidence consisted not only of charred bones and mountains of unclaimed shoes and clothing but also in the silence of the once Jewish Polish and Russian villages

and in the absence of Jewish voices throughout much of post-war Europe.
▶Concentration Camps; Anti-semitism; Jews in Nazi Germany; Pale of Settlement; Nuremberg Laws; Posen Conference

Flag.   The Weimar Republic adopted as a national flag the tricolour of black,
red and gold, which between 1815 and 1866 had been the colours of the Greater
Germany movement. While this design was used as the Weimar Reichsbanner,
it became an object of hatred to nationalists. The national flag from 1866 to
1919 had been a tricolour (the Hohenzollern colours, black and white, allied
to the red of the Hanseatic League). Black, white and red were thus the symbols
of nationalism and were the choice for the flag of the Third Reich. The colours,
red with a white circle and the black swastika inside, were officially adopted as
the national flag in 1935.

Fleischer, Carl (1883–1942).   Norwegian general who commanded a
remarkable stand against superior German forces in 1940. In appalling weather
conditions his Norwegian 6th Division successfully contained the Germans at
Narvik until joined by British forces to assault the town. Such was his resentment
at what he (probably with reason) considered unnecessary British delays that
he was unable to play a full part in Norway's later struggle against the German
occupation.

Flick, Friedrich (1883–1972).   The industrial magnate who controlled
United Steel, Daimler-Benz and Nobel Dynamite, he was a Westphalian who
made his way up to become one of the richest and most powerful men of his
day. Although he gave 50,000 marks to the Nazis in 1932, he gave much more
to the Hindenburg campaign and to Liberal and Centre parties. In 1933–4 he
gave 7,000,000 marks to the Nazis and made a contribution of 100,000 marks
to the SS. He became a Party member in 1937. As the war developed, his
companies came to employ 48,000 slave workers, some from concentration
camps and others driven directly from eastern Europe; 80 per cent of his workers
died. After the war he successfully refused to pay compensation on the grounds
that he had already had to pay the SS camps for the use of labour.

The Flick consortium was broken up by the Allies in 1945.

Flossenbürg.   A concentration camp located in Bavaria commanded in the
early part of the war by *Obersturmbannführer* Künstler, until he was dismissed in
1942 on charges of drunkenness.

Forster, Albert (1902–1954).   Nazi Party *Gauleiter* of Danzig from 1930 and
its Reich Governor from 1939.

Four-Year Plan.   A plan for the economic development of the Reich, whose
aim was to make Germany industrially independent within the assigned term.
Announced at the September 1936 Nuremberg Rally, the plan was placed
under Göring's control. In practice it meant assigning to Göring the position

of economic overlord, a function he lacked the experience and knowledge to discharge. By the following year his open clash with Schacht's financial plans led to the latter's removal and his replacement as Minister of Economics by Walther Funk. The successes achieved in the attainment of autarky were those of German industry, particularly in the fields of synthetic rubber and fuels, rather than Göring's plan. Yet after the expiry of its first period, the plan was continued into the war years.

Though Göring continued nominally in control, with Erich Neumann as his ministerial director, his authority was greatly diminished in March 1942 by Hitler's appointment of Albert Speer as controller of armaments. Though Göring was able to insist on a face-saving formula by which Speer was technically subordinate to the Reichsmarschall and merely a representative of the Four-Year Plan, it was in fact evident to industrialists that the plan was no longer the key blueprint in the German economy.

Franco. ➤Spanish Civil War; Hendaye

Frank, Hans (1900–1946). Governor-General of occupied Poland from 1939. After brief service in WWI and in Epp's *Freikorps*, Frank joined the German Workers' Party, the forerunner of the Nazi Party. While a student he took part in the 1923 Beer Hall Putsch. He became legal adviser to the Nazi Party from 1929 and ran its internal disciplinary court 'USCHLA'. He drafted the *Gleichschaltung* of the legal system and founded and became President of the Academy of German Law. He proclaimed that 'love of the Führer has become a concept in law'.

Following the defeat and occupation of Poland in 1939 and the seizure of territory by both Germany and Russia, he was made Governor-General of the remainder. Frank set out to destroy the nation, wiping out Jews, intellectuals and professionals in order to make the Poles simply a source of slave labour. Under his rule over three million Jews were killed and tens of thousands of Poles sent to forced labour. He ruled Poland from his palace in Krakow until he fled to Germany before the Russian advance in 1944. He detailed his work in forty volumes of diaries which are a source of much information on early Nazi history and include the possibility that Hitler's ancestry included the Graz Jew Frankenberger, which Hitler had ordered him to investigate secretly in 1942. Hans Frank pleaded guilty to the charges against him as one of the major war criminals at Nuremberg and was hanged.

Frankfurter Zeitung. Influential German newspaper which somehow managed to demonstrate a degree of independence from the strict Nazi line. It is probable that Göbbels believed this was necessary to impress the foreign press with whom the reputation of the *Frankfurter Zeitung* had always been high. ➤Press in the Third Reich

Freiburg Circle. An anti-Nazi discussion group based on Freiburg University. Patriotic and right-wing, the group was led by the historian Gerhard Ritter.

Freikorps. Private armies of ex-soldiers raised by their former regular officers at the end of WWI. Many began in the chaos of 1918 in eastern Europe when German troops, no longer under central command, fought against Russian communists or the claims of the new Polish and Lithuanian states. The then Captain von Schleicher (a later general and Chancellor of Germany) of the political department at German army HQ secretly equipped and paid for the *Freikorps* units at first to protect Germany's eastern borders and then to put down revolution at home.

Freikorps men were tough front-line soldiers who used the tactics developed in 1918, based on small self-sufficient units rather than large army formations. They had a wide range of fighting skills and weapons and maintained the best of wartime comradeship, often electing their own leaders. The communist government of Bavaria in 1919 was crushed by some 30,000 Freikorps soldiers under Epp, using ruthless methods and killing 600 or more in May that year. Hitler, in Munich at the time undergoing the process of demobilization, witnessed the massacre. Workers who tried to form socialist regimes in cities or regions like the Ruhr, and particularly the Spartacists in Berlin, were bloodily repressed by the Freikorps. In contrast to this, the Ehrhardt Brigade occupied Berlin in March 1920 to enable a right-winger, Dr Kapp, to declare himself Chancellor.

Munich became a refuge for *Freikorps* men as their groups gradually broke up. Many were recruited to the SA, including men from the Ehrhardt Brigade who used the swastika symbol on their helmets. The *Freikorps* were dissolved in 1921, but their last descendants were ceremoniously stood down in Munich on the tenth anniversary of the Beer Hall Putsch, in November 1933. A roll call of their units was made ('Baltic', 'Ehrhardt' etc.) and their flags laid to rest in the Nazi Brown House.

Freisler, Roland (1893 – 1945). The President of the Berlin *Volksgerichtshof* (People's Court) from 1942. He is known to have been one of the select group attending the 1942 Wannsee Conference which worked out the plans for the extermination of the Jews.

Freisler qualified as a lawyer, having been a prisoner in Russia, and joined the Nazi Party in 1925. He became Hitler's favourite legal executioner, trying the Scholls in 1943 and those accused of taking part in the 1944 Bomb Plot. Films were made of the trials in Berlin, showing his ranting style and his calculated bullying of prisoners before sentencing them to slow and awful deaths. As a prisoner of the Soviet Russians after WWI he is said to have come to admire their methods and particularly the tactics of the Soviet prosecutor Vishinsky. He was killed during a court session by a bomb dropped from a USAAF Flying Fortress during a daylight raid on Berlin in February 1945.

Frick, Wilhelm (1877–1946). Nazi Party bureaucrat. A senior Munich police officer and Nazi, he was to have been the new chief of police if the 1923 Beer Hall Putsch had succeeded. When it failed he was tried and sentenced for his part in the attempt, but was released in 1924. A Reichstag member from 1924, he was at that time aligned to the Gregor Strasser radicals. In 1931 he became Minister of the Interior in the state of Thuringia, the first Nazi to hold such an office. At this time he was one of the Party's 'Big Five' with Hitler, Göring, Göbbels and Strasser. He became Reich Minister of the Interior in January 1933, operating the Enabling Act, and drafted the *Gleichschaltung* laws which removed the rights of individual German states.

Frick continued as Minister of the Interior, closing down non-cooperating churches and signing the *Anschluss* with Austria in 1938, but his opposition to the wide powers of the SS led to his displacement as minister by Himmler in 1943. He was rewarded with the post of Protector of Bohemia and Moravia from 1943 to 1945. At Nuremberg he was tried as one of the major war criminals, found guilty and hanged in 1946.

Friedburg, Hans Georg von (1895–1945). The Admiral who signed the surrender of the German Navy on Dönitz's orders at Rheims in May 1945. A WWI U-boat officer, his promotion to naval High Command had been due to his good contacts with the Nazi Party. He was made Commander-in-Chief of the navy when Dönitz became Führer.

Friends of the *Reichsführer* SS. A circle of bankers and industrialists meeting regularly in Berlin. The purpose of the group was to act as unofficial patrons of the SS, making donations and even equipping whole Waffen SS units. In return, the Friends would receive honorary rank in the SS. Much more important, however, was the fact that influence with Heinrich Himmler could oil the wheels of commercial and industrial activity in the Third Reich. Most direct of the advantages to the industrialist-patron was his access to cheap concentration camp labour for which he paid six marks per day per man to the SS.

Fritsch, Werner Freiherr von (1880–1939). Army Commander-in-Chief under the Minister of Defence, General Blomberg, from 1934 to 1938. Fritsch had been a brilliant staff officer before he was appointed to command. He supported Blomberg's direct allegiance of the army to Hitler. In 1934 on the eve of the Röhm Purge he put the army on alert and confined all troops to barracks, ensuring that they stood by and allowed the destruction of the SA. With Blomberg and the Foreign Minister, von Neurath, however, he questioned Hitler's war plans against Austria and Czechoslovakia. As a general staff officer of the old school, while welcoming Hitler's dictatorship, he was hostile to the Nazis – and particularly to the SS, whose military aspirations he could not accept. But the SS framed him with charges of homosexuality in 1938, using the evidence of a small-time criminal who claimed to have seen the general with a male prostitute. Fritsch was cashiered from the army, even though a secret military court found him not guilty and established that the man seen under guilty circumstances was an old cavalry captain with the similar-sounding name of Frisch. Werner von Fritsch rejoined his regiment as its honorary colonel and went to fight with it in Poland. He was killed in action in September 1939.

Fronterlebnis.   A school of post-WWI German writing based on the experience of camaraderie at the front. The style and content were on the whole much favoured by the Nazis. ➤Literature in the Third Reich

Führer.   Hitler assumed the title 'Führer' or 'leader' in direct imitation of the Italian fascist leader Mussolini, who styled himself 'Il Duce'. Hitler's close associate Esser was the first to use the title in public in 1923. Only in 1931, by Göbbels' ruling, did its use become compulsory in the Party. Göbbels' object was the same as that for developing the greeting 'Heil Hitler!': to establish the unthinking worship of the Party leader. The word 'Führer' was much used in Nazi Party titles and the Party *Who's Who?*, published in 1935, was called the *Führerlexikon*. Hitler's political philosophy in *Mein Kampf* expounds the *Führerprinzip* (the leadership system), showing contempt for democracy and advocating a dictatorship with decisions taken by a leader and by an élite group whose commands the people must obey. Nazi Germany thus had 'Führers' at many levels of command, each subject to the authority of a Führer above. When, in August 1934, on Hindenburg's death, Hitler combined the offices of Chancellor and President, 'Führer' became his official state title.

Führer Headquarters.   Hitler demonstrated his leadership and absolute control of the war machine by centralizing power in his command posts. While he used a specially converted railway train (as in Poland in 1939) for himself, staff officers, secretariat and signals equipment, he also from time to time established headquarters buildings to which he assigned cover-names drawn from his dramatic imagination.

> **Felsennest** (Cliff Nest) at Bad Münstereiffel, about thirty miles from the Belgian border (1940)
>
> **Adlerhorst** (Eagle Eyrie) at Ziegenberg near the Ardennes (1940). Hitler abandoned this HQ on the grounds that it was too luxurious. Later in the war it was rebuilt by Speer with bombproof shelters and used as Rundstedt's headquarters for the 1944 Ardennes offensive. Hitler himself returned to it briefly from December 1944 to mid-January 1945
>
> **Wolfsschlucht** (Wolf's Gorge) at Bruly-le-Peche, France (6–25 June 1940). He is said to have left when he found the swarm of gnats irritating

> **Tannenberg** (named after the 1914 German victory over the Russians)
> near Freudenstadt in the Black Forest. Used at the end of the French
> campaign, 1940
> **Wolfsschanze** (Wolf's Lair) at Rastenburg in East Prussia (1941–44).
> The scene of the July 1944 Bomb Plot.
> **Werwolf** (Werewolf) his headquarters at Vinnitsa in the Ukraine (July
> 1942)

From mid-January 1945 until his death in April 1945, Hitler's headquarters, which he never left, was the **Führerbunker**, built in the grounds of the bombed Reich Chancellery in Berlin.

Führerlexikon.   *Who's Who?* and *Who Was Who?* in the Nazi Party, combined in one volume published in 1934. It contained the names of no women.

Führerprinzip.   ►Führer

Fuller, John (1878–1966).   British general and military thinker. His *Memoirs of an Unconventional Soldier* (1936) impressed more tank officers in Germany than in Britain. Undoubtedly he was among the four or five military analysts who can be said to have paved the way for the new use of independent armoured formations – the *Blitzkriegs* of 1939, 1940 and 1941, and the spectacular armour-led advances of Patton and Montgomery in 1944/5.

Funeral Demonstrations.   One of the few ways, early in the Third Reich, for Germans to show their anti-Nazi feelings with reasonable safety. Thus hundreds of citizens attended the funeral in 1934 of Breslau trade unionist Hans Alexander who had died in a concentration camp. Similarly in the following year, large silent crowds attended the funerals of Johannes Stelling, former Social Democratic Prime Minister of Mecklenberg, and Fritz Husemann, a coalminers' leader who was murdered (it was widely believed by the Nazis) in the Ruhr.

Funk, Walther (1890–1960).   Minister of Economics from 1937 to 1945. A financial journalist who joined the Nazis in 1931, Funk became a valuable link with industry. He warned Hitler to keep clear of the radical anti-capitalism of Feder and that failure to align with Hindenburg would lose the support and votes of industry and commerce. He followed Schacht as Minister of Economics in 1937, but his ministry was much reduced in power by Göring's authority over the Four-Year Plan to rebuild Germany's economic strength. In 1939 he was appointed President of the Reichsbank and was thus responsible for the Third Reich's wealth, and the SS loot, which was deposited under the account name of 'Max Heiliger'. Since he never attended a board meeting, the real control of the bank was in the hands of the Deputy President, Emil Puhl. After the Reichsbank was bombed in February 1945, he authorized the removal of the reserves, and in April saw the last consignment delivered to Munich.

Thereafter he lost track of them. He was arrested and tried as one of the 22 major war criminals at Nuremberg. An interrogator described him as 'a tubby homosexual suffering from diabetes and afflicted at the moment with bladder pain'. He was suffering from alcoholism and probably from venereal disease he had contracted earlier. He was sentenced to life imprisonment, but released from Spandau prison, on health grounds, in 1957.

G

Galen, Clemens August Graf von (1878–1946).   The 'Lion of Münster'. Cardinal Archbishop of Münster who made an effective public protest against Nazi racialist policies, Galen came of an aristocratic family; an earlier Galen had been the soldier-prince Bishop of Münster in 1650. He had conventional political views and indeed welcomed aspects of Hitler's nationalism, giving a blessing to the troops who marched into the Rhineland in 1936. He was, however, opposed to Nazi racial doctrines, publishing a critique of Rosenberg's *Myth of the Twentieth Century* in 1934, with the result that his diocesan magazine became immensely popular in a country where papers opposing Hitler had all been banned.

In 1941, he spoke out in a sermon against the Nazi practice of euthanasia (the killing of those deemed unfit or genetically unsuitable). His protest was so effective that Göbbels had to warn Hitler against ordering his arrest. Galen saw euthanasia as a crime and informed the civil police of the Nazis' actions. The protest halted euthanasia and has come to be known as the only effective public protest in the Third Reich. Later in the war he preached that vengeance was un-Christian; this was at the time of massive air-raids by the Allies, however, and he lost popularity. After the July 1944 Bomb Plot he was arrested and sent to Sachsenhausen concentration camp; no link with the conspirators was found, however, and he was released in 1945. He returned to Münster and in March 1945, to Hitler's fury, drove out to meet the Allies and surrender the city.

Galland, Adolf (b. 1911).   Ace fighter pilot and commander of Luftwaffe fighters from 1941 to 1945. A keen pilot who had practised as a glider pilot while Germany was forbidden to build aircraft by the Versailles Treaty, he joined the German commercial airline Lufthansa in 1932. The manager of Lufthansa, Milch, was secretly building up a team of men who would become the basis for a future air force, and Galland transferred to the new Luftwaffe when it was formed in 1935. He served as a pilot in the German Condor Legion which fought for the nationalists in the Spanish Civil War, where he flew over 300 sorties and developed tactics for the new Messerschmitt single-seater monoplane fighter. In the Battle of Britain he became recognized as an outstanding fighter leader. He was awarded the Knight's Grand Cross with Oakleaves, Swords and Diamonds and was credited with over 100 victories. In 1942 Galland became the youngest officer to hold the rank of general in the German armed forces, having taken command of all fighter aircraft.

By 1944 the Luftwaffe had attained its largest force of fighters. With over 3,000 aircraft under his command, Galland's plan was to swamp the USAAF daylight raids. Hitler feared, perhaps correctly, that this might instead result in the wrecking of the Luftwaffe and overruled the plan. Göring put all the blame for Luftwaffe failures on Galland and removed him from high command. He ended the war in charge of the new Me262 jet fighters which had come into the air too late to win a victory.

Gällivare.   Site of the Swedish mines whose iron-ore production was vitally important to German industry. It was to protect this source of iron ore, menaced by the prospect of an Allied invasion, that Hitler, probably reluctantly, agreed to a pre-emptive strike against Norway on 9 April 1940. The effect of Hitler's move was, strategically, to surround Sweden with German forces and ensure that the Gällivare output continued to flow to Germany for the rest of the war.

Gau.   The old Frankish term for a political division within a nation, used to describe Nazi Party administrative regions, each headed by a *Gauleiter*. In 1938 there were 32 Nazi Party districts; by 1942 there were 43, the members increased by the *Anschluss* with Austria and those parts of Czechoslovakia and Poland which had been taken into 'Greater Germany'. *Gauleiters* ruled only in Greater Germany. In occupied lands Nazi rule was through a Reich Commissioner or Governor. In December 1942 all *Gaue* became Reich Defence Districts, and all Gauleiters also Reich Defence Commissioners.

Gau	*HQ*	*Gau*	*HQ*
Baden	Karlsruhe	Hamburg	Hamburg
Bayreuth	Bayreuth	Hesse-Nassau	Frankfurt am Main
Berlin	Berlin	Carinthia	Klagenfurt
Danzig, West		Cologne-Aachen	Cologne
Prussia	Danzig	Hesse-Kassel	Kassel
Düsseldorf	Düsseldorf	Magdeburg-Anhalt	Dessau
Essen	Essen	Mark Brandenburg	Berlin
Franconia	Nuremberg	Mecklenburg	Schwerin
Halle-Merseberg	Halle	Main-Franconia	Würzburg
Moselland	Coblenz	Sudetenland	Reichenberg
Upper Bavaria	Munich	South Hanover-	
Lower Danube	Vienna	Brunswick	Hanover
Lower Silesia	Breslau	Thuringia	Weimar
Upper Danube	Linz	Tyrol-Vorarlberg	Innsbruck
Upper Silesia	Kattowitz	Wartheland	Posen
East Hanover	Lüneburg	Weser-Ems	Oldenburg
East Prussia	Königsberg	Westphalia North	Münster
Pomerania	Stettin	Westphalia South	Bochum
Saxony	Dresden	Westmark	Neustadt

Salzburg	Salzburg	Vienna	Vienna
Schleswig-Holstein	Kiel	Württemberg-	
Swabia	Augsburg	Hohenzollern	Stuttgart
Styria	Graz		
Overseas	Berlin		

***Gauleiter* (District leader)**.   Senior Nazi Party administrative figure in a *Gau* (►*Gau*).

***Geheimes Staatspolizei*.   ►Gestapo

Gehlen, Reinhard (1902–1979).   The head of German army intelligence on the Russian front from 1942. He earned a reputation as a reliable predictor of Russian moves and took care to present his reports in clear language and layout. At the end of WWII he put his mass of material and contacts in Eastern Europe into American hands and, with US assistance, opened the Gehlen Bureau, a major Munich-based intelligence organization.

Genocide.   A term now often trivialized for propaganda purposes but originally applied to the Nazi attempt to destroy European Jewry. The destruction of a cultural or racial group, a people or nation (►Final Solution).

German–American Bund.   A pro-German and specifically pro-Nazi movement in the US. Founded in 1935 by Fritz Kuhm, the Bund's Madison Square rallies and the unrestrained pro-Nazi sentiments of its leader provoked much American resentment. Hitler therefore disowned the Bund and at least claimed to forbid anyone to send it funds.

The Bund made little impression on the majority of Americans of German stock and disappeared immediately the US entered the war in 1941.

German States (*Länder*).   Until Hitler unified the Reich with the *Gleichschaltung* process, Germany was a federation of states, large and small, with three independent cities, the Hansa towns originally in a medieval trade league.

Land	Area (square miles)	1933 population (millions)
Prussia	113,750	38.2
Bavaria	29,486	7.4
Saxony	5,856	5.0
Württemberg	7,534	2.6
Baden	5,819	2.3
Thuringia	4,541	1.6
Hesse	2,968	1.4
Mecklenburg-Schwerin	5,068	.7

Oldenburg	2,479	.6
Brunswick	1,418	.5
Anhalt	906	.4
Lippe	470	.2
Mecklenburg-Strelitz	1,130	.1
Waldeck	438	.06
Schaumburg-Lippe	130	.05
Hansa towns:		
Lübeck		.1
Bremen		.3
Hamburg		1.1

Neither the military division of Germany into Commands nor the Nazi Party division into *Gaue* corresponded with the traditional states. The process of *Gleichschaltung* ensured that the Reich was uniform without local variation.

Gestapo.   The secret police (*GEheimes STAatsPOlizei*) of the Third Reich. Its origins lie in Prussia, which comprised two-thirds of the land and population of Germany. Before 1933 each state had its own police; and the Prussian Minister of the Interior, the Social Democrat Karl Severing, had ensured that his police had been purged of both left- and right-wing elements. When Göring took over the Prussian ministry in 1933, he replaced Police Department 1A, responsible for political matters, with a new secret police department (*Geheimes Polizei Amt*), to be staffed by men loyal to the Nazi Party. From this organization, its name marginally changed, sprang the *Geheimes Staatspolizei*, the Gestapo. Nazi careerists now took the senior posts in the Prussian police and an extraordinary jockeying for power began, involving Artur Nebe of the Kripo (criminal police), Heinrich Müller, Rudolf Diels (an expert on communists) and Kurt Daluege (an SS man), now the head of Orpo (*Ordnungspolizei*) responsible for public order.

Everywhere in Germany secret police departments were being formed and staffed by SD men, and Himmler suggested that *Gleichschaltung* could now be applied to the police forces and that he should become chief of the German police. Göring was not deposed, but the organization under him was captured by the SS; Diels was moved out of Berlin to the provinces; Daluege and Nebe retained their posts, while Heinrich Müller (soon to be known as Gestapo Müller) took over the Gestapo. In February 1936 the Gestapo was given formal national status, and in September the Berlin HQ at Prinz Albrechtstrasse became the national headquarters. Himmler now placed the Gestapo under Heydrich as Department IV of the RSHA (the state security organization), with Müller as operational chief.

Essentially the Gestapo were policemen, but they were the instruments of Nazi methods which allowed and encouraged terror to gain and keep control of the state and the people. By 1943, at its largest, there would have been 45,000

Gestapo men in contact with their regular 60,000 agents or the 100,000 informers on SS files. When they moved into war-occupied territories to carry out their work they wore, not police uniforms, but civilian clothes or SS uniform. So thoroughly were they enmeshed with the whole SS operation that it is often difficult to distinguish which act was carried out by the Gestapo, which by the SS/SD and which by Kripo attached to an SD office. The *Einsatzgruppen* (the task forces which moved behind the advancing German army in Russia rounding up and killing Jews, partisans and communists) were under SD control. Their officers were drawn from the Gestapo and the Kripo, while the bulk of the troops were Waffen SS or Orpo men.

As Nazi power spread so did the fearsome reputation of the Gestapo. Backed by the system of concentration camps and by his right under the law to extract confessions by beating, the Gestapo man in his leather overcoat and dark, snap-brim hat became a figure of terror first to liberal and Marxist Germans and German Jews and then to the subject populations of Nazi-occupied Europe.

At the Nuremberg trials the Gestapo was one of six organizations indicted for crimes against humanity (the leadership of the Nazi Party, the OKW, the SS, the SA, the Reich cabinet and the Gestapo). Despite evidence supplied by Gisevius (who had been sent to work for the Gestapo in 1933 and before he left had in horror taken notes of its criminal actions), Allied jurists found great difficulty in identifying those who were responsible in law for the organization's manifold crimes: the SD hid behind the Gestapo and, in turn, the Gestapo sought to hide behind the SD. Gestapo men denied being anything other than policemen, claiming they had never heard of *Einsatzgruppen* and had taken no part in the tortures, lynchings and shooting of hostages they were accused of. But the case was made and the hunt for Gestapo officials went on. Perhaps not surprisingly, many of the senior Gestapo escaped arrest; many were believed to have prepared their escape routes many months before the fall of the Reich. Gestapo Müller, the man who undoubtedly knew most about the *Geheimes Staatspolizei*'s operations and scope, disappeared at the end of the war, having burnt his files and destroyed all photographs of himself.

Girls in Nazi Germany. ➤Youth Organizations

Gisevius, Hans Bernd (1904–1974). Anti-Nazi vice-consul in Zürich. Gisevius was a lawyer in the Prussian Ministry of the Interior in 1933 and saw the effect of the Nazi takeover, the increase of irregularities in police procedures and the cover-up of criminal acts of the Gestapo. He began compiling dossiers and to call for action against wrongdoers. To survive, he moved from job to job in the ministries. General Witzleben gave him entry to the OKW where he met senior officers, among them Oster of the *Abwehr*, who were beginning to form anti-Hitler groups. Canaris had him posted to Zürich as vice-consul. Here he made contact with British intelligence and with Dulles (head of OSS Europe). He was in Berlin at the time of the failed July 1944 Bomb Plot and was obliged to go into hiding. Dulles managed to send him forged documents with a Gestapo metal identification pass, and he reached safety in Switzerland in January 1945.

He gave evidence at the Nuremberg trials for the defence of Frick and Schacht, evidence which proved damning for others who tried to plead ignorance or claimed the impossibility of protesting against criminal acts. 'Everything was possible in the Third Reich,' he said, indicating that there could have been more opposition and less submission to Hitler.

Gleichschaltung. The co-ordination or unification of the Reich. A series of laws passed by the Nazi government after 1933 whose object was to create a highly centralized one-Party Reich by the destruction of the privileges and traditions of the old German states. An Enabling Act was first passed by the new Reichstag giving Hitler dictatorial powers for four years. There followed a mass of legislation creating the Nazi state. By the end of March the first Unification Law placed state legislatures under Nazi control. The independence of the fifteen German states and the three Hansa towns was removed and a Reichsstatthalter from among the senior Gauleiters appointed to each. In practice, all sovereign powers were transferred to the Reich Minister of the Interior. Political acceptability became the measure for advance and even survival in the 'New' Germany: in April the Law for the Restoration of the Professional Civil Service and the Law on Admission to Legal Practice disqualified civil servants and lawyers on political grounds. Special courts were established to try political offences and in Berlin a People's Court (►Freisler, Roland) was charged with trials of high treason.

In June and July opposition political parties of the Weimar Republic were abolished by decree and labour unions were subjected, one by one, to Unification decrees and brought under Dr Ley's Labour Front (*Deutsche Arbeitsfront*, DAF). (It is notable that they were not put under the socialistic Nazi Factory Cell Organization which was under Strasser's influence.) The introduction of the new Front was combined with May Day celebrations; the 1 May holiday was taken over as Nazi Labour Day; union offices were occupied by SA units; and many union officials put into concentration camps. In a parallel attack on the independence of the professions, they were reorganized under 'fronts' or 'Academies' and the old professional bodies dissolved. The media, radio, music, journalism and drama were brought under Göbbels' Reich Chamber of Culture and non-conformist writers silenced. ►Göbbels, Josef Paul

Gleichschaltung was a devastating assault on the political, social and cultural institutions of the old Germany; for the time being, only industry and the armed forces were exempt. While greater German unity resulted and class and professional differences were reduced, it was at massive cost to the rights of the individual.

From the stream of legislation new power groups developed: the Party, the Labour Front, the SS-SD and Gestapo rivalled the older but still strong industrial and military groups. It would be many years before the armed forces and industry were fully subjected to the will of the Nazi leaders, but the legislative explosion which had come to be known as *Gleichschaltung* provided every weapon necessary for the final takeover of the German state.

Gleichschaltung Chronology

1933

March	5	Reichstag elections; Nazi working majority
	12	Hitler speaks on *Gleichschaltung*: 'The Co-ordination of the Political Will'
	21	Reichstag opens. Decrees on: amnesty for all Nazis who committed offences during the 'struggle'; punitive measures against malicious gossip; setting up of special courts (*Sondergerichte*)
	22	Enabling Law passed, giving special powers to Chancellor Hitler for four years. (This is renewed for a further four years in 1937)
	29	Lex van der Lubbe gives retrospective sanction to execution by hanging for arson
	31	First Co-ordination Law of States and Reich establishes new state and local assemblies, with membership in same proportions as Reichstag parties
April	7	Second Co-ordination Law appoints state governors
	8	Law on the Reconstruction of the Professional Civil Service, making no distinction between Reich, state or local cadres, gives transferability between each; all underqualified, disloyal, or Jewish staff are to be dismissed
May	2	All labour unions dissolved. Labour Front established
	19	Establishment of Trustees of Labour
	20	Seizure of assets of Communist Party
June	1	First Law for the Reduction of Unemployment
	9	Law on Payments Abroad
	12	Law on Betraying the German Economy; notification of assets abroad
	14	Law on the New Formation of the German Peasantry
		Decrees dissolving political parties:
	22	SPD
	27	DNVP
	28	State Party (formerly the DPP)
July	4	DVP
	4	Bavarian People's Party
	5	Centre Party
	8	Concordat between Germany and the Vatican

July	*14*	Law against the Establishment of Parties
	15	Reich Regulations for the Corporate Reorganization of Agriculture
September	*13*	Law on Reich Food Costs
October	*1*	Reich Entailed Farm Law stabilizes small farms
	14	Reichstag dissolved
November	*12*	National Referendum: 95 per cent approve Nazi policy
December	*1*	Law to Secure Unity of Party and Reich

Globocnik, Odilo (1900–1945). SS *Brigadeführer*, at one time in overall command of the Polish extermination camps. Born in Austria, Globocnik found an early outlet for his innate violence in the Austrian Nazi Party and rose to become *Gauleiter* of Vienna after the *Anschluss*. As police chief in Lublin he founded a line of extermination camps along the Bug River. Unstable to the point that he terrorized his own concentration camp commanders, Globocnik committed suicide on his arrest by Allied troops in 1945.

Glücks, Richard (b. 1889). Inspector of concentration camps. In 1936 Glücks joined the SS staff of Theodor Eicke, the first Inspector of concentration camps, and in 1940 was appointed to succeed him. He was reported last seen near the Danish border in 1945 and thereafter vanished without trace.

Göbbels, Josef Paul (1897–1945). Chief propagandist of the Nazi Party and Nazi Propaganda Minister. Born of Catholic Rhineland working people, Göbbels as a youth was quick-thinking and a passionate nationalist. But a crippled left leg (the result of a childhood illness) made him unfit for war service. Short, unattractive to women and embittered by his disabilities, he nevertheless achieved academic success, winning scholarships and a university grant. He completed his doctorate in philology at Heidelberg in 1921. His aim was to live from writing and he moved in radical circles, being drawn towards communism (or the 'national bolshevism' then current). He wrote for nationalist papers, the *Völkischer Beobachter* in particular, and was attracted to the radicalism of Gregor Strasser, whose secretary he became. He had however become an ecstatic admirer of Hitler during the 1923 Putsch trial and was won over from Strasser's radical group, Hitler persuading Göbbels to make a public break from Strasser in 1926. By way of reward, still in his twenties, he was made the Party's Gauleiter of Berlin, where he drew the Strasserites back to Hitler. With control of the Berlin SA he developed a tough, street-fighting, fearsome party, menacing to his political opponents and to the elected government struggling to maintain public order. Göbbels represented intellectual sophistication in the Nazi Party but, more importantly, as a North German he helped give the Party a broader national appeal. He founded his own paper *Der Angriff* (the *Attack*) in Berlin in 1927 and continued to voice the radical side of Nazism until the Röhm Purge of 1934. He became Party propaganda chief in 1928 and was elected to the Reichstag in May of that year, while openly deriding it as an institution and claiming that the Nazis would use it only as long as it served them. In Berlin he introduced 'Heil Hitler!' as the regular form of greeting between Party members. He thrust Nazism at the Berlin public with noisy anti-semitism, his thugs smashing Jewish shops and attacking Jews in the streets. His SA men were encouraged to provoke fights with communist street bands who were all too keen to do the same, thus ensuring that the public saw issues in terms of one side or the other, with no middle way possible. This, in Göbbels' view, was the function of political violence.

In January 1933 he took charge of the Party's Reichstag election campaign in the small state of Lippe and doubled the Nazi vote, making it a well-publicized demonstration of the growth of Nazi strength. He then organized SA and SS parades in Berlin where von Papen and Schleicher were still jockeying for power. The outcome was that Hindenburg called Hitler to the Chancellorship.

Göbbels had been promised a place in Hitler's government, but the first January 1933 Cabinet was given the appearance of a broad coalition without Nazi domination, and Göbbels stayed in his Party propaganda post. For the second 1933 election in March, he stage-managed a great demonstration at the Berlin church where the Prussian Emperor, Frederick the Great, was buried. The old President, Hindenburg, was brought in to be seen to give his fatherly blessing, and the blessing of old Germany, on the new era and its leader, Hitler.

Göbbels now entered the Cabinet, creating a new Reich Ministry of Information and Propaganda. In his hands were now concentrated all writing, music, theatre, dance, painting, sculpture, film and radio. With *Gleichschaltung*, culture too was to be brought into line. He created a Reich Chamber of Culture with chambers and academies for every field of cultural activity. Above all he took a close interest in Germany's film industry (and often a closer interest in its actresses). German films were famous throughout the world and the industry continued to produce technically fine work, but (with the exception of Leni Riefenstahl's films) little of lasting value was made. Most of Göbbels' ministry's output was dull. Although he managed to keep the world-famous conductor Furtwängler and the composer Richard Strauss in Germany, he lost the great novelist Thomas Mann, with a host of other intellectuals, writers, artists and actors, to the wave of emigration from Nazi Germany.

Göbbels also put a major effort into radio broadcasting and encouraged the manufacture of a cheap people's radio set in 1933. He obtained huge and ever-growing audiences for his propaganda through the radio, and began the world's first regular television service in March 1935. Although restricted to closed-circuit showing in Berlin, it kept going until near the end of the war.

Göbbels was not a widely popular figure, though he competed with Göring in giving spectacular parties and surrounding himself with glittering people, particularly young film-actresses with whom he enjoyed sexual adventures. His wife Magda lost patience with a long affair with the Czech actress Lida Baarova and in 1938 demanded a divorce. Hitler intervened; Baarova returned home and the rift was healed. Göbbels did not amass riches like other Nazi leaders, but he enjoyed a luxurious lifestyle. Just as his official position provided him with a supply of mistresses, so his ministry paid his bills.

Once Hitler had used him to get into power, Göbbels' key importance lessened; the myth-making propagandist was no longer needed. He did not organize, he only issued Hitler's orders, such as that for Crystal Night's anti-Jewish riots. He continued as Berlin Party Gauleiter and Reich Minister; with the war, however, much of the Third Reich's propaganda came not from his ministry but as military communiqués. He developed broadcasting services directed against Germany's enemies, but they failed to carry the conviction of the BBC. The most famous of his foreign radio personalities was the English-language broadcaster William Joyce, known in England as 'Lord Haw Haw' and hanged there after the war for treason.

After the defeat at Stalingrad, Göbbels took a stand for total war, calling for full support and devotion from the German people in a fight to the death. Thus, from 1943, Göbbels created a new role for himself. He toured bombed cities (which Hitler never did), organizing the relief convoys that moved into the raided towns with food, blankets and first-aid. By the end, he became not only prominent once again but even popular.

On the day of the July 1944 Bomb Plot, Göbbels acted quickly and effectively to control the situation in Berlin. He ordered the guard commander, Otto Remer, to come and take his orders, having convinced him that Hitler had survived. The civilian Göbbels then assumed the role of a military commander and ensured that orders were issued throughout Germany in the name of the Führer.

It was under Göbbels' total war orders that German manpower was fully mobilized for the first time. He increased the working week to sixty hours, raised the age-limit for calling up women to work to fifty, and closed down theatres and concert halls, combing out administrative bodies for men to go into the army.

In January 1945 Hitler moved finally to his Berlin headquarters and Göbbels' effectiveness began to collapse with Germany. In April he moved with his wife and children into Hitler's bunker. The day following Hitler's suicide, Göbbels poisoned his wife and children and shot himself.

The rise of the Nazi Party and the war itself gave Göbbels the opportunity to demonstrate his mastery of the techniques of mass communication. An orator of exceptional talent and power, he used the new medium of radio with consummate skill to sustain and advance the myths of national socialism. Among so much intellectual mediocrity in the Nazi leadership, Josef Göbbels was bound to stand out. ➤Music, Cinema, Art

Gobineau, Arthur, Comte de (1816–82). French writer on racial theory. His *Essai sur l'inégalité des races humaines* ('Essay on the inequality of human races') was published in 1853 and 1855. Many of its propositions on race and racial degeneration entered the European popular consciousness about the time of Hitler's youth and were, often in garbled or partial form, incorporated into his racial theory. ➤Race

Golden Party Badge (*Goldenes Parteiabzeichen*). A golden badge personally awarded by the Führer for services to the Nazi Party. Its holders, known popularly as 'Golden Pheasants', were limited to a few hundred, mostly Old Fighters or new Hitler favourites such as Albert Speer.

Gördeler, Carl (1884–1945). Mayor of Leipzig, 1930–37, and civilian leader of resistance to Hitler. Appointed Reich Price Commissioner and Controller of Foreign Exchange in 1934, Gördeler at this time had some hope that Hitler would become a benevolent dictator. Rapidly disillusioned, he publicly opposed rearmament and anti-semitism and refused to pull down the statue of the composer Mendelssohn in Leipzig or to fly a swastika flag over the city hall.

As the overseas representative of the Bosch company, he used his contacts with Britain, France and the USA from 1937 to warn their governments against Nazism. In Britain, where he met Churchill in 1938, he urged that territorial concessions might be made to Germany to help in her recovery from the indignities of the Versailles Treaty. In Germany he tried to influence others by drawing up plans for a future Germany and was soon identified by Canaris as a man who would help overthrow Hitler. By 1940 Gördeler had correctly decided that only the armed forces could overthrow Hitler, and he devoted much of his efforts during the war to trying to persuade reluctant senior officers that this was their real line of duty. The Allied Atlantic Charter of 1942 which foresaw a disarmed Germany under occupation came as a severe blow to his optimism, however. Nevertheless in 1943 when Gördeler visited Sweden he again sent messages to Churchill (to which there was no reply). Although it was assumed among some conspiratorial groups that he and General Beck would be the leaders of a new Germany, younger officers like Stauffenberg and his collaborators found Gördeler over-conservative and out of touch with the liberal and social elements. At the failure of the July 1944 Bomb Plot, Gördeler, already by this time a fugitive, was arrested in August and interrogated at length. He was hanged at Plötzensee in February 1945. ➤Provisional Government List

Göring, Hermann (1893–1946). The flamboyant Reichsmarschall, next to Hitler the most prominent Nazi leader. Born in Rosenheim, Bavaria, to minor gentry he joined an infantry regiment in WWI but arthritis made him unfit for his duties. By pulling strings he became a fighter pilot and established himself as one of Germany's aces with twenty-two victories. He commanded the crack Richthofen squadron and was awarded the 'Pour le Mérite' medal for bravery.

After the war he earned a living as a pilot, flying in air shows, then for the

Fokker company and subsequently for the Danish government. He had great charm, was a good horseman and a crack shot. When he crash-landed while working in Sweden he swept his hostess, Carin von Kantzow, off her feet and she went through a divorce in order to marry him.

He returned to Germany in 1923 and joined the new Nazi Party, his fame and powers of leadership soon making him the commander of its strong-arm unit, the SA. In the November 1923 Beer Hall Putsch, which he helped plan, he was in charge of all SA operations. He marched with the leaders, Ludendorff and Hitler, to the Odeonsplatz and when the police opened fire he was hit in the thigh and groin. From a private clinic in Munich, Carin Göring took him to safety in Austria. For some years Göring lived in exile in Italy and then Sweden, recovering from his wounds but with the recurrence of arthritis his treatment led him to become a morphia addict.

The amnesty offered to the participants in the Beer Hall Putsch enabled him to return to Germany. Rejoining the Nazi Party he became a Reichstag deputy in 1928 and, as the Nazis recorded massive electoral successes, President of the Reichstag from 1932. In Hitler's first cabinet in January 1933 he was a minister without portfolio and Prussian Minister of the Interior, which gave him control of Germany's largest police force. He was the first Nazi on the spot on the night of the Reichstag Fire and he took charge of the trial of van der Lubbe and the communists accused. But he was obliged to see all but one of the five accused acquitted and was even forced by one, the Bulgarian Dimitrov, into a defence of the Nazi government.

His wife died in October 1931 and in 1935 he married the actress Emmy Sonnemann, remarkable for her vulgarity and Wagnerian appearance. The wedding was the greatest social event of the Third Reich, combining Christian and Nazi-pagan ritual.

He now developed his newly acquired estate, renaming it Karinhall after his first wife. Here he lived a life of luxurious fantasy in which the servants wore antique costume and the 'national' art collection (for he had, untypically for a leading Nazi, a considerable knowledge of art) was assembled under his protection. When the new Luftwaffe was made public in 1935, he was appointed Commander-in-Chief. At this stage he pursued his public duties, especially those connected with the Luftwaffe, with vigour and efficiency.

In 1936 he became Commissioner Plenipotentiary for the Four-Year Plan. In November 1937 he succeeded Schacht as Minister of the Economy. He founded the Reichswerke Hermann Göring, a corporation financed from the Four-Year Plan to make the steel that private industry was reluctant to manufacture. It was 70 per cent government-financed and served to increase his personal fortune. He was now rapidly expanding his power in the economy, the armed forces and political life. In February 1938 he was appointed Field Marshal (following the Blomberg and Fritsch affairs which he had helped engineer). During the next year, 1939, he was made Chairman of the Reich

Council for National Defence and named as Hitler's successor. He planned the Luftwaffe's role in the invasions of Poland, Norway and France; in 1940, when Hitler made nine of his generals Field Marshals, Göring was given the unprecedented rank of *Reichsmarschall*.

He had reached the height of his career. The slide, when it began in 1940, was rapid, as his Luftwaffe failed to substantiate his boast to remove the British RAF from the skies. His tactical error had been to switch from attacks on RAF airfields and radar and to concentrate on the bombing of London.

Neither did the Luftwaffe prove all-conquering in Russia, and Göring's inability to prevent the Allied bombing of German towns confirmed his decline. Self-indulgence softened him and more ambitious Nazis – Himmler, Bormann, Göbbels and Speer – began to bypass him and reduce his importance.

On Hitler's birthday in April 1945, Göring left the Berlin Bunker, claiming urgent tasks in south Germany. When he telegraphed Hitler, offering to take command of the surviving German forces, Bormann interpreted this to Hitler as a treasonable act. He was ordered to be arrested and stripped of all offices and honours. Hitler's Last Will expelled him from the Party. In May 1945, from the SS house where he was detained, he despatched Field Marshal Brauchitsch to General Eisenhower to ask for protection from the SS. Then, dressed in a special uniform, he drove off to surrender, graciously acknowledging the salutes of the German soldiers walking to their imprisonment.

At the 1946 Nuremberg trial, the effect of imprisonment and a normal improved diet showed: he was the star of the trial and clearly the leader of the accused. He was found guilty on all counts and condemned to death. On the day before his execution was due in October 1946, the guards found him in his cell dead from poison. Somehow (and still no one can explain how) he had managed to conceal about him a phial of cyanide on which he had bitten.

He married twice:

Göring, Carin (1889–1931). Born Baroness Fock of an aristocratic Swedish family, she dissolved her marriage to Count von Kantzow to marry Göring when he was working in Sweden in 1922. She died of tuberculosis and in her memory Göring named the estate he acquired when the Nazis came to power Karinhall.

Göring, Emmy (1893–1973). Born Sonnemann she was a provincial actress built on the lines of a Wagnerian heroine. Her talent lay in flamboyance complementary to Göring's: they matched each other's vulgarity. Their marriage in 1935 was a huge and gaudy spectacle, performed by a bishop and witnessed by Hitler. As a leader of Nazi society she was not always popular and made the error of snubbing Eva Braun. She remained loyal to Göring to the end, and is even suspected of having passed poison to him in his cell at Nuremberg. After the war she was banned from the stage and lived her life out in a Munich apartment.

Greim, Ritter Robert von (1892–1945). Hitler's last promotion to Field Marshal. A WWI pilot who had won the 'Pour le Mérite', he flew Hitler to Berlin to witness the outcome of the Kapp Putsch there in 1920. Thereafter he stayed closely connected to Hitler and the Nazi Party and when the Luftwaffe was formed in 1935 Göring gave him command of its first fighter squadron. His war record as a pilot was good and he rose to command an air fleet in Russia in 1943.

In April 1945 he flew to the Führer's Bunker in Berlin with the woman pilot Hanna Reitsch and was told that Göring's arrest for treason had been ordered (►Göring) and that he, Greim, was to command the Luftwaffe. He was promoted Field Marshal on the spot.

Although wounded, he was flown out of Berlin, under Russian artillery fire, to Dönitz's headquarters at Ploen. There he transmitted to Himmler Hitler's dismissal and curses for having treacherously sought peace through Count Bernadotte (►Himmler). Hobbling on crutches, Greim was then flown back to his headquarters in Bavaria where he continued to talk in optimistic terms about victory. He was taken prisoner by the American army but took poison, dying in Salzburg in May 1945.

Grese, Irma (1921–1946). Concentration camp guard. From the age of 19, Irma Grese worked at Auschwitz as a guard over female prisoners. A sadist who was promoted to control blocks of women prisoners, Grese was condemned to death and hanged in 1946.

Grimm, Hans (1875–1959). An unrepentant nationalist author whose 1926 book *Volk ohne Raum* ('People without Space') provided the Nazis with one of their most effective slogans. Grimm died in 1959 having constructed his apologia for the Nazi era (its effective construction of a barrier against communism) in *Answer of a German* (1949).

Grosz, George (1893–1959). German painter. The work of Grosz savagely attacked the militarism and profiteering he had witnessed in his youth. In the 1930s he left Germany for the USA where he became an American citizen. Some of his paintings were included by the Nazis in their exhibition of 'degenerate art'.

Gruppe Herbert Baum. A Communist and Jewish resistance group which in 1942 succeeded in setting on fire a Göbbels exhibition, 'The Soviet Paradise'. All its members were traced and arrested by the Gestapo. At least fourteen were killed and their families transported to the extermination camp at Auschwitz.

Gruppenführer. SS Major-General. ►Rank

Grynszpan, Herschel (1919–?). The seventeen-year-old boy who killed Ernst vom Rath in Paris in November 1938 and who was thus the immediate cause of the Crystal Night attacks on Jews in Germany. With thousands of other Jewish people, his family had just been forcibly deported as stateless persons from German Silesia to Poland. In revenge he waited outside the German embassy, hoping to shoot the Ambassador. It was the Third Secretary, vom Rath, who came to the door to see the visitor and was shot. Grynszpan was arrested by the French, but they were in no hurry for a public trial and his case dragged on. In 1940 he was handed over to the Germans and held in Sachsenhausen and in Moabit prison, Berlin. Surprisingly, at the end of the war he was still alive. He was last heard of living in France under a new name. His father, who also survived the Holocaust, was a witness at the Eichmann trial in Israel in 1961.

Guderian, General Heinz (1888–1954). Specialist in the use of armour and *Blitzkrieg* tactics. Born at Kulm (Chelmno in Polish) the son of an army officer, Guderian was originally commissioned in the infantry and served as a staff officer in WWI. He continued to serve in the shrunken post-Versailles *Reichswehr* and was posted to a telegraph battalion at Koblenz. There his work with radio communications and the possibility of faster controlled movement on the battlefield is said to have been his first introduction to the concept of independent armoured warfare. Certainly from the beginning Guderian was a leading member of the *Reichswehr* school of thought which argued for the establishment of armoured forces, supported by motorized infantry and mobile artillery. German interest in the independently acting armoured unit was excited by the British theorists, Captain Liddell Hart and General Fuller. With the election of Adolf Hitler, enthusiasts for independent armoured units like Thoma, Reichenau and Guderian began to receive serious encouragement. Much impressed by a series of manoeuvres and demonstrations, Hitler sanctioned the new *Wehrmacht*'s first tank battalion in 1934. From this point Guderian received rapid promotion, and in 1938 was appointed General of Armoured Troops. By September 1939, when he led XIX Army Corps into Poland, the Wehrmacht had seven Panzer divisions operational. Tactical doctrine was now to be put to the test: armoured units, self-supporting on the battlefield, were not to be divided and assigned to the mass of advancing infantry. Instead they were to strike *ahead of* the main advance, achieving deep penetration of the enemy's line and dislocation and disruption of his rear areas. It was soon discovered that, even when the terrain was less than ideal for armoured units, speed and unrelenting pressure by the tank commanders could achieve striking results. In Poland valuable lessons were learnt by Guderian: techniques of tactical air support were developed and, above all, the morale-shattering effect on the enemy of headlong armoured advance was established. In six weeks *Blitzkrieg* became a reality.

With the adoption of Manstein's plan for the invasion of France, Guderian was given a further opportunity to reveal the full potential of the Panzer divisions. In May 1940 Guderian's XIX Panzer Corps destroyed the fatally dispersed French forces at Sedan and, supported by the Luftwaffe, forced the crossing of the Meuse and struck out across France. In a matter of weeks, the numerically superior French army was defeated and the British Expeditionary Force pushed to a calamitous evacuation at Dunkirk.

When in June 1941 Germany attacked the Soviet Union, Guderian in command of the 2nd Panzer Group repeated his achievement in the first months of headlong advance. But the intervention of the Russian winter and the effectiveness of the Soviet counter-attack in early December brought the long unbroken line of Guderian's successes to a halt. On Christmas Day 1941 he was relieved of his command for carrying out a withdrawal in contravention of Hitler's specific order.

In March 1943 Guderian emerged from retirement to become Inspector of Armoured Troops. Though now suffering from ill-health, he was able time and again to re-equip the Panzer arm and maintain it in the great battles on the Eastern Front during 1943 and 1944.

Though blunt and outspoken in his criticisms Guderian was not, perhaps surprisingly, suspected of complicity in the July 1944 Bomb Plot. Indeed before the end of that month he was promoted Army Chief of Staff, a post he held until his dismissal by Hitler on 28 March 1945.

His successes as an innovative general were great, but he seems never to have seriously questioned the political objectives of Nazi policy. He was, like many other German generals, a gifted but blinkered soldier.

Guernica. The small Basque town in northern Spain in which 1,600 people died in a German bombing attack. In April 1937 Guernica's population stood at only 7,000, but it was the centre of Basque culture, its old oak tree the customary place for Spanish kings to swear to preserve Basque rights. The Monday of the air-raid was a market day; in the afternoon, German Heinkel 111s and Junkers 52s bombed and machine-gunned the town for over three hours. The truth became a matter of international dispute. At first it was claimed that the town had been burnt by the Basques themselves, later that it was Soviet aircraft which had carried out the raids. After the war Basque exiles tried, unsuccessfully, to bring a case against Germany at Nuremberg. But Göring's admission in 1946 that the Luftwaffe had bombed it as an experiment in urban destruction essentially closed the debate. Today, Guernica is known principally through the painting by Pablo Picasso and as a symbol of the destructiveness of air warfare.

Guns or butter. From a much-quoted phrase of Göring in a speech on the Four-Year Plan for rearmament in 1936. 'Would you rather have butter or guns? Should we import lard or metal ores?'

Gürtner, Franz (1881–1941). Hitler's Minister of Justice from 1933 until his death. A Bavarian lawyer with a medal-winning career in WWI, he joined the German Nationalist Party (DNVP) in 1919. As Bavarian Minister of Justice 1922–32, he protected Hitler, seeing him as a fellow nationalist. His prosecution of Hitler after the 1923 Beer Hall Putsch (during which Gürtner had been one of Hess's VIP prisoners) was notably lenient and in 1925 he persuaded the state government of Bavaria to legalize the Nazi Party and to allow Hitler, now released from prison, to speak in public again.

Von Papen made him Minister of Justice in the pre-Nazi government of 1932 and he continued in this office into Hitler's first January 1933 cabinet, appearing as a symbol of continuity. Although he was responsible, in the process of *Gleichschaltung*, for dismantling the old system of justice and the creation of Nazi courts, there have been suggestions that, as a conservative lawyer, he was not fully in agreement with all that he was ordered to do and that his death in 1941 was not from natural causes.

Gypsies in the Third Reich.   In 1935, gypsies were classed as an alien strain (*Fremdrasse*) under the Nuremburg Laws and were seen as a threat to the purity of the German race. Even before the Nazi accession to power, gypsies were the subject of surveillance in Germany (as they were in several other European countries) but from 1933 the Research Centre for Racial Hygiene in Berlin became the centre for identification and classification. Six tribes of gypsies were identified: Sinti (German gypsies), Rom (Hungarian immigrant gypsies), Gelderari, Lowari, Lalleri (descendants of gypsies from Bohemia-Moravia) and Balkan gypsies.

By 1936, the first steps had been taken against Germany's gypsies when they were forced to live in residential camps, on pain of being sent to a concentration camp if they left. In 1938, the decree *Bekämpfung der Zigeunerplage* (Combating the gypsy plague) was promulgated. In March 1939, special identification papers were issued to gypsies, those of mixed blood (*Mischling*) being recorded separately from those with 'pure blood'.

As Germany began to expand, it inherited gypsy minorities in its captured territories. By 1939 the population of gypsies in the Reich was estimated at 30,000. Deportations to Poland (from the Austrian Burgenland and from Germany itself) began in 1940.

As the war progressed, German gypsies became subject to an increasing number of civil disabilities. Entitlement to welfare benefits was removed and gypsy children were expelled from schools. By 1941, sterilization had been introduced.

In December 1942, those with mixed gypsy blood were moved to a special compound of Auschwitz. There, children could stay with their families and the rigours of the prison regime were modified. Himmler was not in favour of the total extermination of gypsies. He wished to preserve the Sintis and Lalleris in a reservation in Bohemia-Moravia for research purposes, but Bormann was able to veto this plan. By 1944, 'pure-blooded' gypsies were being sent to

Auschwitz to be subjected to the experiments of Dr Mengele. Over 20,000 gypsies were killed there, 2,900 perishing on the day the gypsy compound was destroyed on 3 August 1944. By the end of the war, three-quarters of the gypsy population of the German Reich had been exterminated.

In occupied Europe the fate of the gypsy population varied from country to country. Bohemia-Moravia at first confined its gypsy population to camps such as Lety or Holodin. But in 1944, these camps were closed, the remaining inmates being sent to Germany. Only 600 gypsies survived in this area. By contrast the Slovakian leader, Mgr Tiso, was reluctant to order persecutions and all but a few hundred Slovakian gypsies survived. In Hungary, deportations and executions of gypsies only began in late 1944. Nevertheless it has been estimated that some 31,000 gypsies fell victim to the Arrow Cross Gendarmerie.

In the USSR, extermination of gypsies was undertaken by *Einsatzgruppen* units of the SS. In Estonia and Latvia, the gypsy population was almost totally exterminated. Many gypsies were deported to the former Jewish ghettos in Riga, Kaunas and Minsk, where many would die of starvation. It is estimated that over 30,000 died in the USSR.

In Yugoslavia persecution was particularly savage. The Croatian Ustasa government began deportations and executions in late 1944. A figure of 26,000 to 28,000 has been quoted, almost the entire population. Many died in the Zemun camp near Belgrade, where gypsies from Serbia were also sent. By 1942, the Germans claimed the gypsy problem in Serbia too, had been solved.

By contrast, Bulgaria spared her gypsy population and gypsies in Macedonia (which came under Bulgarian rule in 1941) were spared. In Albania, many gypsies avoided detection by becoming Moslems, frequently co-operating with the Italians and Germans against the Serbs and Croats.

In Western Europe, fewer gypsies perished. But, as in Eastern Europe, the scale of loss varied from country to country. Denmark and Norway's gypsies survived virtually untouched, but almost all of Belgium's small population was killed. In France, over 30,000 were rounded up into camps, a process facilitated by the Vichy government's programme of compulsory registration. Deportation to the east followed and some 16,000 to 18,000 died.

Total gypsy losses in Europe are hard to ascertain, but a figure of over 200,000 has been quoted. Only a few survivors received compensation after the war.

H

Hacha, Emil (1872–1945).   President of the federal state of Czechoslovakia after Beneš, from November 1938. Demands for independence in Slovakia and Ruthenia, encouraged by the Germans, led to his declaration of martial law. When Germany professed alarm and anxiety for Germans in Czechoslovakia, Hacha went to Berlin in March 1939 to plead with Hitler not to invade. Hitler brusquely announced he had already given orders to march and left Hacha to be forced into signing a surrender by Ribbentrop and Göring. Hacha, in poor health, gave way and German troops marched into Czechoslovakia.

Hacha was Hitler's guest of honour at his birthday celebrations that April. He urged the Czechs to collaborate with the Germans and he remained nominal head of state of Bohemia and Moravia, which became a protectorate of the Third Reich. He died in prison in June 1945, after the liberation of Czechoslovakia.

Halder, Franz (1884–1972).   German general appointed Chief of the General Staff in 1938. Immensely capable, he was responsible for the military planning (but not the conception) of the 1939 Polish campaign, the Western offensive of May 1940 and the (abandoned) Operation Sealion, the invasion of England. Much of the early German success in Barbarossa, the 1941 invasion of Russia, was due to Halder's preparations. He was dismissed in 1942 after a disagreement with Hitler on strategic issues. In 1944 he was arrested and sent to Dachau, suspected of having taken part in the July Bomb Plot. Freed by the American armies in 1945, he was called to give evidence at the Nuremberg Trials, where he developed his own 'Stab-in-the-back' theory, arguing that without Hitler's interference Germany would then (1945) have been in a military position to demand an 'honourable' peace.

Franz Halder's record of anti-Hitler activities seems to be based on his belief that Germany was being led by Hitler to military humiliation rather than on moral objection to Nazism. Thus he plotted to arrest Hitler at the time of the Czechoslovakian crisis and approached the Vatican in 1939. But immediately after the great military successes in France in 1940, he appears to have accepted that Germany's fate was – and even should be – in Hitler's hands. Franz Halder is an interesting example of the ambivalence with which many senior German officers looked on Hitler.

Hammerstein-Equord, Kurt Freiherr von (1878–1943).   Commander of the German army from 1930 to 1934. Of the traditional officer class, he expressed the army's doubts concerning Hitler's suitability as Chancellor to President

Hindenburg (who himself said that he had no intention of making the Austrian corporal either Minister of Defence or Chancellor of the Reich). He was removed from command in 1934 and replaced by von Fritsch. In retirement he maintained contact with German conservatives, particularly Gördeler, the Mayor of Leipzig. When senior army officers, notably Beck, von Witzleben and Halder were ready in 1938 to confront Hitler with the danger of his war plans, Hammerstein was among them; but the British appeasement policies led to the conspiracy's collapse.

He was recalled in 1939 and in 1940, but was again retired when doubts arose about his loyalty. He was linked with many officers later involved in the 1944 Bomb Plot, but died in Berlin before the conspiracy took place.

Hanfstängl, Ernst Franz Sedgwick ('Putzi') (1887–1976). Hitler's rich companion in the early 1920s. A Harvard graduate with an American mother, from a well-known Munich family, he had become a friend of Hitler in 1921, loaned him money, introduced him to Munich society and entertained him by playing the piano and clowning. He was part of a social world hitherto unknown to Hitler. He was made 'foreign press adviser' to the Nazis. At the collapse of the 1923 Beer Hall Putsch he and his American-born wife, Helene Niemeyer, hid the wounded Hitler in their home. But as the Nazi movement grew in popularity and power, Hanfstängl's value to the party lessened. In 1937 he left Germany on hearing rumours of a plot to kill him and lived in the USA. During WWII he was for a while an adviser to Washington on Nazism. He returned to Germany after the war.

Harzburg Front. A political alliance of the right against the government of Chancellor Brüning in 1931. Hugenberg, the industrialist and nationalist (DNVP) leader, called a meeting at Bad Harzburg in Brunswick, of nationalists, Pan-Germans, the Stahlhelm, landowning Junkers and industrialists. Among them were Schacht, Fritz Thyssen, Seldte and Hitler. Hugenberg's intention was to show that he could deploy Nazi power to the benefit of the right in general. Hitler however believed he could get power without using the Front and, by refusing to combine with the nationalists, broke it up to the Nazis' eventual gain.

Hassell, Ulrich von (1881–1944). Aristocratic Prussian diplomat who was ambassador in Rome from 1932 to 1938. He had not approved of the Axis and Anti-Comintern pacts (made by Ribbentrop's office rather than the traditional Foreign Ministry) and he was dismissed in February 1938 when Hitler cleared out opponents from the army and civil service. He joined Beck, Gördeler and others in anti-Hitler plotting and tried to persuade senior officials and generals to join them. Hassell believed in the restoration of a Hohenzollern monarch and in 'Greater Germany'.

After the July 1944 Bomb Plot he was arrested and hanged. His diaries, which had been buried in Bavaria, were published after the war and are a valuable source of information on his resistance contacts.

Haushofer, Karl (1869–1946). Professor of Geopolitics at Munich University. A teacher of Rudolf Hess during his days as a Munich student, Haushofer continued to influence Hess's ideas as he progressed in the Nazi hierarchy. An exponent of a theory of geopolitics which saw the continental power of Germany superseding the oceanic power of a declining British Empire, Haushofer nevertheless believed in the essentially complementary nature of British and German power. While in prison in England Hess would claim that his dramatic flight in 1941 was influenced by Haushofer's ideas.

Haushofer was increasingly disturbed by his reputation as a leading Nazi philosopher and as the 'man behind Hitler's ideas of *Lebensraum*'. He committed suicide shortly after the end of the war.

Haw-Haw, Lord. ➤Joyce, William

Heidegger, Martin (1889–1976). Existentialist philosopher. A rector of Freiburg University in April 1933, Heidegger embraced Nazism but refused to burn books or dismiss anti-Nazi staff. His attempt at combining academic with Nazi standards failed and he resigned in February 1934. After the war he was banned from teaching until 1951 and aroused anger by not condemning the Nazis' anti-semitism.

'Heil Hitler!' 'Heil!' ('Hail' or 'Long live . . .') had long been used in German as a call of acclamation. Hitler adopted the raised-arm salute in imitation of the Italian fascist salute. After his release from Landsberg prison in April 1924 the crowds called 'Heil Hitler!' (and 'Heil Ludendorff!'). The first Party use was in July 1925 at a parade of 5,000 uniformed Nazis in Weimar, and the SA commander Pfeffer von Salomon ritualized the salute and shout from then on. Göbbels, when he became *Gauleiter* of Berlin in October 1926, made the formula the regular greeting between Nazis.

Heiliger, Max. The name under which Reichsbank President Walther Funk authorized a bank account to be opened into which the SS industries (SS-WVHA) put the untaxed funds and deposited the gold and jewellery robbed from their victims. Much of this wealth was lost at the end of the war with the Nazi gold reserves, but some was rechannelled into post-war SS escape organizations.

Hendaye. Location in south-west France of a meeting between Hitler and Franco on 23 October 1940. The subject under discussion was Spain's participation in the war on the German side. Hitler's requirements were for Franco to declare war on Britain in January 1941 and launch an immediate attack on Gibraltar. Successful occupation of the rock would effectively deny the Mediterranean to the Royal Navy.

Franco's conditions were that he should be liberally supplied with arms and fuel by Germany and that Spain should be rewarded by the acquisition of the French North African Empire. Discussions continued for over nine hours but essentially neither side trusted the other and the talks broke up without an agreement for Spain to enter the war.

Henlein, Konrad (1898–1945). Czechoslovak pan-German nationalist. After WWI service in the Austrian army, he became a gymnastics teacher and head of the Czechoslovakian 'German Gymnastics Movement' (1923). By 1933 he had founded the Sudeten German Party, with an organization and ideology based on the Nazi Party. The new Party was funded by the German Foreign Office and Henlein was used to create the crises of 1938, visiting Germany for instructions between March and September (when Chamberlain flew to Munich). When the Czech government offered to accede to all Sudeten demands, Henlein broke off negotiations on a minor pretext: at this juncture a peaceful settlement would have ruined Hitler's plans to annex the Sudetenland. The final crisis now developed rapidly: Hitler made speeches threatening violence; Sudetenlanders rose against the Czech government; martial law was declared and Henlein fled to Germany. A '*Sudeten Freikorps*' was raised and, supported by SS detachments, occupied two frontier towns in Czechoslovakia in late September: the Sudeten uprising had begun.

In March 1939, when Hitler marched into Czechoslovakia, Henlein was rewarded by being made head of the Civil Administration of Bohemia and Moravia. In 1945 Czech resistance forces arrested him and he committed suicide.

Henry (Heinrich) the Fowler (876–936). Duke of Saxony who, although never crowned, was accepted from 916 as Emperor of the Holy Roman Empire. He defended the German territory of the empire, building castles and fortifying cities. He defeated the Wends, Hungarians and Danes and added Lorraine to his German lands. The thousandth anniversary of his death was celebrated by Himmler who shared his first name and believed that he was a reincarnation of his spirit.

Hermann, Lilo (1909–38). A student involved in anti-Nazi activities. Sentenced to death for high treason, she was the first woman executed by the Third Reich.

Herrenvolk **(The master race).** A concept, fed to the Nazis by several strains of European thinking, that the Aryan, Teuton or German was a member of a master race. ➤Gobineau, Arthur, Comte de; Chamberlain, Houston Stewart

Hess, Rudolf (1894–1987). Deputy leader of the Nazi Party and for a period next in succession to the leadership of the Reich after Hermann Göring. Born in Alexandria, the son of a German merchant, Rudolf Hess served as a young man in the same regiment as Hitler during WWI and later as a junior officer in the Imperial Air Force.

After the defeat he volunteered to serve in the *Freikorps* under Ritter von Epp and at Munich University he came under the influence of the 'geopolitician' Professor Karl Haushofer. His right-wing views already formed, he joined the emergent Nazi Party and marched with Hitler in the Beer Hall Putsch, was tried by the Bavarian government and imprisoned with his leader at Landsberg. It is almost certainly during this period in prison, when he was taking Hitler's dictation of *Mein Kampf*, that the closeness between the two men was formed. On their release from Landsberg Hess (with Göring still abroad) was now to play a leading part in the re-formation of the Nazi Party. By 1932 he had been appointed Chairman of the Central Political Commission of the Party and an *SS-Obergruppenführer*. As the Party entered its period of power, Hess became Deputy Leader, Reich Minister without Portfolio (in June 1933), a selector of all senior Nazi officials two years later and, in 1938, a member of the secret Cabinet Council. In the following year he was appointed a ministerial member for the Defence of the Reich and named to follow Göring in the leadership succession. It was a dizzying rise to power for a man of very modest intellectual abilities. A tall, dark-browed, intensely proud man, Rudolf Hess burned with a religious fervour for his leader. There is little doubt that he took his own introductory words at the Nuremberg rallies, 'Hitler is Germany – Germany is Hitler', as literal truth.

It was this loyalty to the Führer and this credulousness which led to the flight to Britain on 10 May 1941 which astonished the world. By 1939 the great days of Rudolf Hess were already over. Generals and admirals now filled the Führer's conference rooms, Heinrich Himmler and Göring were in constant attendance. Discussions were no longer of Party matters but of strategy and war. In this new atmosphere Hess felt himself cut off from Adolf Hitler, excluded from the centre of Nazi power. There seems little doubt that Hess's flight to Scotland was made with the intention of recovering his position with Hitler. His reasoning – and even at this stage it is doubtful if Hess can be considered completely sane – was that Adolf Hitler had many times expressed regret that the two principal 'Aryan' nations of Europe were at war. With the attack on Russia only a month away, Hess believed a diplomatic coup was possible. For some still unaccountable reason he believed that if he could speak to George VI he might persuade the British king to dismiss Churchill, make peace with Hitler and align with Germany against Russia.

If the exploit was conceived in folly, it was executed with skill and courage. Parachuting over Scotland, at exactly the point planned, on landing Hess gave his name as Captain Horn and asked to be taken to the Duke of Hamilton whom he had met at the Berlin Olympic Games. He was in fact taken straight into custody and remained there until he moved to Nuremberg for his post-war trial.

The flight was thus totally unsuccessful. Optimistic British journalists speculated for a while on the possibility that Hitler had encouraged his deputy, but there is no evidence whatsoever for this. On the British side the propaganda possibilities were mishandled. An astonished British cabinet could hardly believe its luck and failed to exploit the bare fact that the Deputy Leader of the Third Reich was 'suing for peace'.

Rudolf Hess was tried for war crimes, found guilty and sentenced to life imprisonment at Nuremberg. Long after his death on 17 August 1987 the world will continue to see him, not as the uniformed *Stellvertreter* at the podium of a Nuremberg rally, but as the shuffling figure in the prison garden, Spandau's last prisoner.

Heusinger, Adolf (b. 1897).   A general staff officer present at the Rastenburg Bomb attempt in 1944. Arrested and tried by the People's Court, he survived the experience to become a senior officer of the post-war West German army.

Hewel, Otto Walter (1900–1945).   Son of a wealthy conserves manufacturer whose business was ruined in the currency collapse, Hewel was an early Nazi supporter, taking part in the Munich Putsch of 1923. He was jailed at Landsberg and is said to have corrected the final text of *Mein Kampf*.

Ribbentrop's Foreign Ministry representative at the Führer HQ, Hewel is believed by his wife to have perished in the bunker in April 1945.

Heydrich, Reinhard Tristan Eugen (1904–42).   Chief of the Reich Security Head Office and Protector of Bohemia and Moravia. Born in Halle, Saxony, the son of the founder of the Halle Conservatory, Heydrich himself numbered among his many skills and talents the ability to play the violin at concert level. But Reinhard Heydrich inherited more than the musical ability of his father. In a contemporary *Lexicon of Music and Musicians* the elder Heydrich's name is accompanied by the note 'real name Süss'. The clear implication is that Heydrich senior was Jewish, and throughout his life Reinhard Heydrich sought to suppress details of his Jewish ancestry. From his mother's gravestone he is said to have erased the suggestive forename Sarah.

As a young man Heydrich had served as an officer in the German navy but in 1931 he was dismissed by an Honour Court (presided over by Admiral Canaris) for dishonourable conduct towards a young woman.

Joining the Nazi Party in 1931 as an unemployed ex-officer, Heydrich was introduced to Himmler via his wife's contacts. Many elements in Reinhard Heydrich appealed to Heinrich Himmler: his considerable organizational abilities, his Nordic appearance, his total ruthlessness, the intensity of his antisemitism and, finally and ironically, the fact that he was himself either Jewish, partly Jewish or afraid of being considered Jewish. Perhaps Himmler saw in this fact the means by which he would control his talented associate. Certainly from 1931 he was prepared to promote Heydrich until he became the second most powerful man in the RSHA. He was appointed *Obergruppenführer* SS in 1941 after a career in which he had become Chief of the SD, the SS security police, and had organized the *Einsatzgruppen*, the SS murder squads which followed the German armies into Russia.

In July 1941, Göring ordered Heydrich to submit a comprehensive draft for the achievement of the 'final solution to the Jewish problem'; the Wannsee Conference was clearly part-result of this Göring instruction. Yet it is difficult to see Wannsee any longer as the opening move in the extermination of the Jewish people. At least one extermination camp had been constructed before the date of Wannsee (January 1942). Whatever the precise administrative details, it is certain that Heydrich organized the machinery of genocide in which Eichmann played an executive role. Perhaps in reward for his efforts, certainly in recognition of his considerable talents, Heydrich had been appointed, in September 1941, to succeed Neurath as Protector of Bohemia and Moravia. His administration began in brutality but within months adroitly combined carrot and stick. Reports from Prague showed that Czech industrial production was rising as Heydrich issued additional ration cards and clothing on a productivity basis. The message coming from the Reich Protector in the Hradcany Palace was clear: collaborate and prosper, or resist and perish.

The decision in London to attempt the assassination of Heydrich took place in the early months of 1942 and is to this day shrouded in mystery. Reinhard Heydrich was the only Nazi leader the Allies attempted to assassinate. Inevitably historians have asked why Heydrich, when it was clear that his death would result in massive reprisals against the Czech people. A member of the British government at the time claims that this was precisely the object of the assassination. The argument ran that a period of unrestrained brutality against the Czech people would destroy for ever the fragile co-operation which London feared was growing up in Czechoslovakia and which could be extended to other occupied countries.

It is true that the crucial failure of the German administration of the occupied territories was its inability to secure (or even its unwillingness to try to secure) the freely given co-operation of the occupied peoples. Possibly London exaggerated the importance of what Heydrich was doing in Prague, but the intention, it is claimed, was clear: the assassination of Heydrich would bring reprisals which would divide German administration and Czech worker for ever.

In late spring 1942, a section of Czech soldiers flew from London and were parachuted into Czechoslovakia outside Prague. Significantly, the Czech resistance, hearing of the plan to murder Heydrich, urgently requested the Czech government in London to persuade the British government to abandon the assassination attempt.

The British were unmoved. In Prague the assassination squad struck on 27 May 1942: his open car in which he rode unprotected and unescorted was machine-gunned on the Kirchmayer Boulevard. Heydrich, injured, pulled his pistol and was about to pursue the Czech soldiers when another member of the group hurled a grenade towards him. Pieces of the metal springs and the horsehair stuffing of the car's upholstery penetrated the Reich Protector's body and he died on 4 June in a Prague hospital.

The reprisals were as were feared, or possibly hoped for. After the Czech assassins and their helpers had been traced to the crypt of a Prague church and had died in a heroic battle against SS units, the terror began. The village of Lidice, tenuously connected with the operation, was razed to the ground and its inhabitants murdered. Thousands of Czechs were deported to the Austrian concentration camp of Mauthausen. The hostility of the people of Czechoslovakia towards the occupiers was secure for ever.

The abilities and personality of Reinhard Heydrich have been a matter of considerable comment; it is doubtful that he was even a Nazi in the sense that he was devoted to the ideology of National Socialism. His work for the Nazi state was carried out with an efficiency and lack of pity which often assured success. But even in his destruction of European Jewry he showed no commitment to a grotesque anti-semitism. There is, however, one exception to his disinterested ruthlessness: he hated the Christian churches with a fervour beyond anything else visible in his life, his pathological detestation evident in his administrative memoranda as much as in his conversation. Like Hitler himself he greatly looked forward to the day (which they both recognized would have to be after the war was won) when the Gestapo could deal with 'the black crows', the priests and pastors of the Christian churches.

Many believe that he might have succeeded or even supplanted Hitler as Führer. Certainly had he done so the world would have faced a formidably calculating opponent.

Hierl, Konstantin.   A major in the army's Political Department in Munich who ordered the ex-soldier 'political education officer' Adolf Hitler to attend a meeting of the new German Workers' Party (DAP) of Drexler and Harrer. Hierl later became a Nazi himself and was for a time a senior Party member, taking charge in 1928 of the branch which was planning for the new Nazi state.

Hilferding, Rudolf (1877–1941).   SPD Minister of Finance in 1923 and from 1928–9. As a Marxist economist and a Jew he was marked down for arrest by the Nazis, but in March 1933 he fled to Denmark, and from there to Switzerland and France in 1938.

In 1934 he wrote the 'Prague Programme' as a policy for the SPD in exile. In February 1941 he was arrested in southern, unoccupied France and handed over to the Germans. He was killed a few days later in prison in Paris.

Hilfswilliger ('Hiwi').   'Auxiliaries' recruited from Russian, often Ukrainian, prisoners of war, who were issued with a nondescript uniform and given menial duties. It has been pointed out that these prisoners did not necessarily have any commitment to the German cause; escape from the inhuman conditions in which they were held was sufficient motivation to 'volunteer'.

Himmler, Heinrich (1900–1945). The Reich Leader of the SS from 1929. He was born in Landshut, Bavaria, and studied at the Technischehochschule in Munich, becoming a laboratory technician. As a member of one of the nationalist movements, the *Reichskriegsflagge* organized by Röhm, he was one of those called out for the 1923 Beer Hall Putsch, being the flag-bearer of the group that occupied the War Ministry building. After the débâcle he moved back home to Landshut where he sold advertising space in the Party paper, the *Völkischer Beobachter*. During 1925 he acted as general secretary to Strasser. In 1926 he received the minor appointment of Deputy Leader of the small bodyguard group called *Schutzstaffel*, the SS, but his Party career still allowed him time to run a smallholding chicken farm where he carried out breeding experiments, developing his politico-eugenic theories. He had married Magda Boden, but his devotion to Party work meant that they lived most of their time apart. In January 1929 he took over the SS, now numbering 280, as *Reichsführer* SS. It was still a branch of the SA, but Himmler knowingly concentrated on its growth in size and breadth of function. First he put forward new recruitment plans to sieve through the large number of ex-*Freikorps* and unemployed-bourgeois volunteers, bringing in biological criteria and the concept of racial purity. Thus he gradually asserted the separation of the SS from the SA. One effect of this was that the army, which saw the SA under Röhm as a rival, tended to side with the SS as a force.

When Hitler became Chancellor in January 1933, Himmler added the post of *Polizeipräsident* (police chief) of Munich to his duties. This seemed only a modest post to some, but he was, with his SS assistants Heydrich, Daluege and Schellenberg, gradually taking control of the whole German police system in all states except Prussia, where Göring had taken the Ministry of the Interior. He finally achieved power over all police in 1936.

For the next ten years Himmler's life was devoted to expanding the role of the SS. After Heydrich's death in 1942, Kaltenbrunner took on the administrative weight of the SS and Himmler, being often present at Hitler's military planning sessions, wormed himself further into the Führer's confidence than Göring or Göbbels. From 1941 Bormann had taken Hess's place in running Hitler's secretariat and he now saw Himmler as his rival for power. By the beginning of 1942 Himmler's SS empire was reaching its zenith. He had absorbed Göring's Prussian secret police, the Gestapo, and made it a nationwide force, parallel to his Party intelligence and security organization, the SD; within weeks of their establishment, the new concentration camps had been put under his men and a branch of the SS, the *Totenkopfverbände* (the Death's Head units), was formed to run them; following the invading German armies into Russia, Himmler's

Einsatzgruppen task forces were murdering Jews, gypsies, communists and partisans by the thousand; his armed SS squads had been turned into the Waffen SS and fought now as great armies; his SS empire had its economic section, owning industries and, by making themselves tax-exempt, becoming hugely profitable. At the same time Himmler continued to concern himself with the perfecting of a future German élite through his SS. Not only would they be of guaranteed Aryan stock, but they would be encouraged to breed the new élite, through his *Lebensborn* (Source of life) network of maternity homes. Most important of all to Himmler, however, would be the purity of their thought. Apart from the SS-financed research organization, the *Ahnenerbe*, he ordered the rebuilding of the old castle of Wewelsburg as a shrine to a Germanic civilization in which the holy order of the SS would be founded. This was done at immense expense and, from 1934 on, senior members of the SS met there several times a year in conference; there his assistant Karl Wolff would usher each SS leader into a monastic cell, where he would be surrounded by treasures from old Germany and was supposed to steep himself in Germanic mysticism. The leading twelve higher SS officers were assigned places, beneath their fake-medieval coats-of-arms, around a circular Arthurian table.

There can be no doubt of Himmler's responsibility for the carrying out of the Final Solution. He is almost alone among the leading Nazis to have put the concept of the extermination of the Jewish people into words. In several recorded speeches he lectured concentration camp officers on their responsibility for destroying a whole people. Yet at the same time he authorized an SS unit (►Morgen, Konrad) to investigate incidents of 'brutality' in Sobibor, Majdanek and Auschwitz.

After the 1944 Bomb Plot he was able to remove rivals, such as Canaris, on the slightest ground of suspicion. Himmler's final step to power followed the Bomb Plot when Hitler, no longer trusting his generals, gave Himmler the military appointment of Commander-in-Chief of the Army Reserve (*Ersatzarmee*). In 1944 Himmler seemed to have reached the pinnacle of Nazi power: he was given command first of Army Group Upper Rhine to face the American army, then transferred east to command Army Group Vistula in January 1945. With his lack of military experience he found himself helpless in face of the momentum of the Russian advance.

By now the Allied armies were squeezing Germany on both fronts. In Berlin, Bormann's position close to Hitler was unchanged, and Bormann argued that, as the war moved on to German soil, the Party itself (and not just the *Wehrmacht*) was responsible for military leadership. As the army became discredited in defeat, the Party *Gauleiters* took charge. It was Bormann therefore (rather than Himmler) who commanded the last-ditch *Volkssturm*. By now even Himmler saw that the end was coming. Since October 1944 Schellenberg had been urging him to make contact with neutral nations to obtain peace terms for Germany. But it was not until February 1945, when the Swedish

Red Cross representative Count Bernadotte visited Germany, that Himmler showed interest in the dealings. In April, Himmler met Bernadotte, but for a moment he hesitated; he begged Hitler to leave Berlin to fight in southern Germany. Hitler, having heard of Himmler's peace moves, dismissed him from all posts.

The final Dönitz government saw him as a liability. Hoping to escape arrest, Himmler took the name and documents of a dead village policeman, Heinrich Hitzinger, but at a routine check by British military police his nerve crumbled and he admitted to being Himmler. He was arrested, but before he could be interrogated he was found to have taken poison. ►SS

Hindenburg, Paul von Beneckendorff und von (1847–1934). President of Germany from 1925 to 1934. A veteran of the Prussian wars against Austria (1866) and France (1870–71), Hindenburg had retired in 1911 but was recalled at the outbreak of WWI in 1914 to become the commander of the German armies on the Eastern Front where he was credited with winning a spectacular victory over the Russians. He became Chief of Staff of all German armies in WWI from 1916 and retired in 1918.

He was recalled to public life in 1925. As President of the Republic he upheld the Weimar constitution, appointing Brüning (of the Catholic Central Party) Chancellor. Always inclined to the conservatives, he was persuaded to dismiss Brüning in 1932 and appoint the conservative von Papen. Even so, Brüning urged him to stand again in the presidential elections, due that year, as a counterbalance to the extremism of Nazis or communists. In March 1932 an election failed to give him the required absolute majority: Hindenburg winning 18.7 million votes (49.7 per cent); Hitler, 11.3 million; Thälmann, the communist, 5 million; and Düsterberg of the nationalists 2.6 million. By the rules of the election the last candidate was eliminated and a second round was held in April. This time Hindenburg won 19.4 million votes (53 per cent), Hitler 13.4 million and Thälmann 3.7 million. Hindenburg was re-elected, but the Nazi vote had increased significantly. He was now persuaded to appoint Hitler Chancellor in January 1933, although he had previously told the army commander Hammerstein that he would never bring the Austrian corporal to power.

Hitler, Adolf (1889–1945). Führer of the Third Reich.

Ancestry. Family origins were in the Austrian Waldviertel region near the Bohemian border, an area of poor, backward peasantry, ignorance and inbreeding. No information is available earlier than 1837 when Maria Anna Schicklgruber gave birth in House 13, Strones, to an illegitimate child, Alois Schicklgruber, later to become Hitler's father. The Schicklgruber birth certificate left a blank space for the father's name. Hitler's grandfather's identity was thus unknown – or unrecorded. In 1842 Maria Anna Schicklgruber married

Johann Georg Hiedler. Her son, however, continued to be known as Alois Schicklgruber.

The Czech name Hidlar or Hidlarceck appears in the Waldviertel area from the 1430s; only very much later is it recorded in various Germanic forms, among them Hiedler. The origins of Adolf Hitler's surname became even more confused when, in 1877, the birth certificate of Hitler's father, Alois Schicklgruber (now aged 40), was taken to the local priest who agreed, for an unknown reason, to an illegal entry in the blank space: Johann Georg Hiedler. However, the priest misspelt the name, thus Hitler. From this date Alois Schicklgruber, customs official, is known as Alois Hitler. His son, born 20 April 1889 by his third wife, Klara Pölzl, is therefore known to the world as Adolf Hitler by dint of rustic intrigue.

The question arises: who was in fact Adolf Hitler's paternal grandfather? Hitler himself ordered a covert investigation (1942) by lawyer Hans Frank, the reaction to a blackmailing letter Hitler had received hinting at dark family secrets. Frank later testified at Nuremberg that Hitler's grandfather was an Austrian Jew named Frankenberger for whom Maria Anna Schicklgruber had worked as housemaid. (There is some evidence of continuing payments made to Maria Anna from the Frankenberger family for some years after she left their employ.) A further Gestapo investigation is believed to have failed to produce corroboration. The truth is probably that Hitler did not know for certain the identity of his own grandfather. Throughout his life, however, he took great care to disguise his origins. The psychological importance of Hitler's background lies in his own fear of being partly Jewish. It is an irony of history that in terms of SS entry (where positive proof of non-Jewish background to 1715 was required) Adolf Hitler would have been rejected for membership.

Childhood (1889–1907). It has been said that Hitler's childhood was emotionally suspended between an indulgent mother and a harsh, over-strict father. Hitler talked, probably truthfully, of numerous beatings with his father's belt. Certainly his mother was indulgent and ambitious for her son. After public school he was sent at the age of eight to the monastery school at Lembach; it was Klara Hitler's wish that her son become a monk. In practice the spoilt, resentful child was soon expelled and the family moved to Leonding. Hitler attended the Gymnasium at nearby Steyr and left at 16 without having graduated. He was clearly an indifferent pupil, probably too arrogant to learn the subjects he was offered. The one teacher he admired was a pan-German who rejected the Austrian Empire under which they lived; the one friend he appears to have made was August Kubizek who would share part of the next stage of his life.

Youth (1907–14). In September 1907, Hitler, aged 18, was stunned when he failed to gain entrance to the Vienna Fine Arts Academy, staying in Vienna with his godparents, Johann and Joanna Prinz. His mother died in December in Linz, having been in the care of the Jewish Doctor Bloch. His guardian,

Mayrhofer, took charge of the estate and gave Hitler a small allowance.

In February 1908 Hitler moved from Linz to Vienna, staying with Frau Zakrey at Stumpergasse 29, where he was joined by his friend, now a music student, August ('Gustl') Kubizek. They spent much time together walking about the town, visiting the opera and theatres, Hitler planning Wagnerian operas or the rebuilding of Vienna. He was not poor; his inheritance and his student's pension (his father having been a state official) provided for him adequately. There is evidence of one romantic attachment, to a girl named Stephanie Jansten, but it seems that he worshipped her from afar – she was quite unaware of him.

In September he again tried and failed to enter the Academy. In November he moved into an apartment at Felberstrasse 22. He was now reading voraciously, but probably easily digested pamphlets rather than works of history and economics. He is reported to have enjoyed particularly the periodicals of Lanz von Lieberfels (whom he sought out) praising racial purity and at the same time instilling the fear of 'race impurity'. He probably at this time also read accounts of the work of the anti-semitic Houston Stewart Chamberlain.

In August 1909 he moved to a cheaper room at Sechshäuserstrasse 58, leaving his friend Kubizek. The next few months of his life are mysterious: there is no evidence that his allowance had ceased, yet in September he moved on again, living rough with tramps and sleeping out or in shelters, until December when he was accepted into a poorhouse. Here he met another drifter called Hanisch who showed him how to survive poverty, making them both a living by selling postcards of Vienna scenes that Hitler painted. In February 1910 he moved to the Home for Working Men at Meldemannstrasse 25. At this time yet again he tried and failed to qualify for the Academy. Later this year his godmother Joanna gave him a substantial sum of money before she died, early in 1911. This led to a dispute between him and his half-sister Angela, resulting in Hitler giving her some of the money and part of his income. He continued to live in the Home for the next few years, living mostly off his painting, yet (again mysteriously) holding his godmother's money in reserve.

In May 1913 Hitler was well past 21 and overdue for Austrian military service. He moved from Vienna to Munich in Germany, where he found a room in the house of a tailor, Popp, at Schleissheimerstrasse 34, on the edge of the students' and artists' district of Schwabing. He continued the same way of life as in Vienna, making a lonely living from his paintings of scenes in the city. In January 1914, however, he was summoned to report for military service in Austria, and the Munich police obliged him to return. At Salzburg he was found to be medically unfit and was allowed back to Munich. In August he joined the crowds demanding action against Russia and calling for a pan-German movement against Russia and Serbia. The Austrian Empire had already declared war against Serbia since the heir to its throne had been assassinated at Sarajevo. A photograph of Hitler in August 1914 shows him celebrating Germany's involvement in the war. By the summer's end he was an infantry volunteer in the 16th Bavarian Regiment, known as the List Regiment after its founding colonel.

War Service (1914–19). By October, Hitler's regiment was at the front before the town of Ypres. By his own choice he served in the dangerous role of regimental message-runner, for the rest of the war refusing promotion beyond the rank of corporal. In the regiment were Lieutenant Wiedemann and Sergeant Amman, both of whom later became Nazi Party members. During the first years of the war the regiment stayed in the front line, taking part in the Battles of the Somme from the summer of 1916. In October, Hitler was injured in the thigh and sent to a military hospital in Berlin. On recovering, he was sent to the reserve battalion in Munich, returning to his regiment in March 1917 in time to take part in the Battle of Arras. He took leave in December, visiting Berlin and Dresden.

The List Regiment participated in Ludendorff's April 1918 offensive, when Hitler was awarded the Iron Cross, First Class, for his bravery. The award to a soldier of his rank was unusual and marked him out as a distinguished front-line soldier. He took his last leave in September, visiting Berlin and Austria before going back to the fighting near Ypres. He was blinded by gas in October and sent to a hospital in Pasewalk in eastern Germany, until discharged fit and posted back to the Munich barracks in November 1918.

The war had ended by the time he reached Munich, and Germany was in chaos and revolt. The new Republic's army decided to defend itself against subversion, and Hitler witnessed first the rule in Munich of a Bavarian socialist government and its subsequent crushing by central government troops with its Freikorps allies. (It is not known which side Hitler took in these events.) In February 1919, still a corporal awaiting his discharge from service, he was selected for training as an 'education officer'. He was given some political instruction to add to his already well-formed nationalistic and anti-semitic prejudices. In September his army intelligence employers sent him to investigate a small new group, the DAP (German Workers' Party). It was this roomful of right-wing radicals whom Hitler transformed into the election-winning Nazi Party within an astonishing thirteen years.

Politics and Power (1919–39). By 1921 Adolf Hitler had advanced to the leadership of the Party, had changed its name to the National Socialist German Workers' Party (NSDAP) and was learning to impose his extraordinary personality and unique brand of political showmanship on people other than the discontented working class in Munich. In particular this is the period when he learned to speak to large audiences, to stir their feelings of nationalism, of resentment and anti-semitism. In a typical speech he would throw at his listeners the intellectual detritus of the nineteenth century – blood, race, Jews, capitalism, communism would be his subjects, but all bound together by a true ferocity of commitment.

It was not only his former army employer, Captain Röhm, who recognized Adolf Hitler's astonishing gifts as a speaker.

Yet his talents were not confined to public speaking. Hitler saw art – or rather graphic design – with an eye untrammelled by intellectual complexity. His sense of design – first in the selection of the swastika, then in the colours red, black and white – produced an overwhelmingly powerful Party symbol. In later years uniforms, badges, rallies, architecture and even the design of Party documents would all become part of the extraordinary imagery of the Nazi Party and the Third Reich.

In 1923 the Beer Hall Putsch proved Adolf Hitler's first setback. In later years, by a brilliant process of instant mythologizing he would transform defeat into victory, using a near-farcical attempt to seize power in Munich to create instant history for the Party. But in 1923 it was defeat and Landsberg prison which Hitler faced. His peculiar resilience is shown in this low point in his political fortunes. In the outside world his party was banned and its structure disintegrating. Inside Landsberg, Hitler behaved like an honoured guest, receiving political visitors and writing *Mein Kampf*. In December 1924 he emerged from prison to rebuild his party.

But even as Hitler worked with an energy which he would never again produce to reconstruct the Nazi Party, a critically important schism was revealing itself. So much of the earlier appeal of the Party involved the fusion of two elements, nationalism and socialism. The political sleight-of-hand, successfully achieved by Hitler when the Party was simply Bavarian-based, was to maintain that fusion. Now that the Party was growing, however, a different view was emerging in northern Germany, a view which stressed the socialist element in Party ideology much more strongly than Hitler, who had little interest in it, was prepared to accept.

The first crisis with the Party's left wing came at the Bamberg Conference of 1926 when Hitler successfully forced down Gregor Strasser. It was however only the first battle in a vital struggle which would not end until the Röhm Purge in 1934 when the Party's left wing was decisively beaten and its leadership murdered.

Hitler's own view was blatantly opportunistic. What moved him was nationalism, race, anti-semitism and the achievement of power. He had added or accepted socialist elements into the Party programme and was capable of addressing the German *Mittelstand*, the lower-middle class, directly and with an apparent depth of feeling. But he had already decided that the Party needed industry and commerce for much more than the funds they were able to provide. He had chosen the electoral road to power. While his followers fought in the streets, Adolf Hitler was meeting soldiers and businessmen, the conservative heart of Germany, talking, placating, reassuring. And with each election the Nazi Party, now nationally based, was increasing its representation in the Reichstag.

In this frenetic ascent to the status of a national figure, Adolf Hitler had little time or inclination for a private life. It is probable that in only one area, the company of women, did his interests not overlap or coincide with his political ambitions. His intensely secretive nature in financial and sexual matters makes it difficult to discover his preferences. Certainly in his sexual leanings there are persistent suggestions of a darker side to his nature. He was prepared to admit that he enjoyed the leg-shows of the Berlin musical comedy in the 1930s until he himself decided his attendance was not suitable. His earliest mentioned love was in his Vienna days when he adored, but did not approach, the tall blonde Stephanie Jansten. In the early days of the Nazi Party, 1920–23, he was believed to have had an affair with Jenny Haug, the sister of his driver. In 1924 or 1925 he was reported to be mooning over a sixteen-year-old in Berchtesgaden called Mitzi Reiter. But Adolf Hitler's proclivities, it is suggested, went far beyond leg-shows and an attraction towards sixteen-year-olds. Undoubtedly he was in love with his niece Geli Raubal, with whom he seems to have had some sort of physical intimacy; the circumstances surrounding her suicide are obscure, but there were accusations of his having made unusual demands on her. Two women, Renate Müller, an actress, and Henny Hoffmann, the daughter of his photographer Heinrich Hoffmann and later the wife of von Schirach, are claimed to have beaten or abused him for his sexual satisfaction. Rumour linked him to other women admirers: Leni Riefenstahl the film-maker, the actresses Mary Rahl and Anny Ondra (who married the boxer Max Schmeling), and Unity Mitford, the English aristocrat, who worshipped him. There was even talk that he might marry Winifred Wagner, the daughter-in-law of Hitler's spiritual mentor, Richard Wagner, when she was widowed in 1930. Little is known about his relationship with Eva Braun, whom he married as his Empire collapsed around him.

From the elections of 1933 and the Nazi assumption of power, the days of Adolf Hitler's peacetime leadership of Germany were days of supreme indulgence. The very structure of the state led inexorably to his near deification: the organization of Party rallies, the speeches of Gauleiters up and down the country, the pride and gratitude of Germans at the 1936 Olympic Games, the subservience of the smaller European heads of state, the anxiety of generals to please the former corporal, of princes to be seen in the company of the rough-accented, middle-class boy from Austria.

It was an astonishing personal triumph which was to have a deep impact on his foreign policy. By 1936 it is certain that Adolf Hitler believed in the *actual* invincibility of his will. He spoke of it more often and discussed it as an abstraction which could only be admired. He invoked it before Mussolini, Daladier and Neville Chamberlain. He used it as a bludgeon on Kurt Schuschnigg, to force his acceptance of the *Anschluss* with Austria.

By 1939 Adolf Hitler was convinced that no individual could stand in the path of his will. He is reported to have been utterly astonished at Chamberlain's decision to go to war over Poland.

Warlord and supreme commander (1939−45). Long before the tide of war turned against him, Adolf Hitler had been changed by the conflict. It is possible to see, beyond the great victories in France in 1940, the gradual ebbing of his confidence, the increasingly desperate reliance on his will alone.

Defeat in the Battle of Britain played no very visible part in the erosion of Adolf Hitler's confidence. But once he had turned eastwards, it was the winter of 1941 that dealt the first great hammer-blows. The generals were almost unanimous in favour of regrouping on a winter line. As winter and fresh Russian troops intervened before Moscow, Hitler remarked: 'The recognition that neither force is capable of annihilating the other will lead to a compromise peace.' He meant a peace which would be decisively in his favour, but a compromise nevertheless.

Then the winter disasters of 1941 struck: at the beginning of December, General Zhukov's counter-offensive before Moscow struck at an exhausted German army ill-equipped for a winter campaign. In this grim situation Hitler ordered no retreat beyond local withdrawals; it was perhaps more an act of stubbornness than of will. But it was, despite the extreme suffering it imposed on his soldiers, undoubtedly the right military decision. It is now generally agreed that if Hitler had allowed the army before Moscow to retreat, a tactical withdrawal might well have turned into a full-scale rout.

The near disaster of the winter of 1941 (and the remarkable recovery of the initiative in the summer of 1942) provided Hitler's flagging confidence with new belief in the power of his will. From now on he was to rely utterly on what he saw as an exercise of the will and what his generals increasingly saw as a denial of military reality. In the Stalingrad winter of 1942/43 he had nothing more to offer his soldiers than a blank refusal of permission to withdraw. It had worked once, even the doubters now agreed, but it was no substitute for generalship.

By the spring of 1944 the certainty of an Allied landing in the West was preoccupying the Führer; when and where were subjects for constant discussion. In the event, Hitler came closer to choosing the Normandy location of the landings than any of his generals. But now in six months the decline was rapid. Generalship which was based on the philosophy of no retreat handicapped the commanders on the spot. A Christmas offensive in 1944 was shrouded in misty unreality as to its aims and possibilities. But a new theatrical element had now been revealed in the Hitler personality − or, more likely, an old element had resurfaced. As the ring closed round Berlin and disaster followed, Hitler had no taste for surrender. Rather he was preparing what has been called a strategy of grandiose doom. A scorched-earth policy would destroy the German infrastructure. Deliberately he invited disease and starvation to follow him. As the Red Army began to shell Berlin and the whole Third Reich was overcast by the red glow of burning buildings, Adolf Hitler wrote his Testament: he personally was responsible for nothing, neither military defeat nor the deaths of millions of his fellow countrymen and untold millions of others; he had been betrayed; the German people had proved unequal to his leadership and they would deserve the future he foresaw for them.

Hitler Youth (Hitler Jugend). ➤Youth Organizations

Hoffmann, Heinrich (1885–1957). Photographer to Hitler and the Nazis from 1921. He had been a photographer with the Bavarian army and his photography of the 1923 Beer Hall Putsch provides the only visual record. He was Hitler's introduction to the fringes of Munich's intellectual society. His daughter married the Hitler Youth leader von Schirach after (it is rumoured) an affair with Hitler.

Eva Braun was also introduced to Hitler by Hoffmann while she was employed as a photographic assistant in his Munich shop. His business became highly profitable as the Nazis came to power and he published volumes of his pictures as 'court photographer' to Hitler. After the war he was tried in 1947 for profiteering and heavily fined. He continued to make money, however, from his memories of Hitler until he died.

Hoheitsabzeichen. The eagle badge worn by all ranks of the armed forces, in cloth for soldiers, metal for more senior ranks and gold for general officers. In printed form, the national eagle was widely used on official letterheads and became familiar and sinister throughout the occupied countries on wall posters and proclamations.

Holidays in Nazi Germany.

30 January	Day of Power (on which Hitler became Chancellor, 1933)
24 February	Party Foundation Day (1920)
16 March	National Mourning Day (an older celebration given a new date; used as 'Heroes' Remembrance Day')
20 April	Hitler's birthday
1 May	National Labour Day, taken over from the old May Day
2nd Sunday in May	Mothering Sunday, becoming the day when medals were given to prolific mothers
Summer solstice	A pagan revival with bonfires in the evening and memorials to party martyrs
9 November	Anniversary of the 1923 Putsch (and the occasion for Crystal Night)
Winter solstice	Designed to detract from Christmas and the traditional 'Sylvester Eve'

The Christian festivals of Easter and Christmas continued, but were not 'Party' days. The annual Nuremberg rally became another Third Reich festival.

Hollywood Exiles. The group of talented German and Austrian film makers (directors, producers, cameramen, composers of film music and actors) who emigrated to Hollywood when the Nazis came to power.

In June 1933 publication of the *Arierparagraph* banned all Jews from the film industry, stressing that 'it is race not religion that is decisive'. From that moment any member of the *Filmwelt* (the film community) who was of Jewish origin or was unable to stomach tyranny left Germany. The vast majority went to Hollywood, often via Paris; some of them, Fritz Lang in particular, despite personal invitations from Hitler to continue making pictures for the Third Reich.

Menschen am Sonntag (*People on Sunday*), a documentary made in 1929 by Robert Siodmak (later famous for his Hollywood thrillers *Spiral Staircase* and *The Killers*), had a script by Billy Wilder and photography by Fred Zinnemann, both of whom were to win Oscars in their later, American careers. Other well-known directors who preferred to work in America were Henry Koster, Douglas Sirk, Max Ophüls, Otto Preminger and William Dieterle. Among the performers were Conrad Veidt, Peter Lorre, Oskar Homolka, Elisabeth Bergner and Marlene Dietrich, while Kurt Weill and Franz Waxman were among the best-known composers.

There is no question that the presence of these talented European directors made a considerable contribution to American cinema in the 1930s and '40s, in particular to that kind of film known to critics as 'film noir', in which American down-to-earth realism was tempered by a more subtle European cynicism. ➤Cinema

Holocaust.   Term applied by many historians to the wholesale persecution and destruction of the Jews of Europe during the period of the dominance of the Third Reich. ➤Final Solution; Pale of Settlement; Concentration Camps

Homosexuality in the Third Reich.   Homosexuality had already been outlawed in Germany under section 175 of the Reich Penal Code of 1871, but in the liberal climate of Weimar Germany, and especially of Berlin with its café life, bars and cabaret clubs, there had been proposals for repeal.

Persecution of homosexuals varied in intensity throughout the period of the Third Reich. While many members of the performing arts enjoyed an unofficial immunity, castration was included in the range of punishments applied to others.

After the Reichstag Fire of 27 February 1933, decrees were issued against public indecency and homosexual bars were closed. Magazines like *Die Insel* or *Der Kreis* were banned and on 6 May 1933 the liberal Magnus Hershfeld Science Institute was closed down. But homosexuality was undoubtedly present in Nazi organizations, and especially the SA, where some of its leaders, like Edmund Heines, Karl Ernst, and Ernst Röhm himself were homosexual. Allegations of homosexuality were used to justify the Night of the Long Knives and in the following weeks a purge of homosexuals was conducted by Lutze, the new SA Chief of Staff.

In 1935, section 175 of the Reich Penal Code was revised. The concept of the 'unnatural sex act' was replaced with a broader one of 'sex offence' which included 'self gratification' where one male had contact with the body of the other with sexual intent.

Declared 'national pests' (*Volksschadlinge*), homosexuals were subject, by 1936, to nation-wide registration and reported acts were to be presented to the Reich Office for the Combating of Homosexuality and Abortion. Penalties for those who were members of the SS and Hitler Youth were severe.

On 29 October 1937, Himmler issued a decree imposing a night curfew and ordering those homosexuals found guilty of repeated offences to be placed under police supervision. By 1940, the Reich Office had information on 41,000 suspected homosexuals.

In August 1941, Hitler denounced homosexuals and called for harsher punishment. From now on those convicted in the SS and Hitler Youth could face the death penalty. Yet there appeared to be no uniform code of conduct for the regular forces. The Luftwaffe issued a guide to combat homosexuality, but only the Army took action. Up to 1944, over 7,000 soldiers had been convicted and sentenced to detention in a concentration camp.

Homosexuals in concentration camps faced an increasingly harsh regime. In 1938 homosexual prisoners in Buchenwald lost their political status, and had to carry out hard labour in the quarries. They were required to wear a reverse triangle in pink on their prison uniforms. Frequently subject to brutal treatment at the hands of Kapos (trustees), for many the only way to alleviate their conditions was to become a concubine (*Piepel*). Many homosexuals were subject to medical experiments, such as those of Dr Jensen, who specialized in hormone transplantation.

Although lesbians were imprisoned in camps such as Ravensbrück, persecution was generally on a much smaller scale. They were not perceived as dangerous, but after 1933 many women were forced from the professional positions they had acquired during the Weimar Republic years and the Women's Movement was abolished. The Nazi State saw the woman's role as a domestic one, limited to homemaking and the bearing of children.

As the area of the Third Reich increased, Reich Penal Laws on Homosexuality were extended to cover the new territories. Austria and Bohemia-Moravia (where the Bund Youth movement, very active in the Sudetenland, was heavily persecuted) had the homosexuality legislation after 1939. In contrast, during the early years of the occupation of Poland, homosexual activities were generally overlooked. In the Latin countries of Europe, there was no legislation in place which outlawed homosexuality, and there was no systematic persecution. In Holland there were convictions during the occupation but on the whole the Dutch courts were reluctant to prosecute under Article 248b of their own code.

No reliable figures are available for the number of homosexuals killed under the Nazis.

'Horst Wessel Song'. ➤Wessel, Horst

Höss, Rudolf (1900–1947). Commandant of the Auschwitz extermination camp. Rudolf Höss entered the army at the age of 17 in WWI and won an Iron Cross. In 1919 he was in the Rossbach *Freikorps* with Martin Bormann; they were jointly indicted for the murder of a man whom they accused of betraying Germany in the French-occupied Ruhr. Höss was jailed in 1924 and released in 1928. With Bormann as a sponsor, he was invited to join the SS in 1934 and worked in Dachau concentration camp, transferring to Sachsenhausen in 1938. From 1940 to 1943 he was commandant of Auschwitz and was noted for his brutal efficiency: he was the first to use Zyklon-B gas for extermination. So successful was Höss that he was posted to the SS headquarters department controlling concentration camps, WVHA, as Deputy Inspector General.

In 1945 he avoided arrest and worked on a farm until detected. He was called as a witness for the defence of Kaltenbrunner at Nuremberg, trying to show that extermination was only carrying out orders. He gave evidence of the care with which over two million people had been killed under his command at Auschwitz, the system for disposing of bodies, for collecting gold teeth and rings for the SS treasury and women's hair for upholstery. Höss was hanged by the Poles in Auschwitz camp in 1947. He had resented any suggestions that he was a sadist. 'I am completely normal,' he wrote in his autobiography, 'I led a completely normal life.'

Hossbach, Friedrich (1894–1980). Hitler's army adjutant from 1934 to 1938, he made the notes of the 1937 meeting between Hitler and his army, navy and Luftwaffe commanders, known as the 'Hossbach Memorandum'.

Hossbach returned to military duties at the time of the Blomberg and Fritsch crisis in 1938. Promoted general in 1942, he was given command of 16 Panzer Corps in the following year. By January 1945 he had risen to be commander of the Fourth Army but suffered the fate of so many of Hitler's generals when he was dismissed for conducting a retreat contrary to Hitler's explicit orders.

Hossbach Memorandum. In November 1937 Blomberg and Raeder, the Minister of Defence and the commander of the navy, asked Hitler for a meeting on rearmament, to share materials and arms between the three services. Hitler brought them together with Göring, as commander of the Luftwaffe, Fritsch for the army and von Neurath the Foreign Minister. Colonel Hossbach, Hitler's military adjutant, took the notes, hence the name given to the conference.

Hitler did not speak of the allocation of resources, but for two and a half hours gave his vision of future wars, calling it his 'last will and testament'. He spoke of the need for Germany to be self-sufficient, even given the shortage of raw materials. It might be possible to achieve autarky in coal and synthetic textiles, he said, but not in all metal ores and certainly not in food. Europe had rising standards of living and it was not possible to raise food production to meet the level of its demand.

He defined Germany's main problem as *Lebensraum* (living space). Greater living space must be found for Germany, to relieve problems of 'tension' or 'sterility', by taking territory in Europe. First Czechoslovakia then Austria would be conquered and space made by clearing out non-Germans from the land: 'The German problem can only be solved by force.'

The two countries which would see Germany as a threat were France and Britain (not, in spite of his professed anti-Bolshevism, Russia), but they had weaknesses: they could become embroiled in the Spanish Civil War; they both had internal and imperial difficulties to preoccupy them. In the case of Britain, he cited the constitutional struggle in India, the growth of Japanese power in the east and of Italian power in the Mediterranean and East Africa. He saw France's internal political difficulties as her major weakness.

Hitler suggested three possible situations:

The first was that by 1943 or 1945 at the very latest Germany must be fully rearmed for after that other countries' rearmament programmes would have built up strength and Germany's weapons would become obsolete. They could not wait longer to solve the *Lebensraum* problem.

The second arose if France's internal difficulties involved its army, then the time for action against Czechoslovakia would come.

Thirdly if France were at war with another country, then both Czechoslovakia and Austria could be taken.

Hitler said that he believed that Britain and probably France had already assumed that Germany would clear up the Czech question and that Britain's imperial difficulties would make her unwilling to become entangled in a long European war. She would not therefore be planning for a war against Germany. This attitude would also influence France, who would not contemplate an attack on Germany which would be halted by German West-Front fortifications, nor through Belgium and Holland, without British support. Germany would of course keep strong forces in the west during the invasions of Austria and Czechoslovakia.

The occupation of Czechoslovakia and Austria would gain Germany food-stuffs for five or six million people if the compulsory emigration of three million from these lands was practical. Further, Germany would be provided with men for an extra twelve divisions. Italy would not object to the elimination of Czechoslovakia, but Hitler could not be sure of her attitude on Austria. Swift action would be decisive, and this would counter intervention by Russia (who would probably be more concerned with Japan). If the second opportunity arose, it must be taken at once, but Hitler saw the third as more likely, particularly with the present tension in Spain and the Mediterranean, and he thought this might be as early as 1938.

Hitler thought that the Spanish Civil War might last another three years and it was in Germany's interest to prolong it. He foresaw war between Italy and a Franco-British alliance as possible; and this would give an opportunity for the German occupation of Austria and Czechoslovakia. Again Hitler stressed the need for speed, using the word *Blitz* (lightning).

Blomberg, Fritsch and von Neurath were stunned and openly criticized Hitler, warning him of the dangers of war with France and England. By February of the following year Hitler had arranged the resignations of Blomberg and Fritsch on trumped-up accusations of immorality and had von Neurath replaced by Ribbentrop.

On at least two further occasions Hitler revealed plans for war. On 23 May 1939, in the new Reich Chancellery in Berlin he assured senior officers that: 'Further successes can no longer be won without bloodshed', and declared that 'no stock can be taken of declarations of neutrality.'

On 22 August 1939 at Berchtesgaden he declared his preference for war now. 'So strike! Object? Destruction of Poland. Execution: harsh and ruthless. Close your hearts to pity.'

By now the fate of Fritsch and von Blomberg and the appeasement policies of France and Britain had left their mark. On these last two occasions there is no evidence of public objection to the contents or tone of the speeches by any of the senior officers present.

Hugenberg, Alfred (1865–1951). Media magnate and right-wing politician. A Reichstag deputy for the nationalist DNVP from 1920 and its Chairman from 1928 until it was disbanded in 1933. Hugenberg controlled UFA, Germany's largest film company, and in addition a number of provincial newspapers. He had been a director of Krupp's and his range of holdings in other concerns ensured that his wealth survived the disastrous inflation of 1923. His links with heavy industry provided him with substantial funds for his political campaigns. He campaigned against the 1929 Young Plan to ease the weight of reparations and put the resources of his papers at Hitler's disposal for this purpose. In 1931 Hugenberg brought right-wing interests and parties together in the 'Harzburg Front'; but Hitler withheld his full support and it never established itself as an important grouping in German politics. Appointed Minister for Economics and Agriculture in Hitler's first cabinet of January 1933, Hugenberg was replaced in June by Walter Darré as Minister of Agriculture, and by Dr Karl Schmitt, the Director General of the powerful Allianz insurance company, as Minister of Economics.

The Hugenberg newspaper empire was bought out by the Nazis in 1943 for many millions of marks. After WWII Hugenberg was not subject to charges and was allowed to retain his fortune.

I

IG Farben.   A cartel formed after W W I by leading companies of the German chemical industry. Originally (1916) the recognition of a 'community of interest' between the chemical giants B A S F, Bayer, Hoechst and five smaller companies in the face of American competition, the full terms of the cartel were agreed in 1924.

The largest single company in Germany between the wars and an enormous concentration of economic power, IG Farben was a vital factor in Hitler's calculation of Germany's ability to wage war. Despite early mistrust between IG and the Nazi Party, the company enthusiastically devoted itself to the task of making Germany self-sufficient in vital strategic materials. This military-industrial partnership was best symbolized by Carl Krauch, from 1938 Göring's Plenipotentiary General for Chemical Production and, simultaneously, a senior member of the IG managing board. During this period, IG produced for the war effort almost all Germany's synthetic lubricating oils and gasoline, synthetic rubber (Buna), poison gases, explosives, methanol, sera, plasticizers, dyestuffs and nickel. In 1940 Hitler himself presented Krauch with the Knight's Cross for victories won 'on the battlefield of German industry'.

In 1943, under pressure to further increase synthetic oil and rubber supplies, the company established IG Auschwitz, the largest producing plant in the world. Built by slave labour from the neighbouring Auschwitz concentration camp, the IG plant was operated by workers who were selected for extermination when they were no longer able to fulfil work quotas. Taken to the neighbouring camp they were gassed with an IG product – Zyklon-B.

At the war's end many of the directors and executives were tried and found guilty at Nuremberg, and the IG cartel was broken up into its three major constituents.

Industrialists in the Third Reich.   ▶Keppler, Kirdorf, Krupp, Messerschmitt, Thyssen

Industry in the Third Reich.   Whatever the international factors involved, the basis of Germany's apparent prosperity after 1933 was clearly the *Wehrwirtschaft* – the war economy. Some rearmament was already taking place before Hitler came to power but the increase in military demand and the final open commitment to rearmament massively fuelled the German economy.

The figure of Dr Hjalmar Schacht was dominant in this first period. His reward for rallying industrialists to the Hitler cause was his reappointment in

March 1933 as president of the Reichsbank, and in August 1934 as Minister of Economics. He was instrumental in mobilizing the resources of the Reichsbank and in devising new stratagems for the financing of rearmament. Little more than a month after Hitler had announced, in March 1935, conscription of an army of 36 divisions, Schacht was appointed Plenipotentiary-General for the War Economy. The direction of the German economy had thus been clearly indicated and in September 1936 with the inauguration of the Four-Year Plan Germany took a further step in the devotion of its economy to total war.

German economic life in the Third Reich was organized under the Reich Economic Chamber in *Reichsgruppen* (National Groups), of which the Industrial Group was the most important. Increasingly German industrial concerns realized the importance of a direct link with government purchasing departments and directorships were given to senior Nazi Party members for liaison purposes. While Dr Schacht remained as Minister of Economics (until 1937) or president of the Reichsbank (until 1939) industry was more or less able to hold off the march of party directors, but with the appointment of Funk in Schacht's place and the outbreak of war SS and Gestapo directors became more common. From the late 1930s the demands of the Four-Year Plan, the desire for autarky and the pace of rearmament brought industry increasingly into a profitable but certainly subordinate position to the state.

At the same time, the late 1930s and the early war years saw important changes in the structure of German industry. After 1933 the power of the cartels had been enormously strengthened and the process of industrial concentration proceeded apace. Laws of October 1937 dissolved all corporations with a capital under $40,000 and prohibited the founding of companies of less than $200,000. From a figure of 9,500 joint stock corporations in 1932 the number declined to 5,400 in 1941.

In contrast the great firms were favoured and the Economics Ministry took powers to organize new cartels and to force companies to join them. Autarky, the pursuit of economic self-sufficiency, provided an important guiding line under the Four-Year Plan, the office of which encouraged Krupp to finance the Buna project for synthetic rubber, induced IG Farben to set up the Brabag company to produce petrol from lignite and required research and development into synthetic fibres.

Those large industrial groups, like IG Farben, which co-operated fully, reaped healthy profits. Between 1938 and 1943 the labour force of this vast cartel expanded 50 per cent while its profits rose 150 per cent. Not all industries so successfully reacted to the state's demands. The more conservative steel industry at first vacillated until forced by the state to finance (in effect) its own competition in the form of the massive National Hermann Göring Works.

During this period of the Third Reich the major changes in German capitalism have been listed thus: an increase in undistributed profits; the subordi-nation of stockholders' to directors' interests; a reduction in the importance of banking capital; the control of distribution by monopoly industry; and the domination of the industrial scene by the chemical industry and certain of the metallurgical industries.

The last years of peace and the first years of WWII proved an immensely profitable period for German industry: in the three years before 1942 industrial expansion was equivalent to the fifty preceding years. By 1941 much of this expansion was achieved with the aid of foreign slave labour. The IG Farben works at Auschwitz is only the best known example of the massive use of compulsion in labour supply: in 1944 Krupp was using 70,000 foreign labourers from over fifty camps in the Essen area and smaller concerns throughout German industry benefited from the use of cheap foreign labour.

Reservations about the regime and even the increasingly disastrous course of the war were slow to surface among senior industrialists. Only one, the Krupp director Ewald Löser, is known to have been actively involved in the July 1944 Plot.

In 1942 Albert Speer was appointed to the post of Minister of Armaments and War Production. Within the year he had become the virtual dictator of German industry. His production miracles were achieved through committees of manufacturers, some 6,000 honorary administrators replacing the former state and army purchasing agencies. But by 1944 the days of Hitler's Reich were clearly numbered. Allied bombing was being directed more specifically towards industrial targets, the Soviet army was approaching in East Prussia and the Morgenthau Plan seemed at least some indication of the Western Allies' intentions towards German industry.

The end now came quickly. Large concerns – even Krupp's – began to press demands for war-damage compensation and the rapid recovery of debts from the Reich. Investment in new plant was curtailed. Germany's industry had at last seen the writing on the wall.

It was almost too late. In the last days of the war, as part of a claimed scorched-earth policy but more in fact from a vengeful nihilism, Adolf Hitler ordered the wholesale destruction of the infrastructure of German industry. Only now was the state openly thwarted. Working with some *Gauleiters* and German industrialists, like Roland of Krupp, Albert Speer deliberately refused to obey. At the last moment Germany's industrial base was preserved, more or less intact, to await the new miracles of the post-war '*Wirtschaftswunder*'.

Iron Cross.   Originally a Prussian award for military valour instituted in 1813 and having three grades: the Second and First Class, and the Grand Cross. Another old Prussian award, 'Pour le Mérite' (instituted in 1740), was also in existence up to 1918. The French title, however, was already offensive to German nationalists; when in 1939 Hitler revived the Iron Cross medal, he created new Germanic classes above the First: the Knight's Cross (Ritterkreuz) which went in degrees upwards: 'with oakleaves', 'with oakleaves and swords' and 'with oakleaves, swords and diamonds'. Above that was 'golden oakleaves' awarded only once, to the air fighter ace Colonel Rudel. A 'Grand Cross of the Iron Cross' was created and given to Göring alone.

Iron Front.   A loose association of anti-Nazi parties devoted to securing the re-election of Hindenburg in the elections of 1932. In two elections of that year Hitler stood against Hindenburg for the presidency of the republic. Although losing both polls, Hitler nevertheless gained 30.1 and 36.8 per cent of the vote.

Italian Campaign, The.   ➤Appendix IV

J

Jena Stop-over, The.　During the intrigues for power in the Weimar Republic which brought the year 1932 to an end, Hitler had failed to secure the workable Reichstag majority which would gain him the chancellorship. In a bid to become Chancellor, General Kurt von Schleicher now suggested to Hindenburg that the Nazis might join him in a government. A telegram was sent to Hitler by Schleicher inviting him to Berlin. Nazi Party morale was at a low ebb after the recent poor election results. Perhaps Hitler seriously considered the possibility of serving under Schleicher, a concession which might well have destroyed the myth of Nazism and the purity of its demands. Certainly Hitler boarded the Berlin night-train from Munich. One account claims that he was hauled off the train at Jena by Göring and others who opposed the Schleicher option. What is certain is that at a meeting the following day, though Strasser strongly supported an alliance with Schleicher, Hitler, backed by Göring and Göbbels, carried the day by his refusal to join a government in a subordinate capacity.

Jews in Nazi Germany.

1933
April　　　Official boycott of Jewish shops
1935
September　Law for the reconstitution of the professional civil service
　　　　　　Nuremberg Laws promulated
November　Law of Reich Citizenship; definition of 'Jew' and *Mischling* (mixed race); Aryan a precondition for public appointments. First Decree on the Law for the Protection of German Blood and Honour; marriages between Aryan and Jew or *Mischling* forbidden
1936　　Olympic Games result in a calculated reduction of anti-semitic campaigns
1937　　Confiscation of Jewish businesses without legal justification
1938
March　　*Anschluss* in Austria: all racial laws in Germany applied to Austria
April　　All Jewish wealth to be registered
June　　Destruction of Munich synagogue
　　　　　Third Decree, demanding registration of all Jewish businesses
August　　Destruction of Nuremberg synagogue
　　　　　Decree requiring first name of either 'Israel' or 'Sarah' from 1939

October	Passports for Jews to be stamped 'J'
	Expulsion of 17,000 ex-Polish Jews
November	Vom Rath, of German embassy in Paris murdered by Herschel Grynszpan
	'Crystal Night' pogrom, more than 20,000 Jews imprisoned. Decrees eliminate Jews from the economy and demand a collective fine of over 1 billion marks to pay for the destruction. Expulsion of all Jews from schools
December	Aryans to take over all Jewish companies

1939

April	Confiscation of all Jewish valuables
	Law on Tenancies, foreseeing all Jews living together in 'Jewish Houses'
September	Curfew forbids Jews to be out of doors after dark. At the same time, their potential for treachery is underlined by the confiscation of all radio sets

1940

February	First deportation of Jews from Germany, mainly from Pomerania
October	Deportations from newly occupied Alsace-Lorraine, Saar and Baden

1941

March	Jews used for forced labour
September	Yellow star compulsory
	General deportation of German Jews starts. Term 'submarine' used to mean those Jews who succeeded in staying on in Berlin during the war. At the same time 'bounty hunters' develop, men who make a living from the Gestapo by tracking down and denouncing Jews

1942

January	Conference on 'Final Solution' at the Berlin suburb of Wannsee
April	Jews banned from public transport
September	Food rations for Jews reduced

1943

February	Deportation of last highly qualified Jews in Berlin armaments works starts
1944	As Russians advance, concentration camp inmates marched to the west

1945

January	Russians liberate Auschwitz
April	Estimated that 250,000 German Jews had perished since 1939, some 50 per cent of the pre-war German-Jewish population

➤Anti-semitism

Jodl, Alfred Josef Ferdinand (1890–1946). Hitler's chief of Wehrmacht operations from 1939. A professional soldier who was a general staff officer in the 1930s, he had rejoined the regular army after WWI and associated with nationalist and anti-democratic racialist groups. Although he did not entirely approve of Nazism, he saw himself as a military expert working for his superior, and he thus easily adapted to the regime from its beginning. Jodl took up his post as chief of operations in October 1939 and held it until the fall of the Third Reich. He opposed the dismissal of field marshals Halder and List in 1942 and asked for a field command, but Hitler kept him on the staff. He was standing near Hitler when the bomb exploded in the July 1944 Plot, but escaped serious injury. In May 1945, on behalf of Dönitz's government he signed the unconditional surrender of Germany to the Allies.

Jodl was an outstanding staff officer, but his sense of obedience to orders blinded him to their evil. He was tried among the major Nazi war criminals at Nuremberg, found guilty and hanged. It is probable that the Russians demanded the death penalty and that the British were prepared to let him die in return for the court's lenience to Speer.

John, Otto (b. 1909). A young lawyer working for Lufthansa who, through Klaus Bonhöffer, became a member of resistance groups in Germany. His duties allowed him to travel to Spain during WWII. In 1944, after the failure of the July Bomb Plot, he managed to get to the British embassy in Lisbon and thence to England, where he worked for the BBC's German language services. After the war he returned to Germany and was employed by the Federal Office for the Protection of the Constitution. His background made him hated by General Gehlen who was creating a secret service based on his former Third Reich colleagues. In the course of their rivalry, John was abducted by the East German authorities and, when returned, charged by the Federal Republic with treachery.

Johst, Hanns (1890–1978). The Nazi poet and playwright who was the source of the quotation (often wrongly ascribed to Göring): '*When I hear anyone talk of culture I reach for my revolver.*' This was a line in *Schlageter*, a nationalist play about a man killed by the French during their occupation of the Ruhr after WWI.

Johst became president of the Nazi Party poets' organization in 1929 and advanced in honours as the Nazis took power. In 1933 he replaced Heinrich Mann as President of the Academy of German Poetry and became in 1935 President of the Reich Chamber of Literature.

After the war in 1949 he was first cleared of Nazism by being declared only a 'fellow traveller'. Reclassified within months as a 'major offender', he was imprisoned and had his property confiscated. ➤Literature in the Third Reich

Jost, Heinz Maria Karl (1904–51). SD man and leader of an *Einsatzgruppe* in the east. A Nazi since 1928 and a member of the SD from 1934, Jost worked in Spain during the Civil War, and with forces occupying Czechoslovakia and Poland in 1939. He set up a large SD department with sections to cover America and elsewhere, but came into 'territorial' conflict with 'Gestapo' Müller, and was replaced in 1941 by Schellenberg. He was one of the last of the war criminals to be hanged, at Landsberg in 1951, by the American forces.

Joyce, William (1906–46). Known also as 'Lord Haw-Haw', he broadcast from Germany to Britain during WWII.

New York-born and raised in Ireland and England, Joyce joined the British Fascist Party in 1933 and went to Germany immediately before the outbreak of WWII. He offered his services to Berlin and was put to broadcasting to Britain, where the braying tone of his voice earned him his nickname. It is difficult to estimate whether his propaganda achieved any of its desired effects. It was certainly widely listened to, but probably more in amusement than credulity. William Joyce was arrested in May 1945 and accused of treason. Although he claimed German citizenship, he had kept his British passport, and this fact was exploited by the British to secure a conviction for treason. He was hanged in Wandsworth prison in 1946.

Jubilation, Stage Three (*N–S Jubel Dritte Stufe*). The top level of applause at a stage-managed Nazi meeting.

Judenfrei. Free of Jews, in the sense of cleansed free. Used to describe cities or areas where total Jewish deportation had taken place.

July Bomb Plot. The unsuccessful 20 July 1944 attempt on Hitler's life. By the end of 1943 the Gestapo and SD had succeeded in dispersing much of the anti-Hitler opposition within Germany. Himmler's first major coup led to the arrest of Dietrich Bonhöffer, Josef Müller and Hans Dohnanyi in April 1943. More serious for the military opposition, suspicion fell on Hans Oster. He was placed under close Gestapo surveillance and before the end of the year transferred from active service to the reserve. At the same time General Beck had undergone a serious cancer operation and General von Hammerstein had died. In addition, Schellenberg, the leading SD investigator, had penetrated several opposition discussion groups. In January 1944 Moltke and members of Frau Hanna Solf's circle were arrested, and Canaris, head of the *Abwehr*, was dismissed in the following month.

By early 1944 therefore the German opposition was in disarray. If Hitler were to be deposed or killed, a new driving force was necessary. It was in the personality of Count Claus Schenk von Stauffenberg that this driving force was to be discovered. A south German, born in 1907, whose father had been chamberlain to the last king of Württemberg, von Stauffenberg had joined the 17th Bamberg Cavalry in 1926. Fearing a communist seizure of power in the Weimar Republic, he had inclined, like many thousands of officers, to a measure of support for Hitler as the lesser of two evils. Meanwhile his army career progressed rapidly, and in 1938 Stauffenberg had been invited to become one of the 187 members of the élite General Staff.

During the early years of the war von Stauffenberg fought with German armies in France, Russia and North Africa. In Tunis he was severely wounded in April 1943, losing an eye, his right arm and two fingers of his left hand. At some time during his convalescence he appears to have come to the decision that Hitler had to be deposed, that deposition meant assassination and that young officers like himself had a duty to act. Stauffenberg was already aware of the somewhat formless opposition to Hitler. He had been in touch with anti-Nazi groups from before the war. In 1939 he had been approached by Count Friedrich von Schulenberg to influence the Commander-in-Chief, Brauchitsch, against Nazi policy, but at this stage Stauffenberg had refused. It is possible that, like many of his military colleagues, the young career soldier found the approach of war and the high glamour of victory too seductive.

By 1942 Stauffenberg was certainly aware of the opposition flowing from within the army in Russia. By the end of the year he was urging General von Manstein to join the anti-Hitler conspiracy. Perhaps it was his discovery that so many of the senior officers with whom he came into contact were evasive in their reaction that made Stauffenberg request active service in North Africa. Certainly there is evidence that he was already unimpressed by his elders' plans. Later he would learn of the attempts of younger officers to murder Hitler. By the time Stauffenberg lay severely wounded in Tunis, two of these attempts on Hitler's life had already failed. Von Tresckow and Lieutenant von Schlabrendorff had failed to kill Hitler with bombs planted on the plane in which he was returning from Russia in March 1943 (the Smolensk Plot). Later that month a change in the Führer's schedule saved his life when two bombs were placed in his overcoat pockets.

From the time he returned to duty, in the second half of 1943, Claus von Stauffenberg appears to have assumed a leading role in the new plot against Hitler's life. It was now recognized that there were two immediate stages to the operation – the assassination of Adolf Hitler and the quite separate seizure of the German state in the face of SS forces which would be loyal to Himmler, Göring or whoever attempted to take command. In the summer of 1943, Beck and Gördeler, now recognizing Stauffenberg's leading role in the conspiracy, asked him to plan for the seizure of power and in particular for the seizure of Berlin after Hitler's death.

'Operation Valkyrie', as it was to be known, was both a brilliantly devised cover-story and a plan for the seizure of Berlin at the same time. Perfectly openly, as Chief of Staff to General Olbricht of the German Army Office in Berlin, Stauffenberg prepared a contingency plan for the troops of the Berlin garrisons to seize key government buildings, telephone and signal centres and radio stations in the event of a revolt of the hundreds of foreign slave labourers working in the Berlin region. That was the cover; but Valkyrie could equally be directed against SS troops attempting to restore Nazi authority after the assassination of the Führer. For Stauffenberg and the conspirators the latter was of course the intended scenario.

The general indications were favourable. Although the SS had strong forces at their disposal in the Berlin region, *Wehrmacht* training schools offered good quality troops at Döberitz, Krampnitz, Jüterborg and Wunsdorf. The Berlin police force under the command of Count Helldorff could be relied upon and the Commandant of the City of Berlin, General Paul von Hase, was a committed anti-Nazi. The major uncertainty lay in the attitude of General Fromm, the Commander of the Home Army.

But the trigger of the whole conspiracy remained the successful assassination of Hitler. Three attempts were made (by Bussche, Kleist and Stauffenberg himself) before the summer of 1944. But now with the dismissal of Admiral Canaris from his *Abwehr* post, the conspiracy suffered from lack of information on Hitler's movements. From 1 July 1944, however, the situation changed again. Stauffenberg was appointed Chief of Staff to General Fromm, the head of the Home Army. In this new appointment he would now have plentiful access to Hitler at his Rastenburg headquarters.

The Wolf's Lair, as Hitler called his East Prussian headquarters, consisted of a huge compound protected by electrified fencing with watchtowers at frequent intervals. Conferences were held in the Gästebaracke, a large but simply built wooden hut, with concrete-cased walls but its original tar-paper roof. At each end of the hut were three windows, but the dominant feature of the hut was the large oak map table placed in the middle of the room. On the morning of 20 July 1944 Claus von Stauffenberg had been required to attend at Rastenburg to report on the state of the Home Army. Among the conspirators there was a clear sense of now or never. On 17 July, Rommel had been injured when a British fighter aircraft had strafed his car in northern France. Two days earlier, General von Falkenhausen, a supporter of the conspirators, had been summarily relieved of his command. Much worse, on the very day Rommel had been injured, Carl Gördeler had been arrested with lists for the projected provisional government of Germany (►Provisional Government List).

The conference had been put forward half an hour from 1.00 p.m. because Mussolini was due to arrive for a meeting with Hitler early in the afternoon. Stauffenberg entered late with Field Marshal Keitel at 12.37 p.m., having minutes before broken the capsule which activated the time-bomb in his briefcase. The timing gave von Stauffenberg five minutes to plant the bomb. The closest he could get to where Hitler was studying the latest reports was about twelve feet away. Next to a staff officer named Brandt, he placed his briefcase to rest against a strongly built oak table-leg.

The bomb exploded at 12.42 p.m. The light roof and windows of the conference hut were destroyed immediately. In the chaos someone remembered seeing Hitler's hair burning. Claus von Stauffenberg himself was already clear of the hut, certain that everybody at the conference was dead. Only when he arrived in Berlin at just after 4.00 p.m. did he realize to his astonishment that Hitler had not been killed.

The conspiracy now fell quickly apart. Göbbels in Berlin acted with resolution, demonstrating to the Berlin Guard Commander, Remer, that Hitler was still alive by linking them by telephone. General Fromm, as much to allay suspicions of his own involvement as from any sense of loyalty to Hitler, had Stauffenberg shot at midnight in the courtyard of the War Ministry.

Operation Valkyrie was stopped in its tracks. The only serious German attempt to remove Hitler and the Nazi Party from power had failed. Months of vengeance followed. Suspects were arrested and tortured; while many held out with the greatest courage imaginable, a few disclosed further names. These in turn were arrested, often with their families, and tortured. No group of men and women could have surmounted this onslaught. After the trials, held before the notorious Roland Freisler, Judge of the People's Court (*Volksgerichtshof*), sentences were carried out by firing squad or axe or even by strangling with piano wire. Hitler watched home movies of the hangings of the principal conspirators throughout the night of their deaths.

Among the main conspirators and associates killed in the long aftermath of 20 July 1944 were: Colonel General Ludwig Beck, Admiral Wilhelm Canaris, Father Alfred Delp, Hans von Dohnanyi, Dr Carl Gördeler, Ulrich von Hassell, Count Wolf Helldorf, General Höpner, Dr Julius Leber, Graf Helmut von Moltke, General Hans Oster, Field Marshal Erwin Rommel, Colonel Claus von Stauffenberg, General Karl von Stülpnagel, General Henning von Tresckow, Adam von Trott zu Solz, Joseph Wirmer, Field Marshal Erwin von Witzleben and Peter Yorck von Wartenburg.

Jünger, Ernst (b. 1895). A writer who kept clear of the Nazis despite Göbbels efforts to have him write for the Party since he was a holder, from WWI, of the 'Pour le Mérite'.

Justice in Nazi Germany. Hitler's revision of the laws of Germany did not affect civil laws, such as those on wills, torts, commercial contracts; but criminal law was massively restructured. By 1945, forty-three crimes carried the death penalty. Judges who did not conform to the practice of Nazi justice were removed from office; only conformists survived. Their role was to maintain not 'the state' but the Nazi view of the state, preserving the existing *völkisch* (traditional 'Aryan' and Germanic) elements, punishing anything like anti-Nazi behaviour and getting rid of any obstruction to the Party's will. Prosecution lawyers were given added powers and importance in court, while lawyers for the defence were weakened. From 1937, beating suspects (officially on the buttocks) was a legally sanctioned part of police interrogation. The age at which a death sentence might be received was reduced in 1941 to fourteen. In 1940 over 900 German civilians were executed after sentencing by the courts, and by 1943 the number had risen to over 5,000 in the year. To ensure the operation of Nazi justice, from 1942 judges and prosecution were allowed to confer without any defence lawyer being present.

From March 1933 Special Courts (*Sondergerichte*) were set up to try political offences without a jury. In 1934 the People's Courts (*Volksgerichtshöfe*) were established to try cases of high treason, but with a jury drawn exclusively from Nazi Party members. This was the court over which the vicious Roland Freisler presided in Berlin and which condemned those accused of complicity in the July 1944 Bomb Plot. On the lowest level, Nazi Party 'courts' (USCHLA) were also established in each *Gau* as early as the 1920s, to maintain Party discipline, using as sanctions loss of employment, expulsion, social banishment or, from 1933 when Hitler came to power, imprisonment and death.

Civil prisons continued to receive prisoners sentenced by the courts or held in civil police custody. All who came to the attention of the Nazi Party policing system – whether Gestapo, SD or criminal police (Kripo) – were liable to be served with a 'protective custody' order and consigned indefinitely to an SS-run concentration camp. Between 1934 and 1945, People's Court judges sentenced to death 7,000 of the 16,000 brought before them.

In October 1986, West Germany finally dropped legal proceedings against the 577 judges and state prosecutors of the Third Reich's People's Courts. Investigations had started only in 1954 and were properly under way only in 1965; by 1986 the accused were either dead or too infirm to stand trial, and the evidence was becoming harder to substantiate as surviving witnesses died. Many see in this dilatory approach the reluctance of one legal system to condemn its predecessor. ➤*Gleichschaltung*; Freisler, Roland

Jüttner, Hans (1894–1965).   In 1940 he became Chief of Staff of the newly formed Waffen SS and from 1942 head of the Operational Department of the SS which controlled the Waffen SS. He insisted on military standards and disciplined Eicke, the Commander of the Totenkopf division, who believed that his unit could be run on the basis of pseudo-revolutionary flair. Jüttner's concept of the Waffen SS as an imperial guard accorded ill with Eicke's anti-militarism, and Jüttner tried unsuccessfully to remove Eicke from his command. Until the end of the war the struggle between the two views of the SS continued. Jüttner's imperial guard concept depended on separating Waffen SS units from concentration camp guards and policemen. In the last resort Jüttner earned Himmler's disfavour as a senior SS officer whose separatist view of the Waffen SS was unacceptable to the Reichsführer.

K

Kaas, Monsignor Ludwig (1881–1952). Catholic priest and Centre Party leader from 1928. He was concerned with the defence of his church rather than of the Republic; thus he collaborated with Hitler, who promised a Concordat with the church, by recording his Reichstag vote in favour of the Enabling Act. Chastened by the results of the Enabling Act and *Gleichschaltung*, he left Germany in 1933 on the dissolution of the Centre Party, taking up a senior post in the Vatican, with special responsibility for Germany.

Kahr, Gustav von (1862–1934). The leader of the right-wing nationalist Bavarian People's Party, Kahr was Prime Minister of Bavaria from 1920 to 1921, after the collapse of the Kapp Putsch in Berlin had encouraged the army to overthrow the socialist government in Munich. In 1923 he was made State Commissioner with full emergency powers to suppress rightist outbreaks. Hitler had tried to induce Kahr to join him in the Beer Hall Putsch, but Kahr equivocated and withdrew his support as soon as he could. He was mistrusted and even hated for his role in these events and was forced to resign the post of commissioner in February 1924. In the Röhm Purge of 1934 he was a listed victim. His body was hacked to pieces and thrown into a swamp near Dachau; he was seventy-one years old.

Kaltenbrunner, Ernst (1903–46). Head of RSHA, SS Security, Gestapo and SD after the assassination of Heydrich. His height (6ft 7in.) and his scarred face gave him an intimidating appearance.

Born in Austria near Hitler's birthplace, he attended school in Linz with Eichmann. Joining the Austrian Nazi Party in 1932, he became the leader of their SS units. When imprisoned with other Nazis after the 1934 attempted Putsch in which the Austrian Chancellor Dollfuss was killed, Kaltenbrunner organized a strike and obtained his own release and that of his companions.

At the *Anschluss*, when Hitler marched into Austria, Kaltenbrunner formed his SS men into 'auxiliary police' and indulged in an instant campaign attacking Jews and all he saw as enemies. He arrested prominent Austrians, including the Chancellor, von Schuschnigg, and Baron Louis von Rothschild. His energy, shown in company with that of another SS leader, Odilo Globocnik, earned him the post of Minister of State and command of the SS in Ostmark (as Austria now became known), while Globocnik was made *Gauleiter* of Vienna (until his reputation for brutality led to his transfer to Poland to run the extermination camps there).

Kaltenbrunner's loyalty earned him Himmler's recognition and the appointment in 1943 as Heydrich's successor over the heads of others who saw themselves as better qualified. When Hitler ordered the dissolution of the *Abwehr* (the army intelligence organization) in 1944, Kaltenbrunner took it over with the same zeal with which he ordered the Gestapo, SD and concentration camp regimes of violence.

He was arrested in Austria and, in the absence of the dead Himmler and the vanished 'Gestapo' Müller, he was included among the major war criminals tried at Nuremberg. He was found guilty of crimes against humanity, although he protested at his trial that he was only a substitute for Himmler. He was hanged in October 1946.

Kamerad. The usual form of friendly address between members of the Nazi Party.

Kampfbund. ➤Battle League

***Kampfzeit* (Time of struggle)**. Part of the carefully created instant mythology of the Nazi Party was the account of a heroic past, a period of intense struggle against overwhelming odds. The concept appears unendingly in Hitler's account of his own life (*Mein Kampf*) and in his reminiscences of the early days of the Party. The *Alte Kämpfer*, the Old Fighters, were particularly honoured by the regime and the *Kampfzeit* was taught, after 1933, as part of the school curriculum.

Kapp Putsch. In March 1920 the Ehrhardt *Freikorps* Brigade marched into Berlin, protesting against the government's acceptance of the Treaty of Versailles, the disarmament terms of which would have meant their own disbandment. A right-wing journalist, Wolfgang Kapp (1868–1922), was proclaimed Chancellor and the putschists declared the liberal Weimar government overthrown. A general strike of workers in Berlin proved that the Putsch had little popular support, however, and the regular army disassociated itself from the *Freikorps*. The Putsch collapsed after five days and Kapp fled to Sweden.

The right-wing Putsch attracted interest in Bavaria, and Hitler is said to have been flown by his army employers to observe it.

Karinhall. Göring's house and hunting estate north of Berlin, named after his first wife, the Swedish aristocrat Carin von Kantzow, *née* Baroness Fock.

Katyn Massacre. The massacre by the NKVD (Soviet Security Forces) of between 4,000 and 15,000 Polish officers and others at Katyn Forest, near Smolensk in the western Soviet Union in the spring of 1940. The opportunity to capture large numbers of Polish officers came in 1939 when, in accordance with the secret protocol of the Russo-German Pact, Soviet forces moved into Poland to meet German forces advancing from the West. The story of Katyn evolved in a sense, backwards, first reaching the international stage when the

German army discovered and revealed the massacre in 1943. The Soviets hotly denied the accusation and when they had reoccupied the territory, exhumed and displayed the Polish bodies as evidence of a *Nazi* massacre (January 1944).

The responsibility for Katyn became a sensitive political issue between Stalin and the Western Allies long before the war ended. The truth was finally established beyond any doubt only when Mikhail Gorbachev admitted Soviet responsibility shortly before the fall of the Soviet Union.

***Kazetlager* (*KZ Lager*).**   Common abbreviation for the German for 'concentration camp'.

Keitel, Wilhelm (1882–1946).   Chief of Staff of the OKW, the High Command of the armed forces, from 1938. Born at Helscherode in central Germany, Keitel served in the artillery in WWI and in 1919 with one of the Freikorps until reposting to the Weimar army. In 1929 he headed the army organization department and in 1933 was chairman of the Reich Defence Council. He was appointed to the War Ministry under Blomberg in 1935; when Blomberg was forced to resign in 1938, Keitel took over the new post at OKW. He was promoted Field Marshal after negotiating the French surrender in 1940.

Keitel attended all significant German conferences on the conduct of the war and signed operational orders, including those for the execution of hostages and prisoners of war. Following the attempt on Hitler's life in July 1944, he sat as a member of the 'Court of Honour' which sentenced to death many high-ranking officers. A loyal worker for Hitler, Keitel continued to the last under the Dönitz government, organizing the surrender of the German army before his arrest by the Allies.

Keitel's subservience to Hitler became a byword in the army where he was known as 'Lakeitel', a coinage from 'lackey Keitel'. On Hitler's orders he issued the *Nacht und Nebel* decree in December 1941 by which those said to endanger the Third Reich were to vanish 'into night and fog' (i.e. be killed without trial). It was responsibility for this order that led to his inclusion among the major war criminals. He was sentenced to death and hanged at Nuremberg in 1946.

Keppler, Wilhelm (1882–1960).   An engineer and industrialist who was a member of the Nazi Party from the 1920s and a useful intermediary with the bankers and anti-Schleicher conservatives. In 1931 he brought together a group, known as the Keppler Circle, to support and fund the Party. Elected to the Reichstag, he was made a Commissioner for Economic Affairs in 1933, and in 1936 he was appointed adviser to Göring on the Four-Year Plan. He was attached to the German embassy in Vienna before the *Anschluss* and became Reich Commissioner to Austria from March to June 1938. He was employed in the Ministry of Foreign Affairs during WWII and became chairman of many SS businesses. After the war he was sentenced to ten years' imprisonment for his part in war crimes. He was released in 1951.

Kerrl, Hans (1887–1941). A Nazi lawyer who was a follower of Strasser in the 1920s. He remained a close (perhaps the only) friend of Göbbels. In March 1933 he was appointed Reich Commissioner for Justice, implementing the ban on Jewish lawyers. He became Reich Minister for Church Affairs in July 1935 and was responsible for keeping the Evangelical Church under government control. He died in Berlin in December 1941.

Kersten, Felix (1898–1960). A masseur who treated Himmler for stomach pains in 1939 and was then recommended to treat Hess, Ley and Ribbentrop. He became wealthy in the process and a part of the Himmler entourage. He claimed to have worked with Schellenberg in mediating with the Swedes for the release of prisoners from concentration camps.

His post-war memoirs (*Totenkopf und Treue*, translated into English in 1947 as *Memoirs*) and evidence at trials are a major source of information on Himmler and his plans. He recorded that Himmler saw a future when all European *and* American Jews would be exterminated, when German would be the official language of all Europe, and Roman Catholicism would be eradicated in favour of a pagan Nordic faith.

Kesselring, Albert (1885–1960). Luftwaffe and army Commander. Arguably the most successful German general in WWII.

A Bavarian-born regular soldier, Kesselring served as an artillery-man and a general staff officer in WWI. In order to take a post with the newly formed Luftwaffe, he learned to fly at the age of forty-eight. When the Luftwaffe's first commander, General Wever, was killed in an air crash in 1936, Kesselring took over as Chief of Staff. He commanded Luftflotte 1 in Poland in 1939, and in 1940 led Luftflotte 2 in the campaign against the West. During the Battle of Britain it can be argued that he underrated the RAF's ability to resist daylight attacks, probably his only serious tactical error in a unique career. From the west, Kesselring was transferred to Russia where he commanded Luftflotte 2 with great ability. By 1942, now a Field Marshal, he was appointed to the Mediterranean theatre as Commander-in-Chief South. It was in this role during 1943 and 1944 that he was to fight the classic defensive campaign in Italy against a stronger, better-equipped enemy on which his reputation as a general rests. In March 1945 he had already opened secret negotiations with the American Allen Dulles for a separate surrender when Hitler transferred him to the Western Front. But by now no generalship of whatever quality could save the Third Reich, and Kesselring surrendered to American forces on 6 May 1945.

In 1947 a British court found him guilty of ordering the execution of 335 Italian civilians and he was sentenced to life imprisonment. The conviction was in fact an extreme interpretation of the concept of a commander's responsibility for the acts of his troops. In no army in WWII could it have been applied so rigorously, given the command conditions in the last days in Italy when the campaign was characterized by intense partisan activity and drives by SS formations which had become a law unto themselves. Many British jurists and senior officers became concerned at the court's verdict. Kesselring's British opponent, the Allied commander in Italy Field Marshal Alexander, was among those who expressed serious doubts, as an indirect result of which Kesselring was released from prison in 1952, officially on grounds of ill-health.

Kirdorf, Emil (1847–1938). A coalmine owner and extreme nationalist who contributed to Hitler's funds from 1929. A ruthless anti-union and anti-socialist employer who hoped that the Nazis would support his interests, he ran the 'Ruhr Treasury', a group aimed at protecting fellow industrialists.

Kith and Kin. The system under which, legally, the Gestapo might arrest, torture or put to death members of a suspected person's family. In a speech of August 1944 Himmler invoked an ancient German practice of putting a whole family under a ban to justify the Nazi 'kith and kin' system. 'They [our German forebears] said: "*There is traitor blood there; it will be exterminated.*" '

The 'kith and kin' system was widely used by the Gestapo commission investigating the July Bomb Plot.

Klausener, Erich (1885–1934). Leader of Catholic Action in Berlin. In 1933 under Hitler's first government he was made Reich Communications Director. But he angered Hitler by contributing to von Papen's Marburg speech in 1934 in which Nazism was attacked for, among other things, its anti-Christian practices. Within two weeks he was killed in the Röhm Purge. His wife's lawyers unwisely made claims for damages; they were consigned to Sachsenhausen concentration camp until they withdrew all claims.

Kleist, Field Marshal Paul Ludwig Ewald von (1881–1954). From an aristocratic Prussian family; he was a successful Panzer commander in France and the Balkans, and particularly in the Caucasus, 1941–2, where he persuaded local people (Azerbaijani, Kalmuck and others) to collaborate with the Germans. Kleist had been one of the generals relieved of their command when Hitler took over command of the army in 1938; but he was reinstated and achieved spectacular success, nearly reaching the oilfields of the Caucasus in 1942. For his Southern Russian victory he was promoted Field Marshal in 1943. In 1945 he was captured by the British and, after interrogation, handed over to the Russians. He died in a prison camp in Russia.

Kleist-Schmenzin, Ewald Heinrich von (1890–1945). A Prussian land-owner, staunch monarchist and an acquaintance of Admiral Canaris, head of the *Abwehr* (military intelligence). Canaris and Oster chose him as an emissary to London in August 1938 to speak to the British Foreign Office on behalf of

General Beck. Kleist met the head of the Foreign Office, Vansittart. He warned him that Hitler was intent on war and that many generals known to Kleist would oppose Hitler if they could get any support from England. Kleist also saw Churchill, but the latter had no official position at the time; and the reaction from Chamberlain, the British Prime Minister, was one of unease and doubt. It was in part this meeting which prompted Chamberlain to meet Hitler himself. This he did in September at Munich.

Kleist remained in touch with the conservative resistance to Hitler, and his son, Lieutenant Heinrich von Kleist, offered to carry a bomb into Hitler's presence early in 1944, but the opportunity did not present itself. Kleist was arrested in the round-up of suspects after the 1944 July Bomb Plot, brought before Freisler in the People's Court in Berlin and sentenced to death. This was the last sentence passed by Freisler: a bomb from an American aircraft killed him as he left the court. Von Kleist-Schmenzin was beheaded in April 1945.

Kluge, Field Marshal Günther Hans von (1882–1944).   A WWI artillery and General Staff officer, he had risen to the rank of general and commander of a military district in 1934. In 1938 he was one of the officers suspended at the time of the Blomberg–Fritsch crisis.

In 1939 he was recalled to command the 4th Army which took the Polish Corridor and which in 1940, under Rundstedt (and with Rommel as a Panzer divisional commander), invaded France. He was rewarded by promotion to Field Marshal. With the 4th Army he led the attack on Moscow in 1941 and, although forced to fall back after his main advance, he was given command of Army Group Centre, replacing von Bock in December. Hitler gave him as a gift RM 250,000 in October 1942.

Invalided out of action after a car crash in 1943, it was not until the following year that he was fit for command, and in July 1944 he was sent to succeed Rommel in the west. His new command was short-lived, however. In August he was relieved of all duties for failing to uncover or warn of the July Bomb Plot. He had refused to join the plotters, although he had promised help if Hitler was killed. Ordered back to Germany, he committed suicide by poisoning himself.

Koch, Karl (1903–45) and **Ilse** (1906–67).   Concentration camp commandant and his sadistic wife. Married in 1936, the Kochs were posted to Buchenwald concentration camp in 1939 where he was appointed camp commandant and she became an SS female overseer. A large, reddish-blonde woman, Ilse Koch soon gained a reputation for extreme sadism and an unrestrained sexual appetite. She is undoubtedly best known for her collection of lampshades made from the tattooed skin of camp inmates she had personally selected for execution.

Her husband Karl was no less a criminal sadist but, by an irony of SS practice, he was judged to be criminal by his SS peers. The subject of an

SS-Gericht (SS Court) investigation conducted by Dr Morgen, Koch – by this time commandant of the camp at Lublin – was sentenced to death for embezzlement and the illegal killing of two prisoners, Krämer and Peix.

While her husband was hanged for his crimes by his own colleagues, Ilse Koch continued her work at Buchenwald until the camp was liberated by US troops in 1945. At her first trial in 1947 an American court found her guilty of murder and sentenced her to life imprisonment, but General Lucius Clay reduced her sentence to four years. In 1948 she was the subject of a Senate investigating commission and was again brought to trial in 1951. Judged to be 'a perverted, nymphomaniacal, power-mad demon', Ilse Koch was again sentenced to life imprisonment. In 1967 she hanged herself in her cell in Aibach prison.

Kolbe, Maximilian (1894–1941).   A Roman Catholic priest in Auschwitz concentration camp who in 1941 chose to take the place of a Polish prisoner condemned to death. His offer was accepted by the authorities and Father Kolbe died. He was beatified in 1971.

Kolberg.   Film of epic proportions made, on the express instructions of Göbbels, in 1944. The last and most costly of all films made in Nazi Germany, *Kolberg* was Göbbels' final, and unsuccessful, attempt to equal the scale of *Gone with the Wind*, a picture he admired and envied. Based on an incident in the Napoleonic Wars in which the inhabitants of a small Prussian town defended it against the French army with heroic valour, *Kolberg* was directed by Veit Harlan, had a budget of RM 8.5 million and an enormous set built near the site of the actual town. The film did not begin production until 1943 when the battles on the Eastern Front were making a maximum demand on troops and material resources. Despite this, Göbbels ordered whole army units to be assigned to the film as extras, found 6,000 horses, turned the production of munition factories over to making blanks for the muskets and commandeered 100 railway trucks to bring salt to the set in order to simulate snow.

The première was scheduled to open the Atlantikfest at the city of La Rochelle on 30 January 1945 (the twelfth anniversary of the Nazi takeover of power). La Rochelle at this time was completely encircled by Allied forces and the print of the film had to be parachuted into the city. History does not relate how it was received.

Korherr Report.   The work of SS statistician Richard Korherr. The Korherr Report, commissioned in January and completed in March 1943, gave the first total figures of the extermination of the Jews. Korherr was also responsible for uncovering facts on the *Lebensborn* system of SS maternity homes, which showed them as less than efficient. His truthfulness was not tactful and the head of the SS RuSHA, Hildebrandt, slapped his face publicly in August 1943.

Progress report of Jews killed to January 1943

Germany, Austria and Sudetenland	147,000
Bohemia and Moravia	69,000
Poland	1,274,000
France	41,000
Belgium	16,000
Netherlands	38,000
Norway	500
Yugoslavia	61,000
USSR (figures 'incomplete')	635,000

KPD. ➤Communist Party of Germany

Kraft durch Freude. ➤Strength Through Joy

Kramer, Josef (1906–45). One of the most notorious of the camp commandants, the so-called 'Beast of Belsen'. As an SS member, Kramer entered Eicke's fledgling concentration camp service in 1934. He served in Natzweiler camp and in the last months of Auschwitz commanded the extermination centre there before being transferred in November 1944 to Belsen. The camp in north-west Germany had, up to this stage of the German collapse, been a detention camp holding Jews who (in theory at least) were to be exchanged for German nationals abroad. By a grisly irony it was also classified as a *Krankenlager*, a reception camp for sick prisoners. From November 1944, conditions in the camp deteriorated rapidly. Evidence was offered at Kramer's later trial that he was responsible for selling off camp food supplies; more likely, the desperate food shortages in the last months of Belsen were the result of an increase in numbers from 15,000 to nearly 50,000. In the conditions of the time it is unlikely that *any* level of rations for the new arrivals would have reached the camp. The result was the complete break-down of administration. On an outbreak of spotted fever Kramer tried to close the camp but was refused permission. When British troops liberated the site, 13,000 corpses were found, lying unburied in pits or in scattered heaps among the emaciated survivors. Many who saw the newsreel material of that appalling first day of liberation will retain a lasting image of Josef Kramer, stocky and well fed among the dying inmates, his cheek scarred beneath the dark stubble, a man neither shocked nor stricken by conscience, a man simply awaiting new orders. He was tried and found guilty of war crimes, and was executed in November 1945.

Kreisau Circle. Resistance group named after the estate owned by their leader, von Moltke. Conferences held in 1942 and 1943 tried to establish fundamental principles on which a new Germany might be founded when the Third Reich collapsed. Church and state relations and universities were first discussed, then decentralization of the state and the redevelopment of parties and labour unions (a broad reversal of *Gleichschaltung* was envisaged). They proposed war crimes trials and the re-establishment of the rule of law, to be administered by provincial commissioners with strict reconstruction guidelines. They envisaged not a radically changed society but, to a large extent, a remake of the old Germany. They opposed a *coup d'état* against Hitler, but meetings were held with Beck, Gördeler and Hassell. As individuals (though not as a group), many members supported the July 1944 Bomb Plot. In the purge which followed, leading members of the Kreisau Circle – von Moltke, von Trott zu Solz and Yorck von Wartenburg – were all executed.

Among the most prominent members of the Kreisau Circle:

Protestants: Helmuth James; Count von Moltke; Peter, Count Yorck von Wartenburg; Horst von Einsiedel; Carl Dietrich von Trotha; Adolf Reichwein; Otto von der Gablentz; Theodor Stelzer; Adam von Trott zu Solz; Hans-Bernd von Haeften; Harald Poelchau; Eugen Gerstenmaier

Catholics: Hans Peters; Hans Lukaschek; Paulus von Husen; Augustin Roesch, SJ; Alfred Delp, SJ; Lotharn König, SJ

Socialists: Carlo Mierendorff; Theodor Haubach; Julius Leber

➤ Resistance for names of other groups.

Kretschmer, Otto (b. 1912). German U-boat commander who, before his capture in 1941, was credited with sinking over 300,000 tons of British shipping, including three armed merchant cruisers and a destroyer.

Kriegsschuldlüge. The lie of Germany's war guilt. A favourite topic of Nazi orators, it referred to Article 231 of the Versailles Treaty. ➤Versailles Treaty, Article 231.

Kroll Opera House. Location of the Reichstag after the original building had been burnt down in the Reichstag Fire of February 1933. It was here that the Enabling Act was passed in the first Reichstag session after the 5 March elections.

Krupp von Bohlen und Halbach, Alfred (1907–67). The son and heir of Gustav Krupp, he was an enthusiastic supporter of Hitler's war and in charge of Krupp's munitions and weapons production during WWII. Under his direction Krupp's moved to new factories in German-occupied lands; using conscripted or slave labour and the labour of concentration camps. The older Krupp's works in the Ruhr were heavily bombed, and he asked the state for compensation. He was made Minister of War Economy in 1943.

Captured by the Canadians in 1945 and sentenced at a later Nuremberg tribunal to twelve years in prison with the confiscation of all his property, he was nevertheless released from Landsberg in 1951 and his property and companies (valued at millions in any currency) restored to him.

Krupp von Bohlen und Halbach, Gustav (1870–1950). The inheritor of the huge industrial and munition-making concern, from 1931 he occupied a key position as Chairman of the Association of German Industrialists. He had opposed the political rise of the Nazis and warned President Hindenburg against them; but, by the time Hitler became Chancellor, Krupp was an enthusiastic supporter, following Schacht's lead. He saw that Hitler had destroyed the political left and the unions, had proclaimed the need for rearmament and had removed the threat of radicalism (in the person of Strasser) from the Nazi Party. Reassured, Krupp now donated heavily to the Adolf Hitler Fund administered by Bormann. Under his son's management, the Krupp's works prospered in the Third Reich. The huge slave-labour force used by Krupp's brought the son to trial after the war. The father, Gustav, was not brought to court because of ill-health.

Kursk Salient.   The greatest tank battle of WWII. After the disaster of Stalingrad in the winter of 1942/3, Hitler regrouped his armies, hoping to destroy a huge army of Russians who had taken Kursk, a city 100 miles north of Kharkov and 100 miles south of Orël – both held by the Germans. In July 1943 Field Marshals Kluge (from the north) and Manstein (from the south), with 1,000,000 troops and 2,700 tanks, attacked. But the Russians, possibly warned by the 'Lucy' spy ring in Switzerland, were ready. The Luftwaffe failed to establish local air-superiority and German tanks suffered from rocket attacks from the air. Kluge's attack from the north failed and within a few days Manstein too was defeated.

KZ Lager.   Concentration camps ➤Concentration Camps.

L

Labour Charter. A law of January 1934 which aimed to set out the relationship between capital and labour in the new German state. Not a doctrine the radical wing of the Nazi Party would approve, the Labour Charter established the balance against the German wage-earner, to the marked benefit of the industrialist. Based in many respects on Mussolini's 1927 Charter of Labour the Nazi charter offered the German worker the token right to be elected to the *Vertrauensrat* (the confidential council).

Labour Front (DAF). The sole labour union organization of the Third Reich, the Front was set up in 1933 after Hitler had made a May Day speech announcing that he would bring peace to the world of labour. SA men immediately took over the offices and assets of every union and a single Labour Front was established, with all officials drawn from the Nazi Party. Leipart, the chairman of the former council of the unions (the ADGB), desperately offered union collaboration and conformity with Nazi laws, but this offer was rejected. The Front received full powers under the Labour Laws of January and October 1934.

While workers may have welcomed Hitler's promise of industrial peace, the Labour Front deprived them of any bargaining mechanism; the employer was 'leader' and the workers 'followers'; wages were set by the Front and compulsory deductions made for income tax and for obligatory charities such as Winterhilfe, or instalment payments for the future Volkswagen. From February 1935 every worker had a 'work-book', recording his employment record, and no one could be employed without one. From 1937 the Labour Front had full control of wages and ensured that the pay freeze, decreed in 1933, was effective; thus workers had little or no effective increase in wages in the face of increased costs of living (▶Trustees of Labour). The Labour Front had become a gigantic state prison from which workers had no way out. At the same time, based on the funds seized from the original unions, the Labour Front became an immense business which financed the *Kraft durch Freude* (Strength through Joy) movement.

Yet it is highly doubtful whether more than a small minority of politically conscious German workers felt the restraints of the system. The Nazi achievement of much higher rates of employment affected German workers more directly in this pre-war period; and, perhaps even more so, the whole brilliant package of Nazi rallies, parades, graphics, speeches and music directed the German worker's attention away from the legal framework within which he was constrained.

Labour service (*Reichsarbeitsdienst* – RAD).   Introduced by a law of 26 June 1935, RAD enforced six months' labour service for all men between the ages of nineteen and twenty-five. Men called for labour service worked mostly in agriculture or public works; women, who were later included, were used in domestic service and traditionally female agricultural tasks.

The immediate effects of RAD were to reduce the unemployment figures at a time when this was crucial to Hitler's popular standing.

Lagarde, Paul Anton de (1827–1891).   German philosopher whose work foreshadowed National Socialism. A noted Arabist, Lagarde became professor of Oriental Philosophy at Göttingen in 1869. His political works advocated a national moral cleansing and were racist and deeply anti-semitic in content. In his most inflammatory writings he rejected 'humanitarian principles' when dealing with Jews and can be considered, through his influence on Rosenberg, a direct contributor to Nazi genocidal policies.

Lammers, Hans Heinrich (1879–1962).   Head of administration in the Reich Chancellery from 1933 to the end of the Third Reich. A long-serving civil servant who pleaded at Nuremberg that he only obeyed orders.

Lammers was appointed for his efficiency rather than his politics. In 1940 he accepted senior SS rank; and, with Keitel and Bormann, by 1943 formed the close inner circle, the Committee of Three, which filtered all problems before they reached Hitler. Lammers saw this as a means of improving the efficiency of administration of the Reich. To Bormann it was an instrument of power. In the last days of the Reich, Lammers was with Göring in Bavaria, with whom his arrest was ordered by Hitler in April 1945.

Land.   The fifteen states in the Third Reich. The boundary and term were adopted from the Weimar Republic and represent much earlier political divisions in Germany. In the Third Reich each *Land* was subject to the administration of a *Reichsstatthalter*.

Landbund.   The farmers' association of the Third Reich ➤Agriculture in the Third Reich.

Landsberg.   The Bavarian town where Hitler was imprisoned after his arrest in 1923, following the failed Beer Hall Putsch.

In Landsberg prison, Hitler was given special treatment, wore his own clothes, was provided with his own rooms and diet, and allowed free association with the forty other Nazis imprisoned with him. He had as many visitors as he chose and Landsberg became his 'school of higher education'. He began dictating *Mein Kampf* to his faithful fellow-prisoner and secretary, Rudolf Hess, and was still working on the first volume when he was released in November 1924.

After WWII Nazi war criminals were held in Landsberg prison and the last executions of those condemned at Nuremberg, the six Einsatzgruppen leaders, were carried out there in 1951.

Larsen, Leif (1906–1990).   Member of the Royal Norwegian Navy's Special Service Unit. After the German invasion of Norway in 1940, Larsen achieved almost legendary status through his work in running men and arms from Britain to occupied Norway. Larsen was involved in attempts of extraordinary heroism to sink the German battleship *Tirpitz*, at that time sheltering in Altenfjord, and he emerged from the war one of the most decorated men in the Allied forces. It was the relentless efforts of men like Larsen throughout occupied Europe that tied down large numbers of German soldiers in police and occupational roles while the Third Reich was desperately short of manpower on the Eastern Front.

League of Nations.   Established in January 1920 on the ratification of the Treaty of Versailles, its stated object was to keep international peace and provide an arbitrating body for disputes. Although the idea came from US President Wilson, the USA did not become a member. Germany was admitted and given a permanent seat on the Council after the Treaty of Locarno in September 1925. This was seen by the supporters of the Weimar Republic as a triumph for its Foreign Minister, Stresemann. But nationalists in Germany, the Nazis among them, saw the League as an agency of the Allied powers, enforcing the Versailles territorial settlements. Hitler took Germany out of the League in October 1933, having demanded immediate parity in armaments. Russia joined next year, but the League took no effective action against German rearmament. This failure, followed by failure to stop either Italy's attack on Ethiopia, or the Japanese invasion of China, or to intervene in the Spanish Civil War, lost the League any influence it might have had.

***Lebensborn* (The Source of Life)**.   Fanciful title given to the system of maternity homes and welfare for the mothers of SS-fathered children.

The *Lebensborn* organization was a social welfare system in a period when contraception and abortion were illegal and the divorce rate had increased. It was designed to handle the growing number of illegitimate children and to ensure that the children of SS men and suitably Aryan girls should be well cared for. Although the specially provided homes should have given first-rate conditions for SS parents, an investigation by the thorough and reliable SS researcher Richard Korherr showed that they had encouraged no higher SS birthrate than the current German national average and that the common corruption in SS organizations had led to an infant mortality *higher* than average: 8 per cent against the national 6 per cent. The *Lebensborn* homes were not, as has been suggested, a chain of SS brothels – although the arrangement permitted and encouraged the bedding of suitable girls with SS men for the purpose of stock-rearing rather than for simple pleasure. Nor (to the extent supposed) was the system a cover for the kidnapping of Aryan-looking Polish children, although by the beginning of 1942 this practice was decreed and had begun.

Lebensraum (Living space).   A slogan of German expansionism which was used also for demands for a colonial empire long before WWI. Hitler believed in the claim that Germany was over-populated and needed more farmland to support itself – an idea linked with autarky (the need for a nation to be self-sufficient). Further, expansionists believed Germany had a natural right to some of the lands on her borders and could not accept their control by minor nations. Given the Nazi theory of race, it seemed natural to demand land from the inferior Slav peoples of Poland and Russia. The SS set up a department, the RuSHA, to plan for and carry out the settlement of German people on lands forcibly vacated.

Leber, Julius (1891 – 1945).   A socialist Reichstag deputy who had helped overthrow the Kapp Putsch in Berlin in 1920 and was a constant opponent of Nazism. From 1933 to 1937 he was in concentration camps; on his release he made contact with the Kreisau Circle, Gördeler and von Stauffenberg. He was arrested shortly before the July 1944 Bomb Plot on suspicion of being in touch with communists, was tried by the People's Court and hanged in January 1945.

Leibstandarte SS.   The SS unit specifically charged with the protection of the Führer.

Leibwache.   In the violent politics of the Weimar Republic, many (perhaps most) political leaders employed bodyguards (*Leibwache*). Hitler's *Leibwache* developed into the SS Stabwache and later still into the Stosstruppe, before its final manifestation as the Leibstandarte Adolf Hitler, a full-sized bodyguard regiment. ➤SS: Groupings and organizations

Lettow-Vorbeck, Paul von (1870 – 1964).   WWI general, the hero of the East Africa campaign, 1914 – 18. Returning home to Germany in March 1919, he paraded his men through Berlin in uniform, carrying their arms, as the only undefeated German army. Their brown tropical shirts were later copied by the new SA who made their shirts from a consignment which had not reached East Africa; hence Brownshirts.

Von Lettow was a Reichstag member from 1920 to 1930. As a general much admired by the British in 1935 he was offered the ambassadorship to London by Hitler. He refused and thereafter was watched and harassed by the SS, but there is no evidence of a resistance movement gathering about him, and he was allowed to survive the aftermath of the July 1944 Bomb Plot.

Leuschner, Wilhelm (1888 – 1944).   Trade Unionist and leading member of the resistance. A moderate in German politics in the 1920s, he became deputy president of the Trade Union Association in the year the Nazis came to power.

In May 1933 when Robert Ley occupied the offices of Trade Unions, Leuschner was arrested along with other leading German Trade Unionists.

After his release he became engaged in resistance work and maintained contacts with a wide range of resistants. In 1938 he was connected with the Heinz plan to assassinate Hitler which was abandoned on the news of the Munich Agreement. During the war he worked with Beck and Gördeler to bring about the downfall of Nazism. Arrested as one of the July Bomb Plot conspirators, he was hanged in September 1944.

Ley, Robert (1890–1945). A Rhinelander who became a Nazi in 1924 and followed Hitler rather than Strasser. He was rewarded by being made Gauleiter of Cologne from 1928, and in 1932 he replaced Strasser as Party organization leader. On the Nazi election victory of 1933, Ley took over the trades union movement, as leader of the Labour Front (DAF). With confiscated union funds, he started the immense *Kraft durch Freude* (Strength through Joy) movement, the system of workers' advance payments for the Volkswagen and the élite Party training schools, the *Ordensburgen*.

With his violent anti-semitism, his reputation for drunkenness and his vulgar ostentation, Ley exemplified the coarse, corrupt face of Nazism. Hitler trusted him to the end, however, and gave him command of a mythical *Freikorps Adolf Hitler* in April 1945.

Captured by the Americans, he was selected to be tried among the major criminals at Nuremberg. He wrote to Henry Ford in the USA asking for employment when it was all over, but hanged himself in his cell before judgement.

Lichterfelde Barracks. Headquarters near Berlin of the *Leibstandarte* SS Adolf Hitler, the Führer's bodyguard regiment.

Lidice. Czechoslovakian village which was the scene, in 1942, of a violent reprisal for the assassination of Reinhard Heydrich. ►Heydrich

'Lili Marlene'. A popular song of WWII, often heard by the British 8th Army in North Africa on the radios of the Afrika Korps. The British 'captured' it, and through them it became internationally famous. The song had started as a poem, 'Lili Marleen', by Hans Leip written in 1923. Set to music by Norbert Schulze in 1936, it was made popular in Germany by a record made during the war by the Swedish singer Lale Andersen.

Lindbergh, Charles Augustus (1902–74). US aviator who became world famous in 1927 for the first solo flight across the Atlantic in his aircraft *Spirit of St Louis*. In the mid-1930s he was inclined to look favourably on Nazi Germany and Göring used him to publicize the growing might of the Luftwaffe. Lindbergh's assessment of German air power played some part in persuading Joseph Kennedy, US ambassador to Britain, that the RAF would lose command of the sky and thus that the British would lose the war. By this time, however, Lindbergh was in no position to make public statements; he had already been transferred (it is suggested on Roosevelt's own order) from the reserve to active air duty.

List, Wilhelm (1880–1971).   An army general who remained loyal to the Nazi view of the 1938 Blomberg–Fritsch crisis.

One of the field marshals created in 1940, he led the Balkan campaign of 1941 and had command of an Army Group in southern Russia. In 1942 Hitler abruptly dismissed him for lack of success. He was not one of the senior officers approached by conspirators.

Literature in the Third Reich.   Like all the other arts of the period, theatre, cinema, painting and music, literature was profoundly affected by the Nazi assumption of power. The new tone was set by the 'Burning of the Books' in May 1933. Many of the most eminent German writers (such internationally known figures as Thomas Mann, Emil Ludwig, Leon Feuchtwanger, Stefan Zweig and Erich Maria Remarque) went into exile, along with equally well known dramatists like Ernst Toller and Bertolt Brecht. But the existence of a large reading public in Germany ensured a good living for those authors who were prepared either to act as advocates of Nazi attitudes or to remain totally apolitical.

Among the more successful authors receiving official patronage from the Party were: Hans Grimm, whose best-selling *People without Space* (first published 1926) was a fictional justification of *Lebensraum*, and Hans Carossa, whose novels adroitly managed to avoid raising any of the issues which were at the centre of life in Nazi Germany. Heinz Steguweit, Edwin Eric Dwinger and Wermer Beumelburg were leading examples of the Fronterlebnis school, their novels almost entirely concerned with the camaraderie of the trenches during WWI. Borries von Münchhausen (a descendant of the swashbuckling heroic liar, Baron Münchhausen) wrote chivalric works in ballad form mostly set in East Prussia. Like a number of other supporters of the regime, he killed himself in 1945.

Another important and (to the Party) valuable form of writing consisted of the regional novel. Sometimes this emphasized the rich elements of Christian, usually Catholic, religiosity in peasant life. Ernst Wiechert specialized in this kind of writing, as did H. Kunkel. Rather similar but essentially pagan in tone was the *Blut und Boden* ('blood and soil') style of novel, of which Herbert Bohme was a leading exponent.

Some authors, like Erich Kästner (author of *Emil and the Detectives*), stayed in Germany but were forbidden to publish. Others, like Friedrich Georg Junger, were banned; yet again, others, like Albrecht Haushofer (whose well-known poems, *Moabiter Sonette*, were written in prison), were executed as anti-Hitler conspirators.

Perhaps the ultimate comment on the literature of the Third Reich is that – despite a huge increase in public libraries from 6,000 in 1933 to 35,000 in 1943 and a rapid growth in the number of publishers and book shops – the best-selling book throughout the whole period was *Mein Kampf*, which sold more than 6 million copies. ➤Book burning; Göbbels, Josef

Locarno Pact. A non-aggression treaty of 1925 between Germany, France and Belgium, guaranteed by Britain and Italy. The demilitarization of the Rhineland was recognized as permanent and German, French and Belgian post-Versailles frontiers were mutually accepted. Finally, Germany was brought into the League of Nations. Stresemann, for Germany, seemed to have brought Europe to an age of peace. An atmosphere of optimism generated later talk of an 'eastern Locarno' to agree on German–Polish borders, but this was something that no Weimar government dared do. While Strasser saw Locarno as an Anglo-French plot to use the Germans as cannon fodder against the Russians, Hitler (in *Mein Kampf*) welcomed the idea of an alliance with Britain against Russia. In 1935 (after Locarno had been reaffirmed at Stresa) Hitler openly announced German rearmament; in March 1936 he renounced Locarno and sent troops into the Rhineland.

Lochner, Louis P. Head of the Associated Press Bureau in Berlin. From at least 1939 Lochner established contact with the German resistance at the highest levels. In 1941 he was asked by a meeting of resistants including trade unionists Haberman and Letterhause, Otto John and Klaus Bonhöffer (on behalf of Canaris and Beck) to brief President Roosevelt on the aims and principles of the Resistance. The secondary object was to establish direct radio contact between Washington and themselves. Detained in December 1941, Lochner was only repatriated in June the following year. By then the complex relationship of the Soviet Union and the Western Allies demanded that Washington ignore any approach from the German resistance. More than that, the maintenance of this delicate balance of distrust between the Soviet Union and the West required that the US withhold any recognition that there *was* a German resistance.

Lord Haw-Haw. ➤Joyce, William

Lubbe, Marius van der (1909–34). A Dutch bricklayer, associated with anarchists, he was found in the Reichstag building at the time of the Reichstag Fire in February 1933. He was tried publicly and sentenced to death under a special retroactive law, the Lex van der Lubbe. The Nazis chose to execute him by beheading as a signal to the world that old Germanic traditions were being brought back. Was this half-blind, subnormal man indeed the arsonist, or was he set up by the Nazis? The debate is still going on.

Lublin. Location of a concentration camp, also known as Majdanek. Lublin was fitted with gas chambers in the autumn of 1942. By the end, 200,000 people had been murdered there. ➤Concentration Camps

Lucy.   The code-name for a group under Sandor Rado which transmitted information to Russia from a base in Switzerland, until the Swiss authorities broke it up in 1944.

Rado was a Hungarian who had fled from his country after the post-WWI communist government of Bela Kun had fallen. He became a journalist in Austria and Germany, running a Russian-assisted news agency until it became too dangerous under the Third Reich. In 1936 he was sent by Russian intelligence to open an agency in Switzerland. Rado became a 'head agent' for the Russians with the code-name 'Dora'. In 1942 he was offered a source of information on German actions against Russia, provided he did not track the source back. This he called the 'Lucy Ring' and began transmitting its information to Moscow (who admitted its accuracy but suspected it of being from the *Abwehr* and therefore not trustworthy). The key figure in 'Lucy' was a Protestant Bavarian journalist, Rudolf Rössler, who, horrified by the Nazis, had left Germany for Switzerland in 1934 and was used by some officers of Swiss army intelligence to leak out anti-Nazi information. But the quality of the information (including details of the German army's offensive plans in April 1943) went beyond that available to Swiss intelligence. Further sources have been suggested, including Canaris of the *Abwehr* (German military intelligence) with Gisevius as his courier. It has also been suggested that 'Lucy' was used as a channel for selected items of British intelligence learnt from decoding German signals through the 'Enigma' operation at their Bletchley Park centre. At the end of WWII Rado and others of the Lucy Ring were tried by the Swiss and sentenced to imprisonment. When Rado returned to Moscow he was imprisoned by the Soviets for reasons unknown and was not released until the post-Stalin era.

Ludendorff, Erich (1865–1937).   Military hero of both East and West Fronts in WWI; Chief of Staff to Hindenburg. In 1919 he fled from Germany, but returned to set up an anti-republican group in Berlin where he conspired in the Kapp Putsch in 1920. Hitler brought him into the Beer Hall Putsch in Munich in 1923 and he was tried with Hitler and the others, but to his outspoken indignation he was found not guilty and left the court to shouts of 'Heil Ludendorff!'

In 1923 and 1924, while the Nazi Party was banned, he joined with Gregor Strasser in the 'National Socialist Freedom Party'. He later served as a Reichstag Nazi deputy, but his politico-religious views moved further away from Hitler and his relations with the Third Reich were only ceremonial until his death.

Luftwaffe.   The air forces of the Third Reich. Although military aircraft were forbidden by the Treaty of Versailles, the Weimar Republic began early to plan an air arm. As early as 1923 General von Seeckt, as commander of the army, arranged for aircrew training in Russia, while in Germany gliding clubs were encouraged in order to build a reserve of potential pilots.

At the same time, though military aircraft were forbidden, the design and manufacture of civil aircraft was permitted. Hugo Junkers had designed transport aircraft at the end of WWI and developed the first all-metal transport mono-plane. The Junkers factory employed as a manager Erhard Milch whom Junkers moved into the state-subsidized airline Lufthansa to be its chief executive in 1929. Conditions now existed for the rapid development of a German military air arm. Lufthansa already possessed a large flying school and signals and meteorological stations at all airports. By the time of the Nazi takeover in 1933 Milch, with Göring as Minister, controlled everything they needed for a military air force. By March 1935 they were ready for the public announcement of the formation of an air force, the Luftwaffe.

The first Luftwaffe Chief of General Staff, Wever, was killed in an air crash in 1936, before his plans had got underway. He had a background as an artillery officer and, unlike the glamorous fighter pilots of WWI, Göring and Udet, who in fact dominated the formative years of the Luftwaffe, Wever would undoubtedly have developed a stronger bomber force.

In the event the Luftwaffe's main combat aircraft were Messerschmitt's single-engine BF109 and the twin-engined Me110. The mainstay of the Luftwaffe in its early days was the Junkers 52 transport plane which was in service with Lufthansa by 1932. It was tried in Spain as a bomber, but not found successful. More successful was the Dornier D017 bomber, originally a high-speed mail plane, and the Heinkel He111, which were faster than the fighters they met in Spain, but much slower than the British fighters of 1940. The most versatile bomber was the Junkers Ju 88 which came into service in 1939 and in its later versions was in action throughout the war, as bomber, fighter-bomber and, equipped with radar, as a dangerous night-fighter.

The Junkers Ju 87, the two-man, single-engined 'Stuka' divebomber, with its fixed undercarriage and strengthened wing, was successful in Spain and in the early 1939 and 1940 campaigns of WWII, but it was slow and of short range and highly vulnerable to the RAF's Spitfires and Hurricanes.

The Messerschmitt jet fighter, the Me262, had been on the drawing board since 1938, but Hitler's blindness to technical innovation led to its production being delayed so that it appeared only in the last months of the war.

The Luftwaffe maintained control of ground anti-aircraft defences. General Kammhuber as commander of night-fighters from 1940 deployed the radar and defensive searchlights and guns for the air defence of the Reich until he was dismissed and replaced in 1943 with Luftwaffe General Schmid. Anti-aircraft batteries (Flak) were also Luftwaffe formations. Göring's declaration in August 1939 that British bombers would never reach Berlin ('Or you can call me Meier!') was therefore based on his command of all the air defences of the

Reich and, as the bombers made their way through, his reputation collapsed.

Parachute troops came under Luftwaffe command. Although much acclaimed before WWII as the key to modern warfare and demonstrated in manoeuvres in the 1930s by the Russians, they were used only as special forces by the Germans, attacking Western Front forts in 1940, Crete in 1941 and, under Skorzeny of the SS, in snatching Mussolini out of captivity. They were often used as shock troops or reorganized as infantry. Their General, Student, had command of an Army Group in the west in 1944–5 which included both army and Luftwaffe troops. Göring's other army, the 'Hermann Göring Panzer Division', although virtually part of the army, remained officially listed as Luftwaffe.

The early Luftwaffe bombing successes (Guernica in 1937, Warsaw in 1939 and Rotterdam in 1940) were against targets with little defence. In 1940 its attacks on Britain (the 'Battle of Britain') aimed to draw the RAF fighters out to defend coastal shipping and to destroy them in the air and on their airfields. But this priority was abandoned under political pressure, and the Luftwaffe was directed to attack London and other cities. The Luftwaffe now found that their technical advances were equalled or outmatched by the British in radar and aircraft performance, and heavy German losses ensued. During 1941 the German air attack on Britain slowed down and Hitler's war planning was directed towards Russia. The failure of the Luftwaffe to destroy RAF Fighter Command marked the watershed in the air war. The Luftwaffe was to remain a formidable fighting force wherever it was deployed, but the crucial battlefield now changed to the skies over Germany itself. At first the RAF's night raids presaged little of the might of the Lancaster and Halifax bombers. By 1943 large formations of the US 8th Air Force had joined the bombing campaign against the Reich. In 1943 when the RAF dropped 'window' (metal strips which confused radar interception) Kammhuber was dismissed and Schmid was forced to develop new tactics of night-fighting with radar-equipped fighters or head-on attacks at the massed formations of USAAF daylight bombers.

In the Russian campaign the Luftwaffe was markedly superior in aircraft design and pilot training; most German ace fighter pilots made their large scores on this front (Major Erich Hartmann was credited with 352 victories). Although the Russians later developed effective ground-attack aircraft, the Luftwaffe retained air superiority in the east until 1945.

The Luftwaffe surprisingly retained high morale to the end and, unlike the army, never had an SS rival organization for Hitler to prefer. When von Greim flew into Berlin with the famous woman pilot Hanna Reitsch in April 1945, Hitler performed his last act of promotion, making him Field Marshal and commander of an air force which, in practical terms, no longer existed.

Lüger, Karl (1844–1910). The mayor of Vienna 1897–1910, when Hitler lived there as a youth. In *Mein Kampf* Hitler called him 'the last great German to be born in Ostmark [Austria]'.

Lüger was a leader of the fiercely anti-semitic 'Christian-Socialist' Party of the Austrian Empire. Although he had been elected Mayor of Vienna, the Emperor had at first refused to appoint him. Hitler admired him for his manipulation of all possible institutions or means to achieve his ends. His mass-membership Party was the origin of a 'German Workers' Party' in the Austrian Empire, which defended the German-speaking artisan against cheap Czech labour and was an ideological forerunner of the Party in Munich which Hitler transformed into the Nazi Party.

Luther, Martin (1895−1945).   Policy adviser in Ribbentrop's Bureau and later in the Foreign Ministry. In May 1940 he was appointed the Ministry's liaison with the SS. A strong anti-semite, he attended the Wannsee Conference on behalf of his Ministry, but seems to have misunderstood the significance of the 'Final Solution', since he was reported to be worried about the large-scale resettlement needed. With Schellenberg, head of SS foreign intelligence, he tried to oust Ribbentrop from his post as Minister, but Himmler would not co-operate. His plot was discovered and he was sent to Sachsenhausen concentration camp. He was liberated by the Russians, but died soon after, in May 1945.

Lutze, Victor (1890−1943).   SA leader in Hanover. He reported secretly to Hitler on Röhm's plans to make the SA a National Socialist army and was used by Hitler to draw up murder lists for the Night of the Long Knives. Lutze accompanied Hitler to Munich to arrest Röhm and after the SA leader's death was promoted to be the next leader of the SA. But it was an SA which was now to decline rapidly in importance in the Nazi state; never again would it, even remotely, be in a position to challenge the army or Hitler's leadership of the Nazi Party. Lutze, by now a minor figure in the hierarchy, was killed in a car crash in May 1943 when on a food foraging expedition outside Berlin.

M

Madagascar. As a solution to what the National Socialists insisted was the 'Jewish Problem', the idea of deporting Jews to the large island of Madagascar came up from time to time before the war. As a proposal it was probably as serious as many of Himmler's fantasies. By 1941, however, the Madagascar option was no more than a smokescreen for the true nature of the Final Solution. ►Anti-semitism

Madam Kitty's. Berlin brothel run by the SD and staffed by SS girls. Foreign statesmen were taken there (Count Ciano was a frequent visitor) and conversations were recorded by dour Gestapo men working in the basement. It is doubtful if anything of value to the Third Reich's war effort emerged from Madam Kitty's. The recordings are believed still to exist in the former East Berlin police archives.

Mailed Fist (*Eiserne Faust*). One of many groups formed in 1919 to terrorize supporters of the Weimar Republic and to destabilize the state. It was as a member of the *Eiserne Faust* that Adolf Hitler met the leaders of the German Workers' Party.

Majdanek. ►Lublin

M.A.N. Resistance group and anti-Nazi organization. In 1934 and 1935, some 700 Social Democrats were arrested in Bavaria. The anti-state activities had been centred on the M.A.N. heavy engineering plant at Augsburg and the wave of arrests persuaded the Gestapo that dissent had been eradicated. But the workers there, led by Bebo Wager, reorganized to form an effective resistance unit, with contacts in Austria, Italy, Hungary and Switzerland. Wager's M.A.N. group was unusual in contemplating *armed* resistance from an early stage, and by 1940 they were collecting arms and training.

The numbers involved in the M.A.N. group are unknown but are likely to have been significant. When the Gestapo struck again in 1942, fifty of the leaders of the unit were said to be arrested. Bebo Wager was among them. He was executed, still working on anti-Nazi literature while in jail, in August 1943.

Mann, Thomas (1875–1955). Outstanding German novelist of the twentieth century. Winner of the Nobel Prize for Literature, 1929; author of *Buddenbrooks* 1901, *Death in Venice* 1913, *Magic Mountain* 1924, *Doctor Faustus* 1947. A convinced democrat and believer in old-fashioned German liberalism, he left Germany in 1933. His books were burnt and German nationality taken from him. Obtaining Czechoslovak papers, he lived in Switzerland and the US, lecturing at Princeton in 1938. He died in Switzerland.

Manstein, Field-Marshal Fritz Erich von (1887–1973). Recognized by most historians to have been one of the most brilliant Nazi military strategists. As a major-general and Chief of Staff to von Rundstedt in Army Group South in 1939, he suggested the invasion plan of France which was used by Hitler with spectacular results. In June 1941 in the invasion of Russia he commanded 56th Panzer Corps on the northern flank and made swift advances. Later that year he took command of the 11th Army on the south-east front which cut through the Crimea and took Sevastopol. In July of the next year Manstein was promoted to Field Marshal, and that autumn was given command of Army Group Don. He tried unsuccessfully to relieve the 6th Army, nominally under his command, which was besieged at Stalingrad. Throughout 1943, Manstein achieved some success (using tactics contrary to Hitler's thinking) in stabilizing the Russian bid to reclaim territory. His strategy at Kursk in July, however, proved a disaster involving heavy tank losses, and his continuing disagreements with the Führer finally led to him being relieved of his command on 25 March 1944 with a courtesy award of the Swords of the Knight's Cross. In Liddell Hart's view, he was the Allies' most formidable military opponent, combining 'modern ideas of manoeuvre, a mastery of technical detail and great driving power'.

Marburg Speech. In June 1934 the Reich Deputy Chancellor, Franz von Papen, gave a public speech at Marburg University criticizing Nazi methods and calling for a return to freedom.

Von Papen was not a Nazi and his speech was largely written for him by conservatives who had come to power with Hitler and had hoped to control the new leader. He condemned the brutal implementation of *Gleichschaltung* and spoke against the attacks on free speech. Although the speech caused much talk, few heard it or read it, for Göbbels refused to broadcast it or have it printed. The main writer of the speech was Edgar Jung, with some contributions from Erich Klausener; within a week, both were murdered in the Röhm Purge.
➤Papen, Franz von

Maurice, Emil (1897–1979). Hitler's companion, bodyguard and chauffeur in the early days of the Party. Trained as a watchmaker, he lived a life of riot and rowdiness, joining the Nazis in 1919. He took part in the 1923 Beer Hall Putsch march and joined the fugitives when it failed. He was arrested and imprisoned with Hitler in Landsberg, where he acted as secretary, taking *Mein Kampf* in dictation until Rudolf Hess took over this role. After their release from prison, Maurice continued as Hitler's chauffeur and was close to his daily life. Hitler feared that Maurice had become Geli Raubal's lover and after the suicide of Geli they became somewhat distanced. Nevertheless in 1934 Maurice was with Hitler on the raid on Röhm and his colleagues, shooting the homosexual Heines and the boy found in his bed. Like others of Hitler's tough friends from his earlier life, he was rewarded with a sinecure far from the corridors of state power: Maurice headed a Munich handicraft workers' guild.

Mauthausen.   A concentration camp located near Linz in Upper Austria. Austrians, Dutch, Italian and Hungarian Jews were sent there from its inception in 1939 onwards. Although it was not an extermination camp (►Sachsenhausen), over 40,000 deaths were recorded in the Mauthausen *Totenbuch* (record of deaths).

Mayer, Helene (1910–53).   A great woman fencing champion who won the Olympic Games Gold Medal for Germany in 1928. She studied law in California from 1932 and, although she had a Jewish mother, she was invited to represent Germany in the 1936 Games, where she won the Silver Medal. She gave the Nazi salute on receiving the medal but returned to the USA where she settled for the rest of her life.

Medals and awards: Adolf Hitler.   As Führer, Adolf Hitler wore only his Iron Cross, First Class (proof of his true front-line heroism), awarded in August 1918. He had previously won the Second Class Iron Cross in 1914. Other medals awarded him in WWI were: a Military Cross 'Third Class with Swords', September 1917; the Regimental Award for Outstanding Bravery and the Medal for the Wounded, both in May 1918; and the Service Medal, Third Class, August 1918.

Mefo Bills.   A financial device invented by Dr Schacht to make payments to arms manufacturers engaged in secret work for German rearmament. The bills were accepted by all German banks but no reference to them was allowed in published accounts. Nevertheless twelve billion marks in Mefo (an acronym for *Metallurgische Forschung* – metals research) bills were issued before the outbreak of WWII, and much of German trade with Eastern Europe was financed by this method.

***Mein Kampf* ('My Struggle')**.   Adolf Hitler's attempt to set out his political dreams. Begun in Landsberg prison with Hess acting as secretary, Volume One was published in 1925 with sales of 9,400. Volume Two followed in 1928 and a cheap edition in 1929. Sales rose to 50,000 in 1930, 90,000 in 1932 and to over one million in 1933. Turgid and appallingly crude, the book reveals Adolf Hitler's political ambitions. Believing in the superiority of a Nordic or Aryan race which was responsible for all that was valuable in modern civilization, he saw a conspiracy, led by the Jews, to spoil the purity of Aryanism by crossbreeding with inferior races. France was indicted as the stronghold of international Jewry; Germany was the most outspoken Aryan power, and WWI was a Jewish conspiracy to destroy that power. Bolshevism (like freemasonry, socialism and democracy) was seen as a trick of the Jews to achieve world domination. Hitler's programme, set out in *Mein Kampf*, was to make a strong Aryan nationalist state, suppressing dissident parties, exiling the Jews and uniting all Germanic people. Expansion should not be through African or Asian colonies but by conquering new lands from the lesser Slavs, and the settlement of German peasants in Eastern Europe and the Ukraine. France would have to be destroyed and, to do this, alliance with Britain and Italy would be necessary. The Nazi publisher Max Amann cut Hitler's original title to two words only from 'My Struggle for Four and a Half Years against Lies, Stupidity and Cowardice'. The royalties, even before the Nazis came to power, made Hitler a wealthy man.

Although widely read in German, only an abridged translation was available in English until 1939, and few people in America or Britain were aware of its full contents.

Meinecke, Friedrich (1862–1954). An eminent liberal historian whose work on the Prussian state was nationalist in tone. But because he had defended the Weimar Republic's right to exist, he was removed from all academic posts when the Nazis came to power. He survived the Third Reich in poverty and was able to write an objective account of how the Nazis had corrupted the leading German academics and soldiers on taking power.

Memel. Baltic seaport with a substantial German-speaking hinterland which was taken from the defeated German Empire and transferred to the new state of Lithuania by the Treaty of Versailles. A local Nazi Party flourished in the 1920s, and demands were made to rejoin Germany. On his successful seizure of the Sudetenland in 1938, Hitler demanded the return of Memel. Lithuania immediately conceded and Memel was returned to Germany in March 1939.

Memorial Day Plot. An attempt on Hitler's life made in March 1943. After the failure of Operation Flash, Tresckow's Smolensk attempt to kill Hitler, the conspirators chose the Heroes' Memorial Day ceremony at the Zeughaus in Berlin the following week, where not only Hitler but some of the other leading figures in the regime were expected to be present. This plot also failed, as had the Smolensk attempt, because of technical problems with the bomb.

Mengele, Joseph (1911–1979?). The notorious Auschwitz doctor in charge of racial experiments, 1943–5.

To create a race of blue-eyed Aryans, he experimented on the living and the dead, specializing in twins, dwarfs, hunchbacks and any physical oddity. Onto twins he grafted skin, bones or organs, and then made comparative post-mortem autopsies. Experimented upon by a medical mediocrity, his victims died painful and totally pointless deaths. No information of medical value is known to have emerged from the tortures inflicted on those Mengele still called his patients. To the camp he became known as 'the Angel of Death' from his selection duties on the entry ramp as transports arrived.

He escaped to Latin America after the war and became one of the most hunted of war criminals. Confessions by his friends and family in 1985 led to the examination of the remains of a man drowned in Brazil in 1979, which were judged to be those of Mengele.

Messerschmitt, Willy Emil (1898 – 1978).   The designer of the Luftwaffe's most widely used fighter aircraft.

As a boy in Frankfurt he had made a glider from the design of a famous early airman, Friedrich Harth. During WWI he was given the opportunity to work with Harth, and in the 1920s he raised the money to buy the Bavarian Aircraft Works and began the design and production of aircraft. Although he was a friend of Rudolf Hess, who had been a wartime pilot, he was not liked by Milch, the head of Lufthansa and the man in charge of German aircraft production. Nevertheless his design for a fighter plane was accepted for the new Luftwaffe in 1935. The Me109 (properly known as the BF109, since it came from the Bayerisch Flugzeugwerke only later known as Messerschmitt) was an all-metal single seater. It entered full production in 1938, although it was first used operationally in Spain in 1937. Several modifications were made and the aircraft remained in production until 1945. The Me109 was in action throughout WWII.

Messerschmitt also designed the twin-engined Me110 as a long-range fighter. It was this aircraft that Hess used for his flight to Scotland in 1941. Many other aircraft came from the Messerschmitt drawing board, including a huge six-engined transport and a rocket-powered fighter. His last wartime plane came into service too late to have its full effect; the world's first jet fighter, the Me262, flew only in small numbers from 1945, outclassing any Allied fighter. Its design was begun as early as 1938, but Göring's production plans for the Luftwaffe ruled it out and Hitler's irrational and negative attitude to developments he did not understand delayed it until too late.

Messerschmitt Me262.   In February 1945 as the Anglo-American air-raids became heavier and German air defence less able to stop them, Hitler agreed to the formation of a special squadron of Me262 jet fighters under Galland with the cream of pilots to man it. The Me262 was the first operational jet fighter in the world and could fly at 540 mph at 20,000 feet. Armed with rockets, it could attack the American daylight bomber formations without their defending piston-engined fighters getting near it. The only feasible Allied counter-measures were to bomb the airfields or to keep standing formations of fighters near them to attack the jets before they could take off.

Fortunately for the Allied air offensive the Führer impeded the development of the Me262 by confusing the role of fighter and fighter-bomber. Albert Speer gives the jet aircraft as an acute example of the deadening effect of political intervention on scientific development in the Third Reich.

Milch, Erhard (1892–1972).   Luftwaffe Field Marshal. Milch's father was Jewish, but he was 'Aryanized' by a statement from his mother that another man had fathered him. After service in WWI as an observer and squadron commander, Milch went into the Junkers aircraft organization and in 1929 became chief executive of Lufthansa. In 1935 he became Inspector General of the new Luftwaffe. He controlled the Condor Legion in Spain, 1936–8, and developed tactics for the new aircraft types. During the Battle of Britain he commanded Air Fleet 3, based in Scandinavia. He succeeded Udet as Luftwaffe Director of Armaments in 1941, but his plans for increasing the bomber fleet were ignored by Göring, who saw him as a rival. He was sentenced at Nuremberg to life imprisonment, but was released in 1954.

Mischling **(People of mixed race)**.   In Nazi racial doctrine, half Jews and quarter Jews represent some difficulties since deportation or extermination of half Jews was also deportation or extermination of half Aryans. ➤Anti-semitism

Mit brennender Sorge **('In Deep Concern')**.   Papal encyclical of 14 March 1937, issued by Pope Pius XI to express the Vatican's dissatisfaction with the Nazi application of the terms of the Concordat between Berlin and the Holy See signed in July 1933. ➤Churches in the Third Reich

Mitford, Unity More Valkyrie ('Bobo') (1914–48).   Aristocratic British supporter of Adolf Hitler. The daughter of Lord Redesdale, sister of the author Nancy Mitford and sister-in-law of the British fascist leader, Sir Oswald Mosley, Unity Mitford was a wayward aristocrat who was studying art in Munich in 1935 when she was introduced to Hitler. He was impressed by the striking golden-haired girl who spoke out with the arrogance of her class. She became his frequent companion, giving rise to rumours that she was the Führer's mistress. When Britain declared war on Germany in September 1939 she went into a Munich park (the *Englischer Garten*) and shot herself in the head. Severely injured, she was cared for on Hitler's orders and sent back to England through Switzerland. She never recovered fully and died of the wound eight years later.

Mittelstand **(The lower-middle class)**.   The *Mittelstand* of small shopkeepers, clerks and factory foremen was the target group for much Nazi recruiting in the 1920s. Economically squeezed by inflation and, later, unemployment, they were prepared to believe that the Jews were responsible and, equally, that the Nazi Party was the only political organization with the will to address the situation.

Molotov, Vyacheslav (1890–1986).   Soviet Foreign Minister throughout the war. Replacing Litvinov (as People's Commissioner for Foreign Affairs) in 1939, Molotov was the executor of Stalin's labyrinthine policy. He was negotiator of the Russo-German Non-aggression Pact in August 1939. During the following year, when German military successes were placing new strains on the Soviet-German relationship, Molotov discussed a four-power (Germany, Russia, Italy and Japan) pact with Hitler in Berlin. The proposal stumbled, however, on the Soviet Union's requirement that German troops should withdraw from Finland. In 1941, when 'Barbarossa' was launched, it was Molotov who announced the attack to the Soviet people.

Molotov's long career at Stalin's side culminated in the arrest of his Jewish wife. It was said that he was too cowardly to mention the problem to Stalin. After Stalin's death, Molotov lost favour in the Khrushchev era and was only totally rehabilitated two years before his own death. He was described by Churchill as effective and 'totally ruthless'.

Molotov Cocktail.   A simple petrol bomb reputedly used by partisans against German forces in Russia and the Balkans. Named after Vyacheslav Molotov.

Moltke, Helmut Graf von (1907–45).   Legal adviser to the OKW. A great-grandnephew of Field Marshal von Moltke of the Franco-Prussian War (1870–71), he was born of a British mother on the Moltke family estate at Kreisau. Here, in the early years of Nazi power, a group of high-minded gentry began to meet, forming what became known as the Kreisau Circle. They discussed what new social order would emerge after Nazism, Moltke adding trades unionists and socialists to the circle which was otherwise aristocratic. They had no plans to overthrow Hitler or the Nazis, for they were essentially pacifist and Christian. Nevertheless Moltke did hold secret meetings with Kirk, the US Chargé at the embassy in Berlin in 1939 and 1940, to try and persuade him of the existence of an effective German opposition to Hitler. He was not successful. Taken by the Gestapo in January 1944 for warning a friend about to be arrested, he was tried for treason and hanged in January 1945.

Montoire.   Meeting of Hitler and Marshal Pétain on 24 October 1940. In secret accords Pétain agreed to support Germany in every way short of military involvement: 'The Axis Powers and France have an identical interest in seeing the defeat of England as soon as possible.' In return for Vichy support, France was to be accorded 'the place to which she is entitled' in the new Europe. It can be argued that Pétain had no choice but to pay lip-service to Hitler's ambitions. Certainly the ancient Marshal had succeeded at Montoire in keeping France out of the war, and Hitler himself professed in later years to believe that he had been 'deceived' by Pétain.

Morell, Theodor (1890–1948).   Hitler's physician. After curing the Nazi photographer, Heinrich Hoffmann, with an injection of the newly available sulphanilamides, Morell was invited to examine Hitler. His diagnosis of 'intestinal exhaustion' appealed to the health crank in the Führer and for the following nine years Hitler submitted to his treatment. A mixture of relatively harmless items like 'bulls' testicles' and more dangerous amphetamines, Morell's treatments may well have contributed to Hitler's later condition which resembled a form of Parkinson's disease.

Though put aside by Hitler in 1944, Morell had become a rich man promoting his own vitamin remedies and even securing the German army contact for lice powder. Though rejected by Hitler and despised by Eva Braun, Morell survived the war to die at Tegernsee in 1948.

Morgen, Konrad (b. 1909).   An assistant SS judge whose function was to look into irregularities in concentration camp administration. Dr Morgen's function accurately encapsulates what most sane people would consider an extraordinary ambivalence in SS attitudes towards its role as exterminator. Amid the transports of Auschwitz or Treblinka, amid the gassing and the burning of bodies, Dr Morgen's brief was first to ensure that *no brutality took place*. His investigative role in combating theft by guards or SS officers is easier to understand. In both functions Morgen acted scrupulously within his brief. In camp after camp he indicted and obtained sentences against SS men for brutality. But his targets were not restricted to lowly members of the general SS. In 1943 he discovered that Karl Koch, the commandant of Buchenwald, had embezzled over 100,000 marks, had falsified documents and concealed murders. Morgen returned with his report to SS headquarters where it went up to Kaltenbrunner (head of security, RUSHA) who in turn sent it to the legal department – each official trying to pass it on rather than handle it – until it reached Himmler. Himmler ordered action to be taken against Koch. Subsequently Morgen was sent to inspect the four extermination camps built by Christian Wirth (Belzec, Majdanek, Sobibor and Treblinka) and returned with 800 cases of corruption and murder. Dr Morgen survived the war to disappear into post-war obscurity.

Morgenthau Plan.   A plan devised by President Roosevelt's Secretary of the Treasury, Henry P. Morgenthau, to reduce Germany, after her defeat, to an agricultural economy. The announcement of the plan at the Quebec Conference of September 1944 (although quickly rejected by F.D.R.) was a serious error on the part of the Allies which enabled Göbbels to present the plan as the alternative to fighting to the last man.

Motor Racing in Germany.   Shortly after coming to power, Adolf Hitler watched an Italian victory at the Berlin Grand Prix at Avus. Angered at the absence of German participation, he directed funds to two companies to construct Grand Prix cars. The two companies selected were Mercedes Benz, based in Stuttgart, and Auto Union, a smaller company based in Chemnitz. Mercedes Benz called on the services of Rudolf Uhlenhaut, an outstanding engineer, and Alfred Neubauer, a German-domiciled Austrian, as team manager. Auto Union employed Dr Ferdinand Porsche, an Austrian who would later be involved with the development of the Volkswagen.

Germany's most distinguished driver, Rudolf Carraciola, led the Mercedes Benz team up to the outbreak of the war, with Manfred von Brauchitsch, nephew of General Walter von Brauchitsch, as second driver. Auto Union called on the services of the Austrian, Hans Stuck.

In common with other sports in Nazi Germany, motor racing was organized on Nazi lines. In 1934, Adolf Huhnlein was appointed *Sportskorpsführer* of Motor Sports, rapidly becoming a familiar Nazi figure all over Germany. Military parades and much officialdom were a feature of meetings, but standards of track-marshalling and organization were high.

In July 1934, the Mercedes Benz W25 and the Auto Union A Type made their international debut at Monthlery, in the French Grand Prix. Mechanical problems, however, eliminated nearly all the German cars. But by the end of the season, German cars were dominant and Stuck won the German Grand Prix. In 1935 Rudolf Carraciola was acclaimed European Champion, after an outstanding season for Mercedes Benz.

In 1936, Auto Union swept all before them, with Bernd Rosemeyer being acclaimed European Champion. By contrast, Mercedes Benz could manage only one major victory. In 1937, they regained their dominance with the immensely powerful W125 and Carraciola was again proclaimed European Champion.

The next two years saw Germany dominant in the sport. Carraciola became champion again in 1938 but his pre-eminent position in the team was now under challenge from Hermann Lang, a former mechanic, and the English driver Richard Seaman. Seaman won the 1938 German Grand Prix (much to the embarrassment of Huhnlein), but was fatally injured in the closing stages of the Belgian Grand Prix the following year. The Czech crisis of 1938 nearly caused the Donnington Grand Prix in England to be cancelled. With the Munich Agreement signed, the race took place and was won by Nuvolari, driving for Germany.

1939 saw Hermann Lang the leader. On the day England and France declared war on Germany, Nuvolari drove an Auto Union car to victory in the poorly-supported Yugoslavian Grand Prix at Belgrade, which brought the curtain down on international motor racing for six years.

Muchow Plan.   An organizational structure for sections of the Nazi Party membership devised by Reinhold Muchow. One of the *Alte Kämpfer* and a leader of the Berlin Gau, Muchow worked to perfect a vertical Party structure covering everything from a section (several streets or eighty blocks in size) to a basic Party cell of half a dozen members. ➤Nazi Party

Müller, Friedrich Max (1823–1900).   German philologist who invented the term 'Aryan' to describe a group of Indo-European languages. Before he died Müller warned unsuccessfully against extending the meaning of his neologism to race or racial characteristics. ➤Race

Müller, Heinrich (b. 1896). Bavarian police expert on politics and the surveillance of communists. Selected by Heydrich to take over the Gestapo from Göring's man, Diels, Müller had already had a long, unpublicized association with the Nazis, although he had avoided compromising his position by joining the Party. He is believed, for instance, to have been called in by Bormann to cover up the possible scandal of the suicide of Hitler's niece and probable lover, Geli Raubal.

As head of the SS RUSHA Amt IV, the bureaucratic office that was Gestapo headquarters, Müller directed the department run by Eichmann that carried the Final Solution into action. His position remained unchanged to the end and the promotions and changes that followed the murder of Heydrich in 1942 did not affect him; he continued to serve under Kaltenbrunner. Mass murder and the running down and detaining of political suspects were daily administrative acts to him. He shunned the limelight, and there are no satisfactory photographs of him.

He is believed to have planned an escape long in advance, and the mystery of his disappearance remains. It has been suggested that he was in touch with the Russians (and indeed that he may have had contact with their secret police for many years). Müller was last seen in Berlin in the last weeks of the war and then he vanished. ➤Gestapo

Müller, Josef (b. 1898). Munich lawyer and a devout Catholic who used the Vatican to make contact with the British.

He was known as 'Joe the Ox' (*Ochsensepp*) not because of his physique but because as a peasant schoolboy he had driven oxen. He became prominent in the nationalist Bavarian People's Party and a well-known adviser to church institutions. He was picked by the Vatican to warn the Austrian bishops of the dangers of working with the Nazis after the 1938 *Anschluss*. Oster of German military intelligence saw him as a reliable envoy on behalf of the German resistance and arranged to send Müller to the Vatican as an *Abwehr* officer in 1939.

His contacts with the British were discovered by the SD and he was arrested in April 1943. His marriage was (inaccurately) rumoured to have been conducted by Pope Pius XII, and this story probably helped his survival. Held first in Buchenwald, he was moved from camp to camp, until liberated by the US army from Dachau in 1945.

Müller, Ludwig (1883–1946). 'Reich Bishop', and armed forces chaplain who was outspokenly nationalistic and anti-semitic. He became a leading figure in the association of German Christians and a friend of leading Nazi army officers, notably von Reichenau. With this support, Müller was elected Reich Bishop of the Protestant Church in 1933. The Protestant opposition to this Nazi group came to be known as the Confessional Church. Led by other bishops and outspoken men like Pastor Niemöller, in 1934 the Confessional

Church declared itself the only legitimate church. Müller remained a titular bishop, without influence in state, Party or church. He killed himself in 1946. ►Churches in the Third Reich

Munich Agreement.   An agreement signed in September 1938 between Germany, Italy, France and Britain ceding the German-speaking Sudetenland of Czechoslovakia to Germany. In August, Hitler had mobilized his army and threatened to attack the Czechs. Chamberlain flew to Berchtesgaden to dissuade him and, with Daladier, recommended that the Czechs should make some concessions. On a second flight to Germany, Chamberlain met Hitler at Godesberg near Bonn, where Hitler now presented him with greater demands. War seemed inevitable, and the Anglo-French advised the Czechs to prepare for it. But Mussolini suggested another meeting at Munich, where Hitler slightly modified his demands. Chamberlain and Daladier judged them accept-able, though neither Czechoslovakia nor Soviet Russia, bound by treaties to France, were present at this meeting. The lands were handed over without any consultation with their inhabitants. Chamberlain flew back to London and declared that he had obtained 'peace for our time'.

The German generals were taken by surprise. A number of them, such as Fritsch and Beck, had long assumed that Hitler's bluff would be called by Britain, but by September they themselves had both been replaced, Chamberlain's appeasement policy having given Hitler the opportunity to dominate the generals. In March 1939 Hitler marched into the remainder of Czechoslovakia unopposed. Czech President Beneš resigned and in England led a Czech government in exile.

The leading personalities at the Munich meeting were:

Germany: Hitler, Ribbentrop, Göring, von Neurath, Abetz (Ribben-
trop's representative in Paris), Himmler, Hess and Keitel
UK: Chamberlain, Henderson (Ambassador to Germany) and Dunglass
(later the British Prime Minister Douglas Home)
France: Daladier, Alexis Léger (Foreign Minister) and François-Poncet
Italy: Mussolini and Ciano

►Appeasement

Music in the Third Reich.   During the Weimar Republic, Germany retained its reputation as the West's most active centre of music, of musical experiment and performance. Atonal music, developed in the later works of Richard Strauss, Hindemith, Schönberg and Alban Berg, was an entirely Germanic phenomenon. But while experiment flourished, the more traditional composers were far from ignored. There were important festivals (Wagner at Bayreuth, Mozart at Salzburg), while performances of the other great classical and romantic composers were given added lustre by the five great conductors of the period: Felix Weingartner, Wil-helm Furtwängler, Otto Klemperer, Bruno Walter and Erich Kleiber.

With the advent of Nazi power in 1933 this glittering scene underwent almost total eclipse. Atonality was condemned as decadent and a stream of musical emigrants – composers, conductors and performers – began to leave for friendlier environments. Among the most famous were the composers Schönberg, Hindemith and Kurt Weill, and the performers Artur Schnabel, Lotte Lehmann, and Elisabeth Schumann. Of the great conductors, Walter, Klemperer and Kleiber left the Third Reich, banned as non-Aryans, and Weingartner returned to Austria. Wilhelm Furtwängler, however, remained.

The official Nazi line was expressed through the medium of a Reich Chamber of Music whose first president was Richard Strauss, though he resigned in 1935, perhaps because of official displeasure at his collaboration with the Jewish librettist, Stefan Zweig. Hitler, to whom the works of Wagner had always been a source of inspiration, became deeply involved in the Bayreuth Festival, awarding it a large annual subsidy and complete tax exemption. The Festival became an important event in the Nazi calendar and was extensively used in Nazi propaganda.

Before 1939, ideology had already penetrated art. Musicologists in the Third Reich became involved in complex ideological discussions on the necessity for important works to be composed in a major rather than a minor key; similar ideological concerns even led to performances of Schumann being played 'in a heroic manner'.

In the field of popular music, American jazz and swing particularly attracted the hatred and scorn of the Nazi musical establishment. The saxophone was banned as a symbol of Negro decadence – though it is true that when Jack Hylton's dance band played at the Berlin Press Ball in 1937 both Göring and Göbbels danced to the music. In the darker days of the war, jazz (particularly in Holland and France) would become symbolic resistance music.

Among the most successful and approved younger composers in the Third Reich were Werner Egk and Carl Orff. Egk's *The Magic Violin* proved enormously popular and represented virtually a new kind of folk opera. Both Egk and Carl Orff received the Party stamp of approval when they were commissioned to write music for the 1936 Olympic Games. Thereafter, Orff went on to write many successful works, including *Carmina Burana*, based on medieval themes, and his best-known opera *Die Kluge* ('The Clever Woman'), composed in 1941–2.

Mussert, Anton (1894–1946). Dutch Quisling leader. Founder of the national socialist movement in the Netherlands, Mussert was named by the occupying power in 1942 leader of the Dutch people. In a nation so fiercely anti-Nazi, Mussert's following was not large. As the war ended he was arrested and, after a trial at which he was charged as a collaborator, hanged at The Hague in 1946.

Mussolini, Benito (1883–1945). Italian fascist dictator whose takeover of the Italian state by his 'March on Rome' in 1922 impressed Hitler and was the inspiration for his 1923 Beer Hall Putsch. Mussolini's use of slogans, black uniforms, special salutes and his Party's national organization were a model for the early Nazis. However, once Hitler had become Chancellor of Germany, the importance of Mussolini to Hitler decreased. Their interests in Austria conflicted and Hitler was determined not to be the second-best leader in Europe. He ensured Italy's collaboration in the Spanish Civil War in 1936 and that Italy signed both the Rome–Berlin Axis that October and the Anti-Comintern Pact in 1937. The first time the two dictators met was in Venice in June 1934 (a fortnight before the Röhm Purge). Hitler was made to feel uncomfortable and inferior, since he appeared dressed simply in a raincoat and a soft hat, while Mussolini received him in full uniform. But when Mussolini came to Germany in September 1937, as an ally, he was treated to a view of the new Nazi might with military parades.

In 1940 as the Germans were proving victorious in France, Mussolini declared war on Britain and France, and the two dictators met in early October to share the triumph. But a further meeting revealed their rivalry, for Hitler's plans for the Balkans excluded Italy. To regain ascendancy, Mussolini ordered the disastrous invasion of Greece.

The balance of power now lay heavily with Germany. In January 1941 Hitler summoned Mussolini to Berchtesgaden. With his eyes on Russia, Hitler was prepared to help Mussolini not only in Greece but also in Libya where the British had nearly destroyed the Italian army. By 1943 Italy was no more than a client state of Germany, with German generals in command in Italy and North Africa and with the Balkans under German control. The dictators' thirteenth meeting was in northern Italy in July 1943 when Anglo-American forces were already in Sicily and ready to invade the Italian mainland. On his return to Rome, Mussolini's government revolted and arrested him; the veteran Italian General Badoglio formed a non-fascist government.

A humiliating postscript remained to Mussolini's career. Hitler sent SS Major Skorzeny to rescue him and brought him to northern Italy to head a new Italian state, a puppet of Germany. The last meeting of the two dictators was in July 1944 immediately after the Bomb Plot: the Italian with no real power and the German facing a revolt by his own officers.

In April 1945 Mussolini was caught by Italian partisans as he tried to escape to Switzerland. With his mistress, Clara Petacci, he was shot, then their bodies were taken to Milan and strung up by the heels.

Mylius Group. Extreme right-wing anti-Hitler group led by Dr Helmuth Mylius. The group was joined by members of the *Jungdeutscher Orden*, Schwarze Front, Stahlhelm; supporters of the former SA leader Walther Stennes; by one of the murderers of Liebknecht and Rosa Luxemburg and by Captain Ehrhardt of the Ehrhardt Brigade. In 1935 over 160 men were infiltrated into the SS, but the Putsch and plan to assassinate Hitler was never carried out, were mainly because the Gestapo had infiltrated the infiltrators. Mylius himself narrowly escaped arrest. When war broke out he was able, with Manstein's help, to obtain the protection of a military post and ended hostilities as a reserve major.

***Myth of the Twentieth Century*.** ➤Rosenberg, Alfred

N

***Nacht und Nebel* (Night and Fog).**   A Hitler order of December 1941 (issued through Keitel) that the Gestapo and SD should seize any person they thought dangerous in Germany or occupied lands, and that these prisoners should be made to vanish into *Nacht und Nebel*. No questions were to be answered about the prisoners' whereabouts or fate; indeed no confirmation or denial would be issued to those seeking news of missing relatives. The object of the order was deliberately to initiate a new dimension of fear. People arrested were lost to the outside world. Keitel wrote: 'Effective and lasting intimidation can only be achieved by capital punishment or by means which leave the population in the dark about the fate of the culprit.' The *Nacht und Nebel* order was a major accusation against him at Nuremberg.

Napolas.   ➤Education in the Third Reich

National Socialist.   ➤Nazi

National Socialist Factory Cells.   A Nazi factory workers' organization (the NSBO) existed in the 1920s and expected to take over organized labour on the Nazi accession to power in 1933. But the Party leadership had in fact already decided that there would be no role whatsoever for organized labour in the new Reich, not even for the NSBO. Thus by the end of the year, large numbers of NSBO members had been denounced as 'Marxist gangsters' and consigned to concentration camps. This was of course part of the process by which the Nazi Party shed its radical wing. After the Night of the Long Knives, the NSBO was represented by the murderers of Gregor Strasser as a private army built up by him as a challenge to Adolf Hitler. In December of that year, the NSBO was forbidden to intervene in national or local labour affairs and was allowed to decline into an ineffective cardboard organization.

Naujocks, Alfred (1911–60).   SD 'dirty tricks' specialist. In his youth a street-fighting SA man, he joined the SS in 1931 and became Heydrich's trusted agent. In August 1939 he led a squad in Polish uniforms across the Polish border to provide 'evidence' of provocation for Germany's attack on Poland. In November he succeeded in abducting the British secret service man Payne-Best at Venlo. Dismissed by the SD for disobedience, he joined the Waffen SS in 1943 and was responsible for the murder of Danish resistance men. In November 1944 he deserted to the Americans, but later escaped from custody. He was suspected of running the SS escape-route 'Odessa'. He died in 1960 in Germany without having been brought to trial.

Nazi. A widely used acronym derived from the letters of *Nationalsozialistische*.

Nazi Party. The NSDAP – the *Nationalsozialistische Deutsche Arbeiterpartei* (the National Socialist German Workers' Party).

Chronology 1919–33

1919	Anton Drexler, Dietrich Eckart, Karl Harrer form the German Workers' Party (*Deutsche Arbeiterpartei*) in Munich.
September	Adolf Hitler, employed by the army as an 'education officer', to report on possible subversive movements, is sent to a meeting of the Party and joins it as member number 7.
November	Hitler persuades this tiny group to hold a meeting at the Hofbräuhaus Beer hall. He speaks there and finds highly effective his passionate outpouring of abuse against enemies, mingled with dire threats and promises of retribution. He speaks at further meetings, each one with a greater attendance.
December	Hitler opens a permanent Party office and demands better organization.
1920	
February	With Drexler and Feder, a man with personal theories of economic reform, a Party programme, the '25 Points', is issued, at the Hofbräuhaus. Hitler achieves an audience of 2,000 and several hundred new members are enrolled.
April	The Party changes its name to the *Nationalsozialistische Deutsche Arbeiterpartei* (NSDAP, the National Socialist German Workers' Party). Its name is not yet abbreviated to 'Nazi'. Among the new members are men like Alfred Rosenberg, a refugee Baltic German, full of anti-semitism and anti-Bolshevism, and Captain Röhm, still a serving officer, who brings in other serving soldiers and *Freikorps* men.
October	The Party forms a group, many of them from the *Freikorps*, to keep order at their meetings. Organized by Emil Maurice, they are called the 'Storm Group', the *Sturmabteilung* or SA.
December	Röhm persuades his former commanding officer, General von Epp, to help raise the money to buy the Party the twice-weekly paper, the *Völkischer Beobachter*, probably using secret army funds. Hitler ignores the old Party committee and works with his new friends, Röhm, Hess, Göring and several other people of a richer class which he was now meeting through Hanfstängl.
	General Ludendorff is made aware of him as a likely demagogue who might play a part in his own nationalist dreams. He introduces Hitler to the Strasser brothers who have links with disillusioned socialists and radicals throughout Germany.

1921

January   The first 'National Congress' of the NSDAP is held in Munich. Although the attendance is poor, the papers report Hitler and he becomes a recognized part of Bavarian politics.

July   The first leadership crisis in the NSDAP. Hitler offers to resign in the secure knowledge that the Party following will disappear without him. He humiliates the Party committee which is disbanded, and Hitler is recognized as sole leader.

1922

October   The Italian fascist Mussolini takes power in Italy, providing an example of a successful Putsch accompanied by striking propaganda symbols: the black-shirted supporters, the raised-arm salute and the title of *Duce*, 'leader'.

Hitler uses the full force of the SA to demonstrate his power, driving the communists out of the small town of Coburg in a series of street brawls, and is acclaimed by his supporters as the Mussolini of Germany.

1923

November   The NSDAP with its large number of dissatisfied ex-soldiers and *Freikorps* men and its strong anti-socialist feelings, now has 70,000 members in Bavaria. Munich is a centre of anti-central-government feeling and Hitler and the Party gamble on a Putsch, to be led by Ludendorff and supported by the army and the current Bavarian government.

Hitler leads the Beer Hall Putsch with Ludendorff but is not supported by either the army or the Bavarian government, and the Putsch fails.

Hitler is jailed in Landsberg and the Nazi Party and SA are banned.

1924   Hitler has special privileges and many visitors in Landsberg. He nominates Rosenberg as the leader in his absence, who forms the GVG (*Grossdeutschland Volksgemeinschaft*) Party, while the SA groups carry on under the disguise of sports clubs, singing clubs or rifle clubs. With Rudolf Hess as his secretary, he starts writing his political philosophy, *Mein Kampf*.

May   Gregor Strasser, Rosenberg and Ludendorff, acquitted and not imprisoned at the trial after the Beer Hall Putsch, form the Völkisch Block. Streicher forms his own group in Bamberg. Together they take over the GVG and form a 'National Socialist Freedom Party' which wins 32 out of the 472 seats in the national Reichstag elections of May 1924.

December   Another Reichstag election and the NS Freedom Party loses all but 14 of its seats.

| | Hitler is released from Landsberg, but the NSDAP is in ruins. |

1925

February The NS Freedom Party is dissolved.

In the first issue of the *Völkischer Beobachter* since the 1923 Putsch, Hitler announces a 'new' Nazi Party and a meeting to be held at the Bürgerbräukeller.

There is a big crowd at the meeting, but Röhm and Strasser do not attend and Drexler refuses to take the chair. Max Amann, Hitler's publisher, substitutes. The audience cheer Hitler loudly, but he is still banned from public speaking in Bavaria and throughout Germany.

Party headquarters are opened in Schellingstrasse in Munich.

March Strasser agrees to take on the leadership of the Nazis in north Germany.

Röhm, who had put the militant ex-soldiers together in the Frontbann, demands that his SA be separate from the Nazi Party. This leads to a quarrel with Hitler.

April Röhm resigns. Hitler accepts his resignation without further argument.

Drexler leaves the Party and tries unsuccessfully to start a new one.

Summer First SS units formed.

July Amann publishes the first part of Hitler's *Mein Kampf*. From the high point before the Beer Hall Putsch, Nazi Party membership has declined so that there are only 700 Party members in Munich. But in north Germany, Strasser's campaign, with his business manager Josef Göbbels, boosts membership and support for Strasser. For the first time the Nazi Party centre of gravity is moving north.

November Hitler's delegate, Feder, is ordered out of a Hanover meeting held by Strasser, Göbbels and Rust.

December Strasser publishes his new Party programme, replacing the '25 Points' of the original Party. It is an open challenge to Hitler's leadership.

1926

February Hitler calls a Party meeting in Bamberg, where he outmanoeuvres and outvotes the Strasser programme. He wins Göbbels and others over to him.

May A general Party meeting in Munich resolves that the Munich Party is the leadership of the movement and that the '25 Points' are immutable. 'USCHLA', the Party disciplinary body, is established.

July The first Party rally is held in Weimar. The new salute with the outstretched arm is used by 5,000 uniformed men: Pfeffer von Salomon had taken charge of the training of SA men for all public displays.

Party membership is now reckoned at 27,000.

A 'Hitler Youth' branch of the SA is formed.

November   Göbbels is made party *Gauleiter* in Berlin.

At the end of the year, the Party membership in Germany is 49,000. Hess is Party secretary.

1927

May   Hitler is permitted to speak in public in Bavaria and Saxony.

July   The Party rally is held for the first time at Nuremberg. It is claimed that 30,000 uniformed SA men are present. Nazi Party membership is put at 70,000.

Göring returns from Sweden, where he has been since 1923, rejoining the Nazi Party for old comradeship and action and not (as he put it) for 'ideological junk'.

Göbbels campaigns to raise funds to get his Berlin party out of debt. He holds large, well-publicized meetings notable for their anti-semitism and insistence on the approaching end of the bourgeois state.

1928

May   In the Reichstag elections Nazis win 12 places. Strasser, Feder, Göbbels and Göring are elected deputies.

Party membership passes 100,000.

Party hierarchy reorganized. Strasser is given the task of attacking the present government, while Hierl takes on planning for the future, making these men the key figures in the party:

> *Political Branch* (Strasser)

Foreign affairs	Nieland
Press	Otto Dietrich
Party cells	Schumann

> *Nazi State Branch*, the 'shadow government' (*Hierl*)

Agriculture	Darré
Economics	Wagener
Race and Culture	Konopath
Interior Ministry	Nicolai
Legal	Frank
Technical matters	Feder
Labour	Schulz

The Party organization is divided into 34 *Gaue*, plus seven more in areas considered 'German' (Austria, Danzig, etc.).

September   Hitler permitted to speak in Prussia.

November	Göbbels takes over the propaganda branch of the Party from Strasser.
December	The second volume of *Mein Kampf* is published.

1929

January	Himmler becomes first *Reichsführer* of an SS whose strength is 280 men.
August	Nuremberg Rally of 60,000 SA men and some 200,000 Nazi supporters.
September	With Hugenberg (DNVP), Hitler drafts a law demanding repudiation of Versailles debts.
October	Law defeated in Reichstag.
December	Hugenberg–Hitler law put to national referendum, getting under 6 million of the required 21 million votes. The campaign fails, but Hitler attracts the attention of the many Germans frustrated by the nation's economic difficulties.
	Party membership 178,000.

1930

February	Death of Horst Wessel, used by Göbbels for publicity.
March	Party membership 210,000.
June	Otto Strasser is expelled from Party.
September	Reichstag elections: Nazis gain 107 seats, the second largest party (SPD 143, Communists 77).
	Hitler appears as a witness in a trial of three officers accused of spreading Nazism in the army. He assures the generals that the SA does not rival the army. But the SA is now over 100,000 men, larger than the regular army.

1931

January	Nazi Party move into Brown House headquarters in Munich. Röhm is reappointed as SA Chief-of-Staff.
October	Hitler officially received by President Hindenburg.
	Harzburg Front meeting attended by Hitler, but he declines to join it.
November	'Boxheim papers' are discovered, with records of Party meeting in Hesse discussing measures to be taken when the Nazis come to power.

1932

March	Presidential elections: Hindenburg defeats Hitler, but without an absolute majority (49.6 per cent to Hitler's 30.1 per cent). The SA, now 400,000 strong, mobilize in Berlin, causing rumours of a Putsch.
April	The SA is banned.
	Second presidential election: Hindenburg re-elected, but Hitler gains votes (53 per cent to 37 per cent, with 10 per cent Communist).

State elections in Prussia and other states. In Prussia, Nazis win 36 per cent of the votes to become the largest party. Göring takes over the Ministry of the Interior, controlling the Prussian police.

June   Von Papen is made Chancellor and lifts ban on the SA.

July   Reichstag elections: Nazis with 230 delegates are the largest party but have no overall majority and only 37 per cent of the total vote. SPD seats reduced to 133 and Communists rise to 89. Klara Zetkin, a veteran Communist and the oldest delegate to the Reichstag, presides over the election of Göring as its President: Göring 367 votes, Löbe (SPD), Reichstag President since 1920, 135, and Törgler (Communist) 80.

August   The SA mobilize in Berlin and Hitler demands from Hindenburg the office of Chancellor. The President of the Republic refuses Hitler the chancellorship.

October   Nazis join with the Communists in a Berlin transport strike.

November   Further Reichstag elections: the Nazis lose seats, falling to 196, while the Communists now stand at 100.

December   Schleicher is named as Chancellor and offers Strasser the Vice-Chancellorship. Strasser urges Hitler to join in a coalition, but they quarrel and Strasser resigns. Hitler takes over the Party's political organization himself, with Ley as his Chief-of-Staff.

1933
January   Schleicher is unable to get a majority in the Reichstag and resigns. Von Papen agrees to join a cabinet with Hitler as Chancellor, himself as Vice-Chancellor and a largely conservative cabinet, with only three of the eleven ministries going to Nazis.

February   Hitler cannot co-operate with the Centre Party and calls for new elections.

Schacht hosts a meeting of industrialists and financiers who pledge support for the Nazi Party.

Göring, as Prussian Minister of the Interior, creates an auxiliary police force of 50,000 mostly SA men.

Communist Party HQ raided and papers produced to show their plans for a revolution.

Reichstag Fire: Hindenburg signs a decree suspending civil rights. Thousands of arrests are made of communists, socialists and liberals. SA, as police auxiliaries carry out the arrests, open temporary concentration camps for their prisoners.

March   The last Reichstag elections are held. The Nazi vote increases but is still only 44 per cent, giving them 288 seats. Combining with Hugenberg's 52 nationalist (DNVP) delegates, the Nazis have a majority. With all 81 communist members and a large number of socialists barred from the Reichstag, Hitler has a strong enough majority to alter the constitution and, through the process of *Gleichschaltung*, introduce the Third Reich.

Nazi Party Headquarters, Munich

1920	Sterneckerbräu
1922–3	Corneliusstrasse 12
1925	(for six months) Eher Verlag, Thierstrasse 15 (later the Party publishing house)
1925–31	Schellingstrasse 50
1931	Barlow Palace, Briennerstrasse 45, rebuilt by Troost as the Brown House

Nazi Party Membership. From its low point in 1925, when, recovering from the failure of the Beer Hall Putsch and the imprisonment of Hitler, it boasted only 700 members, the Party membership increased with Strasser's campaigns in north Germany and Hitler's return to action. By the end of 1926 there were 49,000 members; and its growth continued until, just before the seizure of power at the end of 1932, there were 850,000 members. In the years of the Third Reich from 1933 the Party grew so that one German in ten was a member – some eight million.

The original members up to 1923 had usually been believers in *Völkisch* theories, based on a romantic ideal of the pure nation that Germany could become. Many were war veterans, like Hitler, who missed the front-line trench camaraderie and were frustrated by the immediate economic and political difficulties. Some were attracted to radical solutions, loosely called 'national Bolshevism'; the cause of their difficulties was variously located in the Treaty of Versailles, in France, in the Jews or in the capitalist system. The '25 Points', the first formulation of Nazi Party policies – which were retained to the end – reflect these various motivations.

Between 1926 and 1930 the increase in Party membership came largely from the lower-middle class. But the mood of the Party was also heavily influenced by Germans exiled from their homes in east Europe, men like Rosenberg and Darré. Leaders and followers were united in their hatred of things as they were. At this level, the Nazis were recruiting from the same people as the Communist Party.

Nazi Party Membership Analysis

Nazi membership in 1930 was analysed as:

Occupation	percentage
workers	26.3
white collar	24.0
self-employed	18.9
civil service	7.7
farmers	13.2
miscellaneous	9.9

Age-range	percentage
18–20	0.4
21–30	36.4
31–40	31.4
41–50	17.6
51–60	9.7
60+	4.5

The low proportion of working class (in relation to the total population) has been variously explained, most simply by the suggestion that they were least able to afford the cost of Party membership. The Nazis themselves recognized divisions within the membership. The old members, particularly those who had marched in the Beer Hall Putsch, were 'Alte Kämpfer' and wore the 'Blood Order' badge. They looked down on the 'March Violets' who joined in 1933. While earlier members were typically from south Germany, rural and lower-middle class, the growing Party brought in civil servants and graduate professionals in large numbers. Though the former type remained the core of the Party, the latter took over the leadership of the Party from 1933 on. Numbers of aristocrats were also drawn into the Party. The SS was keen to attract the upper classes, and offered honorary rank to senior civil servants, members of equestrian clubs and relatives of the former monarchy. These awards were not always welcomed by the recipients.

Nazi Party Programme: 25 Points.   The forerunner of the Nazi Party was the German Workers' Party (DAP), a small, radical, anti-capitalist, anti-semitic and nationalistic grouping. Its programme, drawn up by Drexler, Feder and Hitler in February 1920, took the form of 25 points. Hitler declared these to be unchangeable and fundamental to the Nazi Party. He reaffirmed them after the 1926 confrontation with the Strasserites in Bamberg; and they remained the Party programme, though rarely Party practice, until the end of the Third Reich. The following is a summary of the points:

1. The union of all Germans in a Greater Germany
2. The rejection of the Treaty of Versailles and the affirmation of the right of Germany to deal with other nations
3. The demand for additional territories for food production and to settle excess German population ('*Lebensraum*')
4. Citizenship to be determined by race; no Jew to be a German
5. Non-Germans in Germany to be 'only' guests and subject to appropriate laws
6. Official posts not to be filled by political nepotism, only according to character and qualification
7. The livelihood of citizens to be the state's first duty. Should the state's resources be overstretched, non-citizens to be excluded from the state's benefits

8. Non-German immigration to be stopped
9. Equal rights and duties for all citizens
10. Each citizen to work for the general good
11. All income not earned by work to be confiscated
12. All war profits to be confiscated
13. All large business trusts to be nationalized
14. Profit-sharing in all larger industries
15. Adequate provision for old age
16. Small businessmen and traders to be strengthened and large department stores to be handed over to them
17. A reform of land-ownership and an end to land speculation
18. Ruthless prosecution of serious criminals and death for profiteers
19. Roman law, which is materialist, to be replaced by 'German law'
20. A thorough reconstruction of the national education system
21. The state to assist motherhood and encourage the development of the young
22. The abolition of the paid professional army and the formation of a national army
23. Newspapers must be German-owned; non-Germans banned from working on them
24. Religious freedom, except for religions which endanger the German race; the Party does not bind itself exclusively to any creed, but to fight against Jewish materialism
25. A strong central government for the execution of effective legislation

Nazi Party Ranks.   The Party indicated rank mainly through party function.

> *Reichsleiter*   The senior Party officers, e.g. Bormann, Party chancellery; Frank, Party law division; Göbbels, propaganda; Himmler, SS; Ley, Party organization; Rosenberg, Party foreign relations
>
> *Gauleiter*   Senior officer in a Party district. (There was a supervisory rank of 'Landesinspekteur' above this, but it was allowed to vanish in the 1930s.) By 1942 there were 43 Party 'regions' (➤*Gau*) including one for Nazi Party members overseas
>
> *Kreisleiter, Ortsgruppenleiter, Zellenleiter*   District, Locality and Cell leaders

The above levels were the élite of the Party. Below them came:

> *Blockwart*   The immediate representative of the Party to most people
>
> *Parteigenosse Helfer*   'Party Comrade', the ordinary member of the Nazi Party

Nazi-Soviet Non-aggression Pact.   ➤Russo-German Pact

Nazi street fighting.   It was Nazi practice to make political points through violence. As a result, about 400 Nazis were killed in fights up to 1933. In the month of May 1932, ninety-nine were killed and 1,125 wounded in brawls between Nazis and their opponents. In July 1932 a Nazi march and communist meetings were allowed on the same day in Altona, a district of Hamburg. The result was 'bloody Sunday'. The communists shot at the Nazi marchers from the rooftops and the Nazis fought back. Seventeen were killed. The Nazi propaganda machine pictured the Nazis as defenders of decent values and their enemies as decadent thugs whom only force could contain.

Nazi treasure.   The Third Reich amassed vast treasure from its conquest of much of Europe. Some of its leaders, like Göring, collected works of art and seized estates, living ostentatiously. Some, like Göbbels, preferred to make the state pay for their pleasures. The SS, through Oswald Pohl's WVHA division, enriched itself by taking the gold and jewellery from its death-camp victims and depositing them in the Reichsbank: *Aktion Reinhardt* of 1943 brought in $10 million worth of cash, gold and jewels from concentration camps. SS business enterprises, such as their monopoly of soft-drink production, made immense tax-free profits. The Nazi state took the gold reserves of its conquered and tribute nations, Austria, Belgium, Czechoslovakia, France and the Netherlands. It took what it found in Poland and the USSR as it invaded and, after 1943, what could be seized from Italy.

Like the SS, the army, the *Abwehr* and the Foreign Ministry all deposited their loot in the Reichsbank. The vaults of the bank's Berlin headquarters were a massive treasure-house. Walther Funk had succeeded Schacht as President of the Reichsbank in 1939, but he left its running to the Deputy President, Emil Puhl (who accepted the deposits to the bank of his near namesake, Pohl of the SS, under the account name of 'Max Heiliger'). Puhl took care to make himself a director of a Swiss bank; when in February 1945 American air-raids on Berlin hit the bank, Puhl decided it was time to move to safety.

The first move was of art treasures, gold, jewellery and foreign currency, valued then at over $300 million, to mines in Thuringia. But within a month the American army had overrun the mines and this consignment was captured. All remaining Reichsbank reserves were now in Berlin and had to be removed before the approaching Russian army got there. Puhl and Funk decided to take what they could to Bavaria and Austria, where the SS had already begun to hide some funds. 94 per cent of Germany's gold reserves had been lost in Thuringia; the rest, including boxes of gold coins and stores of the special paper needed for banknote printing, was sent by train and road to Munich, where Funk and Puhl received it. The consignment was taken to the mountains for hiding and seems thereafter to have passed through many hands, both German and American.

The SS were determined not to lose all their wealth and twice raided the Munich branch of the Reichsbank for what they regarded as theirs. In late April, as the Russians closed in on Berlin, Kaltenbrunner, head of the SS

RSHA, ordered a raid on the Reichsbank and cleared out the last of the valuables, worth some $10 million then. Nothing has ever been proved, but it would seem clear that the Americans did not recover all the Nazi treasure in southern Germany; some was stolen by American occupation troops, but millions of dollars went into secret SS accounts and were almost certainly used to finance their escape-routes and to set up the survivors in business.

Nebe, Artur (d. 1944). Head of the Kripo (Criminal Police). A senior officer specializing in criminology in the Prussian police who had secretly joined the Nazis before 1933, Nebe emerged from the closet to be made head of the Kripo. His claim was that he had renounced Nazism when Göring ordered him to kill Gregor Strasser in 1934. Certainly he avoided obeying the order yet remained head of the Kripo. Subsequently he made contact with men like Gisevius and was a valuable source of information and warnings of Gestapo movements to German resisters. When the extermination camps in Poland were reported to him, he claimed to be surprised by the news, yet Nebe had commanded one of the Einsatzgruppen in Russia in 1941. As a high-ranking SS officer he was considered as a successor to the murdered Heydrich in 1942 and he was still sufficiently in favour for Himmler to put him in charge of the investigation of the July Bomb Plot in 1944. But Nebe's continued friendship with Gisevius and other conspirators was uncovered and he was among those arrested and executed. He remains a genuinely enigmatic figure, reacting to the dreadful exigencies of the system in a way that those outside it can never comprehend.

Neo-Nazis: Austria. Unlike the two modern German republics, BRD and DDR, the Austrian republic was not required to 'denazify'; it was treated, rather, after the four-Power post-war occupation ended, as a nation which had been the victim of the Third Reich. There was no formal process of expressing regret for the role of some Austrians, or accepting that some Nazi war criminals had also come from Austria, or that Hitler, Kaltenbrunner, Seyss-Inquart and Eichmann were of Austrian birth. It was not widely taught that in 1938 many Austrians had welcomed their entry to the Third Reich. The Freedom Party of Georg Haider still in 1987 had support from some of the 150,000 former Nazis and their families. Despite its generally moderate and liberal policies, its membership includes those of fascist views, unashamed of the Nazi period, and those who still blame economic difficulties on 'the Jews and communists'.

Neo-Nazis: Germany. After WWII, both BRD and DDR passed laws which were intended to prevent any rebirth of the Nazi Party. Several attempts have been made to re-create such a party, notably by von Thadden (in the form of a conservative party of which he became chairman in 1967) or Remer (who had played a key role in suppressing the July Bomb Plot in 1944). There are still some followers of radical Nazism who look for inspiration in their neo-Nazism to Otto Strasser rather than to Hitler. There have also been groups which have re-created some of the trappings and activities of the SA and have committed acts of violent anti-semitism. In the BRD, the Office for the Protection of the Federal Constitution monitors any attempts at reanimating neo-Nazism and there has been little real impact on the nation.

Nero Order.   The Führer decree issued in the last days of the Third Reich for the destruction of the nation's industrial infrastructure. In his account of the part he played in the Third Reich, Albert Speer describes the last frantic days when he persuaded Gauleiters to disobey the Nero Order and preserve what remained after the Allied bombing, as the basis for Germany's post-war future. ➤Resistance

Neu Beginnen.   An underground Social Democrat group which operated in Berlin and the Ruhr after the Nazis came to power. Fritz Erler and Waldemar von Knöringen were leading figures in the group whose operations received support from social democratic exiles in Switzerland and Spain. Their principal publication, *Der Grüne Otto* (Green Otto), brought news of the outside world and its view of Nazi policies. In 1936-7, members were breaking open ammunition and armament trains and reporting to foreign contacts on the extent of German rearmament.

Unusually successful in avoiding the Gestapo, *Neu Beginnen* survived until the great purges of 1944 when, after the arrest of dozens of its members, the leadership core was scattered and the group disbanded.

Neurath, Constantin Freiherr von (1873-1956).   Aristocratic diplomat (German ambassador in Copenhagen 1919-20, Rome 1921-30, London 1930-32). He was made Foreign Minister in von Papen's 1932 'Cabinet of Barons', and like Schwerin von Krosigk stayed on in the Cabinet when Hitler became Chancellor, giving respectability to the new government. He was removed from the Ministry after the 'Hossbach' Conference, where Hitler outlined his plans for conquest at which von Neurath protested. After this he held only titular posts; he was made Protector of Bohemia and Moravia from 1939 to 1941, when he was replaced by Heydrich. At Nuremberg he was included among the major war criminals and sentenced to 15 years' imprisonment, but was released in 1954 on health grounds.

Niekisch, Ernst (1889-1967).   A member of the small National Bolshevist group distinct from the communists. He was chairman of the Munich 'Soviet' in 1918-19 and sentenced to jail. His extreme leftist nationalism influenced Strasser, Röhm and Göbbels. Later he tried to organize an anti-Nazi resistance and for this he was sentenced to jail in 1937; he was fortunate that his arrest and trial were conducted by the police and not by the Gestapo; he was thus sent to a civil prison rather than a concentration camp. He survived in prison until the end of the war.

Niemöller, Martin (1892–1984).   Pastor Niemöller had been a submarine commander in WWI, winning the 'Pour le Mérite'. He was a nationalist and an anti-communist and, at first, thought that Hitler would be good for Germany; but he was soon disillusioned by Nazi attempts at *Gleichschaltung* of churches and the takeover of the Protestant Evangelical Church through Ludwig Müller and Hans Kerrl. His branch of the church, the Confessional Church, came out against the Nazis' actions and their anti-semitism. For this, one of the Church leaders, Dr Weissler, was taken to Sachsenhausen concentration camp and executed. Niemöller was arrested in 1937 and jailed in Berlin for seven months after trial. On release, he was taken into custody in concentration camps until the end of the war, when he was liberated with other prominent prisoners from Dachau.

After the war he wrote: 'First they came for the Jews and I did not speak out because I was not a Jew; then they came for the Communists and I did not speak out because I was not a Communist; then they came for the unionists and I did not speak out because I was not a union man. Then they came for me – and there was no one left to speak out for me.'

Nietzsche, Friedrich Wilhelm (1844–1900).   Noted German philosopher whose works can be said to have influenced Hitler and Nazi thought in general. A brilliant philologist who was offered a professorship at Basel before he had taken his degree, Nietzsche's health was so poor that he was forced to retire just ten years later in 1879. In 1888 he became insane and remained so until the time of his death.

Philosophically, he was a successor to Schopenhauer but developed even more extreme notions of aristocratic élitism. Politically, his views were not dissimilar to Machiavelli's, though in Nietzsche's case the object of his admiration was Napoleon rather than Cesare Borgia. He said of Napoleon: 'We ought to desire the anarchical collapse of the whole of our civilization if such a reward [the emergence of Napoleon as emperor] were to be its result.'

Will was the concept of enormous force to him. 'I test the power of a will,' he said, 'according to the amount of resistance it can offer and the amount of pain and torture it can endure and know how to turn it to its own advantage.' The 'noble man' was to Nietzsche essentially an expression of the incarnate will to power.

Fiercely anti-Christian, claiming to be nauseated by the decadent notions of repentance and redemption, Nietzsche also despised Christianity for denying the value of 'pride, exuberant spirit, splendid animalism, the instincts of war and of conquest, the deification of passion, revenge, anger, voluptuousness, adventure, knowledge'.

Certain aspects of Nazi thought, in particular nationalism, found little place in his philosophy. He believed in an international ruling class in which 'the will of philosophical men of power and artist tyrants will be stamped upon thousands of years'.

Probably his best-known remark concerns women: 'Thou goest to women. Do not forget thy whip,' from *Thus Spake Zarathustra*. This is offered as a self-evident truth – though his actual experience of women was remarkably limited. It is in *Also Sprach Zarathustra* that Nietzsche propounds his theory of the '*Übermensch*' or 'superman' which appealed to Nazis and was erroneously equated to their own *Führerprinzip*. In other directions too, Nazi ideology appropriated elements of Nietzsche. His disdain for the chaotic, cloudy spirit of Germany was ignored, as was his admiration for the Jews; more important to them was what they preferred to regard as a prophecy of the coming of Hitler and the pure Nordic spirit of the new man.

Night of the Long Knives.   Also known as the Blood Purge. ➤Röhm Purge

Nordhausen.   The underground factory in the Harz Mountains south-west of Berlin where the V-2 rocket was assembled by slave labour. On average 100 men a day had died of exhaustion or beatings as they dug the warren of forty-six tunnels, some up to 30 yards high, which were to comprise the V-2 factory and assembly plant. A complex of barrack buildings was built in the pinewoods near the mouth of the main tunnels and here in Camp Dora, the slave labourers were housed in conditions no better than at Buchenwald from which many of them had come. Nordhausen was occupied in April 1945 by the US 1st Army. Within days, US technical officers of 'Project Hermes', the plan for the seizure of German rocket equipment and scientists, arrived at the underground site with orders to ship 100 complete V-2s to the US firing range at White Sands, New Mexico.

Normandy landings.   The cross-Channel invasion of Europe, D-Day, 6 June 1944. Since 1942 the German High Command had expected an Allied attack on what Nazi propaganda had named Festung Europa (Fortress Europe). After the Dieppe raid had been successfully repulsed, German fortifications along the French coast were extended and deepened, until by 1944 they presented a formidable barrier to any landing force. Behind the barrier, which Hitler called the Atlantic Wall, stood fifty-nine divisions, ten of which were Panzer divisions capable of mounting a swift counter-attack on any Allied beachhead that might be established.

Field Marshal von Rundstedt, the commander in the west, thought the Calais area the most likely choice for an Allied landing. Hitler, however, had come to the conclusion that Normandy would be the most-favoured coastal area, with the large port of Cherbourg as the main Allied target. Rommel, who was by now the tactical commander of the coastal areas, inclined to Hitler's view.

Between von Rundstedt and Rommel there was a further difference of professional opinion as to how the Allied attack should be repulsed. Rundstedt preferred a carefully planned counter-attack after the Allied landings had been consolidated; Rommel believed the Germans would have to win the battle on the beaches in the confusion of the first hours of the landing. Once the beachheads had been consolidated, he considered it certain that Allied air power would be able to defend the Allied gains from the prepared German counter-attack of the type in which von Rundstedt placed his faith.

Whatever their view as to the most appropriate tactics to be employed against the landings, neither of the commanders nor the troops under them were prepared for the vast armada which appeared off the coast of Normandy on the morning of 6 June 1944: there were 59 convoys, 21 American and 38 British, over 2,000 transport ships escorted by 700 warships, including 23 cruisers and 5 battleships. In fact, American and British airborne units had already seized the flanks as the seaborne troops in the landing craft approached the beaches: Utah and the fateful Omaha for the Americans; Gold, Juno and Sword for the British and Canadians.

Communications in the German command chain were a compound of bungling and disbelief. Rommel, the proponent of an immediate counter-attack while the enemy were still on the beaches, was back in Germany celebrating his wife's birthday; he was not informed until after 10.00 a.m. that the Allies had landed; thus, what he had characterized as 'the longest day' was almost half over before the German tactical commander could intervene.

By midday, five Allied divisions (two US, two British and one Canadian) were safely ashore. Only at the US Omaha beach landing had the attackers suffered the violent response for which they had trained in innumerable manoeuvres.

By nightfall of the longest day the Allies had nowhere quite achieved the depth of penetration planned; but they had succeeded in landing the colossal number of 155,000 fully equipped soldiers on the continent of Europe. Deception techniques made Hitler retain formations in the Calais area in expectation of the 'main attack' still to come. Perhaps only Rommel – who believed that the result of that first day would determine the outcome of the campaign, and even of the war – realized that although no major battles had been fought, the German forces had nevertheless lost the day.

Normandy to the Rhine: Defeat in the West.   ➤Appendix VI

North African Campaigns.   ➤Appendix III

Norwegian Campaign and the Occupation of Denmark.   ➤Appendix II

Novemberverbrecher **(November Criminals)**.   In Nazi eyes, the men who agreed to conclude the 11 November 1918 Armistice. Implicit in the idea is that traitors anxious to subvert German military successes were responsible for the stab in the back which brought Germany to its knees. ➤Stab in the back

NSDAP.   ➤Nazi Party

Nuremberg Laws. A series of laws against Jews, drafted by Wilhelm Stukart, made public at the 1935 Nuremberg Rally and enforced from September of that year. The first Reich Law of Citizenship recognized two degrees of humanity: the *Reichsbürger*, the Citizen of pure German blood; and, for all other categories of person, the *Staatsangehörige*, the Subject of the state. The Law for the Protection of German Blood and Honour forbade intermarrying between the two groups. Some 250 decrees followed these laws, from 1935 to 1943, excluding Jews from official positions and professions and progressively from economic life, obliging them to wear the 'Star of David' or to live where ordered. The final decree, anticipating the Final Solution, made Jews outlaws in Germany. Those who did remain were eventually forced into hiding.

Anti-semitism had been strong before the advent of Nazism, but it became a rallying call and focus of Nazi philosophy, and the declaration of the Nuremberg Laws was seen by Nazi adherents as part of the recovery of the nation after the 1934 Röhm Purge. ➤Anti-semitism

Nuremberg Rallies. Starting with two parades in Nuremberg in January and August 1923 (held with other groups such as the Battle League), the Nuremberg rallies became a Nazi custom. The third took place in July 1926, associated with 'Party Day'. In 1927 and 1928 the rally grew and in 1933 it celebrated Hitler coming to power. 1934's lasted a full week and was the subject of Leni Riefenstahl's film *The Triumph of the Will*. 1935 was the occasion of the Nuremberg Laws; 1936, 1937 and 1938 – the last – continued as spectacular demonstrations of Nazi power. Hitler used the 1938 rally to heighten world tension during the Munich crisis.

Each rally became grander than the previous one and their staging was calculated to arouse emotions to give frenetic support to Hitler and Nazism. Speeches, marches, parades, flags and music were all combined to bring Germans to a high pitch of nationalistic feeling. Torchlights and floodlights became an established part of the presentation – but even the boundaries of Nazi stagecraft were extended by the dramatic introduction of over 100 powerful anti-aircraft searchlights, mounted to shine vertically in great columns of light. In awe the British ambassador described the scene as 'a cathedral of ice'. From 1934 Albert Speer took on the design of a great auditorium in Nuremberg where the rallies would be staged in what was to be the Nazi Party's capital. Work on this went on during WWII, and it remained a vast desolate monument for years after.

Nuremberg Trials. The international military tribunal which sat in Nuremberg from November 1945 to September 1946 to try the major Nazi figures for war crimes. A United Nations War Crimes Commission had been set up in London in 1943 and in November the Americans, British and Russians declared that Germans responsible for abominable deeds would be sent back to where they had committed them to be tried by the liberated countries. The shock of the killing of American prisoners at Malmédy during the German

Ardennes offensive (1944) convinced America of the need to punish the guilty. Although the British showed caution in case there might be unwanted legal tangles, it was agreed by May 1945 that an international tribunal should sit, with American, British, French and Russian judges and prosecutors. A conference was held in London to agree the methods of the trial (each country having its own quite different legal rules and practices). In August it was agreed that Nuremberg should be the location of the trials, mainly because it had been the site of the great Nazi Party rallies.

Defendants (and organizations such as the Gestapo) were to be tried on four counts: crimes against peace (planning and making war); war crimes (responsibility for crimes during war); crimes against humanity (to cover racial persecution); conspiracy (to commit crimes alleged in other courts). The tribunal's judges were Francis Biddle with John Parker (USA), Norman Birkett and Sir Geoffrey Lawrence (Britain), Henri Donnedieu de Vabres and Robert Falco (France), and Roman Rudenko (who replaced the first nomination, Nikitchenko) with Volchov (USSR). There would be teams of prosecutors from the Allies. The defending lawyers were Germans, who operated under difficulties, not having the resources of the victorious nations and being themselves subject to the rules of the victors. Their most effective defence lay in questioning the existence of any previous international law rather than an attempt to deny or excuse the defendants' acts.

A shortlist of the most notorious surviving leaders of the Third Reich was agreed by the tribunal (Hitler, Himmler and Göbbels were already dead; Bormann was noted as 'missing'); others were added at the insistence of individual nations. In August 1945, a list of twenty-three defendants was published, but it was still disputed. It included Gustav Krupp, the aged father, rather than the active son, Alfred, and the name remained on the list even though the old man was too sick to be brought to trial.

The tribunal also put Third Reich organizations on trial. Thus if an organization were declared criminal, any member of it could be tried on that count alone. The SS (including the Waffen SS), the Gestapo and SD were all declared guilty organizations, as were the senior ranks of the Nazi Party, from that of *Kreisleiter* up. The SA was not declared criminal nor were the General Staff and OKW, although individual officers were to be tried.

Before the trial began, one of the defendants, Robert Ley, the Labour Front leader, hanged himself in his cell. The twenty-one remaining were tried between November 1945 and late September 1946 when the verdicts and sentences were given: death for Göring, Frank, Frick, Jodl, Kaltenbrunner, Keitel, Ribbentrop, Rosenberg, Saukel, Seyss-Inquart and Streicher; life imprisonment for Funk, Hess and Raeder; 20 years for von Schirach and Speer; 15 years for von Neurath, and 10 for Dönitz. Fritsche, von Papen and Schacht were found not guilty. Göring, having secreted or been passed a phial of cyanide, killed himself the day before execution. The remainder of the condemned were hanged in October 1946.

O

Oak (*Eiche*). Code-name for the German military response to the expected invasion of Italy by the Allies.

Oath of Legality. A trial of Nazi officers in the Reichswehr, held in Ulm in 1930, in which Hitler presented himself as a witness. Aware at this time (as many SA leaders were not) of the need to represent the Party as an essentially legalistic organization, he voluntarily took an oath in court to the effect that the Nazi Party would never resort to illegality. ➤*Adolf Légalité*

Odessa (*Organisation der SS Angehörige*). One of the groups which, it is widely believed, financed and arranged the escape of Nazis from Germany after the war. Otto Skorzeny was possibly a key figure, but proof has never been assembled. Little is certain about 'Odessa', but it remains probable that some such escape-route was set up before the war ended and that the vast loot of the SS was moved out through Swiss or Vatican banks, for the support of fugitives in their harried post-war existences.

OKH (*Oberkommando des Heeres*). Developed from the Weimar Wehramt, the army High Command, becoming the Allgemeines Heeresamt (General Army Office). In May 1935 this became OKH (➤OKW).

OKL (*Oberkommando der Luftwaffe*). ➤OKW

OKM (*Oberkommando der Marine*). ➤OKW

OKW (*Oberkommando der Wehrmacht*). Armed Forces High Command. By 1934, Hitler, as Chancellor and President, was nominal Head of the Armed Forces. When War Minister Blomberg was dismissed in 1938 Hitler abolished his ministerial post and took personal command. The new organization became OKW, with Keitel as Chief of Staff and Jodl as Head of Operations. Hitler retained OKW as his own planning staff, with OKH for the army, OKL the Luftwaffe, and OKM the navy (*Kriegsmarine*). In 1941 he gave control of the war in Russia to OKH, retaining his OKW for command of all other theatres. There were thus effectively two military High Commands. In December 1941 he dismissed Brauchitsch from OKH and assumed supreme command. Chiefs of Staff of OKH during the Third Reich were: 1938–42, Halder; 1942–4, Zeitzler; 1944–5, Guderian; 1945, Krebs.

Olympic Games, 1936. Hitler saw in the staging of the Olympic Games in

Berlin a great opportunity to present the smiling face of Nazism to the world. Anti-semitic posters were taken down, the paper *Der Stürmer* was removed and foreigners made welcome. Even German part-Jewish competitors, such as the women's fencing champion Helene Mayer and the Olympic village commandant, were tolerated. Richard Strauss and Carl Orff were commissioned to write music for the Games and artists prepared massive paintings and statues to celebrate them.

A brilliant publicity event was created by Dr Carl Diem who for the first time produced a relay of runners carrying the Olympic flame from Greece across the Balkans and Austria to the German border. From there to Berlin the roads were lined with children waving Nazi flags, villages were bedecked with the swastika as the lone runner passed through. The prosperity of Germany and the enthusiasm of Germans for the new Nazi state were shown on newsreels throughout the world.

At the opening in August, Hitler paraded with 40,000 SA men, a choir of 3,000 sang '*Deutschland*' and the '*Horst Wessel*' song, and a crowd of 110,000 cheered. On the first day Hitler presented medals to German victors in the shot put and women's javelin throw. The Olympic committee felt he should either give medals to all winners or none. He therefore presented no more, since American black athletes were coming to the fore, Jesse Owens alone winning four gold medals. However, the Nazi triumph was ensured: Germany won most gold, silver and bronze medals; a huge finale was staged with the crowds shouting to Adolf Hitler, 'Sieg Heil! Sieg Heil!' and Leni Riefenstahl's internationally acclaimed film recorded the Games and in particular celebrated the stable, confident community which had staged them.

Operation flash.   ➤Smolensk Plot

Oradour-sur-Glane.   Village in France (north-west of Limoges) where the SS 2nd Panzer Division, Das Reich, murdered some 600 inhabitants during the afternoon of 10 June, 1944. The division, which was on its way from its assembly area around Montauban to the new invasion front in Normandy, had already committed a number of atrocities (most notably the hanging of ninety-eight men in Tulle) on its way north. A degree of mystery still surrounds the motives for the Oradour massacre. Certainly the division had been severely harried by resistance fighters as it travelled through the Lot and Correze, but the suggestion remains unproven that the headquarters company had lost the divisional war chest in an ambush outside Oradour and believed members of the village to be responsible.

***Ordensburgen* (Castles of the Order)**.   Residential colleges for the training of a Nazi élite ➤Education in the Third Reich.

Ordnungspolizei (Order police).   Known as the Orpo. The regular police force of the Third Reich.

Organization for the Industrial Economy.   Separate laws of February and November 1934 aimed to restructure the Cartel Organization of 1923 by transferring its powers to the Reich government. The new government powers required all commercial and industrial activity to be represented within the boundary of the *Gau* by a chamber, the director of which was a prominent Nazi businessman.

Ossietzsky, Carl von (1889–1938).   The Nobel Peace Prizewinner of 1935. A pacifist who edited a small weekly paper in which he exposed the secret rearmament of Weimar Germany under General von Seeckt. The *Reichswehr* demanded his prosecution and he was jailed briefly in 1931. In 1933, in the round-up of suspects after the Reichstag Fire, he was put into a concentration camp, where nevertheless he was awarded the Nobel Prize. Incensed, Hitler ordered that Germans should accept no more Nobel prizes.

Ossietzsky died of tuberculosis in Oranienburg concentration camp in 1938. His periodical *Die Weltbühne* is still published, with the same cover, in Berlin.

Oster, Hans (1888–1945).   Chief assistant to Admiral Canaris, head of the Abwehr (German military intelligence) 1938–43. Hans Oster was a regular soldier who had served in WWI and under Weimar. Dismissed in 1932 after a scandalous affair with a fellow-officer's wife, he was immediately brought back into the Abwehr by Halder, serving under General von Bredow. Oster disliked the Nazis, and the murder of Bredow in the 1934 Röhm Purge convinced him they must be opposed. After the replacement of the next head of the Abwehr, Patzig, by Canaris in 1935, his hostility to Nazism brought Oster close to Canaris. He was one of the four officers appointed to examine the charge of homosexuality made against the army commander Fritsch in 1938; another member of the court was the lawyer Dohnanyi, who later worked with him against Hitler.

Canaris used Oster to deal with his contacts in Britain and to pass warnings of Hitler's intentions to Czechoslovakia and Poland. Oster had contact with the senior officers who in 1938 were expected to turn against Hitler; then, on the outbreak of war, he sent warnings of the German invasions of Denmark and Norway, of Belgium and the Netherlands, but the governments concerned ignored his warnings.

In April 1943 the Gestapo arrested Dohnanyi, and Oster was suspended from duty. In July 1944 he was arrested in the aftermath of the Bomb Plot and held in the Gestapo interrogation centre at Prinz Albrechtstrasse in Berlin with others suspected of plotting. He was moved to Flossenbürg concentration camp in February 1945 and hanged, with Canaris, just before the American army arrived in April.

***Osthilfe Skandal* (Eastern Aid Scandal)**.   Pressure from the conservative landowners (*Junkers*) of the great estates east of the Elbe had resulted in financial support from the state. During the early 1930s financial abuses became apparent and Oskar von Hindenburg, the son of the President, spoke for the *Junkers*. It seems probable that the Nazis used the scandal (and the bribe of the estate of Neudeck) to gain Oskar Hindenburg's support in the political manoeuvring of 1933.

P

Pact of Steel.   The Rome–Berlin Axis. ►Axis.

Pale of Settlement.   Area of western Tsarist Russia in which some 2,700,000 Jews lived in 1940/41. By 1943 it is estimated that barely 250,000 had survived. The following is an incomplete list of towns in which the Jewish inhabitants were murdered, mostly by SS special units in circumstances of extreme barbarity:

Town	No. of victims	Town	No. of victims
Dvinsk	30,000	Braslav	1,800
Kovno	3,800	Glubokoye	2,500
Vitebsk	16,000	Troki	550
Vilna	70,000	Vileika	4,000
Rudnya	1,200	Smolensk	3,000
Lida	6,000	Borisov	7,620
Bialystok	5,000	Mir	1,200
Mogilev	4,844	Stonim	10,000
Nesvizh	4,000	Bobruisk	179
Kovel	27,000	Pinsk	30,000
Gormei	4,000	Sarny	3,000
Rovno	22,000	Zhitomir	7,000
Kiev	33,000	Babiyar	100,000
Berdichev	35,000	Vinnitsa	15,000
Poltava	12,000	Dnepropetrovsk	37,000
Mariupol	90,000	Taganrog	2,000
Rostov-on-Don	18,000	Nikolaev	94,000
Uman	30,000	Odessa	60,000

The following is a list of the principal concentration camps within the area of the former Pale of Settlement where many hundreds of thousands of Jews were murdered between December 1941 and February 1943:

Treblinka	800,000	Belzec	650,000
Sobibor	250,000	Chelmno	350,000
Majdanek	250,000		

Of the estimated 250,000 survivors from the former Pale of Settlement in 1943, a further 100,000 are believed to have perished, mostly in concentration camps, in the last two years of the war.

Papen, Franz von (1879–1969).   German Chancellor in 1932 and Hitler's Deputy Chancellor 1933–4. A general staff officer and later a diplomat in WWI, von Papen became a leader of the Catholic Centre Party after the war. He was among those conservatives who believed that they could control Hitler while his demagogic powers were used in turn to control the German masses. Both von Papen and those who thought like him proved mistaken. An Emergency Reich Commissioner in Prussia 1932–33 and Deputy Chancellor 1933–4, von Papen was bypassed and finally outmanoeuvred by Hitler. No longer of real value to the Nazi leadership, von Papen was appointed ambassador to Austria in 1934, and when this post became unnecessary he was given the relatively minor post of German ambassador to Turkey, 1939–44.

He was tried by the Allies at Nuremberg and acquitted. The following year a German court sentenced him but he was released in 1949 after two years in prison.

Party Courts (*Parteigerichte*).   Courts to maintain the Party principle of the *Führerprinzip*. Under the guidance of Walter Buch, the Party courts imposed discipline in the often confused and ramshackle hierarchy of the Nazi Party. Established before the assumption of power, the courts became a formidable means of exerting Party control over the membership. After 1933 they were able to impose loss of employment and prison terms.

Paulus, Friedrich von (1890–1957).   Promoted Field Marshal at Stalingrad just before he surrendered his army to the Russians in January 1943, von Paulus was a regular soldier in WWI who served both the Weimar and Nazi governments. In 1942 he was given command of the 6th Army, poised to attack Stalingrad, but as the year ended his army was surrounded and he was forced to surrender. Von Paulus broadcast from Moscow to German soldiers and was used as a witness by the Russians to confirm the complicity of the General Staff in the attack on Russia and in the orders to conquer land for German colonization. He was released from Russia in 1953 where he had been held as a prisoner of war and died in East Germany in 1957.

Peace proposals from Germany.   When, after the successful *Blitzkrieg* on Poland, Hitler turned to the west in 1940 and occupied Denmark, Norway, the Netherlands, Belgium, Luxemburg and France, he could see no reason why Britain should carry on with the war, and said so when he addressed the Reichstag in July. His expectations of peace were widely shared and the American ambassador in London, Joseph Kennedy, reported to Washington that he expected Britain to make an early compromise. Hitler's speech was not a clear offer of peace, but an expression of regret that he had to make war against the English. But the reaction from Britain surprised him by its refusal to consider his suggestion. Rather than accept this, Hitler let Ribbentrop make indirect approaches through the King of Sweden which were equally ignored.

At the beginning of August, the Luftwaffe dropped leaflets on Britain with 'A last appeal to reason'. Hitler himself made no more attempts to make peace with Britain.

The next peace feeler from the Third Reich came in 1941 when the Deputy Führer, Rudolf Hess, flew to Scotland with the vain idea of inducing Britain to sue for peace. This attempt had no support from any of the rest of the Nazi hierarchy, and had certainly not received Hitler's approval.

By 1944, several important Nazi circles understood that a German victory was no longer possible. Schellenberg, head of SS intelligence, used Himmler's masseur, Felix Kersten, to encourage Himmler to consider ending the war. The 'Egmont Reports' were designed by Schellenberg to show Allied strength and the increasingly vulnerable position of Germany. He was encouraged by Karl Wolff, then Himmler's SS adjutant and liaison officer with Hitler's HQ. Wolff himself later negotiated peace terms with the Allies in north Italy.

In April 1945, with Hitler's health worsening and the military situation hopeless, Schellenberg, on behalf of Himmler, spoke to Count Bernadotte, the Swedish Red Cross representative, who relayed Himmler's peace approach to the Allies. But Churchill and Truman (by then US President) consulted each other by telephone and refused to negotiate separately from the Russians.

Pétain, Henri Philippe (1856–1951).   Head of State of unoccupied 'Vichy' France, 1940–44.

Marshal Pétain was a French soldier with a heroic reputation, the defender of Verdun in 1916 and the commander of the French armies in 1918. In 1940, when the Germans advanced through Belgium, Premier Paul Reynaud hoped to strengthen his cabinet by making Pétain Vice-Premier. As the Germans swept through France and took Paris, the government moved to Bordeaux. Here the cabinet turned against Reynaud and Pétain took office as Premier and sued for peace. The surrender terms dictated to the French at Compiègne included the division of the country into two, an occupied northern and an unoccupied southern zone.

Pétain, now Head of State, governed only one third of France. His rule was conservative and authoritarian and in general totally collaborative with the Third Reich. When Allied forces broke out from Normandy, Pétain fled to Switzerland, but returned to face trial in April 1945. He was convicted of collaboration with the enemy and sentenced to military degradation and death, but the penalty was commuted by General de Gaulle to life imprisonment.

Pfarrer-Notbund.   Emergency league of pastors formed by Martin Niemöller in September 1933 to defend the Lutheran Church against the Nazi German Faith Movement. By Christmas of that year the league had 6,000 members, nearly a third of all Protestant pastors in the country. In 1934 the league agreed its Six Principles of the Synod of Barmen, but thereafter it was heavily persecuted by the Nazis until Niemöller himself was arrested in 1937.

Pfeffer von Salomon, Franz Felix.   Commander of the SA, 1926–30. A Freikorps commander who joined Röhm's Frontbann, Pfeffer was Party Gauleiter in Thuringia and Westphalia until a year after Röhm had left Germany when he was given command of the SA. He added orderliness and traditional army drill to SA formations to try to give parade-ground impressiveness and the glamour of a military appearance. His object was to make the SA an instrument of propaganda rather than a gang of bullies. It was Pfeffer who trained the SA in the mass parades and salutes with the raised arm, and the massed shout 'Heil Hitler!' that became a feature of Party rallies. After the SA mutiny of 1930 led by Stennes in Berlin, and a dispute with Hitler over the nomination of SS (rather than SA) men to the Reichstag, he was relieved of command of the SA. Hitler took it over personally until Röhm returned.

Pfeffer was unsentimental and Prussian rather than Bavarian in outlook, and not taken in by the Hitler image. 'That flabby Austrian', the taut and austere Pfeffer called him.

Phoney war.   A phrase first used by the American press and later adopted by the British to describe the war period, September 1939 to May 1940, during which the Western Front saw little or no aggressive activity. On the German side, the reason for their lack of activity is obvious: their principal formations were engaged in Poland for the first three months and thereafter required refitting before they could be transported to the west. Thus German banners draped across buildings opposite French troops proclaimed '*C'est à votre attaque seul que nous riposterons*' ('We shall only fire on you if you attack first').

Three days after his peace proposal of 6 October 1939, Hitler issued the first directive for his assault in the west. In it he noted German superiority in air power and in the theory and practice of armoured warfare, while at the same time recognizing the French superiority in men and artillery and the potential of Great Britain to contribute decisively within the first year. In short, Hitler required that the phoney war, or *Sitzkrieg*, should be brought to an end by a massive German offensive in the west as soon as the German armies could be transferred from the Polish front.

In Berlin, the disclosure of Hitler's intentions came as a shock to Brauchitsch, the Commander-in-Chief, and General Halder, his Chief of Staff. A coup was briefly contemplated, a march on the capital to depose Hitler. But other officers withheld their support and the opposition of Germany's senior soldiers, as would happen so many times in the next few years, dissolved into a form of technical loyalty.

On the British and French side it is more difficult to account for the inactivity of the phoney war. The Allied leadership was not unaware that the bulk of Germany's first-line formations were in Poland or, as 1940 arrived, refitting and still far from their positions on the Western Front. The immediate answer is of course that the British and French had been infected by the 'Maginot' mentality, defence at all costs, but it is possible that the Anglo-French attitude went deeper, or at least further back in recent history. It is possible to see the Allied reluctance to stir from prepared positions as a continuation of the appeasement of the recent past. The principal appeaser, Chamberlain, was after all still in power in Britain throughout the period of the phoney war. France's appeaser, Daladier, remained Premier until March 1940, and the influence of appeasers in the government continued to affect even the belligerent new Premier, Paul Reynaud. Appeasement then, perhaps (in the developed sense of the word: the desire not to provoke), can be seen to be at the root of the Anglo-French view of military strategy during the phoney war.

The period of inactivity on the Western Front ended dramatically on 10 May 1940 when the German army launched its assault. Within hours the phoney war, '*Sitzkrieg*' or '*Drôle de Guerre*' was forgotten as the German armoured columns, supported by dive-bombers, sliced their way through the Anglo-French armies on their way to Adolf Hitler's greatest military triumph of the war.

Pohl, Oswald (1892–1951). Head of the SS Economic Enterprises section, WVHA. Pohl was one of the early élite in the SD. An ex-navy paymaster, he ran the *Allgemeine* SS administration from 1934, and subsequently all SS administration. He headed his own department from 1939, which developed into the WVHA in 1942, making him the next most powerful SS man after Heydrich. He opposed the headlong extermination of Jews because his factories needed their labour. He was appointed to run the administration of concentration camps in 1942 as their productive capacity became appreciated.

In April 1942 his staff ordered that prisoners sent out to work should not be beaten but should be encouraged with better food and clothing. Nevertheless they were slaves working long hours under harsh conditions. Oskar Schindler (described in *Schindler's Ark* by Thomas Keneally, 1982) is the Pohl paradox in operation, by which a prosperous and (by the standards of the time) not unhappy factory operated with Jewish labour.

His business brought immense riches to the SS. In addition, gold and jewellery seized from concentration camp victims amounted to a holding of gold bars in the Reichsbank – under the account name of 'Max Heiliger' – to the value at that time of ten million dollars. He formed companies, obtained monopolies and recruited to the SS businessmen and administrators more concerned with profit than with the ideas of the SS and Nazism.

Although sentenced to death in 1947, four years were spent in appeals and debate before he was hanged at Landsberg in 1951.

Poison Pill. A book written by Ernst Hiemer, editor of *Der Stürmer*, which contained a rag-bag of crude anti-semitic 'history'. Highly praised in some Nazi quarters (although not by the more intellectual SD leaders), Max Amann stated that it should be read by every German boy and girl.

Poland. A Polish republic was formed in 1918 out of the Polish-speaking parts of Russia, Austria and Germany, which, however, included large areas of minority groups, most notably German. After the Treaty of Brest-Litovsk (imposed by Imperial Germany), the area was fought over in 1918 until 1920, with German Freikorps on one side and Soviet Russians on the other. A particular point at issue was the 'Polish Corridor', land between the Baltic Sea and the centre of landlocked Poland, established by the Treaty of Versailles. Poland thus relied greatly on the political support of France which saw Poland as a counterbalance to possible German resurgence.

In 1934 Hitler signed a ten-year non-aggression pact with Poland, loosening the Franco-Polish alliance. In 1938, when Germany took the Sudetenland from Czechoslovakia, Hitler tolerated Poland's annexation of a small corner of Czechoslovakia. But early in 1939, after Germany had occupied all Czechoslovakia, Hitler extended his demand to Danzig and the Polish Corridor. Despite British and French guarantees of Polish independence, Germany invaded Poland in 1939.

The German armies overwhelmed the Poles, and the Russians entered Poland from the east. Within the month Poland had collapsed. Its government fled to Rumania and, in 1940, to Britain.

The population of Poland contained many German speakers who were welcomed into the Third Reich, but the remainder, in what was known as the Governement-General, were treated as racially inferior people and under Frank degraded to a servant society. In western Poland, Poles were expelled from their lands which Germans resettled as part of the Reich to be known as the Warthegau. ➤Warsaw ghetto rising; Russo-German Pact

Polish Amnesty Decree, 1939. A Führer decree giving full amnesty to SS men and units held by, or about to be arraigned by, the army for atrocities in Poland. The purpose of the decree, which seems to have been intended to signal to the military that it had no jurisdiction over SS special units, appears to have been clearly understood by the army command in Poland and two years later in Russia.

Pope Pius XII (Eugenio Pacelli) (1876–1958). Papal Nuncio in Munich in 1917, and in Berlin from 1920 until he became a Cardinal in 1929. Chief adviser, as Vatican Secretary of State, to Pius XI during the negotiation and signing of the Concordat between the Church and the Nazi state in July 1933. Disillusioned by Nazi failure to observe the agreement, however, Pius XI issued the encyclical *Mit brennender Sorge* in 1937, an outspoken attack on Nazi beliefs and methods. On Pius XI's death, Pacelli was elected Pope in March 1939 as Hitler took Czechoslovakia and moved towards war with Poland.

In November 1939, after the conquest of Poland and as the German army was being prepared to attack western Europe, Josef Müller, an anti-Nazi Munich lawyer, was sent to the Vatican by Oster, leader of the Abwehr-centred conspirators. Müller was granted an audience with the Pope, at which he asked if he could act as intermediary with the British if an anti-Hitler government could be formed in Germany. Assured that this was possible, Müller returned, but General Halder and Oster failed to convince General von Brauchitsch, the army commander-in-chief, to act against Hitler. After this, Pope Pius seems to have been reluctant to involve himself on either side.

Many attacks have been made on Pope Pius XII for his failure to condemn Nazi atrocities (while not hesitating to condemn communist misdeeds). Even though he was well acquainted with Germany and was kept well informed, he did not openly condemn Nazism or Hitler's attacks on other countries. His detestation of atheistic and materialistic communism made it impossible for him not to support the anti-communist elements in Hitler's politics and impossible to give full support to the Allies in so far as communist Russia was one of them. Although he knew of the extermination of the Jews, he told the College of Cardinals in June 1943 that a public condemnation might do more harm than good. However, this public caution did not stop priests, churches and monasteries from providing refuge for thousands of Jews. Many members of the Church undoubtedly felt betrayed by the Pope's silence on the issue of genocide and his refusal to threaten excommunication to any Catholic taking part in the arrest, transportation or murder of the Jewish people.

Posen Conference.   Conference held on 6 October 1943 at Posen (Poznan) at which Heinrich Himmler addressed the assembled *Reichsleiter* and *Gauleiter* of Germany on the subject of the Final Solution. Also present at Posen that day was Albert Speer, although he later claimed that he had left the castle where the conference took place before Himmler delivered his speech.

Following speeches by Admiral Dönitz, Field Marshal Milch and Speer himself, Himmler addressed the conference. In his speech the Reichsführer delivered the first known official admission to members of the Party outside the SS that the extermination of the Jewish people of Europe was in progress. The speech is completely without ambiguity on the subject. Referring to the 'difficult' problem of women and children, he said, 'I do not think that I was justified in exterminating the men while leaving the children to grow up and take revenge on our own sons and grandsons'.

One sentence of the speech, concerning war production matters, was addressed specifically to Speer (and seems to indicate that he was still actually present in the hall).

Himmler's Posen speech is crucial to Speer's case that he did not know the state was engaged in mass extermination. His insistence that he left Posen for an appointment with Hitler in Berlin immediately before Himmler's speech is difficult to substantiate. There is no record of any such meeting on 6 October (although there was a meeting on the following day). But, as Gitta Sereny points out, even if Speer had not heard the Himmler speech himself, he could not possibly have remained unaware of its devastating content.

Post-war chaos, 1918–1920. The years of turmoil during which Hitler emerged as the leader of a new revolutionary party.

1918

March   Treaty of Brest-Litovsk; Russia surrenders to Germany. The independent states of Poland, Estonia, Latvia, Lithuania, Finland, Ukraine and White Russia are carved from the former Russian Empire. (When in November 1918 Germany is defeated by the Allies, the Treaty of Brest-Litovsk is annulled by the 1919 Treaty of Versailles.)

Ludendorff begins an offensive on the Western Front against the Anglo-French armies, now joined by Americans. This is at first successful, but exhausts German reserves.

September   The Allies counter-attack and the German army retreats. Food shortages in Germany (caused by the Allied blockade) lead to riots in towns; soldiers and sailors in Germany mutiny.

November   Revolution in Berlin; the German Emperor abdicates and a new government accepts the Allies' armistice terms (signed in the forest of Compiègne).

In Munich a Bavarian Democratic and Socialist Republic is declared. Uprisings and riots throughout Germany.

1919

January   The Spartacist (communist) rising in Berlin is put down with many killed; the leaders, Karl Liebknecht and Rosa Luxemburg, are killed.

A Soviet Republic is proclaimed in Bremen and put down within the month.

April   The Bavarian Republic is taken over by a Soviet Republic; this is suppressed bloodily by army and Freikorps units.

1920

March   The right-wing Kapp Putsch in Berlin (witnessed by Hitler) is put down by Freikorps, including Epp's unit which uses a swastika symbol.

The domination of the Ruhr by a 'Red Army' of 50,000 workers is ended ruthlessly by the army with Freikorps support.

It is in these chaotic years that the Weimar Republic is born.

Potempa. A village in Upper Silesia where a communist was beaten to death by five Nazis in August 1932. They were tried, found guilty and jailed by the courts of the Weimar Republic, but in March 1934 under the new Nazi legality they were freed 'for the good of the Reich'.

Potsdam Putsch. An attempt in January 1933 by General von Schleicher and other senior military figures to seize power. At the end of his fifty-seven days of power as the last Chancellor before Hitler, von Schleicher is believed to have contemplated a Putsch. While senior Nazis were celebrating the news that Hitler would be Chancellor on the morrow, an emissary arrived claiming Schleicher and von Hammerstein had put the Potsdam garrison on a war footing and were preparing to take control of the person of the ancient President Hindenburg. The coup, if it existed in the sense Hitler later claimed, was avoided by the arrival of General von Blomberg in Berlin in the early hours of the morning of 30 January 1933. Blomberg, summoned by Hindenburg, was appointed Defence Minister in the Hitler–von Papen cabinet which was at that moment coming into being. This new authority empowered him to suppress any military Putsch which might be in progress; his reputation in the army made it certain that the Potsdam garrison would obey.

Pour le Sémite.   A pun based on 'Pour le Mérite', Germany's highest military award in W W I. 'Pour le Sémite' described the yellow star which first German Jews and finally other European Jews were forced to wear.

Press in the Third Reich.   In Germany before the establishment of the Third Reich there were no national newspapers. Local papers, like the Nazi *Völkischer Beobachter* with a Bavarian circulation of 115,000 in 1932, or city newspapers like the *Berliner Tageblatt* (circulation in 1932 about 130,000) dominated the field. With the coming of the Third Reich in 1933, all papers were required to conform and editors were held responsible for the content of their papers. Such newspapers of high reputation as the *Berliner Tageblatt* or the *Frankfurter Zeitung* survived, though not as independent journals; and the latter was closed when it published adverse criticism of the late Professor Troost, Hitler's favourite architect. From 1938, when Otto Dietrich became Reich Press Chief, editors were given official stories to follow. Foreign papers were still on sale in the larger towns of Germany, but were forbidden when war began in 1939. The apparatus of news suppression was operated by the Gestapo; news distortion was the task of the editors of the recognized journals.

In 1933 Max Amann began publishing the Munich-based *Völkischer Beobachter* simultaneously in Berlin, adding a Vienna edition in 1938 and bringing the total circulation to 1,200,000 by 1941. Close to a national newspaper, it became required reading for all Nazis and even more for those who wished to avoid accidental criticism of Nazism. Göbbels' periodical *Der Angriff* ('*Attack*') was started in 1927, basing its layout and design on a Communist Party paper. It was used to give a low-brow explanation of Party theory. Göbbels' more serious Party weekly, *Das Reich*, aspired to a more dignified approach and reached a circulation of 1.5 million. The near pornographic and violently anti-Jewish Nazi Party weekly, *Der Stürmer*, edited by Julius Streicher, boasted a circulation of half a million, but was regarded, even by many Nazis, as no more than vulgar pap for the masses. ➤Göbbels, Josef

Pripet Marshes.   Area of Poland in 1939 in which the Polish army planned to make a stand against German forces. But the advance of Soviet formations (under the agreements signed in the 1939 Russo-German Pact) destroyed any possibility of Polish resistance. The Pripet Marshes entered military history for a second time in WWII when Germany invaded the Soviet Union in 1941, her forces driving north and south of Pripet for Minsk and Kiev.

In 1944 the Pripet Marshes again featured in the fighting when Soviet forces advanced westward, towards Lvov. The area was 'reincorporated' in the Soviet Union in 1945. ➤Russo-German Pact

Prisons.   Prisons remained mostly under the control of the local police (Orpo) and the Ministry of Justice. Those prisons which were not SS-run were safer for the prisoners, and a well-intentioned local administration could ensure that a prisoner at political risk (such as Adenauer) would be given a jail sentence rather than consigned to the SS or Gestapo. Yet executions took place in prisons too, and in vast numbers. Between 1939 and 1945, in 175 major prisons and 51 penal-servitude prisons, 21 execution sites carried out over 21,000 executions: in Berlin-Plötzensee alone, there were 3,000 executions.

Protocols of the Elders of Zion.   A forgery of nineteenth-century origin used by various European organizations to provoke anti-semitic reactions. The document purported to be the minutes of a secret Zionist congress. The congress, according to the forged document, was devoted to the planning of terrorism in European capitals, the undermining of the Aryan peoples and the establishment of a Jewish world-state. In the anti-semitic context of the time, the childish exaggerations were ignored and organizations ranging from Tsarist secret police to Nazi Party speakers were able to quote the *Protocols* and be widely believed.

In the western world too, the *Protocols* were widely published, first appearing in the United States early in the century. In 1921 the London *Times* led the attack on the *Protocols*, denouncing them as a forgery; and in 1935 a Swiss court of law declared them to be without authenticity. This, however, did not prevent their continuing use in the Third Reich where they were widely used in schools to inculcate anti-semitic attitudes among the young.

Provisional Government List.   The final list, drawn up by Dr Carl Gördeler in June 1944 for the proposed German government after a successful attempt on Hitler's life, was as follows:

Dr Carl Gördeler: Chancellor
Wilhelm Leuschner: Vice-Chancellor
General Ludwig Beck: Regent and Commander-in-Chief of the Armed Forces
Count Ulrich Schwerin-Schwanenfeld: State Secretary to the Regent
Jakob Kaiser: Deputy Vice-Chancellor
General Friedrich Olbricht or General Erich Höpner: War Minister

Count Stauffenberg: Secretary of State for War
Field Marshal von Witzleben: Commander-in-Chief of the Wehrmacht
Julius Leber: Minister of the Interior
Johannes Popitz: Finance Minister
Dr Paul Lejeune-Jung: Economics Minister
Ulrich von Hassell: Foreign Affairs Minister
Eugen Bolz: Education Minister
Andreas Hermes or Hans Schlange-Schoiningen: Agriculture Minister
Joseph Wirmer or Dr Carl Sack: Justice Minister
Bernhard Letterhaus: Minister for Post-war Reconstruction
Theodor Haubach: Information Minister
General von Tresckow: Chief of Police

➤July Bomb Plot; Gördeler, Carl

Putsch.   The German word for a forcible takeover of a government, a *coup d'état*. Well-known examples were the 'Kapp Putsch' in Berlin 1920, the 1923 'Beer Hall Putsch' by Hitler, and the supposed 'Röhm Putsch' of 1934 which was the pretext for the murder of dissident Nazis on the Night of the Long Knives.

Q

Quisling, Vidkun (1887–1945). Norwegian politician who collaborated with the Nazis and whose name became synonymous in English with 'traitor'. Before the war he had served as a minister in the Norwegian government (and was an honorary Commander of the Order of the British Empire), but he resigned to start a Norwegian Fascist Party. Under the Nazi occupation of Norway he was appointed Minister President of the State Council (1942), but real power lay with Josef Terboven, the German Reichskommissar. Quisling was tried and executed in 1945, after voluntarily surrendering to the newly restored Norwegian government.

R

Race. 'Blood mixture and the resultant drop in the racial level', said Adolf Hitler, 'is the sole cause for the dying out of old cultures . . . All who are not of good race in this world are chaff.'

This distillation of Hitler's point of view, a grim pointer to the future actions of the Third Reich, was by no means the result of a unique obsession on his part – or even a unique perception drawn from the classic works of the period. There is no need to believe that Hitler had read the Comte de Gobineau's *Essay on the Inequality of the Human Races* (1853–5) or the Anglo-German writer Houston Stewart Chamberlain's *The Foundations of the Nineteenth Century* (published 1899 in German and 1910 in English). By the turn of the century, preoccupation with race had reached a popular level, to be debated in cafés throughout Europe or 'studied' in the cheap pseudo-scientific pamphlets which were available in bookshops in London, Paris, Berlin and Vienna. In this last period of Europe's cultural dominance, Anglo-Saxonism in England, Aryanism in Germany and Celtism in France took hold of the popular imagination, and race was believed to provide a key to the achievements recorded in a nation's history. Anti-semitism throve in Victorian England and more so in the France of the Dreyfus Case. But it was in Germany and the Austrian Empire that intolerance became acute and, moving even further east to Poland and Tsarist Russia, there it was expressed in violent and bloody pogroms, sporadic outbursts against the local Jewish population.

The ironies of German and Austrian anti-semitism have often been pointed out: in the late nineteenth century both Empires had large and often prosperous Jewish populations. More, the Jews of Central Europe were frequently well integrated into the societies in which they lived and, in 1914, were seen to be in the forefront of volunteers to fight for their countries.

Yet it remains true that a vast reservoir of anti-semitism survived the war and was increased in intensity by the defeat. The early Nazi Party was only one of hundreds of nationalist parties in Germany and Austria which seized upon the Jews as the organizers of defeat. No exactitude was necessary in the heated atmosphere of the time of 'Stab in the back', the Versailles Diktat and November Criminals; the Jews were responsible: Jewish capitalists or Jewish Bolsheviks. The whole was fuelled by quotations from the *Protocols of the Elders of Zion*, a forged document which purported to show the Jews plotting to take over the world.

Adolf Hitler was by no means alone in believing that this was possible. To what extent other Nazi leaders, like Göring or Hess, believed it is now impossible to know. But it is clear that Hitler believed that Gobineau's racial degeneration was not only a present danger to the Aryan race – it was the chosen means by which the Jews would destroy the Aryan world. (Rationality must not be looked for. How the Jews were to become the master race by infecting Aryans with their own bad blood is difficult to conceive!) What Hitler required and so often got from his German audiences was an act of faith, a decision to believe.

The accepted nature and extent of the 'Aryan' race remains difficult to assess. Gobineau believed the French to be Aryans; Hitler included the British and the northern Italians. By the end of the war the SS, desperate for recruits, included Croatians under the leaking umbrella.

The term 'Aryan' was coined by the Sanskrit scholar Friedrich Max Müller to replace the earlier term 'Indo-European'. In his work he described the migrations of the Aryan peoples and their irresistible surge into north-western Europe. Müller's interest was principally in linguistic terms and he warned against glib correlations of language and race: 'If I say Aryans, I mean neither blood nor bones, hair nor skull; I mean simply those who speak an Aryan language.'

But a whole culture was already primed to accept its superiority. It was the period of the 'yellow peril' and the 'white man's burden'. No easy boundaries could be ascribed to the Aryan world (especially since Müller, its reluctant inventor, denied its racial existence), but the heartland was clearly the Nordic peoples, and most clearly those about to take up the struggle against Jew and Slav in the Aryan kingdom of Adolf Hitler's Third Reich.

Raeder, Erich (1876–1960).   Commander of the German navy from 1935 to 1943, Raeder had risen as a regular officer to become chief of the Naval Command in 1928. He impressed Hitler sufficiently to be promoted Grand Admiral and given full command of the navy. Not all his relations with Nazis were good, for he had cashiered Heydrich from the Navy in 1931 for misbehaviour with a young woman who claimed that he had promised to marry her. Raeder was responsible for the proposed 'big ship navy', the 'Z-Plan', but it is unlikely he anticipated a war with Britain. When war came, his failure to stop the Allied convoys crossing the Atlantic with supplies and armaments from America infuriated Hitler who forced his resignation and replaced him with the submarine commander, Dönitz.

He was captured in Berlin in 1945 by the Russians who included him among the major defendants at the Nuremberg trial. He was found guilty of having planned war and of having issued orders to kill prisoners. Sentenced to life imprisonment, he appealed vainly for a death sentence. He was released in 1955.

Rank.   The right to wear uniform and to assume rank was an essential part of the appeal of the Third Reich. To the familiar army ranks the movement added Party and SS rankings in mostly unfamiliar terminology. An approximate equivalent is given:

NSDAP	SS	Army	US/British Equivalent
Reichsleiter	Reichsführer SS	Generalfeldmarschal	
Reichsleiter	SS Oberstgruppenführer	Generaloberst	
Gauleiter	SS Obergruppenführer	General	Field marshal and
	SS Gruppenführer	Generalleutnant	general officers
Deputy Gauleiter	SS Brigadeführer	Generalmajor	
	SS Oberführer	Oberst	
	SS Standartenführer	Oberst	Officers of
Kreisleiter	SS Obersturmbannführer	Oberstleutnant	field rank
Kreisleiter	SS Sturmbannführer	Major	
Ortsgruppenleiter	SS Hauptsturmführer	Hauptmann	Junior
Zellenleiter	SS Obersturmführer	Oberleutnant	officers
Blockleiter	SS Untersturmführer	Leutnant	
Bereitschaftsleiter	SS Oberscharführer	Feldwebel	
Hauptarbeitsleiter	SS Unterscharführer	Unteroffizier	Non-commissioned
Oberarbeitsleiter	SS Rottenführer	Gefreiter	officers
Arbeitsleiter	SS Sturmmann	Oberschütze	
Helfer	SS Mann	Schütze	Privates

Rascher, Dr Sigmund (d. 1945).   An SS 'medical experiment' doctor who used gypsies, Jews and 'criminals' for tests which ended in the painful death of his victims. His speciality was the use of decompression chambers to simulate high-altitude flight or low-temperature baths to simulate winter Atlantic conditions. He boasted to Payne-Best, the British agent held at Dachau, that he had invented the gas chamber for mass killing, but by then, in 1943, he was a Dachau prisoner himself for having falsely claimed that his wife had given birth to children after the age of forty-eight. He was shot on Himmler's orders in February 1945.

Rastenburg.   Location of the 20 July 1944 military conference at which a near-successful attempt was made on Hitler's life.

Rations.   The basic weekly food ration in Germany for the non-productive worker, for example a housewife, was (in grammes):

	bread	meat	fats
September 1939	2,400	500	270
April 1942	2,000	300	206
June 1943	2,325	250	218
October 1944	2,225	250	218
March 1945	1,778	222	109

These rations were the highest in Continental Europe at the time. British rations were consistently higher, averaging throughout the war 795 grammes per week for meat and 225 grammes for fats.

Raubal, Geli (1908–1931). Hitler's niece and probably his mistress. In 1928 Hitler had first rented the Haus Wachenfeld on the Obersalzberg above Berchtesgaden and invited his sister Angela Raubal to move in as his house-keeper. She brought with her to Berchtesgaden her two daughters, Friedl and Angela – or Geli, as she was known – blonde and unusually attractive. It can reasonably be assumed that the thirty-nine-year-old Hitler soon fell in love with her. Certainly by early 1929 she was his constant companion at meetings, restaurants, conferences and on walks in the mountains. When later in the year Hitler took an apartment in Munich's Prinzregentenstrasse, the Raubal family came to live with him. Talk about the couple spread rapidly. Many Nazi leaders recognized the attraction exerted over German women voters by a bachelor Führer, and appeals were made to Hitler to discontinue the romance.

Of this there was no possibility, however; they were at the height (or possibly just past the high point) of their affair. There were arguments over Geli's career and, more important, violent quarrels during which Hitler accused her of conducting a parallel love affair with his chauffeur, Emil Maurice. She was certainly attracted by her uncle, the increasingly well-known national figure; whether it was more than that of a young girl flattered and impressed by a famous uncle is unknown. For his part, on the evidence of many Party colleagues, Hitler was in love with his niece.

What exactly happened between the couple is unknown, but it seems certain that the relationship degenerated as Hitler became more and more demanding. He is known to have been furious if she were seen in the company of any other man, and he certainly frustrated her operatic ambitions by refusing to let her go to study in Vienna. This refusal was the subject of a scene between them on 17 September 1931. Neighbours, who heard Geli shouting from the window of the Munich apartment as Hitler left for Hamburg, later attested to the despair in her voice and the abruptness of Hitler's manner. The next morning she was found dead, shot through the heart. After a coroner's investigation a verdict of suicide was recorded.

There is no doubt that Hitler was devastated. He wept publicly at her graveside. Weeks later, at a crucial meeting with President Hindenburg, Gregor Strasser complained that Hitler was still lacking in concentration, his mind on the death of his niece rather than on the momentous political developments in which the Party was involved. None of this supports the Munich gossip that Hitler shot his niece in a fit of jealous rage. Yet Geli Raubal's death remains one of the greater mysteries in Hitler's life. Again, it has been suggested that, despite the coroner's report, Geli Raubal did not take her own life but was in fact a victim of Heinrich Himmler who saw the dangerous direction (for the Party) that Hitler's relationship with his young niece was taking.

Whatever the truth, there is a final sinister footnote to the story. One of the many rumours circulating at the time concerned a letter which Hitler is supposed to have written to his niece. In it, the rumour stated, Hitler confessed to some of his sexual problems, and in particular his sado-masochistic inclinations. This letter, it was said at the time, fell into the wrong hands and was bought back with Nazi Party funds by a Nazi priest, Father Bernhard Stempfle. Only one thing in this story is certain: the fate of the helpful priest quickly followed all those who knew anything of the darker side of Hitler's life, when his body was found in a forest near Munich with three bullets in the chest.

Rauschning, Hermann (1887–1982). President of the Danzig senate in 1933, he resigned in 1934 over Nazi policy towards the free city of Danzig, administered by the League of Nations. In 1935 he stood unsuccessfully against the Nazis in Danzig elections, lost and fled to Switzerland. In 1940 he moved to England and thereafter to the USA, where he took American citizenship. Rauschning was an early, well-known and authoritative anti-Nazi writer; but his book *Conversations with Hitler* must be read with reservations since his real contact with Hitler was certainly less than he wished to imply.

Ravensbrück. Women's concentration camp located some 50 miles from Berlin. Established to hold 6,000 prisoners, the number had doubled by 1944. Medical experiments took place at the camp. At the post-war Doctors' Trial, Herta Oberhauser, the only woman defendant, admitted giving lethal injections to Polish women who had suffered experimentation.

Women were transported to Ravensbrück from all over Europe. Thousands of women from the occupied countries, and from Germany itself, perished there.

Rearmament. The 1919 Treaty of Versailles, articles 160 to 210, had limited the German army to 100,000 officers and men, abolished compulsory service and ordered that all surplus equipment and ammunition be handed over to the Allies. The navy was limited to 15,000 men, with a small number of capital ships; submarines were banned. There were to be no air force and no military aircraft. Fortifications on the Rhine were to be demolished, the General Staff dissolved and no associations or 'clubs' were to have weapons or to practise military training. All these requirements were to be supervised by an Allied Control Commission.

Even before the Treaty was signed, its measures were being evaded. General von Schleicher's department in the Ministry of War was recruiting, financing and equipping the Freikorps to defend Germany's interests on the eastern border with Poland and, later, to defend the Republic against insurrection. The Commander-in-Chief of the army, General von Seeckt, from 1920 set to reorganizing and retraining it in new methods. The army of the Weimar Republic found allies in the new Soviet Union and agreed to secret training programmes and military experiments in Russia for tank and aircraft crews. Successive Weimar governments turned a blind eye to this training and the development of new military tactics. Thus Hitler inherited in 1933 a growing military power with an army – unlike the French, British or American armies – with no vast stocks of old weapons to use up before the commissioning of new equipment could be justified. The new army tactics (later to be called '*Blitzkrieg*') were based on the successes of the 1918 offensive. They did not depend on the classic infantry rifle and no new model was developed, but light, rapid-firing, short-range assault rifles, known as machine pistols, were designed. To evade Versailles rules, German police (*not* soldiers) were armed with a Schmeisser design of submachine-gun or 'machine pistol'. Later use in the Spanish Civil War confirmed the military value of this and it was adopted by the German army in 1938 as the MP38.

In WWI Germany had failed to develop the tank as a weapon, so totally new designs were needed and experimental tank chassis were built as 'tractors' and tried out secretly in Russia, by a Reichswehr/Red Army agreement of 1928, using a training ground at Kazan. By these means the new Mark I tank was ready for Hitler to order into production in 1934.

From 1923, von Seeckt had authorized the secret training and design of an air force, the Luftwaffe. The government supported the development of the commercial airline, Lufthansa, thus ensuring an active aircraft industry. Gliding clubs were encouraged, and by 1932 there were 50,000 members of these. At the same time Lufthansa ran a pilot-training school, training a surplus over its requirements for a future Luftwaffe.

The navy was unable to rebuild its fleet of either surface ships or submarines, but planned for the time when it would be possible. ➤Z-Plan; Anglo-German Naval Agreement

Red Front (*Rote Front Kämpferbund*). The German Communist Party (KPD) equivalent of the SA, founded in 1924.

All main parties had their organized groups of bullies during the Weimar Republic, including the SPD. The Red Front at its height numbered 150,000 men. They wore jackboots, with green tunic, cap and breeches and a red armband. Usually armed with truncheons and only rarely and unofficially with pistols, they frequently co-operated with the Nazis before 1933 in breaking up Social Democratic meetings.

Reich (Empire). Nazi Germany officially styled itself the Third Reich from 1933. The first Reich was the Holy Roman Empire, from 962 to its abolition by Napoleon in 1806. The second Reich, Bismarck's empire, lasted from 1871 to the end of the Hohenzollern dynasty in 1918. The term 'Third Reich' was adopted by Hitler in the early 1920s.

Reichenau, Walter von (1884–1942). An ambitious career officer, he followed his commander General Blomberg into the Ministry of War in 1933, co-operating fully with the Nazis. It was von Reichenau who made the agreement with Himmler which kept the army confined to barracks during the 1934 Röhm Purge, thus allowing the SS a free hand. Afterwards von Reichenau even issued a statement justifying the murder of General von Schleicher. He commanded the 10th Army in the 1939 invasion of Poland and the 6th Army in the invasion of Belgium and France in 1940. His success was rewarded by promotion to Field Marshal in 1940. In Russia in 1941 he was an Army Group commander and issued specific anti-Jewish orders for which he would undoubtedly have been tried had he survived the war. He died in an air-crash in 1942.

***Reichsjugendleiter* (Reich Youth Leader)**. ➤Youth Organizations

***Reichsstatthalter* (Reich Governor)**. The governor of one of the eleven districts formed from territories annexed after 1939.

***Reichsstunde (Patriotic hour)*.** A time chosen by its members at which a patriotic club or association would meet and parade.

Reichstag. The imposing domed building in Berlin, the home of the German parliament until it was burnt down in February 1933 (➤Reichstag Fire). Thereafter the 'Reichstag' met in the Kroll Opera House, Berlin, and it was from this building that Hitler, as German Führer, made many of his principal speeches.

Reichstag: Parties, 1920–33
Number of seats held:

Election	SPD[1]	DNVP[2]	DVP[3]	Centre[4]	DDP[5]	BVP[6]	KPD[7]	Others	Nazis
June 1920	102	71	65	64	39	21	4	84	—
May 1924	100	95	45	65	28	16	62	52	—
Dec. 1924	131	103	51	69	32	19	45	39	—
May 1928	153	73	24	62	25	16	54	44	12
September 1930	143	41	30	68	20	19	77	51	107
July 1932	133	37	7	75	4	22	89	2	230
Nov. 1932	121	52	11	70	—	20	100	—	196
March 1933	120	52	2	74	—	18	81	—	288

NOTES
[1] Social Democratic Party, led by Otto Wels from 1931
[2] German Nationalist Party, led by Hugenberg
[3] German People's Party
[4] Representing the Roman Catholic minority, the Centre Party was led by Kaas
[5] Democratic Party, derived from the pre-war liberals
[6] Bavarian People's Party. Formed in November 1918 by the old Bavarian centre, it worked nationally with the Centre Party
[7] German Communist Party, led by Thälmann

Reichstag Fire. On 27 February 1933, a month after Hitler became Reich Chancellor (►Chronology, p. 1), the Reichstag building burnt to the ground. The next day President Hindenburg decreed all civil liberties suspended in the 'Emergency Decree for the Defence of Nation and State'. In March this decree became constitutional law, giving Hitler dictatorial powers and making Germany a police state.

On the night the fire was discovered, Göring, as Minister of the Interior of the State of Prussia, was quickly on the spot and publicly accused the communists of arson; a weak-minded Dutchman, Marius van der Lubbe, arrested that night in the building, was accused by Göring of being their agent. The Prussian police arrested over 4,000 people as suspects. A show trial was organized in September in Leipzig to prove Göring's case that the communists were guilty. Before the court were van der Lubbe, Torgeler (the leader of the communists in the Reichstag who had surrendered himself), and three Bulgarian communists (among them Dimitrov), who were known agents of the Soviet Comintern. The trial was not the success Göring had hoped for. His decision to allow international observers to be present enabled Dimitrov to goad Göring into outbursts of rage and make it sometimes appear that it was the Nazis who could be accused. In the world's press Göring was ridiculed. All but van der Lubbe were acquitted: the Lex van der Lubbe was passed to give retrospective sanction to the death penalty for arson, and he was executed. Torgeler was moved to a concentration camp but later released. Dimitrov was allowed to return to Russia and became Premier of Bulgaria after WWII.

A 'mock trial' was held in London in 1934 by liberal and socialist groups which was used internationally as powerful anti-Nazi propaganda. Nevertheless, though the real trial in Germany was mishandled for foreign consumption, it was skilfully presented to the German people to create a deep sense of shock which effectively helped the Nazis to consolidate their power. At the same time a lesson was learnt about the undesirability of open courts. In April 1934 the right to try cases of treason was taken from the Supreme Court and given to the new *Volksgerichtshot* (the People's Court), which was established with two professional judges sitting with five others from the Party, SS or army and with no right of appeal from its sentence.

There has been a continuing debate as to who really started the fire. There is strong but inconclusive evidence that an SA detachment was responsible, but on balance it seems that it may equally have been the confused and feeble-minded van der Lubbe.

Reichswehr. The army of 100,000 soldiers allowed to the German Republic by the Treaty of Versailles.

Reinhardt, Fritz (1895–1969). Gauleiter of Upper Bavaria, 1928–30. A Reichstag deputy from 1930, he was appointed State Secretary in the Ministry of Finance in 1933. Reinhardt's main historical significance is as an instructor of Nazi street-corner orators; the level of training he offered was pitched to the low standard of education that was typical of the recruits to the Nazi Party before 1933. Reinhardt was imprisoned after the war and released in 1949.

Reitsch, Hanna (1912–1979). Germany's leading woman test-pilot. Personally devoted to Hitler, Hanna Reitsch held the women's gliding records for duration, distance and altitude in the 1930s. For her war service she held the Iron Cross, First and Second Class, the only woman with this distinction. Her ability and bravery as a pilot were widely recognized. She was remarkable for having test-piloted the V-1 rocket plane before it was used in 1944 as a pilotless bomb against Belgium and England. In April 1945 she flew with General Greim into Berlin to visit Hitler in the Bunker. After Greim had been appointed the new commander of the Luftwaffe she managed to fly out of the burning centre of the city with Russian guns firing at the plane. It was to be her last act of loyalty to Adolf Hitler. Captured by the Americans, she was released without trial in 1946 and resumed her career as an international glider and research pilot.

Remagen. An undestroyed bridge across the Rhine brilliantly seized by a reconnaissance patrol of the US 1st Army. While the major effort to cross the Rhine was being prepared by the British and Canadian 21st Army Group and the US 9th Army in the north, General Patton's US 3rd Army had broken through weak German defences in the Eifel (the German section of the Ardennes) and reached the Rhine at Coblenz. Slightly to the north, however, an armoured patrol of US 1st Army had achieved what every Allied commander dreamed of: they had discovered a basically undamaged bridge across the Rhine at Remagen near Bonn. The discovery was brilliantly exploited. US troops, led by Sergeant A. Drabik of Holland, Ohio, raced across the bridge. An explosion set by Captain W. Bratke of the Wehrmacht blew one of the supports while the Americans were in the act of crossing, but the main charge failed to detonate. In under twenty-four hours, more than 8,000 troops with tanks and self-propelled guns had crossed the Rhine at Remagen.

Remer, Otto Ernst (b. 1912). The major commanding the Gross Deutschland Guard Battalion in Berlin on the day of the failed July 1944 Bomb Plot. When told that Hitler had been assassinated, and ordered by the conspirators to arrest Göbbels, he marched men to the Propaganda Ministry, but Göbbels persuaded him that he was being tricked and connected him by telephone to Hitler. Hitler at once promoted him to colonel and ordered him to put down the rising in Berlin. Remer's fanatical loyalty soon brought him further promotion to Major-General.

In the 1950s he founded a neo-Nazi party in Germany, the Socialist Reich Party (SRP), but this came into conflict with the law and he fled to Egypt.

Renn, Ludwig (1889–1979). Saxon aristocrat, born 'Arnold Vieth von

Golsenau'. An army officer in WWI and Freikorps member in 1919, he became a writer and joined the Communist Party (KPD) in 1928, using the name Renn. He was arrested after the Reichstag Fire with other communists and spent 30 months in prison. He was released and went to Switzerland in 1936. In the Spanish Civil War he fought on the Republican side in the International Brigade. Interned in France in 1940, he made his way via England and the USA to Mexico, where he founded the left-wing anti-Nazi movement in Latin America, Freies Deutschland. He returned to East Germany (DDR) in 1947.

Reparations. As part of the Versailles Treaty, Germany was required to pay reparations for damage to the victorious Allies. In the months immediately after WWI there were enormous and unreal estimates made of damages and of Germany's ability to pay. Eventually in 1921 the sum of 132,000 million gold Marks was fixed. At the time, this was equivalent to $32,000 million. There were also large inter-Allied war debts which added to the financial difficulties – particularly France, who owed Britain over £600 million and the USA $4,000 million. This was further complicated by the new Soviet government in Russia, which refused to acknowledge the huge Tsarist debt, much of it to France. The demand by the Allies for reparations from the new Weimar government became a major issue in Germany, and immediately nationalist parties called for the rejection of Versailles; this was one of the fundamental points of the tiny German Workers' Party in 1919 before it developed into the Nazi Party.

By 1923, the German Mark was rapidly collapsing. French troops marched into the Rhineland in an attempt to enforce outstanding reparations. By November it cost an absurd four billion Marks to buy one dollar. At this low point in German history, Hitler thought he saw his destiny and attempted the Beer Hall Putsch.

A new repayment scheme was worked out in 1924. It was known as the Dawes Plan (after the chairman of the Allied Committee, Charles G. Dawes, 1865–1951, Director of the US Bureau of the Budget and, later, 1925–9, Vice-President of the United States). The plan envisaged a rate of payment by Germany of 2,000 million gold Marks a year. This soon proved to be excessive. Another attempt was made in 1929: the Young Plan (named after the next chairman of the Allied Committee, US lawyer Owen D. Young, 1874–1962) reduced the total to 37,000 million gold Marks and increased the period of repayment to fifty-nine years. This plan was hotly contested in Germany and was the issue on which Hugenberg tried to form the nationalist Harzburg Front which Hitler used as a further step to power.

In 1931, in the face of political and economic crisis, Germany ceased repayments and an international conference in Lausanne in 1932 agreed to give up all further reparations claims.

Resistance.   ➤July Bomb Plot; White Rose; M.A.N.; Neu Beginnen; Eilbek
Comrades; Gruppe Herbert Baum; Freiburg Circle; Kreisau Circle; Rote
Kapelle; Youth Resistance to Nazism; Communist/Socialist Resistance;
Lochner, Louis P.; Mylius Group; Leuschner, Wilhelm; Römer, Dr Joseph

Reynaud, Paul (1878–1966).   French politician who succeeded Edouard
Daladier as Premier, 21 March 1940. He constantly advocated resistance during
the German *Blitzkrieg* which began on 10 May. His support for Churchill's
proposal for an Anglo-French Union caused the defeatists led by Pétain to
unite against him and he resigned on 16 June 1940. He was arrested by Pétain's
Vichy government in September 1940 and was imprisoned; he was one of the
accused in the notorious Riom Trial of 1942.

Rhineland, Reoccupation of.   Hitler's first real *coup de main* in foreign
policy. Comprising all German territory west of the Rhine and a thirty-mile
strip east of the river (which included Cologne, Düsseldorf and Bonn), the
Rhineland had been demilitarized at Versailles. On 7 March 1936, in an
operation code-named Winter Exercise, Hitler ordered a slender German force
to reoccupy the zone, on the ground that the Franco-Soviet Pact had broken
the Treaty of Locarno. Orders to the *Wehrmacht* during this first attempt to
reverse a major item in the Treaty of Versailles were to retreat immediately if
French forces moved to oppose the occupation. In the ensuing crisis Hitler's
resolute stance split France and Great Britain diplomatically and ensured the
international acceptance of his *fait accompli*.

Ribbentrop, Joachim 'von' (1893–1946).   Foreign Minister from 1938 to
1945 whose aristocratic connections – or claims to them, for his 'von' was
disputed by many – were useful to Hitler for a while. He had married Annalies
Henkel, of the wine and champagne family, in 1920 and travelled widely as a
salesman. He joined the Nazi Party only in 1932, but immediately became
useful. It was at his house in Berlin in January 1933 that the negotiations with
von Papen were carried out that made Hitler the agreed chancellor. Ribbentrop
was an effective functionary, but it is doubtful if he ever originated any of the
diplomatic moves that he carried out.

In 1933 he set up the Ribbentrop Bureau under Hess's secretariat in
opposition to the German Foreign Ministry. Staffed by journalists and careerists
usually lacking qualifications, the object of the bureau was to prove Nazi
methods more effective than the traditional foreign service. Such duplication
became common Nazi practice: the establishment of a shadow body alongside
the official organization, just as the SS, with many officers from the non-Junker
non-officer class, paralleled the army.

In May 1935 Ribbentrop proved the success of his methods by concluding
the Anglo-German Naval Treaty without using Foreign Ministry officials, or
even officially informing them. Again independently of the Foreign Ministry,

in 1936 he persuaded Japan to join in an Anti-Comintern Pact, which Mussolini agreed to sign the next year. By this time he had been made German ambassador to London (from August 1936).

In February 1938 Hitler dismissed the traditional Foreign Minister von Neurath who, with Generals Blomberg and Fritsch, had tried to dissuade him from moves against Austria and Czechoslovakia. Ribbentrop was appointed Foreign Minister; he was now at the centre of the Nazi aristocracy and the social standing of Annalies von Ribbentrop lent a glamour no other Party wife could match.

Ribbentrop suggested to the Poles the return of Danzig to Germany and collaboration against Russia. When they failed to agree, Hitler moved into Memel, showing them that diplomacy did not mean debate. The return of Danzig was the immediate reason for the attack on Poland in September 1939.

In the war, Ribbentrop maintained his status, but war had superseded diplomacy and his position carried dignity rather than power. He was arrested in June 1945 and brought to trial at Nuremberg with the major offenders. Like others, he claimed ignorance of concentration camps, racial extermination policies and other Nazi crimes. He was found guilty and hanged.

Riefenstahl, Leni (b. 1902).   Film director best known for her propaganda documentaries. Her first film made at Göbbels' request was a short picture *Sieg des Glaubens* (*Victory of Faith*) which, because of her detestation of Göbbels and the difficulties involved in filming, caused her to suffer a nervous breakdown. However, Hitler personally persuaded her to make another film, a record of the Nazi Party Congress in Nuremberg in September 1934. This was the famous *Triumph des Willens* (*Triumph of the Will*), one of the most remarkable propaganda documentaries ever made. Hitler's purpose was to demonstrate the solidarity of the Party after the Röhm Purge and at the same time to introduce the new Party leaders, important in a pre-television age. It was also intended to impress foreign audiences with the power and efficiency of the Third Reich. In this it succeeded. In 1936 she made *Olympia*, a record of the 1936 Olympic Games held in Berlin. It was released in two parts: *Fest der Völker* (*Festival of the Nations*) and *Fest der Schönheit* (*Festival of Beauty*). Like *Triumph of the Will* it is generally regarded as an astonishing film achievement.

After WWII, Riefenstahl was briefly imprisoned by the French for her role in the Nazi propaganda machine.

Riom Trial.   An attempt by the Pétain government in 1942 to organize a show trial for those like Paul Reynaud accused of leading France unprepared into war against Germany.

Rockets.   The first ever long-range heavy rocket was developed under the aegis of the German army and successfully operated in the last year of WWII.

In March 1944 the SS tried to take over control of the project and arrested the scientists, including Werner von Braun, intending to put rocket research under their *Ahnenerbe* organization. The development of rocketry was also delayed by the planning methods of Hitler who, still convinced of quick victory in 1942, would not give priority to new research into future weapons, the jet plane, atomic bombs or rockets.

Allied intelligence knew of the V-2. A test rocket had flown off-course and landed in Sweden, and pieces of another were smuggled out to Britain by the Polish resistance. Photographic intelligence of the rocket research and manufacturing site at Peenemünde on the Baltic was intense and there were heavy air-raids on it from August 1943. In spite of this, the V-2 was brought into action in September 1944. The V-2 was a formidable weapon: 50 feet long with a warhead weighing one ton, it reached a height of 60 miles and plunged down on its target at a speed of over 3,500 mph. Its range was a little over 200 miles.

Between January 1944 and April 1945, about 6,000 were built. Some 1,265 were launched at the port of Antwerp in Belgium, and 1,050 against London and other parts of Britain.

The V-2 was produced too late to win the war, and its development was in spite of rather than because of Nazism. Werner von Braun and others from Peenemünde were taken to the USA after the war, where V-2 technology far in advance of the rest of the world was used as a major step towards the NASA space programme.

Röhm, Ernst (1887–1934). The leader of the SA, murdered during the 'Night of the Long Knives', the Röhm Purge. Short, overweight and bullet-scarred, his flushed cheeks and savage smile were those of the roistering lecher. Certainly he delighted in the comradeship the army had provided, but he was not the traditionally loyalist German soldier at heart. He was non-conformist, homosexual, an adventurer who by his own admission detested bourgeois normality and felt himself drawn to exploit the chaos which engulfed Germany after the defeat in WWI. A hard, front-line professional soldier, Röhm remained in the army after the war and fought in von Epp's Freikorps to crush the revolutionary government in Munich in 1919. At this time he was secretly employed in the Munich area by the army to establish weapon and ammunition dumps for monarchist and nationalist groups and to organize a special political intelligence unit for the army. It was his unit which recruited the unknown Adolf Hitler to investigate and infiltrate the 'German Workers' Party', and it was from this tiny group that Hitler created the Nazi Party. The development of the early Röhm/Hitler relationship is obscure. At their first meeting Röhm was a Reichswehr captain, Hitler a mere ex-front-line soldier. At some point the relationship changed. Certainly the two men were close friends; Röhm in fact is the only political associate known to have called Hitler by the familiar '*du*'. But Hitler had by now imposed himself on the fledgling Party as leader and Röhm was the organizer of the protection squads which he would finally build into the SA.

During the 1923 Beer Hall Putsch, Röhm led his 'Reich War Flag' group together with SA men to capture the Munich army commander, General von Lossow; but the general ordered Captain Röhm, still a serving officer, to dismiss his men and Röhm complied.

After the failure of the Putsch, he was one of those put on trial. Although found guilty of treasonable acts, he was released and dismissed from the army. Shortly afterwards he went abroad to Bolivia to work as a military instructor.

In January 1931 Hitler recalled Röhm to take over the SA again. Röhm's object was to re-establish its confidence, as (by now) the SA felt neglected in the Party. Röhm however saw the SA as the core of the Nazi revolution and expanded it from 70,000 to 170,000 men by the end of 1931. By 1934 he had achieved a total enrolment of 4,500,000.

But Röhm held genuinely revolutionary views, and his radical ideas alienated the landowning Junkers and the industrialists, whom he would have dispossessed, and the army, who saw the SA as a rival. In the Party, his growing power threatened to rival Göring and Himmler. His bohemian conduct, drinking, homosexuality and loose talk outraged many, both in and outside the Party. The crisis began to take shape when the Nazi Party came to power. Röhm saw the Third Reich as the opportunity for the SA to take its reward. Beyond that, however, he believed that the new state under Hitler was already making too many compromises with conservatives in industry, landownership and the army. At issue was what the SA called 'second revolution' and was later called (in Maoist China) the 'continuous revolution'; by this was meant the struggle against those inertial pressures against change which follow the first seizure of power in a state.

Adolf Hitler saw the threat clearly. After some hesitation he acted with chilling decision. Röhm was first ordered to send the SA on leave for the month of August. On 30 June Hitler travelled to Bad Weissee, where Röhm was staying with SA comrades. Röhm was placed under arrest; offered a pistol, he refused to use it. Within two days he had been murdered in his cell at Stadelheim prison by an SS murder-squad led by Theodor Eicke.

Röhm Purge. 'The Night of the Long Knives' in June 1934 when Hitler ordered the killing of his enemies in the Nazi Party. Even after Hitler had achieved power in 1933 there was an anti-Hitler sentiment among the old Strasserite radicals in the Nazi Party. In addition frustration was felt among the SA, who believed themselves to be neglected and unrewarded and in danger of being displaced by the 'March Violets' who had joined the Party in 1933. There was talk of the 'second revolution', when the old traditional power groups (aristocrats, landowners, industrialists and liberal bourgeoisie) would be swept away. Meanwhile the SA was forced to watch the takeover of the Prussian secret police (the 'Gestapo') by Himmler and the rapid growth of the SS.

Röhm, as head of the SA, had increased its size from the time of his return to command in 1931 from 70,000 to over four million – a much larger force than the army. His view of the SA as the true army of the new Nazi Germany alarmed and dismayed the generals; but Röhm persisted in his claim that it was the SA that was responsible for the defence of the nation, and the Führer's continuing belief in the primary role of the army was misguided. Lutze, the SA leader in Hanover, was horrified at this treason and reported it to Hess, the Party's Deputy Führer, and Blomberg's chief of staff, von Reichenau, who was in touch with Himmler.

Himmler and the SS were by now ready to take on the SA. Already in 1933 they had broken up many of the SA's private concentration camps and disbanded the SA 'auxiliary police' units, ensuring that the SS official role in the new state was accepted.

Pressures on Hitler now mounted. President Hindenburg was clearly dying, and without him the traditionalists and the army might call for a return to monarchism; but the leading candidate for the throne was the Kaiser's son, Augustus Wilhelm, who was a member of the SA. At the same time the Deputy Chancellor, von Papen, made a speech at Marburg University denouncing the methods of the Nazis, their violation of human rights and their anti-Christianity. A purge of the SA would make them responsible, by implication, for all the brutalities of the Nazi past.

The men close to Hitler began making lists of those who should be eliminated in order to protect the regime. Many lists were prepared: Göring, Blomberg, Himmler, Heydrich, Best of the SD in southern Germany, Lutze and others all had proposed victims. One of the lists used by the SS in the purge was Röhm's own list of SA officers due for promotion. In the second half of June events moved swiftly.

10 June	Von Papen's Marburg speech
20 June	A shot fired at Hitler slightly wounds Himmler and is supposed to have been fired by the SA escort
25 June	The 'League of German Officers' disowns Röhm and expels him; the *Abwehr* claims to have secret SA orders to stage a *coup d'état*; the army commander cancels all leave
26 June	Himmler informs senior SS and SD officers of an impending SA revolt; Göring makes a speech against monarchists
27 June	Sepp Dietrich, commanding the SS guard in Berlin, goes to army HQ and is given extra weapons and transport after showing an 'SA execution list' with the name of the very officer he speaks to on it! The rumour spreads that the SA plan to kill the army old guard

28 June	Hitler travels from Berlin to Essen to attend the wedding of the local *Gauleiter*, Terboven
29 June	Beck, a general staff officer, later to rise in power, warns officers at Berlin headquarters to have pistols to hand; the *Völkischer Beobachter* prints an article by Blomberg giving loyalty to Hitler and asking for curbs on the SA; Hitler visits labour camps and goes on to Bad Godesberg near Bonn, on the Rhine, where he is joined by Göbbels; Göring mobilizes his Berlin police and SS units; the SA in Munich are ordered out aimlessly on the streets by anonymous notes, and the *Gauleiter* tells Hitler of this as proof of the SA's dissidence
30 June	Hitler flies at dawn to Munich with Göbbels, his press chief Dietrich, and Lutze of the SA; he orders Schmidt and Schneidhuber, the leading SA officers, to Stadelheim jail, shouting that they will be shot; the *Gauleiter* is given lists of SA men and others in Bavaria to arrest; Hitler drives to Bad Weissee where Röhm and other SA men are staying at a hotel and orders them to Stadelheim prison except for Heines, the SA commander of Silesia, who is taken from his bed with a boyfriend and shot immediately; Göbbels sends a code-word 'Colibri' to Berlin for action; SA leaders in Berlin are taken to the army cadet school at Lichterfelde and shot straight away; Hitler prepares announcements from the Brown House in Munich and flies back to Berlin
1 July	Sunday. Hitler attends a public function, then gives the order to kill Röhm in his cell
3 July	A law is issued legitimizing all the killings
13 July	Hitler makes a speech in the Reichstag explaining and justifying the affair, claiming that only 19 senior and 42 other SA men had been shot, while 13 had been shot resisting arrest and three had committed suicide.

In fact many more than 77 had died, probably more than 1,000: not only Röhm and the other senior SA men such as Ernst of the Berlin SA, but also a music critic called Schmid, shot in mistake for an SA leader called Schmidt. The SS gunmen also killed von Schleicher and his wife, von Bredow (the predecessor of General von Reichenau), Edgar Jung who had written von Papen's Marburg speech, Klausener (the leader of the Catholic Action group), von Kahr, now an old man but still hated for putting down the 1923 Beer Hall Putsch, and Father Stempfle, an old Nazi who probably knew too much about Hitler's relationship with Geli Raubal. Not least of those killed was Gregor Strasser, once the leader of the radical Nazis.

Römer, Dr Joseph (1890–1942). A WWI soldier and commander of the *Freikorps Oberland*. Active in the Resistance from Hitler's accession to power,

Römer's importance seems to be that he ranged widely through the resistance movement, overlapping with communist Robert Uhrig's Berlin Osram works' *Robby Group* on the left, through Adam von Trott zu Solz to the Solf Circle and leading army groups on the right.

Details of the Römer Group itself are understandably obscure. Römer was arrested at least twice before the war in 1933 and again in 1934 when he was held in Dachau.˙Released in 1939 on the intercession of his former fellow officer General Ritter von Greim he immediately renewed his contacts with resistance groups at both ends of the political spectrum. He was finally arrested in February 1942 and executed on 25 September.

Rommel, Erwin (1891–1944). The 'Desert Fox'. A most popular general in Germany who also had a good reputation among Allied soldiers. Born near Ulm, Rommel appears to have had no other ambition than to become a professional soldier. He had distinguished himself as a battle group leader in WWI and later wrote on new infantry tactics. Hitler was impressed by his book *Infantry Attacks* and from 1938 Rommel commanded Hitler's HQ staff, first in Austria then in Czechoslovakia and Poland. After serving as a successful Panzer division commander in the invasion of France in 1940, he was given command of the new Afrika Korps in 1941 and drove the British 8th Army out of Libya into Egypt. In June 1942 he was made Field Marshal. Shortage of supplies, combined with British superiority in air cover and gradually increasing forces, checked his advance as it approached the Nile. Late in 1942 he was decisively defeated at the Battle of El Alamein, and retreated westwards as Anglo-American armies landed in Morocco and Algeria. His forces were compelled to surrender Tunisia in 1943. Escaping the North African débâcle he commanded in Italy until given Army Group Northern France to prepare for the Allied invasion in 1944. Here, unable to check the Anglo-American invasion on D-Day in June 1944 and its advance into France, he begged Hitler to end the war.

The army conspirators of the July 1944 Bomb Plot had hoped to have him on their side, but he had in fact refused to involve himself in an assassination attempt; instead, he preferred to bring Hitler to trial. It is uncertain quite how Rommel's name was connected with the conspirators, but in October 1944 he was at home recovering from wounds received during an air-raid, when he was visited by two fellow generals and told he was to be arrested. He chose suicide and a state funeral, rather than a trial and certain conviction.

In 1942 Germany needed a hero; for its part, Britain needed to show that it had beaten a great general. To praise Rommel was therefore in the interests of both sides, although he had in fact commanded only in North Africa and briefly held a major European fighting command in 1944.

Roosevelt, Franklin Delano (1882–1945). US statesman and President during the crucial period of the rise of the Third Reich and throughout most of WWII. Long before the outbreak of war, Roosevelt had stated his opposition to the aggressive aims of the Axis powers and their totalitarian ideologies. Though it was necessary, especially in the election of 1940, for him to adopt a neutral stance to placate the isolationist element in the USA, Roosevelt clearly revealed his intentions with the Lend Lease Act in March of the following year.

In August 1941 Roosevelt and Churchill met at sea off Newfoundland and framed the Atlantic Charter, a remarkable document in that it was, in effect, a statement of war aims before the United States entered the war. In Berlin the message was received with painful clarity and undoubtedly led to Hitler's greatest blunder, his declaration of war on the United States in support of the Japanese attack on Pearl Harbor.

Plans had already been laid to develop a modern army (the Selective Service Act) of seven million men, a huge air force and a navy which before the war's end would outstrip even Britain's Royal Navy. In the course of the war nearly fourteen million Americans were drafted into the services.

Several meetings with Churchill took place in 1943: at Casablanca in January, at Washington in May and at Quebec in August. At these conferences the policies of unconditional surrender and 'Germany first' (i.e. that the US's principal effort should be directed first against Germany and only later against Japan) were agreed.

In December 1943 Roosevelt and Churchill held their meeting with Stalin at Teheran, where agreement was reached on future military operations against Germany.

The last international conference in which Roosevelt represented the US took place at Yalta in February 1945. By now Roosevelt was a dying man, and the decisions taken here may possibly not have reflected Roosevelt's will and intention when in reasonable health. He died on 12 April 1945, less than a month before the war in Europe was over. To Hitler and Göbbels his death seemed a positive sign from the Nordic gods, but the great advantages of Allied disunity which they expected to flow from it never materialized.

Rosenberg, Alfred (1893–1946). An early Nazi anti-semitic writer whose cloudy and obscure book *The Myth of the Twentieth Century*, published in 1930, was regarded as fundamental Nazi thinking. It argued that liberalism had wrecked the proper ascendancy of the Nordic people, that lesser races had taken power and that it was Germany's duty to subdue them.

Rosenberg was born in Russian Estonia and had fought in the Russian army in WWI. He came to Munich after the Russian revolution, and there wrote for nationalist and anti-semitic extremists like Dietrich Eckart. He became editor of the *Völkischer Beobachter* and joined the Nazi Party. Rosenberg marched with Hitler and Ludendorff in the 1923 Beer Hall Putsch, fleeing when the shooting started. When Hitler was arrested and jailed, he appointed Rosenberg Party Leader in his absence – but Rosenberg was incapable of administering or leading, and the Party began to splinter.

Rosenberg remained influential only as a leader in the kind of thinking that the Party liked. In 1933 he was given a Party rather than a national post, in charge of its foreign affairs department. In 1940 he set up a task force to collect or loot art treasures from conquered Europe, and in 1941 he became minister for the occupied eastern territories.

Although he said he was shocked by Hitler's Final Solution, he did not resign his post and he was generally ignored by both military and SS administrations. He was arrested by the British in 1945 and included in the Nuremberg trial of the major war criminals for his deeds in Eastern Europe, found guilty and hanged.

Rossbach, Gerhard (1893–1967). A notorious, flamboyant *Freikorps* leader who joined the Nazis in 1922 and commanded the Munich SA. He led the infantry cadets in the Beer Hall Putsch, escaping to Austria when it collapsed. From there he returned with a stock of unused ex-WWI East African campaign brown cloth that became the uniform of the SA (hence the name 'Brownshirts'). Although an SA man and a homosexual, he survived arrest in the 1934 Röhm Purge and lived on in Frankfurt as a businessman.

Rote Kapelle (Red Orchestra).   The name given by Admiral Canaris, head of *Abwehr* (German Military Intelligence), to the communist spy network in Western Europe, broken up in 1942. In the 1930s Leopold Trepper (1897–1974), a Jew from Poland who had worked in Palestine as a communist and had later been trained in Russia by Soviet intelligence, made contact with dissident Germans from a base in Belgium. The leading German dissident, Harro Schulze-Boysen, had run an anti-Nazi paper until arrested in 1933; his aristocratic family connections saved him, however, and he was employed in the Air Ministry. By 1938 he was sending information to Moscow on the German Condor Legion in Spain and was able to identify suspected Nazi agents in the International Brigade. Others in the *Rote Kapelle* network succeeded in sending to Russia information on German military supplies and plans, including Hitler's insistence on capturing Stalingrad. By 1942 there were some 100 radio transmitters forwarding information to Moscow.

In August of that year Canaris and his *Abwehr* uncovered the organization and the Gestapo made forty-six arrests including Schulze-Boysen. Radio equipment was taken and operators were horribly tortured. All the men were hanged at Plötzensee, near Berlin, and Mildred Harnack (an American citizen) was guillotined there with the other women captured. The transmitters were taken over by the SD who continued to operate them, sending out false information. Trepper was captured in France but survived interrogation and escaped in September 1943. Kept safe until after the liberation of Paris, he was then flown to Moscow. There he was accused of collaboration with the Gestapo and spent ten years in prisons, eventually being released after Stalin's death and allowed to emigrate to Israel.

The Rote Kapelle was not the only – nor perhaps the most important –

Russian source of information in Western Europe. A more successful one, code-named 'Lucy', operated from Switzerland until late 1943. ➤Resistance; Lucy

Rublee Plan. The plan put forward by the American George Rublee at Evian in 1938 to facilitate the emigration of Jews from Nazi Germany with 25 per cent of their assets. In discussions with the Reichsbank president, Dr Schacht, Rublee proposed a figure of 150,000 Jews for resettlement abroad. But internal quarrels among the Nazi leadership led to the plan being abandoned and to later deportation and murder of many of the Jews who might have been involved.

Ruhr. The heart of Germany's coal- and steel-based heavy industry was occupied by French and Belgian troops in January 1923 because of their claim that Germany had fallen behind in Versailles reparation payments. Although the USA, Britain and Italy did not support the Franco-Belgian move, Germans saw it as an invasion by the Allies. At first there was officially supported passive resistance, until Chancellor Stresemann gave this up following international economic pressure. But resistance and sabotage continued against the occupying forces. One of the saboteurs, Albert Leo Schlageter, was arrested and executed by a French army court in May 1923 and became a hero of German nationalists. Though never a Nazi, he nevertheless became the hero of a Nazi play by Johst and was acclaimed as a Nazi martyr by Göbbels. ➤Reparations

Rundstedt, Karl Rudolf Gerd von (1875–1953). The German commander in the 1940 campaign against the Low Countries and France, and in 1944 commander in the west against the Anglo-American invasion.

Von Rundstedt had fought in France and Turkey in WWI and remained with the army, reaching general in 1927. At the time of the Blomberg and Fritsch crisis, when the Minister for War and the Commander-in-Chief were removed from their posts, von Rundstedt, next in seniority to them, was also sent into retirement. He was recalled, and was in charge of the planning for the German invasion of Poland and given command of Army Group South in August 1939. In May and June 1940 he was the commander of Army Group A which led the main attack into France; it was on his orders that the German armour halted near Dunkirk to allow the Luftwaffe to attack and destroy the British, who managed instead to evacuate most of their troops. After the victory in France he was promoted to Field Marshal. He commanded Army Group South in June 1941, invading the Ukraine, but in December Hitler dismissed him for making a tactical retreat at Rostov. He was reappointed as commander of Army Group West, in France, in March 1942. He commanded the German armies at the Anglo-American D-Day invasion, as they retreated through France to the Rhine, and in their last Ardennes offensive in December 1944. He was dismissed for the third time in March 1945.

At the July 1944 Bomb Plot he was briefly removed from office, but reinstated. He had known and approved of the Plot, but did not join. As a prisoner of war of the British, he was regarded as a man who had fought as a professional and had avoided not only the pomposity but also the misdeeds of other Third Reich generals.

Russian Campaign. ➤Appendix V

Russian Prisoners of War. The Soviet Union had not signed either the Hague Regulations of 1907 or the later Geneva Convention of 1929, so the Germans did not expect the Russians to treat prisoners of war according to these international agreements. In their turn, the Germans felt no compunction in maltreating Russian prisoners who were, at least to the SS, members of a lesser race. Of 5,754,000 Russians captured 3,700,000 died.

About one million captured Soviet soldiers took some form of service (with varying degrees of willingness) with Germany. Many of the non-Russian Soviet nationalities were formed into uniformed military units. In August 1941 a Don Cossack infantry regiment was recruited and many German-speaking '*Volksdeutsche*' were enrolled into the Waffen SS. In 1943 the SS Panzer Grenadier Division 'Galicia' was formed, later becoming an anti-partisan unit, the 1st Ukrainian. The 162 Turcoman Division, raised in 1943, was used in northern Italy.

The Russian general, Andrei Andreivich Vlassov, who was captured in July 1942, was persuaded to accept command of the 'Russian Liberation Army' (ROA), but this was a paper army only and the enrolled men were either working in the Todt organization or in separate auxiliary units until March 1945. Vlassov then found himself in command of two real divisions and ordered them into action on the Eastern Front; there the divisions suffered heavy casualties. In the confusion of the time Vlassov took the remains of his troops to Prague in May and joined Czechs fighting against the Germans.

He was captured by the Russians and hanged. Most of his followers were taken back to Russia. Their fate is uncertain though not difficult to guess at, since their original failure in allowing themselves to be captured was construed as a form of treachery.

Russo-German Pact. In August 1939, with a German attack on Poland set for 1 September, it was imperative for Hitler to have an assurance of non-interference from Russia. With this in mind, the German Foreign Minister, Ribbentrop, contacted the Russians on 15 August, stating that he was prepared to settle by negotiation outstanding problems of Soviet-German relations; he furthermore stressed the extreme urgency of these negotiations. The Russian Foreign Minister, Molotov, replied that he was interested in a non-aggression pact and in a joint guarantee for the Baltic States. However, he stalled the Germans by insisting that preliminary discussions must be held on all matters so that when the foreign ministers met they would be in a position to make concrete decisions. The German ambassador in Moscow, Schulenberg, was instructed to stress both Germany's and Russia's need for the quick signing of a treaty, using as an excuse the ever-worsening Polish 'situation'. In reply, Molotov insisted that a trade and credit agreement be concluded as a precedent to the signing of a pact. He also stated that Russia would require a special protocol with regard to mutual interests in various questions of foreign policy. Impatient with the progress of the negotiations, Hitler intervened on 20 August, sending a personal telegram to Stalin. First he welcomed the signing of the German–Soviet Commercial Agreement (signed the same day) and again stressed that, because of the tension between Germany and Poland, an imminent conclusion to the negotiations was essential. He then asked that Ribbentrop should come to Moscow on 23 August. Stalin, in a telegram to Hitler on 21 August, accepted. Upon the German Foreign Minister's arrival, the details of the pact were soon agreed, and the rest of the evening was spent in feasting and drinking. The details of the pact were: (1) Neither party would attack the other. (2) Should one of them become the object of belligerent action by a third power, the other party would in no manner lend its support to this third power. (3) Neither Germany nor Russia would join any grouping of Powers whatsoever which is aimed directly or indirectly at the other party. The secret protocol Russia had requested was attached to this pact. Spheres of interest were settled with regard to future possible territorial and political transformation in the Baltic states (Finland, Estonia, Latvia, Lithuania) and in the territories belonging to Poland. In the former, the northern frontier of Lithuania was to be the dividing line, and in the latter, the line of the rivers Narew, Vistula and San was to be the approximate boundary – although, future political developments being unpredictable, the map would be redrawn, amicably, upon knowledge of such developments.

The Pact, which confused, severely tested and in many cases overstrained the loyalty of communists throughout the world, enabled Hitler to risk war with France and Britain on the issue of the invasion of Poland. Its signing therefore contributed directly to the exercise of Nazi aggression to which the Soviet Union in its turn would fall victim in June 1941.

Rust, Bernard (1883–1945).   Nazi Minister of Education. A schoolteacher who became a Nazi in 1922 and from 1925 was Gauleiter of Hanover-South, Rust was a follower of the Strasserites and took part in meetings held by the radical wing of the Party. Nevertheless Hitler allowed his return to favour. In February 1933 he was made Minister of Science, Art and Education for Prussia, and in April 1934 Education Minister for the Reich. He committed suicide in May 1945.

S

SA (*Sturmabteilung*). The Brownshirts. Partly uniformed supporters, recruited in Munich by Röhm in 1921, to protect Nazi speakers at public meetings. They were mostly tough unemployed ex-soldiers who frequented Munich beer halls such as the Torbräukeller near the Isar Gate. Many were from the recently disbanded *Freikorps*. The style of uniform, the raised-arm salute and their swastika badge all came from *Freikorps* units. The brown shirts which they and all Party members wore from 1924 came at first from an army surplus consignment intended for the WWI German East African troops.

The SA bodyguards grew in number, acting under Röhm's orders rather than Hitler's. In March 1923, Röhm gave Hitler a special SA troop as HQ guard, identifiable by black ski-caps. In April 1925, after Röhm had left Germany to work in Bolivia, Himmler took over this troop in which the SS had its beginnings.

After the 1923 Beer Hall Putsch, the SA had been banned by the Bavarian state, but Röhm had maintained the organization under the wing of his other body of old soldiers, the *Frontbann*, and they remained in this condition until the re-formation of the party in 1925. In November 1926, Pfeffer von Salomon was made chief of the SA; he was a north German, breaking the Bavarian domination of SA and Party. Under Pfeffer, recruitment to the SA continued, largely from the unemployed, bringing the strength from 2,000 to over 60,000 by 1930. Many joined it in the hope that in time it would be absorbed into the army, and Röhm had encouraged this idea. As it grew, political elements in the SA began to challenge the Nazi Party and demanded a greater say in its running. In particular they insisted on the nomination of SA men as Party candidates in the Reichstag elections. There was much brawling between the rival party bodies, the SA and the SS, and in September 1930 and April 1931 SA mutinies took place under their Berlin leader, Stennes. To restore order, Hitler agreed to SA demands but dismissed Pfeffer and named himself supreme SA leader, demanding a loyalty oath to the Führer from each SA man. In 1931 Röhm was recalled to head the SA.

When Hitler became Chancellor in 1933 there were over half a million SA men and their hopes, and Röhm's ambitions, were high. The radicals in the SA, under the influence of early Nazi thinking, expected an economic rather than a political revolution; Hitler shook them by such actions as restoring to the leadership of the Employers' Association Krupp von Bohlen and Thyssen, and by dissolving the Combat League of Tradespeople (small shopkeepers hostile to the big department and chain stores). It was agreed that the SA, the SS and the much larger Stahlhelm should come under the Ministry of War, with the hope that the SA would be swamped. Instead, this move merely extended Röhm's opportunity to claim that the SA was the true national defence force. The army, Röhm insisted, should be confined to a training function. General Blomberg, the Minister, demanded a ruling from Hitler, who tried to compromise with the factions. Fear of the SA and of Röhm's claims now grew, drawing together the army, the Party and the SS into an alliance. For months Hitler hesitated. Then, warned of danger by Göbbels, Göring and other Party leaders, Hitler sought the connivance of the army and ordered the SS to destroy the SA in the Röhm Purge of June 1934 – the Night of the Long Knives.

After the dramatic restoration of Hitler's power by the purge, the new leader of the SA, Lutze, kept the chastened and now unarmed body in existence as servants of the Party, collecting for *Winterhilfe* or demonstrating to order, parading or smashing Jewish shop windows. It gave useful part-time military training and during the war had a role in air-raid duties. Its transport unit, the NSKK, continued as a national organization, but the day of the radical political bullies had ended with the death of Röhm and the purging of the radical elements. ➤Röhm Purge

***Saalschlachten* (Hall battles)**.   A feature of the Weimar Republic was the political battles fought in halls, assembly rooms or beer cellars throughout the land. Men like Thorn, the SA leader in Hamburg, launched his men against Social Democrat or Communist meetings and expected in turn to have to defend Nazi meetings against communist Red Front commandos or the SPD Erhard Aver Guard.

Saar.   The territory on the east of the River Rhine covering some 1,000 square miles, rich in coal, iron and steel industries. In 1919, by the Treaty of Versailles, the Saar was placed under League of Nations control for 15 years and France given the right to exploit its resources. Germans in the Saar felt they were under foreign rule and it was considered patriotic for students to insult the French-run police.

In January 1935 a plebiscite was held in the Saar; in it, 90 per cent voted for reunion with Germany. Hitler assured France that the last obstacle to friendship was now removed. Without being specific, Hitler appeared to be renouncing Germany's claim to Alsace-Lorraine. But it was part of Adolf Hitler's technique for the conduct of foreign policy that he gave the impression that each step was his last. At the same time, on the home front he would seek to maximize the achievement. Thus, although the result of the plebiscite was a foregone conclusion, Hitler presented it in Germany as a victory for the Third Reich in breaking the shackles of Versailles, and made a triumphal entry into the restored German territory.

Sachsenhausen.   The location of a concentration camp near Berlin. Sachsenhausen deserves consideration as a camp which was essentially a labour camp
rather than one for extermination, but where nevertheless unknown thousands
were killed in the ten years of its existence.

The site at Sachsenhausen was chosen for its proximity to Berlin and in
particular to SS headquarters. A workforce was taken from the nearby temporary
camp at Esterwegen and set to building a new camp in July 1934, and in
September 900 prisoners were transferred there. By the end of the year the
camp commandant, Koch, had 2,000 prisoners. The camp grew in the following
year and the Berlin Gestapo moved their interrogation centre from the overcrowded Columbia House in the city to Sachsenhausen. In 1938 further
prisoners were sent in – gypsies, 'work-shy' vagrants or political suspects from
Austria; in June of 1938 alone, 6,000 arrived. By the end of 1938 there were
8,300 prisoners in the camp under the new commandant, Baranowski.

The day's routine began with roll-call. All prisoners, sick or not, with the
sole exception of those acting as servants in SS houses or working in SS
headquarters, paraded from 5.00 a.m. until the SS were satisfied. There were
two and sometimes three roll-calls every day; if any prisoner was missing, the
parade stood still until he was accounted for.

Outside the camp itself, the SS had built their barracks and headquarters.
Camp guards were trained there and, from 1941, Russian prisoners were used
for practice in hangings. Work parties were marched out to the factories or to
duty in the camp, cleaning, repairing or doing domestic work for the SS.
Prisoners were distributed to the main factories as follows:

Factory	Prisoners
German armaments works	1,660
German earth and stone works	2,200
SS clothing factory	800
SS central equipment depot	500
SS signals and transport depot	2,460

The most unusual work section of Sachsenhausen was in a closely guarded
barrack block near the administration offices, where skilled prisoners were put
to work making counterfeit documents and even banknotes for the SS. This
was Operation Bernhard, from which the forged notes came that were used
for SS secret operations including payment of the spy 'Cicero' and, at the war's
end, the financing of SS escape routes.

During the war years, some prisoners were handed over to SS doctors for
experimental work and their bodies used to test poison gases, phosphorus
burns, the effects of jaundice or of sepsis on open wounds, to evaluate how
hand-grenades wounded men or the speed of death from poisons.

Punishments were awarded for any offence, even for a blink of the eye
while on parade. The most frequent punishments were 'sport', exercises until

the victim dropped. Prisoners were sentenced to a whipping and, tied to a stand, had to count out correctly the number of lashes. Prisoners might be chained to a stake or left hanging by their arms. Camp records show that between March 1941 and November 1942 about 1,000 men were whipped on the block and 600 hanged from the stake. Punishments might be collective: in October 1940 12,000 were made to stand in ranks from 5.00 a.m. until 11.00 p.m. without food or water. When the same punishment was ordered in January 1941, over 400 fell dead of cold. A punishment company had its own barrack block. Men sent to it were unlikely to survive, carrying out useless tasks at high speed (such as loading and unloading cartloads of stones). Of a punishment company of seventy or eighty men, seven to ten would be killed every day and another four or five would die of illness or exhaustion.

The Gestapo reserved one cell block in which special prisoners were kept, often tortured for interrogation or shot. Some cells were kept permanently in darkness.

Outside the wall, the SS built Station Z in 1941, a wooden barrack hut about 90 by 55 feet, used for mass killings. In six weeks from the beginning of September, 18,000 Russian prisoners were killed there by shooting in the back of the head.

At the beginning of 1945 there were 47,709 prisoners in Sachsenhausen. Executions continued. Although the International Red Cross had been able to enter the camp in March 1945 to free Danes and Norwegians, nearly 18,000 were killed in the first three months of the year. In April, prisoners were marched out to the north, thousands dying on the road, before the Russian army could find them.

Salomon, Ernst von (1902–72). A Prussian nationalist of Huguenot origin who fought with the *Freikorps* in the Baltic states and Upper Silesia in 1919. He took part in the murder in 1922 of the Weimar Foreign Minister, Rathenau, whose crime was that he was Jewish and had participated in the signing of the Versailles Treaty. Salomon was jailed for this for five years, but was released in 1928. He wrote *Die Geächteten* (1930) about his *Freikorps* times and was invited to join the Nazi Academy of Arts. During the Nazi era he wrote film scripts for the UFA film company. In 1951 he wrote *Der Fragebogen* (*The Questionnaire*), an account of his life and the age in which he lived in the form of the denazification questions he had been asked.

Saukel, Fritz (1894–1946). Reich Director of Labour (1942–5) whose orders moved five million people from occupied Europe to work as slaves in Germany. Saukel had been a seaman and a prisoner of war in France in WWI. He was one of the earliest Nazis, joining the Party in 1921. He was made Gauleiter of Thuringia in 1925 and became its governor in 1933. In March 1942 Hitler decreed the mobilization of labour, both German and foreign, to meet the labour demands of Albert Speer's armaments and munitions production programme. Speer found the flow of workers too slow and suggested that a tough Gauleiter be found to take on the job. Saukel was chosen and recruited the required five million, including half a million women, as house-workers for German homes. His teams went out on the streets all over Europe, even in allied Italy, to round up men and women, taking them from their homes, from shops and cinemas. Saukel saw himself as an agent supplying workers for factories; he was shocked when arrested in 1945 by the British and put on trial with the major war criminals at Nuremberg. He claimed to have known nothing about concentration camps and protested his innocence until the moment he was hanged, in October 1946.

Schacht, Dr Hjalmar (1877–1970). Economist and President of the Reichsbank. Joining the German Social Democratic Party after W W I, Schacht rose to be President of the Reichsbank, 1923–9. Widely regarded as responsible for curing runaway inflation, his opposition to reparations and the Versailles Treaty led him to the Nazi Party, for which he recruited bankers and industrialists for financial support. He was reappointed to the presidency of the Reichsbank and, as Minister of Economics after the Nazi 1933 victory, he invented financial devices to conceal (and limit) the inflation resulting from rearmament. Never totally committed to the Nazi programme he resigned from political office in 1937 and was replaced by Dr Funk. Jailed in 1944 after the July Bomb Plot, he narrowly eluded the hangman.

At his trial at Nuremberg he was acquitted of war crimes and later resumed an international banking career, becoming adviser to Colonel Nasser of Egypt in the 1950s. Schacht can be seen either as the embodiment of the most amoral qualities of international banking or as one of the fathers of the post-war banking system.

Schellenberg, Walter (1910–52). A bright young graduate who joined the Nazi Party and SS in 1933 and the SD in 1935, and rose to be head of the SS foreign intelligence department in 1941.

Schellenberg had carried out work for the SD in France, Italy and Czechoslovakia before 1939 when Heydrich used him to plan and organize the structure of the SS's RSHA, the Reich's central security department. In 1939 and 1940 he was active in counter-intelligence operations, decoying and capturing the British secret service man Payne-Best at Venlo on the Netherlands border, compiling the SS 'search list' ready for the invasion of Britain, and scheming in Spain and Portugal to capture the English king's elder brother, the Duke of Windsor.

From August 1942 he began to urge Himmler to investigate the possibility of negotiations for peace. Contact was made with US intelligence in Spain towards this end. At the same time Schellenberg had secret meetings with the head of Swiss intelligence in Switzerland to try to uncover spy networks like 'Lucy' working there, but he also used these contacts for his own long-term good. In Switzerland he made indirect contact for the first time with Allen

Dulles, the head of American intelligence, and the Swedish Red Cross. Until the end of the war he maintained these contacts with the knowledge of Himmler. In May 1945, Schellenberg fled to Sweden, two days before the German surrender, and was given asylum there. But he was called back to Germany to give evidence at the Nuremberg trials. He was charged, as a member of the criminal SS and SD, but he was sentenced only lightly and was released in 1951, a sick man.

Thereafter he settled in Italy and began to write his memoirs, *The Labyrinth*, published after his death. This book contains useful information, but Schellenberg was inclined to fantasize (including an account of Himmler's attempt to poison Hitler).

Schicklgruber, Alois (1837–1903). Father of Adolf Hitler. Born in Strones, Austria, the illegitimate son of Maria Schicklgruber, father unknown. Alois Schicklgruber later adopted the name Hitler based on a misspelling by a local priest of the name of his mother's new husband, Johann Georg Hiedler. An averagely successful small bureaucrat in the Austrian Imperial Customs Service, he married first Anna Glasl in 1864; secondly Franziska Matzelsberger in 1883, by whom he had two children, Alois and Angela; and thirdly in 1885 Adolf Hitler's mother, Klara Pölzl. Of their five children only two, Adolf and his sister Paula, survived. In 1895 at the age of 58, Alois Hitler (as he had by then been known for 18 years) retired from the imperial service. His life from then on seems to have been spent buying and selling farms. There is evidence that he drank excessively; he was probably a more than averagely tyrannical father for the time and place; Hitler was to claim later that he was severely and frequently beaten with a belt or dog-whip.

The outstanding mystery in Alois Schicklgruber's life is the identity of his father, and thus of Hitler's grandfather. There is some evidence to suggest that Hitler's unknown grandfather was the young son of a Jewish household in Graz, the Frankenbergers, for whom his grandmother was then working as a housemaid. Certainly after Germany absorbed Austria in 1938, Gestapo attempts were made to destroy the Hitler family documents, possibly to conceal the highly embarrassing information that the Führer of the Third Reich was of part-Jewish descent. In the last resort it must be recognized that the historian is here dealing with a primitive central European peasant community where illegitimacy was common, where different spellings of the same surname offered constant confusion and where inbreeding (and sometimes incest) was widespread. ➤Hitler, Adolf: ancestry

Schindler, Oskar (1908–74). A salesman turned entrepreneur, Schindler moved to Krakow in 1939 where, through his meeting with a Jewish businessman Itzhak Stern, he bought up Rekord, a bankrupt enamel-manufacturing company. By 1940 he was employing 250 Poles, and soon added a number of Jews to his workforce.

Through his contacts in the *Wehrmacht*, and later to the SS, and by offering generous bribes, he obtained sizeable contracts which he handled through his new company Deutsche Email Fabrik.

In February 1943 *Untersturmführer* Amon Goeth arrived from Lublin with orders to remove those who survived the clearance of the Krakow ghetto to the Plaszow Forced Labour Camp, of which he was the brutal and mercurial commandant.

During this period Schindler drew his Jewish labour force from the camp. A sharp businessman and a humanitarian, he treated his Jewish workers fairly, fed them well and battled constantly, at great risk to his own life, to save them from the savage policies of the regime. Successfully resisting attempts by Goeth to have his factory moved into the camp, Schindler managed to remove more than a thousand of his Jewish workers, in the last weeks of the war, to the comparative safety of Brinnlitz in Moravia.

The name of those Jews he was allowed to take with him and who thus survived the Holocaust, formed what became known as 'Schindler's List', the title of a much lauded film by Stephen Speilberg.

Camp commandant Amon Goeth survived arrest by Bureau V of the Reich Security Office for black market activities. But in 1945 he was arrested by the Allies and sent back to Poland for trial. He was hanged in September 1946.

Oskar Schindler's role in saving Jewish lives was recognized in an *ex gratia* payment of $15,000 by the Jewish Relief Organization. After two later bankruptcies in Germany and Argentina he was granted a small pension by the German Finance Ministry. He died in October 1974 in Frankfurt.

Schirach, Baldur von (1907–74). Head of Hitler Youth from 1933 to 1940, von Schirach was the son of an American mother, grandson of a soldier who lost a leg at the Battle of Bull Run. He was the leader of the Nazi student movement from 1928 and took over the enlarged Hitler Youth in 1933. His wife was a noted beauty and was rumoured to have been at one time mistress of Hitler. Gauleiter of Vienna from 1940 to 1945, von Schirach escaped capture at the end of the war and hid in the Austrian Tyrol, posing as a novelist writing *The Secrets of Myrna Loy*. He was arrested and charged with war crimes with the major war criminals at Nuremberg, mainly on account of his administration of foreign workers and his treatment of Jews in Vienna. His wife appealed to the American judge for clemency on the grounds that 'our children love America'. He was sentenced to twenty years' imprisonment.

Schlabrendorff, Fabian von. A prominent member of that group of army officers opposed to Hitler, in 1939 Schlabrendorff was sent to London by Hans Oster of the Abwehr where at meetings with Churchill and Lord Lloyd he confirmed Hitler's intention of attacking Poland.

During the war he became ADC to Major-General Henning von Tresckow and was involved with him in Operation Flash, an attempt on Hitler's life, organized by von Tresckow and General Olbricht. One of the group which recruited von Stauffenberg for the 20 July Bomb Plot, Schlabrendorff was arrested and tortured in the aftermath of its failure. He was saved from certain death when the People's Court was destroyed by bombing in 1945.

After the war he wrote his own account of the army conspiracies under the title *They Almost Killed Hitler.*

Schleicher, Kurt von (1882–1934).   Former Reich Chancellor murdered in the Röhm Purge. In WWI he was a general on the staff of Hindenburg and in 1919 originated the *Freikorps*, the irregular armies of ex-soldiers fighting either to maintain German interests on its eastern borders or to put down insurrection at home.

He served under the Weimar government and became the principal military political intriguer of the period. On the promise to split the Nazi vote in the Reichstag and obtain a parliamentary majority, Hindenburg made him Chancellor in December 1932, in succession to von Papen who had recently replaced Brüning. He tried but failed to encourage Gregor Strasser to lead a breakaway faction from the Nazi Party. He next proposed to dissolve the Reichstag, which would have made way for a military dictatorship. Hindenburg refused. Schleicher resigned in January 1933 and Hitler was called to the chancellorship.

In the Röhm Purge in June 1934, five SS men burst into his house. Kurt von Schleicher and his wife were shot dead. ➤Schleicher Intrigue

Schleicher Intrigue, The.   On 17 November 1932 General von Schleicher succeeded in organizing the downfall of von Papen's cabinet. Subsequent negotiations between Hindenburg and Hitler came to nothing, the old President rejecting Hitler's demands for virtually unfettered power. Schleicher seems to have anticipated this, and he now made a bid for power himself. Informing the President, Field Marshal von Hindenburg, that he, General von Schleicher, believed he could obtain the support of Gregor Strasser and at least sixty Nazi Reichstag members, Schleicher asked for leave to form a government. This time he had gone too far, however. The President refused and called von Papen as Chancellor.

Schleicher, as Minister of Defence, now insisted that the von Papen government could not be defended by the army and police forces at the Republic's disposal. Hindenburg, accepting this argument, again dismissed von Papen and now appointed Schleicher. He was to last as Chancellor for fifty-seven days, and – as he claimed – to be betrayed fifty-seven times per day.

Schmeling, Max (b. 1905).   Germany's heavyweight boxing champion. After a successful career as a light heavyweight, Schmeling won the German heavyweight championship in 1928. Two years later, on a fourth-round foul, he went on to win the world heavyweight championship against Jack Sharkey.

In 1934 in a return fight with Sharkey, Schmeling lost the title on a close and controversial decision.

But Schmeling's career was by no means over. In 1936 he became a Nazi national hero when he knocked out Joe Louis in a non-title fight in the twelfth round. Perhaps unwisely, Schmeling was now made a central figure in Nazi racialist propaganda. In the return bout in 1938 for the heavyweight championship of the world, Louis's determination to win a decisive victory was immediately apparent. Schmeling went down in the first round and was counted out, two minutes four seconds after the start of the fight.

During the war Schmeling served in the German parachute forces, and after 1945 worked as a businessman in Hamburg until his retirement.

Schmenzin. The country estate of Ewald von Kleist-Schmenzin and the location of a number of conservative resistance meetings in 1944. Arrested by the Gestapo, Kleist-Schmenzin was executed in Plötzensee prison only a month before the end of the war.

Schmidt, Paul (1889–1970). Hitler's interpreter. As chief interpreter he was present in Munich at meetings with Mussolini, with Franco and others. His memoirs are a useful background for Nazi diplomatic history.

Scholl, Hans (1918–43). With his sister Sophie he was a student at Munich University and resistance leader of the White Rose movement. They were arrested in 1943 by the Gestapo along with many other resisters and sentenced to death for the distribution of anti-Nazi leaflets. ➤White Rose

Scholtz-Klink, Gertrud (1902–1945). Early Nazi associate member and women's leader in Baden from 1929. In 1934 she was appointed *Reichsfrauen-führerin* (head of all National Socialist women), but her leadership was more token than actual and her views on a woman's function closely mirrored those of the male-dominated Nazi Party and state. At the war's end she successfully hid from the Allies for nearly three years. When finally captured in 1948, she was acquitted of war crimes.

Schörner, Ferdinand (1892–1973). Hitler's last army Field Marshal, the man chosen to be given command of the army in his last political testament. Although Schörner had been one of the officers who put down the 1923 Beer Hall Putsch, his WWI record with his 'Pour le Mérite' medal and his non-aristocratic background brought him into Hitler's favour. In 1944 he was given command of Army Group South in the Ukraine and subsequently Army Group North. In 1945 he took over Army Group Central, which included Berlin. He accepted this final promotion and command of the non-existent Berlin army before flying away to escape to the American army. They in turn handed him over to the Russians who imprisoned him for ten years. As a commander on the Eastern Front, he had been a harsh disciplinarian and, on his return to Germany, he was sentenced to a further term of imprisonment for his orders of summary execution of German soldiers.

Schröder, Freiherr Kurt von (1889–1965). A banker who arranged the von Papen–Hitler meeting in January 1933. He subsequently held several Third Reich banking corporation chairs. In 1945 he was arrested, but released with a small fine.

Schumacher, Kurt (1895–1952). A Socialist member of the Reichstag (1930–33), after which the new Nazi government put him in detention. He continued to be in and out of detention for the whole period of the Third Reich and was, like Adenauer, one of those returned to a civil prison after the 1944 Bomb Plot. He became the post-war leader of the Socialist Party in West Germany.

Schuschnigg, Dr Kurt von (1897–1977). Austrian Federal Chancellor at the time of the *Anschluss*. A member of the Christian Social Party and a deputy on the Austrian National Council, he served as Minister of Justice under Dollfuss and became Federal Chancellor following the latter's murder in 1934. No practitioner of democracy himself at the time, Schuschnigg nevertheless came to represent the independence of Austria during the *Anschluss* crisis of 1938. Unable to divert or outmanoeuvre Hitler, Schuschnigg was arrested at the German occupation of Austria and committed to a concentration camp. Released at the end of the war, he taught political science at American universities and became a US citizen in 1956. ➤*Anschluss*

Schutzhaft. Protective custody under a law of 28 February 1933. ➤Concentration Camps

Schwartz, Franz Xaver (1875–1947). Nazi Party Treasurer. An accountant in Munich city government, he joined the Nazis in 1922, and in 1926 became Party treasurer. This plump, bald man remained one of Hitler's 'old comrades' and a member of his close circle. With Max Amann he helped cover up the scandal of Geli Raubal's death. As Treasurer, he had control of membership subscriptions, so all figures of membership came from his office and were probably falsified to fit his accounts. Under his control all enrolment to the Party was suspended in May 1933, when there were a million and a half applications outstanding. In 1945 he burnt all Party financial documents in the Munich Brown House.

Schwarze Korps, Das. The weekly newspaper of the SS. A mouthpiece for Himmler himself, the *Schwarze Korps* reflected his own attitudes, fantastic, censorious, puritanical.

Schwerin von Krosigk, Graf Lutz (1887–1952). A member of the nobility and a Rhodes Scholar at Oxford, he was appointed Minister of France in von

Papen's 1932 cabinet. He remained as a minister in Hitler's cabinets from 1933 to 1945, representing, he believed, 'decent and traditional Germany'. In the brief Dönitz government in 1945, he was Foreign Minister. In March 1945 he urged Göbbels (then responsible for the mobilization of Germany's last efforts) to secure Germany's future – meaning make peace. He urged contact with the Pope or the League of Nations, believing that the western Allies would respect old figures like von Papen or himself. Schwerin von Krosigk had lived in a condition of unreality and his sentence to ten years' imprisonment in 1949 seemed to him totally unjust. He was released through ill-health in 1951.

***Schwertworte* (Sword words)**.   Key words or synopses of Nazi ideology to be learnt by all young people in the Third Reich.

Scientific Development in the Third Reich.   In 1933 Germany already excelled in scientific research. It might have been expected that with the concentration of power and ambition achieved with the Nazi takeover of 1933 there would have been greater progress than there was. But the Third Reich was not a planned regime; it was always opportunistic, and scientific planning suffered from the varying whims imposed at different levels by the leadership principle. ►Rockets; Mengele; Messerschmitt Me262; Atomic Bomb Research

SD (*Sicherheitsdienst*).   The Nazi Party's own intelligence and security body. Himmler created the SD and appointed Heydrich as head in August 1931 to protect the Party. It was kept distinct from the uniformed SS, the SA's intelligence unit (which was closed by 1932) and the Party's foreign intelligence unit under Rosenberg, which itself came under the SD in 1934.

When Hitler became Chancellor in 1933, the SD's role expanded as enemies of the Party became enemies of the state. In 1934 the Röhm Purge was carried out on the basis of SD information and with the active participation of SD men. By 1936, Heydrich headed both the SD and the Gestapo. In 1939 he formalized this empire under the structure of the Reich Security Administration (RSHA).

Working without uniforms and with a wide range of function, often in parallel to the Abwehr, the SD attracted earnest and intelligent young graduates such as Walter Schellenberg. They plotted unsuccessful revolts in Rumania and Iraq, negotiated for arms in the Argentine, were put as attachés into embassies, including the Vatican, kidnapped the British agent Payne-Best from the Netherlands and killed special prisoners in the occupied territories. They headed the *Einsatzgruppen* (the special action – or extermination – groups in Eastern Europe).

After Heydrich's assassination in 1942 Himmler ran the RSHA and SD, until handing them over to Kaltenbrunner in January 1943. The SD absorbed their military rival, the Abwehr, in June 1944 when its head, Canaris, was removed. From then on, paradoxically, the SD head of foreign intelligence,

Schellenberg, worked with Himmler on the possibility of peace, trying to talk to Allen Dulles (the head of American intelligence) in Switzerland, with the Americans in Spain and with the Swedish Red Cross until the final surrender.

At the Nuremberg war crimes trials, the SD was declared a criminal organization on the level of the Gestapo and membership of it made its men liable to prosecution.

Sealion (*Seelöwe*). The code-name for Hitler's plan to invade Britain.

In June 1940 the very speed of the German army's defeat of the French and British forces left the *Wehrmacht* High Command unprepared for a follow-up invasion of England. Although France had surrendered and the British evacuation at Dunkirk had involved the abandonment of all the BEF guns, stores and vehicles, the German general staff were aware that the victorious German army was in no position to pursue the British across the Channel. More to the point, there is no evidence that, at this stage, Hitler intended an invasion. In May 1940 as the Battle of France came to a successful conclusion, Hitler had expected Britain to come to terms. 'I want nothing from England. They can make peace at any time,' he said to Jodl. And when his naval commander, Admiral Raeder, wished to discuss the possibility of landing troops in England, Hitler showed no interest. As late as the beginning of June General von Rundstedt was told by Hitler that he expected the British to offer peace any day now, at which point he could get on with planning for his major target, Russia.

In July, the German general staff began to plan for an invasion of Britain. Drawing on their experience, they chose to regard it as a large-scale river-crossing operation, with the Luftwaffe to act as artillery. Although Hitler still hoped that the British would (in his eyes) be reasonable, he issued a directive on an invasion which had as conditions: (a) that the RAF be made powerless; (b) that the Channel crossing be swept free of British mines and blocked off at both ends by German mines; (c) that the coastal zone be dominated by heavy artillery; (d) that the British navy be previously damaged or diverted to other theatres, such as the Mediterranean.

Göring as commander of the Luftwaffe gave absolute assurance on the first condition, but Raeder could not honestly make similar promises. The army made provisional arrangements which depended on the Luftwaffe and the navy first carrying out their tasks. In August 1940 there was another directive (issued after Hitler had secretly decided on the plan for Barbarossa, to attack Russia), but its terms remained general and left any date to be decided by Hitler later.

Nevertheless preparations for the invasion of Britain went ahead. The German army and navy began to assemble heavy river barges at Ostend and move them to Calais, Boulogne and Le Havre. Troops were trained to use the barges, and loading exercises took place under heavy RAF attacks. The *Abwehr* and the SS issued information on Britain for the invasion, including a list of people to be arrested at once.

The British believed that an attempt at an invasion was certain and began to put together what defences they could. A civilian part-time army (the 'Home Guard') trained with rifles often donated by groups of citizens in the USA. The threat of invasion, together with the Luftwaffe's air attacks, had the effect of turning Britain from a likely victim of the Third Reich into a determined, though still isolated, enemy.

But the Luftwaffe had failed to clear the way for the German navy to transport assault troops in sufficient numbers across the Channel. After the Luftwaffe's defeat by the RAF in the great air battles of 15 September 1940, Hitler began to turn his attention towards the east. By the beginning of the new year it seemed certain that the military prerequisite of complete German air superiority was unattainable and orders were given by Hitler to discontinue preparations for 'Sealion' on 9 January 1941. ➤Battle of Britain

Second revolution. ➤Röhm and Röhm Purge

Seeckt, Hans von (1860–1936). The Commander-in-Chief from 1920 to 1926 of the post-Versailles German army, limited to 100,000 men. The son of a general, Seeckt was a guards officer who was appointed to the general staff in 1897. After field service in WWI he was seconded to advise the Austrians in 1916 and then the Turks in 1917. He emerged from the war with his reputation untarnished by the defeats of 1918. A believer in new methods of war, he began training the small army of Weimar in mobile shock tactics and worked secretly with the Soviet Union by having German tank and aircraft crews (forbidden to Germany under the terms of the Treaty of Versailles) trained there.

In 1923 he was hated by the Nazis not only because he had a Jewish wife but also because he had an international rather than nationalist outlook and because he was the military power that ordered von Lossow to suppress the Beer Hall Putsch. When asked by President Ebert whether the army would obey the government or the Hitler–Ludendorff Putschists, von Seeckt answered with the words that summed up the Reichswehr role in the new republic: 'Herr Reich President, the Army will obey *me*.' He was retired in 1926 and probably only avoided assassination in the 1934 Röhm Purge by accepting the post of military adviser to Chiang Kai-shek in China from 1934 to 1935. ➤Black Reichswehr

Selbstgleichschalter. A self-co-ordinated or self-disciplined citizen. An important totalitarian concept referring to a member of the new Reich who accepted Nazi tenets immediately and without question. More important still, perhaps, is what was implied but left unsaid: those who were incapable of *Selbstgleichschaltung* were to be removed from society.

Seldte, Franz (1882–1947). With Düsterberg, the founder of the Stahlhelm, the militant ex-servicemen's association, in 1918 and leader of it up to its merger with the SA in 1933. After the failure of the Harzburg Front, Seldte became a minister in the von Papen–Hitler government. He was subsequently Minister of Labour in Hitler's governments from 1933 to the end in 1945 when he joined Dönitz and ran a small group acting as a 'Ministry of Labour' in that fantasy government. At Nuremberg he claimed he had always tried to stand against dictatorship and for a two-chamber system of representative government. He had talked with Schellenberg in 1944 to try and achieve this. ➤Stahlhelm

Sennelager. Extensive German army training grounds near Paderborn.

Septemberlings. Name given to those who joined the Nazi Party after the September 1930 elections. Even more contemptuous in its application was 'March Violets' for those joining on the days following the Nazis coming to power in March 1933.

Seyss-Inquart, Arthur (1892–1946). A Viennese lawyer, covert supporter of the Austrian Nazi Party and advocate of the *Anschluss*. As a state councillor in the Austrian government from 1937, he acted as a German 'Fifth Column', not emerging as a full Nazi supporter until, at Hitler's insistence, Schuschnigg reluctantly appointed him Minister of the Interior in 1938. From this point he controlled the police forces of the Austrian state and was able to prevent their use against Nazi interests. After the *Anschluss*, Seyss-Inquart served as the *Reichsstatthalter* of Ostmark, as Austria was now called. Then for a short period he was appointed deputy Frank in the newly established Governement-General in Poland. His last service to the Nazi state was as *Reichskommissar* for the Netherlands where he earned the hatred of the Dutch peoples for the brutality of his regime. Repenting after the war the 'fearful excesses' of Nazism, he was nevertheless sentenced to death and hanged at Nuremberg on 16 October 1946. ➤*Anschluss*

Shame-signs. Signs erected to carry the names of local people who had not contributed to the Winterhilfe fund.

'Sieg Heil!' (literally: **'Hail Victory!'**). A chant of triumph adopted at Nazi meetings.

Sippenbuch **(Clan book)**. A 'racial record' carried by every member of the SS.

Sitzkrieg. ➤Phoney war

Skorzeny, Otto (1908–1975). An Austrian-born leader of special military operations. 6 foot 6 inches tall and of powerful physique, he was the SS major selected in 1943 to lead the snatch squad that took Mussolini from captivity in the Abruzzi, Italy, back into German hands. The parachutists were Luftwaffe men, but the SS and Skorzeny took the credit. Thereafter Skorzeny raised SS-controlled special service units which were used against Tito in Yugoslavia and against partisans in Eastern Europe. In July 1944 he rallied the SS Tank School against the supporters of the Bomb Plot and in October he kidnapped the son of the ruler of Hungary, as a hostage to ensure continuing support for Germany. In December 1944 he raised and led the 'American' brigade – of English-speaking and American-uniformed and -equipped infiltrators – in the Ardennes offensive. He ended the war as a divisional commander in Bach-Zelewski's Corps.

He was acquitted in 1947 by an American tribunal of unlawful practices in the Ardennes. He claimed that he then founded, in 1948, the 'Odessa' organization, to help former SS men escape overseas. He never returned to live in Germany, instead running businesses in Spain and South America. In 1950 he published his autobiography which claimed credit for perhaps more than he had achieved. He died in Spain in July 1975.

Smolensk Plot (also known as **Operation Flash**). An attempt to kill Hitler, organized by General von Tresckow on 13 March 1943. The plan, involving Gördeler, von Tresckow, General Olbricht and von Schlabrendorff, was for Hitler to be enticed to army headquarters in the Smolensk area, where von Tresckow was serving, and there murdered. In the event it was decided to place two bombs, disguised in a parcel to look like bottles of brandy, on the Führer's plane. But technical problems with the bombs meant that the conspirators waited in vain for news of the explosion. When Hitler landed safely at Rastenburg the bombs were removed by von Schlabrendorff and a new date was fixed, a week later, for another attempt on Hitler's life at the memorial day for WWI heroes at the Zeughaus in Berlin (➤Memorial Day Plot).

Sobibor. Concentration camp established in April 1942 near the frontier of the Ukraine Reich Commissariat. Its output was calculated by its founder, Criminal Police Inspector Christian Wirth, at 20,000 persons per day. In all 250,000 people are believed to have died there. ➤Concentration Camps

Solf Circle. One of the many anti-Nazi groups at which the ideas of the Kreisau Circle were discussed. Hosted by Frau Hanna Solf, wife of a former ambassador to Japan, the group exhibited that degree of indiscretion and scorn for the Gestapo which was not untypical of anti-Nazi aristocrats until quite late in the war. In this case Schellenberg of the SD did not find it difficult to infiltrate a Dr Reckze into the circle. Biding his time until January 1944, four months after the group had been penetrated, Schellenberg was satisfied there was no more to learn. A dozen people were arrested, including von Moltke, and all were executed except Frau Solf herself who escaped through the intercession of the Japanese ambassador.

Sorge, Richard (1895–1944). German journalist and spy for Russia. His main sphere of action from 1933 until 1941 was in Japan. Maintaining the fiction that he was a loyal German, he was even asked to become the local

Führer of all Germans living in Japan. He was arrested in 1941 and executed by the Japanese three years later.

Spandau.   A large prison built in the western suburb of Berlin in the nine-teenth century to house military prisoners. It continued to serve this purpose until 1944, when it was used to house those arrested after the 20 July Bomb Plot and other political prisoners. It was equipped with facilities to stage multiple executions, including guillotines.

In 1946, it was decided to use Spandau Prison to house those given prison sentences at the first Nuremberg Trial. At the end of that trial, Walther Funk, Rudolf Hess and Admiral Erich Raeder were given life sentences, Albert Speer and Baldur von Schirach twenty years each, Constantin von Neurath, fifteen years, and Admiral Karl Dönitz, ten years.

On 17 August 1987 the last remaining prisoner, Rudolf Hess, was found dead in a workshop with an electric flex around his neck. The death was recorded as one of misadventure, but the manner of his death remains controversial. His body was taken to Bavaria for burial, and Spandau Prison was swiftly demolished to prevent it becoming a Nazi shrine.

Spanish Civil War.   In July 1936 a revolt broke out against the Popular Front republican government of Spain, led by officers and soldiers under General Franco. The revolt turned into a civil war as Spain split between Republicans and the insurgent Nationalists. To the world, the war seemed to crystallize into a conflict between communism and fascism.

Hitler supported the Nationalists as part of his anti-communist programme. In November 1936 he sent the Condor Legion to Spain, under Sperrle: about 50 bombers, 50 fighters and an auxiliary squadron, with anti-aircraft and anti-tank units and two tank companies under von Thoma. The total strength of the Condor Legion stayed at about 6,500 throughout, giving (with periodic replacement) a total of 16,000 Germans with war experience in Spain. This was very much less than the Italians, who sent an entire 'Blackshirt' division and trained about 50,000 men.

The international character of the war was marked by the foreigners who came to fight on both sides. Soviet Russia sent the Republicans tanks, aircraft and equipment with a force of staff officers and political advisers. An 'International Brigade' was formed of nearly 40,000 men from a number of countries, including about 5,000 anti-Nazis from Germany and Austria of whom 2,000 were killed.

In April 1937 German aircraft bombed the Basque village of Guernica, killing over 1,600 and giving a chilling foretaste of things to come and a lasting propaganda weapon against them.

The German force left Spain in May 1938, having given battle training and opportunities to test out new tactics to the future leaders of Germany's air force of WWII. Galland and Mölders, the fighter aces and commanders of 1940, were both in Spain with the Condor Legion.

Speer, Albert (1905–1981). Reich Minister for Armaments and Production 1942–5. Speer was born of a middle-class Mannheim family and studied architecture as a young man at the Institute of Technology in nearby Karlsruhe. In 1925 he attended the Institute of Technology in Berlin and became assistant to Professor Tesenow who taught him that 'true culture comes from the womb of the nation'.

In 1932 Speer joined the Nazi Party and shortly after became a member of the SS. He first attracted Hitler's attention by making the technical arrangements for a Berlin Party rally in May 1933. Given the task of making the Nuremberg rally of 1934 a spectacle, he succeeded brilliantly. He was put on the staff of the Deputy Führer, Hess, from 1936, designed the German exhibit at the Paris Exhibition of 1937 and drew up grandiose designs for the Reich Chancellery in Berlin and the Party Palace in Nuremberg.

Even after the outbreak of war, Speer's official connection with the Nazi state was still that of court architect and favourite. His celebrated metamorphosis into Armaments Controller did not happen immediately. The early war years were still occupied with preparing grandiose schemes for city rebuilding; although required at the same time to design a headquarters complex like Ziegenberg for the coming campaign against France, his main responsibility was for the design of the twenty-five 'reconstruction cities' in the Reich.

In February 1942 the death in an air crash of Dr Fritz Todt, Minister of Armaments, dramatically changed Speer's involvement with the Third Reich and led directly to his post-war appearance at the Nuremberg trial of major war criminals. Appointed controller of armaments and minister in Todt's place, Speer now proved himself an exceptionally capable administrator, raising production levels of armaments to previously unattained heights. His autobiography *Inside the Third Reich* is the most complete and authoritative description of the processes of government in the Nazi state.

By the last year of the war Speer's commitment to Nazism had declined, but he continued to produce the armaments on which the state's survival depended. It was probably his rigid pride that demanded he plead guilty at the Nuremberg trial. Sentenced to twenty years' imprisonment for his use of slave labour in his production programmes, he was released from Spandau in 1966.

Spengler, Oswald (1880–1936). World-famous author of *The Decline of the West* (1918–22). Initially popular with the Nazi Party, he was soon disillusioned with Hitler's methods. Daring to speak out against Nazism, he found his work suppressed and himself banned from writing.

Sperrle, Hugo (1885–1953). Luftwaffe Field Marshal. A WWI fighter pilot who in 1919 ran a Freikorps air detachment, he served with the Weimar army until 1933 and was transferred to the new Luftwaffe in 1935. He was in charge of the air forces sent to the Spanish Civil War by Germany in 1936, and on the outbreak of war commanded an air fleet. After a command in North Africa he was transferred to Western Europe. In 1944 he was in Paris at the time of the July Bomb Plot, but there is no evidence of sympathy for the conspirators. At the trials of war criminals in Nuremberg after the war he was acquitted.

SS (*Schutzstaffel* – Defence Unit).   Originally the personal guard of Adolf Hitler which was transformed by Himmler into a state within a state, an army within an army.

Outline history

1925

Summer	First SS units formed

1929

January	Himmler becomes first *Reichsführer* SS, strength 280 men

1930

November	SS independence from SA in practice; strength 400 men

1931

August	SD set up under Heydrich
December	Race and Resettlement Office set up under Darré

1933

March	Himmler police president of Munich
March	*Leibstandarte Adolf Hitler* set up under Sepp Dietrich, forming core of SS-VT (*Verfügungstruppe*, armed), with the remainder as *Allgemeine SS* (general)
March	Dachau concentration camp opened
April	Himmler becomes commander, Bavarian political police

1934

April	Himmler becomes inspector of the Prussian Gestapo
April	Heydrich heads Gestapo
June	SD made sole intelligence service of the Party
June	Röhm Purge
July	SS formally separated from SA

1936

February	Gestapo given national status
March	SS camp guards formed as *Totenkopfverbände*, of 3,000 men
June	Himmler combines offices of *Reichsführer* SS and chief of all German police

1939

September	SS-VT increased from 8,000 to 9,000 and *Totenkopfverbände* to 6,500
September	RSHA (Reich Chief Security Office) formed under Heydrich
October	SS Divisions '*Das Reich*' and '*Totenkopf*' formed
October	Himmler 'Reich Commissioner for the Strengthening of Germanism'

1940

January	Waffen SS (decreed 1939) formed from SS divisions
June	Strength of Waffen SS raised to 100,000; 150,000 by December

1941

June	Four *Einsatzgruppen* (extermination squads) move into Russia behind the invasion
December	Waffen SS with strength of 230,000 men

1942

February	SS administrative organization of its enterprises (WVHA) set up
March	All concentration camps put under WVHA
June	Heydrich killed

1943

August	Himmler made Reich Minister of the Interior

1944

June	Waffen SS strength 594,000, *Allgemeine* SS 200,000, *Totenkopfverbände* 24,000
July	Himmler given command of *Ersatzarmee*, the Reich's reserve military forces
October	Waffen SS at its greatest strength, 38 SS divisions and 910,000 men

1945   At Nuremberg the Allied International Military Tribunal declares the SS (excepting the Waffen SS) a criminal organization

SS: Groupings and organizations. As the SS developed, it grew new branches and associated organizations. First from the armed group of the general (*Allgemeine*) SS, Sepp Dietrich was given charge of a special bodyguard, the *Leibstandarte Adolf Hitler*, which expanded to battalion size; the SS executioners of the Röhm Purge came from this unit. Himmler then proposed to enlarge military SS units to three divisions. After the Minister of War, Blomberg, and the commander of the army, Fritsch, were removed from their posts Hitler had assumed supreme military command. An August 1938 decree added a clear wartime role, as well as an internal political function, to these military SS units (known as SS-VT, *Verfügungstruppe*, signifying SS troops at the disposal of Hitler or the state).

Concentration camp guards, under Eicke, formed a separate SS unit. At first they wore brown rather than black uniforms with an identifying Death's Head Badge. In March 1936 they were officially named the SS *Totenkopfverbände* (SS Death's-head Units) and the force of 3,500 men was used in camps and for 'special political duties' during the action of taking over Austria and Czechoslovakia. In March 1939 the Waffen SS (armed SS) was formed by combining the SS-VT and the camp guards.

As part of his struggle to wrest power from Frick's Ministry of the Interior, Himmler took control of both the Orpo (*Ordnungspolizei*), the regular uniformed police, and the Sipo (*Sicherheitspolizei*), the security police. From this base he was able in 1936 to take over the Gestapo as a national organization and replace the former system, based on the separate German states, with a centralized national police system.

SS: Honorary members. To establish its élite nature and its fundamental difference from the SA, the SS set out to attract members of the aristocracy and upper classes. By 1938 the SS could boast that 18.7 per cent at the rank of *Obergruppenführer*, 14.3 at *Brigadeführer*, 8.8 at *Oberführer* and 8.4 per cent at the rank of *Standartenführer* were drawn from titled families.

'Honorary commanders', with no duties or powers, but the right to wear the uniform, were appointed, such as Seyss-Inquart, Konrad Henlein and Bormann. Elite societies, like the Equestrian Association, were invited to join – which gave the SS the most spectacular horseriding event team in Europe. There were also 'friends of the Reichsführer SS', an élite of subscribing industrialists and, on a lower level, 'sponsoring friends', less eminent people who thus bought favour with the SS.

Since the post-war period of denazification, when most of the honorary members were classified as only *Mitläufer* ('fellow-travellers') and suffered no penalty, there have been occasional allegations that well-known people were members of the SS. A recent press sensation concerned the father of the member of the British royal family, Princess Michael of Kent, an allegation that would have sounded less sinister if the nature of his honorary membership had been understood.

SS: Ritual and romance. SS duties often included guard duties in support of Nazi rituals, such as the Munich commemoration of the dead of the 1923 Beer Hall Putsch or at the massive Party rallies at Nuremberg. In addition they created their own pattern of rituals.

All eighteen-year-old applicants for the SS had their racial purity checked, back to 1715. When cleared, they were accepted in a mass parade on the anniversary of the Munich Beer Hall Putsch of November 1923; then, on Hitler's birthday in April, they took an oath and, after qualifying in sports and the Party catechism, they entered the service of the SS at a ceremonial parade in October at which they were awarded their engraved SS dagger.

To emphasize that they had entered something more than a paramilitary police service – rather a holy order – Himmler had built a replica medieval castle at Wewelsburg near Paderborn in Westphalia where senior SS officers were to gather several times a year to discuss policy and soak themselves in mysticism. When he realized in 1945 that the war was lost and the Third Reich collapsing he ordered Wewelsburg to be destroyed.

SS: RuSHA (*Rasse und Siedlungshauptamt*). The Race and Resettlement Office, the guardian of the ideological and racial purity of the SS. Headed by

SS: RuSHA (*Rasse und Siedlungshauptamt*)

Darré, until Himmler tired of him, finding him too theoretical, and replaced him in 1943 with Hildebrandt.

The RuSHA had a staff of lecturers who reportedly bored SS men with solemn talks on Aryan history. It established standards for entry to the SS; racial appearance (which had to be Nordic), good physical condition and general bearing. No defined intellectual attainment was required. The marriages of SS men were vetted before approval by the RuSHA.

The race experts of the RuSHA had ideal plans for the resettlement of occupied lands with the pure Germans whom they had approved, aiming at an immediate settlement of 840,000, followed by a second wave of 1,100,000 and then an annual resettlement of 200,000 over ten years.

SS: structure

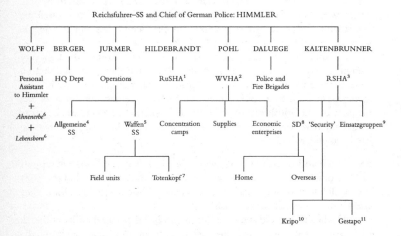

NOTES
[1] Rasse und Siedlungshauptamt: the Race and Resettlement Department
[2] Wirtschaftsverwaltungshauptamt: the Economic Administration Department
[3] Reichssicherheitshauptamt: the Reich Security Department
[4] General SS (the original bodyguard groups)
[5] Armed SS (the military units)
[6] Research institutes; SS maternity homes
[7] 'Death's Head': the concentration camp guards
[8] Sicherheitsdienst: the intelligence department
[9] 'Task groups': the extermination units
[10] KRIminalPOlizei: criminal police
[11] GEheimes STAatsPOlizei: secret state police

SS: Training Schools. The principal SS officer-cadet schools were located at Brunswick and Bad Tolz. Both schools clearly provided a high standard of training, although the rumours that attached to them had little real basis in fact. It is true that a percentage of casualties during training was allowed, but similar levels were officially 'acceptable' in the British commandos. Stories of each SS cadet exploding a grenade balanced on his steel helmet as a graduating requirement can be dismissed.

SS: Uniforms. The SS, while a part of the SA, wore the same brown shirts and breeches as the main force, with different badges and a black tie instead of a brown one. They also wore black ski-caps rather than the brown peaked cap of the Party and SA. With full independence from the SA in 1930, the complete black uniform was introduced: boots, belts, hats and tie, with a special swastika armband. This became the uniform of the Party élite – even civil servants in Ribbentrop's Foreign Ministry took to wearing it to demonstrate their position as honorary SS officers. The concentration camp guards, recruited from 1934 and styled the *SS-Totenkopfverbände* in 1936, wore the SA brown and not the black uniform (only other SS men and officers attached to the camps wore the black).

From the outbreak of war in 1939, to show their integral role as soldiers of the Third Reich, the SS adopted the field-grey of the army, and the striking black uniform was used only for ceremonial purposes.

SS: *Verfügungstruppe* (combat troops). The forerunners of the Waffen SS. The SS-VT were formed out of armed SS groups from the General (*Allgemeine*) SS. The literal meaning of VT is 'troops at the disposal [of Hitler]' for whom Sepp Dietrich in March 1933 had commanded a special HQ bodyguard. This appeared at the 1933 Nuremberg rally as the '*Leibstandarte Adolf Hitler*'. The success of the unit in providing the SS executioners during the Röhm Purge of 1934 emboldened Himmler to propose expanding his SS-VT to the strength of three divisions. General Blomberg, Minister of War, agreed to the SS-VT having a full military role in case of war. The army preferred the SS to the loutish SA and did not anticipate its future growth; they did not perhaps observe that the SS training was not as policemen, but as soldiers.

When the Waffen SS was formed in May 1939, the SS-VT together with the Death's Head SS (the former concentration camp guards) were absorbed into the new body.

SS: Waffen SS. The SS army which, at its height, numbered 40 divisions. From its beginnings in the 1920s, the SS had developed a fully armed unit, starting as a bodyguard for Hitler under Sepp Dietrich, but growing in size (as the SS-VT) to two divisions at the outbreak of war. In 1939 an 'armed SS', the Waffen SS, was formed and during 1940 the SS-VT were converted into it. Since voluntary service with the Waffen SS counted as compulsory military service, the *Totenkopfverbände* (the 'Death's Head' concentration camp guards) were also included in the Waffen SS by an order of March 1940. At this stage the Waffen SS was not a favoured body. The army discouraged recruitment to it and numbers had to be made up with *Volksdeutsche*, men of German origin living outside Germany and not liable for call-up to the German army. With expansion in 1942 and 1943, however, when the Waffen SS constituted a full but separate army corps, volunteers for the oversubscribed Luftwaffe and navy were directed into the SS. Almost all of the *Hitler Jugend* 12 SS Division were so recruited. The expansion continued, but more and more recruits came from outside Germany until it was calculated that of the 900,000 men who served in the Waffen SS, half were non-German. The number who were conscripted or transferred as opposed to SS volunteers cannot be estimated.

The quality of the Waffen SS divisions varied greatly. Seven were top-class fighting formations and after their successes in Russia in March 1943 received preference in equipment and were used by Hitler as his élite army. These divisions were:

1 SS Panzer, '*Leibstandarte*' (originally Hitler's bodyguard)
2 SS Panzer, *Das Reich*
3 SS Panzer, *Totenkopf*
5 SS Panzer, *Viking* (including Flemish and Scandinavians)
9 SS Panzer, *Hohenstaufen*
10 SS Panzer, *Frundsberg*
12 SS Panzer, *Hitler Jugend*

While these were among the best of the Third Reich's soldiers, these divisions of the Waffen SS also contained some of the worst in character. It was *Das Reich* that butchered the French village of Oradour-sur-Glane when their march north was opposed in 1944. And the smear of the concentration camp could never be taken from the reputation of the *Totenkopf* division.

Of the many non-German SS divisions, several Waffen SS divisions were raised by Byelo-Russians, Ukrainians and Cossacks; and 30th SS 'Volunteer Grenadier' Division was turned into the Free Russian Army under Vlassov. In the west, SS divisions were recruited from France (SS Charlemagne), from Holland (SS Landstorm Nederland), from Belgium (SS Langemarck and SS Wallonie) and many Scandinavians went to make up SS Viking.

By the end of the war, many units had strayed far from Himmler and Berger's original Aryan ideal. Necessarily there was a considerable variation in fighting prowess between the units, but it remains true that the Waffen SS constituted one of the most formidable military organizations ever developed.

SS (WVHA: *Wirtschaftsverwaltungshauptamt*) business enterprises. The SS branch which controlled the twenty concentration camps and 165 labour camps, administration and supplies for the Waffen SS, and which had charge of the enterprises which were indirectly (but completely) owned by the SS.

In 1939 the four major SS businesses were: an excavation and quarrying company producing building materials; a company marketing a great variety of products from workshops in concentration camps; a foodstuffs, estates, forestry and fishery company; and a textile and leather company based on Ravensbrück women's concentration camp, producing uniforms for the SS. In addition the SS controlled most of the Reich's soft-drink and mineral-water factories, based on takeovers in the Sudeten; a huge furniture-making complex deriving from former Jewish and Czechoslovak companies; and cement, brick, lime and ceramic companies, mostly from Poland and often using Jewish slave labour. These enterprises all had their subsidiaries, ranging from jam-making to printing and shale-oil production.

WVHA enlarged its activities with contracts for building armaments factories, underground hangars and even, after July 1944, for the building of V-1 and V-2 weapons.

An inherent contradiction in WVHA was that, in the face of the Final Solution, it needed slave labour and found itself advocating the preservation of Jewish workers. First the Dresdner Bank and then the Reichsbank gave huge loans at low interest. With these funds and cheap labour, and the loot from victims of extermination, SS profits were enormous. The disappearance, at the end of the war, of many millions of dollars of SS funds has never been satisfactorily explained.

SS: women's units. Primarily, women were wives and mothers in the Nazi world; however, some were given special honorary SS ranks, others became 'SS sisters' in front-line dressing stations or were employed in the SS as office workers, especially in radio, telegraphy, long-distance telephone work, or as warders in women's concentration camps. The first warders were recruited for Lichtenburg in 1938. Between 1942 and 1945 there were about 3,500 SS women warders in Ravensbrück. They were recruited through newspaper advertisements for 'supervisors of the work-shy', selected with a 'pure Aryan' history and uniformed in grey with black knee-boots and black caps.

From 1943 this recruitment method was insufficient and wardresses were brought in from the normal women's labour service or called up as for war service. Given light work and higher rates of pay than other women, the warders were mostly brutal, or quickly became brutalized, beating and killing with as much enthusiasm as their male counterparts: five were condemned to death by the Americans after the war for their crimes. Such was Hermine Braunsteiner-Ryan, a blonde Viennese who served as a warder in Ravensbrück, having been recruited at the age of twenty-one from a Berlin factory. She was sentenced to imprisonment for her inhumanity in the Majdanek extermination camp. She later married an American, but in 1971 was extradited from the

USA (the first US resident to be extradited for such crimes to be tried again in both Poland and Germany).

The corruption of the SS world was reflected in the wife of the commandant of Sachsenhausen, Ilse Koch, who took pleasure in whipping prisoners and collecting lampshades. She was later judged by psychiatrists to be power-mad, demoniacal and nymphomaniac. In prison after the war she managed to seduce her American army warder and give birth to a baby.

Stab in the back (*Dolchstoss*). The accusation that the German army in WWI was never defeated on the field of battle but had been betrayed – stabbed in the back – by Social Democrats, Jews and profiteers on the home front.

For the German soldier serving on the Western Front there appeared to be some evidence to support this view. The German army was never routed along the line of the front and many of its units returned to Germany intact and carrying their arms. The truth was different, but the stab-in-the-back theory pandered to the wounded pride of the army and to the vast reservoir of anti-semitic, anti-democratic resentment which was building up in Germany in the years immediately after the war.

Nazi propaganda, though not responsible for inventing the term, brilliantly exploited the idea, combining stab in the back with the 'November Criminals' (the signatories of the Versailles Treaty) to damn the Weimar Republic and all its supporters.

***Stahlhelm* (Steel helmet)**. The militant right-wing, nationalist ex-servicemen's association started in the chaos of the German collapse of 1918. Founded by Franz Seldte, co-leader with Theodor Düsterberg until its formal dissolution in 1933. Hindenburg, as the ideal of soldiers, became its President. Von Papen encouraged them as a stabilizing force since they had links with both army and industry which financed them.

In 1923 *Stahlhelm* had twenty-three units, 14,000 local groups and up to a million men. The organization played an increasingly prominent part in Weimar politics. In the March 1932 presidential elections, Düsterberg representing the *Stahlhelm* won 2.5 million votes before withdrawing in Hitler's favour at the run-off. Again, linked with Nazis and others in the Harzburg Front, they successfully urged the dismissal of Chancellor Brüning in May 1932.

Göring first linked them with the SA and SS in an auxiliary police force in 1933, forbidding the Prussian police to interfere with their activities. It was in fact the beginning of total absorption by the SA. On the Nazi assumption of full power Seldte became Minister of Labour in Hitler's cabinet and put the *Stahlhelm* directly under Hitler's control in June 1933. By February 1934 even the once proud name had changed to the deliberately prosaic 'Nationalist League of Ex-Servicemen'. It was an indication of Hitler's success in controlling the right-wing elements in his support.

Stalin, Joseph (1879–1953). Soviet dictator. After a period in which the

Comintern had underrated the importance of the Nazi threat, Stalin seemed prepared to take the lead against fascism; but a lack of enthusiasm from France and Britain for an alliance with the Soviet Union led him to the dramatic change of policy enshrined in the Russo-German Pact of August 1939. The full significance of the pact, which was in effect a division of East European spoils, was not revealed until Russia's occupation of east Poland in 1939. This was followed by the annexation of the Baltic States, the seizure of the Rumanian provinces of Bukovina and Bessarabia and the attack on Finland.

Despite British warnings, the German invasion of Russia in June 1941 took Stalin by surprise, more perhaps in its timing than the attack itself. During the series of defeats between June and December 1941, Stalin seems to have been in some danger of losing his grip; but by Christmas he had reasserted his authority and from then on was directly responsible for the conduct of the war. To the Nazis he now showed himself an implacable enemy; to Britain, and later the US, he was as often a querulous and demanding ally.

But the sacrifices of the Russian people were real. In July 1941 Stalin's historic appeal to scorch the earth initiated a policy of utter destruction in the face of the invader; many millions of Soviet citizens were killed; millions of Jews and Russian soldiers were massacred or died in camps. After the war the claim of 20 million Soviet dead was to become established in the reference books; certainly suffering was on a gigantic scale and losses were colossal. To some historians, however, it seems likely that the Soviet figure of 20 million included some millions dead as a result of Stalin's own pre-war crimes.

In terms of the overall conduct of the war, Soviet policy was aimed at persuading or pressurizing Britain and the US into an invasion of France in 1942. It is uncertain to what extent Stalin understood the military impossibility of the task, but certainly he was able to shape future Allied policy with his veiled threats of an 'understanding' with Germany. Crafty and totally devious, Stalin seems to have played cat and mouse with Churchill and Roosevelt throughout 1943. The Teheran Conference (December 1943) which established Allied military policy for 1944/5 in effect recognized Russia's pre-eminent political position in Eastern Europe. In the nature and location of the Third Reich's last battles is to be found the shape of post-war Europe as Joseph Stalin envisaged it.

Stalingrad, Battle of.   The decisive battle of the war. When Field Marshal von Paulus surrendered in January 1943 with 90,000 surviving German soldiers and twenty-four generals, the world saw for the first time the possibility of the defeat of the Third Reich.

When Hitler's invasion of Russia failed to win victory in 1941, he returned to the offensive in the following year. By July he had moved to his 'Werewolf' headquarters at Vinnitsa in the Ukraine to supervise the advance of his armies to the Volga river and into the Caucasus. Army Group B reached the Volga at the end of August 1942, where Stalin gave special authority to the Communist Party leader there, Khrushchev. General Chuikov was given command of the Soviet troops to defend the key point on the Volga controlling the rail and waterway communications of southern Russia: the city of Stalingrad. In September, von Paulus's 6th German Army had taken most of the city and, controlling the air, he seemed on the way to smashing through the town to the river. But in October and November the Germans fought without succeeding, and the Russians held on with their backs to the river but with their artillery countering the Germans from the far banks of the Volga.

In November Russian counter-attacks to north and south of Stalingrad broke through and von Paulus was surrounded. Hitler had dismissed General Halder as Chief-of-Staff OKH and replaced him with the less imposing Zeitzler, whose warnings he ignored. Reinforcements were sent, including Rumanians and Luftwaffe ground forces. To add to the stresses at Hitler's headquarters, the Anglo-American forces landed in North Africa and the *Afrika Korps* was routed by the British at the Battle of El Alamein.

Supply was now the crucial factor in the battle. Göring claimed he could supply von Paulus with 700 tons a day by air. Within days he had reduced the promise to 300; but even this could not be achieved by the Luftwaffe in the Russian winter. Nor could Field Marshal Manstein's relief army break through to Stalingrad. In January 1943 the Russians offered surrender terms to the Germans, but Hitler ordered his army to fight on. Von Paulus was promoted to Field Marshal. But by February 70,000 German soldiers were dead and the survivors surrendered, from an army which had once numbered half a million men. It was a catastrophic blow to Hitler and the Third Reich.

Stangl, Franz (d. 1971).   Commander of the extermination camp at Treblinka where over 700,000 were killed. At the end of the war he was arrested by the Americans but escaped in 1948 through Italy to Syria (where he was joined by his family) and thereafter to Brazil in 1951, where contacts found him working at the Volkswagen plant in São Paulo. He was identified and arrested in 1967, extradited to Germany and tried. He said: 'My conscience is clear. I was simply doing my duty.'

Apart from organizing death, he delivered to the SS bank deposits $2,800,000, £400,000, 12,000,000 roubles, 145 kilograms of gold from rings, 4,000 carats of diamonds, as well as loads of hair and used clothing for SS factories. He was sentenced to imprisonment in 1970 and died in 1971. ►Concentration Camps

Stauffenberg, Graf Claus Schenk von (1907–44).   The officer who placed the bomb which exploded at Rastenburg on 20 July 1944. Fiercely anti-Hitler in his views, von Stauffenberg entered the broad area of conspiracy through the Kreisau Circle. His attitude to tyrannicide changed, however, in the latter part of 1943 and he began to consider that the assassination of Hitler was vital to a change of government. This was in itself a development of many conspirators' views. By early 1944 von Stauffenberg found himself exasperated by the lack of action among the many groups and 'circles' which made up the German aristocratic or military resistance. Volunteering to carry the bomb himself, he placed it in the conference room where Hitler was present. It was by far the closest any conspirators had come to the destruction of what von Stauffenberg called the 'Master of Vermin of the Third Reich'. ➤July Bomb Plot

Stennes Mutiny.   Mutiny of the SA, named after Walter Stennes, SA Deputy Commander. A former *Freikorps* leader and follower of Strasser's radical Nazism, Stennes had become Pfeffer von Salomon's deputy and leader of the SA in eastern Germany. His men were unemployed and in poverty; in September 1930 his men heckled a speech by Göbbels, the Party Gauleiter of Berlin, and beat up his SS guard. Hitler's persuasion did not work and he feared an SA revolt. He dismissed Pfeffer from the SA and recalled Röhm from Bolivia to command it, demanding a personal loyalty oath from the men of the SA.

In April 1931 Hitler had submitted to a government ban on public demonstrations and was rumoured to be about to dismiss Stennes. Stennes therefore held a secret meeting of SA leaders which declared for him and against Hitler. But his men had no funds and could not sustain a revolt. The Party declared them expelled and Göring took over the Berlin organization with SS men. Göbbels' role in the affair is not clear; it is possible that, as a former radical himself, he may have had some sympathy with the SA.

Stennes was the nephew of a cardinal and had influential friends, among them Göring who managed to prevent Stennes being arrested in 1933 and had him smuggled out of Germany before the vengeful SS could kill him during the Röhm Purge. Stennes aligned himself for a while with Otto Strasser's anti-Hitler 'Black Front', but ended his career as Chiang Kai-shek's bodyguard in Nationalist China.

Stinnes, Hugo (1870–1924).   The Ruhr business tycoon who built a financial and industrial empire linked with Thyssen and Kirdorf. An early backer of the Nazis, he believed that politics were meant to serve his own interests and that the Nazis would be a useful tool to defeat socialists and trade unionists.

Strasser, Gregor (1892–1934).   A radical Nazi, one of the acknowledged leaders of the Party until killed in the Röhm Purge. A big, hard, blond Bavarian who enjoyed good living and classical literature, Strasser had risen from the ranks in WWI, winning the Iron Cross, First Class. He owned a chemist's shop in Landshut, Lower Bavaria. Joining the Nazis in 1920, he rapidly gained promotion in the Party with his organizational skills. In the 1923 Beer Hall Putsch he led 300 men to Munich, but played no significant role in the events. His men dispersed and he was arrested.

While Hitler was in Landsberg prison, Strasser organized with Ludendorff and Röhm a 'National Socialist Freedom Movement'. In the 1924 Reichstag elections this group won 32 seats, but was dissolved when Hitler came out of prison in February 1925.

Strasser worked to expand the Party. In North Rhineland he made the young Göbbels local Party business manager. At this time, north German Nazis saw their leader Hitler as surrounded by the corrupt influence of the 'Munich clique' and Strasser himself became estranged from the old Munich Nazis. He founded a Berlin Party newspaper with Göbbels as editor, to emphasize the socialist side of Nazism and its fundamental working-class attitude. While anti-semitic, the Strasserites did not condemn the Jews alongside the capitalist enemy; nor did they see Bolshevik Russia as necessarily evil, even calling for an alliance with the Soviets against the militarist enemies of the German people like France, imperialist Britain and capitalist USA.

While Hitler's tactics made him side with big business and the remnants of the Hohenzollern aristocracy, Strasserite programmes called for land nationalization, co-operative farms and profit-sharing by workers in industry. Hitler fought against these ideas and, at a meeting in Bamberg in February 1926, spoke so strongly against the radicals that he swung Göbbels to his side and away from Strasser. From now on there was to be no Party criticism of Hitler. The Nazi salute of 'Heil Hitler!' and uncritical mass adulation were to be the rule.

Strasser's claim to ideological leadership was extinguished. His Berlin stronghold was put under Göbbels as Gauleiter who at the same time was given full authority to write Party propaganda. To an extent Strasser was mollified by becoming titular chief of propaganda, and his skills were used by giving him charge of Party organization. In 1928 he became one of twelve Nazi Reichstag deputies.

In 1930 Strasser organized the Party for the Reichstag elections, concentrating on key seats, making the Party the second largest in the Reichstag. But again he quarrelled with Hitler over Nazi Party policy. His younger brother, Otto Strasser, was thrown out of a Party meeting in Berlin and called for other radicals to form a new party with him. Gregor disowned him and remained at the centre of Nazi power, but his position was seriously weakened.

General Schleicher approached Strasser in December 1932, hoping to draw the radicals out of the Nazi Party and induce him to join him in a coalition government. Instead, Strasser went to Hitler; again they disputed policy, but again Strasser was isolated. He resigned his Party posts and moved away from the crisis by going on holiday to Italy. Instantly Hitler smashed the remains of his support by appointing new men to Party organizational positions. When Strasser came back, Hitler refused to see him.

Strasser was now cut off from power and during 1933 was only a spectator as Hitler forced Germany into a dictatorship mould. The atmosphere of suspicion and fear in 1933 led to a rumour that Strasser was plotting with Röhm to overthrow the Führer and he was an early victim of the Röhm Purge in June 1934. Taken from his chemical products factory to the cellars of Gestapo headquarters in Berlin, he was shot by an SS squad.

Strasser, Otto (1897–1974). The younger brother of Gregor Strasser; a Nazi from 1925 but later an outspoken opponent. At first his politics were socialist but he became alarmed at the anti-nationalist and internationalist aspects of radical socialism and communism and followed his brother into the Nazi Party. He took the 'socialist' element in Nazism seriously and, like his brother, demanded the nationalization and state control of businesses and industry. This alienated potential supporters of the Nazis who demanded that the Party denounce the Strasserite policies.

He was expelled from the Nazi Party and in 1930 started a revolutionary socialist party of his own, the Black Front. But the new party failed to attract votes from the Nazis, and Strasser left Germany in 1933. He was hunted unsuccessfully by the SD, moving from Switzerland to Canada. After the war he returned to Germany, still hoping to lead a party, but his anti-semitic neo-Nazi views were unpopular and he found no role in modern German politics.

Strategic Air Offensive. The Anglo-American air attacks on Germany, 1939–45.

The doctrine of the strategic air offensive is now generally recognized to have been developed in Britain in the last year of WWI in part as a justification for the creation of the new independent Royal Air Force. In the US the theory was enthusiastically embraced by Brigadier-General William Mitchell in the 1920s and, in Italy, General Giulio Douhet's book, *The Command of the Air* (1921), contained much of the doctrine of the strategic air offensive. Thus by the 1930s it was widely believed that air power could win wars and that massed bombing planes would always get through to destroy cities. The effect of German air attacks in the Spanish Civil War seemed to support this view. Yet in 1939 neither Germany, Britain, France, Russia nor the USA possessed operational heavy bombers. But while the Luftwaffe had abandoned plans for heavy four-engined bombers, the RAF had already ordered the new heavy aircraft which were to come into service in 1941, and the USA's 'Flying Fortress' was available shortly after the outbreak of war in Europe. Soon after the beginning of the war, therefore, Britain (later to be joined by the United States) was the only combatant with a real heavy bomber force.

When the German air attacks on British cities opened in late 1940, the British leadership felt bound to retaliate. Daylight raids quickly proved too costly. Instead, from May 1940 to the end of 1941, the RAF sent aircraft out on 44,000 night sorties. In this period 45,000 tons of bombs were dropped in raids planned to hit specific targets such as oil-refineries and armament factories. But bombing patterns in these raids proved (on examination of aerial photographs) to be wildly inaccurate. RAF command therefore decided to concentrate on broader targets, such as railway yards or centres of population. As the four-engined Lancasters became available, massive attacks were made from February 1942 on accessible coastal towns such as Lübeck and Rostock. In May, by assembling every possible aircraft, the first RAF '1000-bomber raid' was made on Cologne. This was followed by raids on the industrial Ruhr, Essen and Düsseldorf. The era of area bombing as the RAF called it – terror bombing as the Germans knew it – had arrived. From now on the inhabitants of Hamburg, the Ruhr towns, Nuremberg, Munich, Cologne and Berlin itself would be forced to live with the threat, sometimes nightly, of death from the air. Valuable resources were devoted to protecting the civilian population, but despite the huge numbers killed and injured it is difficult to detect any real breakdown in civilian morale.

From August 1942 the RAF was joined by the USAAF which chose to raid by day in the joint bombing programme. Throughout 1943 there were heavy and continuous raids by night and day on Berlin, Hamburg – where incendiary bombs caused a firestorm in August 1943 and 45,000 civilians died – Nuremberg, Munich, Stuttgart and Frankfurt. It was the conviction (to the exclusion of all argument) of Air Marshal Sir Arthur 'Bomber' Harris that Germany could be brought to her knees by the RAF's destruction of civilian morale. In this light he interpreted his orders from the Casablanca Conference and Joint Bombing directives. Between March and July 1943 the Battle of the Ruhr inflicted widespread damage on Duisburg, Dortmund, Düsseldorf, Bochum and Aachen. On a single night, 29 May, 90 per cent of Barmen-Wuppertal was destroyed. Yet the RAF, despite the high quality of its crews and aircraft, remained more bludgeon than rapier. In the Battle of Hamburg, thirty-three major attacks between July and November 1943, the city was devastated and tens of thousands of civilians were killed.

The reaction of the Nazi leaders differed greatly. Hitler, despite requests from *Gauleiters* of the stricken cities, refused to visit them to see for himself the extent of the damage. Göring, who had said that if the RAF ever raided Berlin 'you can call me Meier' (the equivalent of 'Smith'), made fewer and fewer public appearances as civilian casualties mounted and in many districts of Berlin was widely referred to as 'Meier'. Josef Göbbels, by contrast to the two senior Nazis, was active in visiting damaged areas and certainly appreciated the horrifying extent of the destruction. In his diary entry for 29 July 1943, following one of the heaviest single raids on Hamburg, he records: '[Nearly] 1000 bombers . . . *Gauleiter* Kaufmann spoke of a catastrophe the extent of which blunts the imagination. A city of one million people has been devastated in a manner unknown before in history . . . problems almost impossible to solve . . . food for a million people . . . shelter . . . clothing . . . 800,000 homeless people . . . wandering the devastated streets . . .'

Meanwhile the USAAF under its Commanding General H. H. Arnold favoured daylight attacks by well-armed bombers which could deliver higher degrees of industrial damage and lower civilian casualties than the RAF's night attacks. But the catastrophic raid on Schweinfurt on 14 October 1942 demonstrated that daylight bombing was also beset with practical difficulties; a force of 291 Flying Fortresses was attacked by wave after wave of German fighters. By the time the American force returned to England, sixty bombers had been shot down and 138 had sustained heavy damage. Such a rate of loss could not be sustained.

Fortunately the solution was already under construction. The North American Mustang powered by Rolls-Royce Merlin engines would provide the long-range fighter escort the USAAF desperately needed. From December 1943 when the Mustang became available, Flying Fortresses and Mustangs would, from the beginning of 1944, take command of the daylight skies over Europe.

In 1943 the combined Allied air forces had dropped a total of 200,000 tons of bombs. But both the RAF and the USAAF had been forced by successful Luftwaffe tactics to modify their own approach to the air war. In 1944, however, despite new levels of Luftwaffe fighter production, Allied air strength increasingly asserted itself.

From the Normandy invasion onwards, the two air forces were assigned separate roles. While RAF Bomber Command concentrated on the destruction of the communications systems behind the Normandy front, the US 8th Air Force devoted its efforts to attacking German oil production targets. The trend away from Harris's area bombing became marked; oil targets were now favoured by British commanders (with the exception of Harris) as much as by the Americans. By July, every major oil plant in Germany had been attacked, and by September Luftwaffe fuel supply had been reduced to 10,000 tons of octane against a monthly requirement of 160,000 tons.

From October 1944 to May 1945 the Allied air forces were dominant. Industrial targets lay at the bombers' mercy, yet still Harris directed RAF efforts into town areas where over 50 per cent of Bomber Command's explosives were dropped. The morality of these British actions has been vigorously questioned since the end of the war. This has been especially the case since the USAAF adopted a markedly different targeting policy aimed at industrial weak spots like oil and ball-bearings.

From February 1945, raids were made at Russian request to block the movement of German troops. Berlin, Chemnitz, Leipzig and Dresden were among the selected targets where there were heavy casualties as the war ended. In the great Dresden raid where between 60,000 and 120,000 civilians died, both RAF and USAAF combined to create a firestorm. It was an ignoble end to what, on the British side especially, many see as an ignoble policy. In Germany nobody believed that anything but the highest possible civilian casualties was the object of Allied 'terror bombing'. Regrettably, it is an argument which Sir Arthur Harris's policies in particular make it difficult to refute. An estimated 500,000 people were killed by air-raids on Germany between 1939 and 1945. ➤Air Defence

Streicher, Julius (1885–1946).   The violently anti-semitic writer who edited the Jew-baiting weekly, *Der Stürmer*. An early Nazi who marched with Hitler at the Beer Hall Putsch, Streicher was Party Gauleiter for Franconia from 1925 and became widely known for his corruption, greed, sexual extravagance and sadism. To lash a prisoner apparently gave him pleasure and satisfaction. Dismissed from his post in 1940, he continued to edit his paper as a private citizen, but held no further Party or government post. It was as the loudest anti-semite in Germany that he was put on trial with the other major criminals at Nuremberg, but it was difficult to prove him guilty in strictly legal terms. Nevertheless he was sentenced to death. At the gallows he shouted, 'Heil Hitler!' and 'The Bolsheviks will get you!'

Strength Through Joy (*Kraft durch Freude*, KdF).   A hugely successful and popular Nazi scheme for the leisure and pleasure of workers. It was in imitation of the Italian Fascist scheme *Dopo Lavoro* and was first proposed as *Nach der Arbeit*, 'after work'. The leader of the Labour Front started the scheme because he had large sums of money available from the takeover of trades union funds, but it soon became another Nazi big business, ordering the building of two new cruise-liners and subsidizing the development of the People's Car, the Volkswagen.

The cruise-liners sailed as far as the Norwegian fjords or Madeira and had equal accommodation for all passengers. 180,000 Germans went on cruises in 1938 and the volume of German tourism doubled. New tourist areas in Germany were opened up and Germans saw more of their own country than ever before. It is certainly true that never before had workers enjoyed such opportunities. The organization's sports facilities awarded five million certificates; hundreds of travelling theatre and cabaret groups were put on for workers; group cut-price visits to theatres caused an entertainment boom.

'Strength through Joy' took advantage of the common desire of people to join in activities and left them (as Ley said) with nothing but sleep for their own selves. It was on the whole an immensely successful Nazi organization of inestimable propaganda value to the Nazi state.

Stresa Front.   In April 1935, Britain (MacDonald), France (Laval) and Italy (Mussolini) met at Stresa, Italy, to discuss problems of the Danube basin. They condemned German rearmament, supported Austria's independence and reaffirmed Locarno. It seemed that a community of interest had been established against the new Germany. But the Front soon collapsed, as Hitler had already in March announced the development of the Luftwaffe and in May, while affirming that he had no wish to annex or conclude an *Anschluss* with Austria, he changed the name of the Ministry of Defence to Ministry of War. Shortly afterwards he began the Anglo-German naval talks. The British, seduced by Hitler, failed to consult the other nations of the Stresa Front. London's acceptance of Hitler's naval proposals destroyed Stresa; France signed a treaty of mutual assistance with Russia; Italy, also abandoning any sense of international harmony, invaded Ethiopia. The Stresa Front was dead.

Stresemann, Gustav (1878–1929). The German Chancellor from August to November 1923. During this short period Stresemann faced threats to the Weimar Republic's authority from both the left and the right. Acting impartially he sent troops to suppress communist rebellion in Saxony and Thuringia and the Nazi Beer Hall Putsch in Munich. Although a Nationalist, founder of the Deutsche Volkspartei in 1918, his liberalism was distrusted by right-wingers like Kahr in Bavaria, and the Socialist Party broke away from his coalition in dislike of what they saw as his conservatism.

From November 1923 he was Foreign Minister, dedicated to reconciliation with France. In 1926 he was awarded the Nobel Peace Prize jointly with the French Foreign Minister, Briand. With Schacht he treated with Germany's creditors on the Dawes and Young Plans for reparation payments. He negotiated the Locarno Treaty and German entry to the League of Nations. His achievements in restoring Germany's international status were more widely recognized abroad than in Germany itself.

He died suddenly in 1929 having brought Germany back into the forum of international politics. Hitler saw to it that the Third Reich undid most of his work.

Stülpnagel, Karl Heinrich von (1886–1944). Military Governor of France who led the July 1944 Bomb Plotters in Paris by arresting 1,200 SS and Gestapo and cutting off all communication from France to Germany.

As Quartermaster General of the army from 1938 to June 1940, he was openly critical of Hitler's war plans and would have joined any attempt to depose him. He was chairman of the armistice commission in France in 1940, then commanded the 17th Army in Russia from June to October 1941. He returned to Paris as Military Governor in February 1942.

Although he was responsible for the arrest and execution of French hostages during 1943, he disapproved of the rounding-up of Jews. But Jewish deportations were on the orders of Otto Abetz, the Paris-based German ambassador to France, who outranked him. Deeply involved in the July 1944 Bomb Plot, Stülpnagel tried, through General Speidel, to bring Rommel into the conspiracy and thus inadvertently implicated him. When the plot failed, Stülpnagel was exposed as one of the leading conspirators. Immediately Keitel ordered him to Berlin. On the way back Stülpnagel chose to shoot himself but did not die. He was tried by Freisler's People's Court and hanged in August 1944.

Stürmer, Der. A violently anti-semitic and frequently near-pornographic

Nazi broadsheet run by Julius Streicher. It was claimed by the editor to be the only newspaper read from cover to cover by Hitler.

Sudeten.   The mountainous area between Bohemia and Silesia whose population in 1919 was German-speaking. The Treaty of Versailles, following the old Austrian frontiers, assigned these 3,250,000 people to the new state of Czechoslovakia. The Sudetenland difficulties were used as a pretext for Hitler's further expansion after the Austrian *Anschluss* in 1938. A Sudeten German Party under Henlein was supported by Berlin, and its agitation and German accusations of Czechoslovak maltreatment were the cause of the Munich meeting which ceded Sudetenland to Germany. After WWII most of the German-speaking people were expelled from Czechoslovakia. ►Henlein, Konrad

Swastika.   The hooked cross. The immensely powerful emblem of the Nazi Party, the black cross on a white circular background against red. The history of the swastika in Germany goes deep into nationalistic and anti-semitic movements. The Ehrhardt Freikorps Brigade, for instance, painted large swastikas on their helmets as a distinguishing mark.

The symbol itself comes from 'Aryan' mythology and became a fetish of those who clustered round early Nazism. Hitler made the swastika the most famous symbol of the age, outclassing the Fascist axe and rods or the Soviet Russian hammer and sickle. It was incorporated in the new national flag from 1935. By the 1940s the swastika appeared everywhere under Nazi rule, as much at the head of documents and proclamations as on uniforms or ceremonial banners. As the war progressed, the swastika inevitably came to represent the murderous tyranny of Nazi Germany. Over fifty years later, the image retains an extraordinary degree of power.

Swing.   A banned form of American music which both in the occupied countries (1939–45) and even in Germany itself had strong resistance connotations. ►*Swingjugend*

Swingjugend.   A term for what the Party considered 'deviant' youth, usually urban middle-class boys who danced to American-style music. They seem to have been non-political, but they were non-conforming and favoured long hair. In Hamburg in 1940 over 500 of them were found together at a 'swing' festival. They were arrested and accused of degeneracy and jitterbugging.

Swiss Banks.   A significant but unknown quantity of Nazi gold and other assets passed through the Swiss banking system. British government archives released in September 1996 revealed that gold worth $500 million at 1945 prices was held in Swiss banks at the end of the war. Much of this had been plundered by the Nazi regime from the treasuries of Hungary, Holland and Belgium.

At the Nuremberg trials in 1946 Waltter Funk (President of the Reichsbank) testified that gold looted from Holocaust victims in the form of coin, gold jewellery and even gold teeth had been melted down and stamped as Reichsbank twenty-kilogramme bars before being sent to Switzerland.

In May 1946 the Washington Agreement sought to release these funds. The Swiss Bankers' Association agreed with the Allies to make a one-off payment of 250 million Swiss francs, and after lengthy negotiations, a further *ex gratia* payment of 121.5 million francs. Yet there were undoubtedly other sources of funds (profits from SS enterprises or deposits from individual high-ranking Nazis, for example) flowing from Germany into Switzerland. It has been estimated that, by pleading client confidentiality, Swiss banks have continued to hold nearly three-quarters of what they held at the end of the war.

The voluntary deposit of funds by Jews (particularly Hungarian Jews to whom the Holocaust came later and with more warning) can be seen as a separate issue. These were Jews seeking to protect their assets from confiscation. For many years the banks had refused to release funds without the kind of documentation unlikely to be in the possession of Holocaust survivors or their heirs. Vigorous efforts were made to persuade the Swiss government to release more information and in 1996 the Swiss Bankers' Association signed an agreement with the World Jewish Congress to allow an independent commission to investigate the role of the banks in this affair.

The Swiss banks estimate dormant accounts, the bulk of them certainly derived from Jewish sources before and during WWII, to be worth no more than $32 million. But in October 1996 Holocaust survivors and their heirs filed a class action in New York City for recovery and distribution of $20 billion. ►Nazi treasure.

T

Table Talk.   Hitler's dinner-table or late night ramblings, published in the US as *Hitler's Secret Conversations* (Farrar, Strauss & Co, New York 1953) and in London by Weidenfeld and Nicolson the same year as *Hitler's Table Talk*. The nightly monologue was taken down by secretaries and edited to an unknown extent by Martin Bormann. All the familiar Nazi obsessions are covered, along with comment on smoking, getting married, the importance of a good chauffeur and claims to be a tolerant employer.

The tone of the *Table Talk* is that of a didactic and over-confident parent. There is no expectation of correction or dissent. On subjects as diverse as the Ancient Greeks or American production methods, the Führer can be wrong with impunity, outrageous without irony. On one night in 1942, with Heinrich Himmler present and the chimneys of Auschwitz and Treblinka already belching black oily smoke, Hitler could calmly state that compared with past treatment of the Jews his own methods were much more humane. There is no evidence that either man smiled at the grotesque nature of the claim.

Tannenberg Bund.   An association founded in 1926, of ultra-rightist ex-soldiers led by General Erich Ludendorff. Named after the battle in which Hindenburg, with Ludendorff as his Chief-of-Staff, defeated the advancing Russian forces in 1914, the Bund was anti-communist, anti-semitic and anti-Masonic. Despite Ludendorff's name, the *Tannenberg Bund* failed to achieve the status of an independent party and in the late 1920s most of its activists drifted towards the Nazi Party.

Television.   An early user of television, the Third Reich was unable (in common with the rest of Europe) to develop it during WWII, since it interfered with radar and could have been used for homing purposes by enemy aircraft. A closed-circuit system had started, however, and was maintained during the war in Berlin.

Terboven, Josef (1898–1945).   The Reich Commissioner in occupied Norway.

A member of one of the groups who marched in the 1923 Beer Hall Putsch, Terboven joined the Nazi Party later and became Gauleiter of Essen in 1928 and a Reichstag delegate in 1930. In June 1934 Hitler used attendance at his wedding to disguise his preparations for the Röhm Purge. Terboven rose to be President of the Rhineland state in 1935 and a district Reich Defence Commissioner in 1939.

In April 1940 he went to Norway as Reich Commissioner to supervise Quisling's government. In practice, Terboven ruled Norway throughout the war without reference to Quisling's ideas and he enforced a repressive regime. In May 1945 he committed suicide before capture.

Thälmann, Ernst (1886–1944). The German Communist leader in the Reichstag, 1924–33. Following the Comintern policy line, he concentrated his attack on the Social Democrats rather than on the Nazis, believing that the Nazi paymasters would never permit them to carry out their published programme, nor would the French and British let the Nazis dominate Europe. The enemy, to Thälmann and the German Communists, was, on the insistence of the Comintern, the moderate Social Democrats, the traitors to the working class.

Thälmann's anti-socialist policy did much to enable the Nazis to increase their vote by nearly five million in the presidential election of March 1932, and another two million in the second, April election that year, while the Communist vote fell. In July 1932 the Nazis were the largest party in the Reichstag with the Communists third.

The Reichstag Fire in February 1933 was used by the Nazis as an opportunity to arrest Thälmann and other communists. He was held in concentration camps until 1944, when he was shot in Buchenwald.

Theatre in the Third Reich. As with the other arts, the Weimar Republic provided a fertile soil for theatre, where experimentation and new modes of expression flourished.

Expressionism, as a movement in the 1920s, was headed by playwrights Georg Kaiser, Ernst Toller, Fritz von Unruh and Franz Werfel. At the same time Gerhart Hauptmann, Hugo von Hofmannsthal, Arthur Schnitzler and Carl Zuckmayer were all producing new work, and Bertolt Brecht was at the beginning of a career that was to make him internationally famous.

Max Reinhardt, Leopold Jessmer and Erwin Piscator were dazzling audiences with their imaginative productions and great actors and actresses of the stature of Paul Wegener, Emil Jannings, Heinrich George, Werner Kraus, Kather Gold and Elisabeth Bergner were adding lustre to performances of both the classics and the 'new' drama.

This ferment of experiment and novelty was brought to an end by the advent of the Nazis. Most established directors were banned and nearly all the playwrights were forced into exile or retirement. The same fate overtook a large number of the best-known performers. It was not that the Nazis were uninterested in the theatre; in fact, Nazi theatre policy aimed at widening audiences by arranging for seats to be available through the 'Strength through Joy' and Labour Front organizations at bargain prices. In 1936, for example, there were twenty-five touring companies visiting rural communities, and by 1942 audiences at municipal theatres had doubled compared with 1933.

The Nazi movement did make one specific contribution to theatre art. Known as the *Thingspiel*, it was based on the concept of a revived version of the Teutonic tribal assembly, a mixture of tattoo, pageant and circus perform-ance. Held in specially constructed amphitheatres known as *Thingspielplatten* the pageants often involved Hitler Youth formations, or battalions of the SA. More common in the early days of the Third Reich, the genre did not survive for long and in some sense its role was taken over by the Nazi Party rallies.

Göbbels' policy for the theatre was very similar to that for the cinema: a diet of escapism varied by the occasional ideological piece, and a steady supply of classics. In 1938 for example the theatrical hits were *The Base Wallah*, a comedy of army life, and *A Leap out of the Workaday World*, a light-hearted fantasy. The ideological pieces were of two kinds: historical plays featuring German heroes of the past, such as Barbarossa or Henry IV, or a theatrical version of the *Blut und Boden* theme. These plays celebrated the notion of the farmers' passionate attachment to the soil and made an equivalence of the fertility of human beings and the soil. In *The Giant* by Richard Billinger, an old farmer's daughter, an only child, deserts the farm for the city, but her father, unwilling to admit defeat, creates a new heir by mating with his housekeeper.

The classics, especially Schiller, Goethe, Kleist and the plays of Shakespeare, were performed constantly. Sometimes a certain editorial licence was taken, as when in *The Merchant of Venice* (popular because of its potentiality for anti-semitism), Jessica is made to be illegitimate, thus an Aryan, so that she can marry Lorenzo.

Even in late 1942, when in Russia and North Africa the tide was beginning to turn, Berliners were given the choice of nearly 100 different plays in a season. Only in 1943 and 1944 did the ambitious Nazi theatrical programme begin to shrink under the impact of Allied bombing and the restrictions of total war.
➤Göbbels, Josef

Theresienstadt. A concentration camp located thirty-five miles from Prague. Originally acquiring a reputation as a more humane concentration camp, this view was shattered as the war progressed and Theresienstadt became a transit camp for Jews bound for Auschwitz or Treblinka.

Thierach, Otto (1889–1946). A lawyer who became Minister of Justice in 1942, thus becoming nominally responsible for the People's Courts under Freisler. He was named as Minister of Justice in Hitler's last political testament. Before his trial at Nuremberg could take place, he hanged himself.

Thoma, Ritter Wilhelm von (1891–1948). German Panzer General who commanded the German ground forces of the Condor Legion in Spain (1936), was a tank commander under Guderian in France (1940) and field commander of the Afrika Korps when captured by the British at the Battle of El Alamein (1942).

Thorn. SA leader in Hamburg during the 1920s. He frequently collaborated with the communist Redcommando to disrupt Social Democratic meetings.

Thule Society. Founded during WWI ostensibly for the study of old Germanic literature, it was devoted to extreme nationalism, mysticism and the occult, with an organization akin in its system of branches and secrecy to Masons. The swastika was among the Society's mystic symbols. Eckart, Drexler, Hess and Rosenberg were members. It was a natural source for the cheap philosophy of the new state.

Thyssen, Fritz (1873–1951). Multimillionaire steel industrialist (United Steel Trust). A Nazi Party member from 1923 who helped fund the Party (although the book attributed to him *I Paid Hitler* was a fabrication). He was among the industrialists who petitioned Hindenburg to appoint Hitler Chancellor in November 1932 and demanded, with other businessmen, that Gregor Strasser and the radical SA group be repudiated for their attacks on industry and demands for nationalization. In 1933 he was confirmed as head of the national employers' association but, alarmed and disillusioned by Hitler's progress towards war, he fled from Germany to Switzerland in 1938.

Todt, Fritz (1891–1942). Head of construction for the Third Reich's Four-Year Plan. A civil engineer who joined the Nazi Party in 1922, rose to be an SS colonel and in 1933 was made inspector-general of the road and highway system. Named leader of the Todt Organization in 1933, he was appointed one of the leaders of the Four-Year Plan. From 1940 to 1942 he served as Reich Minister for Munitions. He died in an air accident in February 1942 and was succeeded as Munitions Minister by Albert Speer.

Tojo, Hideki (1884–1947). Leader of the Japanese militarists who, as Premier, brought Japan into the war in 1941. In 1940 as War Minister in Prince Konoye's government he had pressed for the treaty of mutual assistance with Germany and Italy which was signed in September.

As Premier he effectively converted the government into a military dictatorship dedicated to a New Order in South-East Asia. But by mid-1944 the war was turning against Japan and with the US occupation of Saipan, which brought the homeland within bombing range, Tojo and his Cabinet resigned. At the war's end Tojo was found guilty of responsibility for Japan's attacks on her neighbours and was one of seven Japanese leaders condemned to death.

Totenbuch **(death book)**. The records of killings kept in the extermination camps.

Trade agreement with Russia, 1940. In February 1940 a second trade agreement (▶Russo-German Pact) was signed between Germany and Russia. Dr Schnurre, a Foreign Ministry economics expert, negotiated for Berlin while Stalin himself was frequently the principal Soviet representative. A tight bargain was struck which left both parties satisfied with the arrangements. For the Soviet Union, Stalin acquired the cruiser *Lützow*, plans for the battleship *Bismarck*, heavy naval guns, and a selection of the Luftwaffe's highly prized aircraft, the Me109 and 110 and the Ju88. In addition Russia would receive sophisticated heavy machinery, diesel engines, machine tools, chemicals, explosives and ships. It was a formidable collection of the machinery without which modern war could not be waged. In return, Germany was to receive 1.5 million tons of cereals, a million tons of oil and huge quantities of phosphates, cotton and soya beans. Of vital importance was Stalin's promise of Soviet help by acting as a secret buying agent for Germany. This way, Dr Schnurre believed, the British blockade could be reduced in effectiveness.

Treblinka.   An extermination camp located on the Bug River in Poland, its total of 700,000 victims made it the second of the *Vernichtungslager* (extermination camps) after Auschwitz. Situated near a railway junction seventy-five miles from Warsaw, the camp began operations in July 1942 when the first transports arrived from the Warsaw ghetto. By the end of the first few months, escaped prisoners had brought back to the Jews of the ghetto the truth about the camp. From the very first days that truth was charged with horror: there was no industry attached to the camp, no hope of a stay of execution to be gained through slave labour. The sole purpose of Treblinka was extermination. Gassing specialist Christian Wirth had installed thirty gas chambers initially for use with carbon monoxide, and aimed at the destruction of 25,000 people a day. In practical terms the techniques of 1942 were unable to cope with the immense task of killing that number per day. From July 1942 each daily transport from the Warsaw ghetto carried 5,000 people. On arrival, the prisoners were stripped and directed (or beaten if they showed reluctance) along the Himmelstrasse, the Heavenly Way, at the end of which the bathhouses fitted with gas nozzles were ready to receive them. In 1987 the trial of John Demjanjuk revealed the appalling sadism of Ivan the Terrible who stood at the bathhouse entrance. Karl Franz, the commandant, regularly set his ferocious Saint Bernard dog to savage the faces of Jews whom he had had hung upside down in his private execution square. Yet the point was made by prisoners that relatively few of the SS guards serving in the camps were sadists. Most – and perhaps this is the more serious accusation – were indifferent to the fate of the men, women and children who passed down the Himmelstrasse.

Höss, the Auschwitz commandant, boasted that few victims in his camp were aware of their fate; at Treblinka, he claimed scornfully, the prisoners usually knew. We know now that this was the result of Jewish efforts to send messages from the camp not only to Warsaw but to the Jewish ghettos. Almost certainly for this reason the Treblinka inmates, the 700 – 1,000 Jews who worked for the Germans until they in turn were gassed and replaced by others, were willing in 1943 to stake their lives in rebellion. In June 1943 a camp revolt was abandoned when it was discovered that the stolen hand-grenades could not be detonated, but in August a group of prisoners used kerosene to spray buildings instead of disinfectant. Igniting the buildings, they attacked the guards with grenades and armed themselves with guns snatched from them. It was in every sense a hopeless rebellion. No more than fifteen German, Baltic and Ukrainian guards were killed by the group of 700 working prisoners. All but 150 who broke out were killed at once; only twelve managed to get away alive. The rest of the escapees were caught and killed.

Tresckow, Henning von (1901–44). Senior operations officer of Army Group Centre in Russia who planned in 1943 to end the war by killing Hitler.

In 1934, as an army officer, he had taken the oath of loyalty to Hitler. He supported the idea of a Greater Germany, but while on the planning staff for the invasion of Czechoslovakia he objected to the actions of the SS and Gestapo. After the fall of France in 1940 he hoped that the war would end and a Greater Germany be achieved, but the Russian campaign and the orders to kill all Russian commissars turned him to active opposition to Hitler. A number of attempts on Hitler's life were planned and, in the Smolensk Plot, came close to success. On another occasion Colonel von Tresckow found the fire-eating Colonel von Böselager ready to lead a field security regiment which would kill Hitler and his SS bodyguards on a visit to Field Marshal von Kluge's headquarters. Von Kluge, however, refused to take part in the assassination.

Von Tresckow made many attempts to secure a posting to Hitler's headquarters but was forced in the end to cede the first place to von Stauffenberg. Tresckow himself remained on the Eastern Front, where he waited for news of the success of the July Bomb Plot. On hearing of its failure he killed himself.

Triumph of the Will. ➤Riefenstahl, Leni

Troost, Paul Ludwig (1878–1934). Hitler's first favourite architect with whom he discussed grandiose building plans. Troost had designed the luxurious interiors of transatlantic liners and applied this style to the monuments of the Third Reich. Typical of the style were two 'classic' temples for Munich's Königsplatz, in memory of the victims killed during the 1923 Beer Hall Putsch, which were built in 1935. He redesigned the Brown House (the Party headquarters in Munich) and the House of German Art.

On his death in 1934, Albert Speer took over the role of 'architect fantasist' for Hitler.

Trott zu Solz, Hans Adam von (1909–44). German Foreign Office official. Member of the Kreisau Circle of anti-Nazi German aristocrats and Christians. By 1938 already deeply involved in the idea of resistance to Hitler, Trott travelled to Washington and made contact with State Department officials, vainly asking for support for the German resistance movement. His journey to England in the following year was equally fruitless. As a former Rhodes scholar,

Trott zu Solz approached senior Oxford contacts to persuade them of the existence of a German opposition to Hitler and Nazism. His object was to gain British government support for an alternative German government to Hitler's. At this stage no discussion in Germany had resolved how this change of government might take place. Tall, personable and totally sincere, Trott zu Solz was nevertheless suspected in Oxford of being a Gestapo plant.

In 1943 he travelled to Switzerland to meet US agent Allen Dulles, but was considered more concerned with the intellectual justification of resistance action than with the moral and practical problems of tyrannicide.

Returning to Germany, he took part in Kreisau Circle discussions and figures in the diaries and accounts of the time as a prominent resister to the regime.

After the July 1944 attempt on Hitler's life, he was among the many hundreds arrested. He was tried, found guilty of treason and strangled with piano wire on 26 August 1944.

Trustees of Labour.   By a law of 19 May 1933 thirteen departmental offices were set up throughout the Reich, each headed by a 'Treuhänder der Arbeit' – a Trustee of Labour. The function of the new officials was defined as the 'negotiation of work contracts between employer and labour' – a clear usurpation of trades union functions in the Weimar Republic by the Nazi state.

Typhoon (Taifun).   Code-name for the attack on Moscow in late 1941.

U

Udet, Ernst (1896–1941). WWI fighter-pilot ace and professional flyer after the war. With Milch he built the Luftwaffe, joining, when it was created in 1935, as Inspector of Fighters and later as Director of Armaments. He was an enthusiast for fighters and dive-bombers and was responsible for the introduction of the Messerschmitt BF109, the 'Stuka' Junkers Ju87 and the twin-engined bomber Ju88, but neglected the development of heavy bombers. A man of brilliance but not an administrator, he became depressed by the Luftwaffe's failure in the Battle of Britain (1940) and by criticisms of technical failures. When Milch temporarily overruled his plans to produce a new fighter plane, the Fw190, and stopped Messerschmitt's work on a jet fighter, Udet shot himself in November 1941.

Ulbricht, Walther (1893–1973). A founding member of the German Communist Party, Ulbricht went to Russia for training and returned as a party organizer in 1928, when he became a member of the Reichstag. In 1933 he escaped to Paris before the Nazis could arrest him with other communists. In 1936–38 he was in Spain with the International Brigade on 'intelligence duties' (investigating suspected Trotskyites or other enemies of the Party). From Spain he went to Russia, returning in the wake of the Russian army in 1945 to become a founder of the new German Communist Party and head of state of the DDR (East Germany).

Unemployment. High unemployment and the dissatisfaction of the German people with the government of the time are commonly given as reasons for the Nazis' success at the polls in 1933. On taking power they succeeded in a variety of ways in reducing unemployment:

Unemployed	
June 1933:	5,400,000
January 1934:	3,700,000
January 1935:	2,900,000
January 1936:	2,500,000
January 1937:	1,800,000

By the spring of 1937, with the 'Four-Year Plan' under way, there were fewer than one million unemployed.

This reduction was achieved by a number of means, mostly through public works programmes. The previous Weimar government had had a quarter of a million men employed in programmes which the Nazis boycotted in principle, but which in 1933 they took over and transformed, by *Gleichschaltung*, into their own. Superficially these schemes were not unlike the programmes started at the same time in the USA under Roosevelt's 'New Deal'. They instituted an emergency work programme (*Notstandarbeit*) for reforestation, land reclamation, dam building, motorways, etc., giving short-term heavy labour work. They made a year of work service compulsory for registered unemployed from 1935, and by introducing compulsory military service the same year achieved further reductions in the numbers.

From 1939, with forced labour from the conquered lands to the east, German employment statistics become less meaningful. During the war, supposedly at a time of manpower shortage, the amount of domestic foreign service available to the German middle-class household increased and the Todt Organization's vast schemes of wartime building were supported by huge armies of slave labour with inhumanly wasteful management.

Universities in the Third Reich.   There is every indication that the higher academic establishment in general welcomed the coming of the Third Reich. In March 1933, 300 occupants of professorial chairs addressed a manifesto to the voters asking for their support for Adolf Hitler. Students felt much the same. In 1931, 60 per cent of all Prussian students demanded that an *Arierparagraph* (a clause calling for the exclusion of Jews) should be included in the constitution of the university. In 1931 anti-semitic riots broke out at most of the major universities including Berlin, Cologne, Hamburg, Munich and Vienna.

In May 1933 the celebrated ritual burning of the books took place at some universities, with orations from such eminent professors of literature as Professor Bertram of Cologne and Professor Naumann of Bonn. The physicist Professor Jordan, responsible with Heisenberg and Born for the founding of quantum mechanics, claimed that he saw the *Führerprinzip* (leadership principle) demonstrated in the molecular structure of matter.

Although the academic establishment displayed little real resistance to Nazi tyranny, there were some notable exceptions. Bultmann and Soden, powerful figures in the theological world, continued the work of Karl Barth, expelled for his 'unsound' views. Litt publicly challenged Rosenberg's theory of the race soul, and Professor Huber of Munich was executed for his part in the White Rose conspiracy.

What evidence there is suggests a steady deterioration of standards at the universities owing to the ideological strait-jacket imposed by the Party but, more importantly, by the wholesale dismissal of Jewish and liberal academics; a total of 1,200 were dismissed from their posts in the first two years of Nazi rule. The effect was devastating for Germany; the famous Göttingen school of quantum physics was broken up, and this led quite directly to the prior development of the atomic bomb by the American universities to which the scientists had fled. Student protest was confined, in general, to complaints against compulsory group lectures on Party matters and to the attempted break-up of their fraternal organizations known as corporations. The Nazis disapproved of the practice of duelling – a notorious student pastime – on the grounds that a man's honour was no longer his own affair but that of the whole community.

Yet serious dissent surfaced early. An accurate assessment of its scale is not possible, but the evidence of the White Rose and the Edelweiss movements is sufficient to underline the fact that not all German students conformed and that many were willing to give their lives to resist.

US naval policy and the Third Reich, 1939 – 1941. Before the US entered WWII, President Roosevelt's naval policy was to keep the sea routes to Europe open and to refuse to be intimidated by the Third Reich's submarine blockade. From December 1939, in enforcement of this policy, the USS *Tuscaloosa* was detailed to maintain a pan-American neutrality zone between Bermuda and Puerto Rico. But in other areas it could be argued that US policy was less concerned with strict neutrality. To deliver armaments and supplies to Britain under the March 1941 'Lend Lease' agreement made between Roosevelt and Churchill, American shipping used the North Atlantic. The Germans declared a blockade, by submarine, and the US countered with a security zone and a 'Pan-American Neutrality Patrol'. In April 1941 Raeder wanted to attack US merchant shipping, but Hitler replied that 'Under no circumstances does the Führer wish to cause incidents which would result in the US entering in the war.' But the situation remained tense and Roosevelt's attitude continued to be deliberately provocative. In September 1941 when the US destroyer *Greer* was attacked by a U-boat, the President announced a 'shoot on sight' order and warned Axis shipping out of the US defence zone. In October the USS *Kearney* was attacked and the USS *Reuben James* sunk. Thus when Hitler declared war on the USA in December 1941, the US navy in the Atlantic was already on a war footing.

USCHLA (*Untersuchungs-* und *Schlichtungs- Ausschüsse*). To repair the weakened Nazi Party in 1926, Hitler set up USCHLA, the 'Committee for Investigation and Settlement', as its disciplinary body. It was not concerned with such matters as dishonest business practices, immorality or gambling, but with offences damaging to the Party, particularly disobedience to Party orders or any disrespect to Hitler. Expulsion from the Party was USCHLA's harshest punishment, and after 1937 this also meant consignment to a concentration camp.

V

V-1 (*Vergeltungswaffe 1* – Reprisal weapon 1).   A fast pilotless flying bomb carrying a one-ton warhead. Psychologically one of the war's most effective weapons, the V-1 buzzed (thus to Londoners becoming the 'buzz-bomb') like an angry hornet, the engine cutting out dramatically over the 'target'. Thereafter those on the ground waited for the contact explosion of the warhead. In the summer of 1944, more than 8,000 V-1s exploded on London. Many were shot down over Kent and some were even 'returned' by RAF fighters nudging their wingtips to redirect them back across the Channel. Although the weapon failed in its attempt to destroy British morale, it was nevertheless responsible for over 5,000 killed, 40,000 wounded and 75,000 houses damaged or destroyed. For V-2, ➤Rockets.

Valkyrie (Operation Valkyrie).   A contingency plan, devised by anti-Nazi conspirator von Stauffenberg, for Berlin garrison troops to seize key points in the capital in the event of a revolt by the thousands of slave and foreign workers billeted in and around the city. The importance of Valkyrie is that it was in fact a brilliantly devised cover-story whose real purpose was to organize the seizure of Berlin once the conspirators' first object – the assassination of Hitler – had been achieved. ➤July Bomb Plot

Vassiltchikov, Marie.   Russian-born aristocratic diarist who lived throughout the war in Germany and Austria. Among her friends were many who died in the Gestapo terror after 20 July 1944.

VE-Day.   Victory in Europe Day, 8 May 1945. It was also of course the last day of the Third Reich.

Versailles Diktat.   The view was widely held in Germany after WWI that the Versailles Treaty was an imposed settlement of great injustice. As an emotive phrase it was used in nationalist speeches alongside 'November Criminals' and 'the war-guilt lie'.

Versailles Treaty.   The peace treaty signed in June 1919 ending WWI. The Treaty set up the League of Nations, reduced German territory by returning parts to France, Belgium and Denmark, creating Czechoslovakia, Poland, Hungary and Lithuania, and setting up Danzig as a 'free city'. In addition the Treaty assured Austrian independence. The German Rhineland was to be occupied for 15 years and the Saar to be administered separately until 1935.

German colonies were to be shared among the Allies under League of Nations mandates. Germany was to recognize her war guilt and pay reparations to the Allies ➤Reparations.

On the purely military level, Germany was to disarm, abolish universal and compulsory military service, keep an army of not more than 100,000 men and a small navy with no submarines. There were to be no military aircraft, nor any aircraft manufacture. No tanks or heavy artillery were to be manufactured and armament factories were to be dismantled.

The terms were harsh: all German colonies, one-eighth of Germany's European territory, one-tenth of its European population and most of its iron and steel industry were taken. A feeling of injustice exploded in Germany. Reparations were seen as vindictive, although in the years to come the Dawes Plan and the Young Plan modified them. But many of the articles of Versailles were soon perverted or undermined: the *Freikorps* was an immediate response to the disarming of the army, and there were immediate schemes for clandestine rearmament. After the Locarno Pact of 1925 alterations to the Treaty of Versailles were made, but it remained, for Germans of all groups, a unique act of savage vindictiveness.

Versailles Treaty, Article 231. The war-guilt clause in the 1919 treaty. After WWI the victorious Allies felt strongly the need to establish the guilt of Germany and her allies for the outbreak and the destructiveness of the war. Two elements were combined here: first, by forcing Germany to take responsibility for the war, any doubt as to the legitimacy of the Allies' pursuance of the war was obliterated; the Allies could not be responsible for the tragic losses if Germany were responsible for the war. Secondly, the Allied nations – and in particular France, the greatest sufferer – required a practical justification for the vast extent of the reparations the French intended to demand from Germany.

Article 231 of the Treaty therefore required Germany to accept responsibility for causing all loss and damage which the Allied governments and their nationals had suffered as a result of the war imposed upon them by Germany and her allies.

The Article was, for German nationalist parties, including the Nazi Party, a subject for scornful rejection throughout the Weimar period.

Vichy. After the fall of France, the government of the unoccupied southern zone was established in July 1940 in the small spa town of Vichy. The terms of the armistice signed at Compiègne left northern France and the Atlantic coast under German occupation and the remainder under the rule of a French government under the leadership of Marshal Pétain.

After the Anglo-American landings in North Africa in November 1942, the Germans occupied all France, while maintaining the façade of the Vichy government. The Vichy police, the *Milice*, was commanded by Darnand, a much-decorated WWI soldier with extreme right-wing and anti-semitic views;

it was created in 1943 to work with the Germans in uncovering the French resistance, hunting Jews and rounding up men for forced labour in Germany. The *Milice* collaborated with the SD and Gestapo units of men like Klaus Barbie. As France was liberated in 1944 some 5,000 collaborators were summarily executed and possibly another 15,000 were killed in the weeks after liberation. Vichy leaders were tried for treason. Laval was executed in 1945, Marshal Pétain, ninety years old and either deaf or unable to comprehend the court proceedings, was condemned to death, a sentence commuted to life imprisonment by his one-time protégé, General de Gaulle. ➤Montoire

***Völkerchaos* (The chaos of races).** The mix of peoples of different origin brought about, especially in the Mediterranean lands, by the process of historical change. It was the struggle against what they saw as this ethnic confusion that formed the basic emotional appeal of Nazism.

***Völkisch*.** Literally 'of the people'; but the term gained a special meaning in Germany where it was associated with extremist nationalists and anti-semites. The Völkisch Block was a coalition of groups in Bavaria in 1924 under Strasser and Ludendorff. Similar groups existed in north Germany. The excesses which are now linked with Nazism had their roots in *Völkisch* policies, hence the saying 'Buchenwald began in Berlin', where *Freikorps* men, wearing the swastika on their helmets, helped crush a left-wing rising in 1918–19 at the breakup of the Hohenzollern Empire.

***Völkischer Beobachter* (Nationalist Observer).** Originally a rundown twice-weekly Munich newspaper consisting largely of anti-semitic, nationalistic gossip, it was bought for the Nazis, possibly from secret service funds, through Epp. In 1923 it became a daily, with financial backing from prosperous Munich families, including the Hanfstängls. Max Amann took over the business management of the paper and Rosenberg became its editor. It was banned after the 1923 Beer Hall Putsch, but reappeared in February 1925 as Hitler was rebuilding the strength of the Nazi Party.

Up to 1933 the *Völkischer Beobachter* remained a Munich paper with a circulation of no more than 127,000. But it was the spearhead of Amann's press empire which was to outgrow Hugenberg's. It became the first national German newspaper, being published simultaneously in Berlin from 1933 and in Vienna from 1938. A professional editor, Wilhelm Weiss, increased the circulation by 1941 to about 1,200,000. It remained a paper with a popular rather than an élitist style, but subscribing to it became a symbol of loyalty to the Party. It was widely used as a tool in the educational system, many of its articles being standard texts for study. During the Third Reich the *Völkischer Beobachter* daily represented 'received truth'. ➤Press in the Third Reich

Volksgrenadier Divisions. From September 1944 Himmler's Reserve Army formed new divisional units from recruits combed out of industry, or from remnants of units broken up in battle. These divisions, numbering about fifty at the most, were half the strength of a normal infantry division but with increased automatic firepower and increased use of the 'Panzerfaust' (a light anti-tank weapon). They were mostly used to hold the West Wall (the defended line built west of the Rhine in the 1930s and known as the 'Siegfried Line' to the Allies).

Volkssturm.   The last-ditch defenders of the Reich, formed in October 1944. All men aged from sixteen to sixty were organized in their districts, with few uniforms, with little training and with any weapons that could be found, under the leadership of any available officers from the SS, SA, NSKK or Hitler Youth. Units of this home defence force varied greatly in quality. Young boys of the Hitler Youth were reputed to have fought with great ferocity in the last days of Berlin. The *Volkssturm*, intended to fight in their own areas, might have made a significant defence contribution had they not been thrown into the last battles of the Reich whenever there was a desperate need.

Volkswagen.   The 'People's Car' which the Nazi Labour Front promised savers under its *Kraft durch Freude* scheme. Dr Ferdinand Porsche (1875–1952), a car designer famous for racing cars, especially the Auto Union, developed plans between 1933 and 1934 to build a cheap car. Hitler announced the project in 1935 and in 1938 a factory was built at Fallersleben near Brunswick to produce it. Over 330,000 workers subscribed 280 million Reichsmarks for the car. But by 1939 Germany was at war and the People's Car was postponed. During the war, however, the factory produced a modified vehicle, the Type 82VW, a military vehicle used in the same way as the Jeep. The factory, considered for reparations, was rejected by the British, and the famous 'Beetle' Volkswagen came on sale at last in 1946.

W

Waffen SS (Armed SS). ►SS: Waffen SS

Wagner, Richard (1813–83). German operatic composer. In *Tannhäuser* (1843–4), *Lohengrin* (1846–8) and the *Ring* cycle, the *Ring des Nibelungen* (1869–74), Wagner used Teutonic legend and history to serve a personal mix of attitudes to love and death, mysticism, heroism and nationalism. For these reasons his music was immensely popular with the Nazi movement and especially with Hitler himself.

Wandervögel **(Birds of passage)**. Originally a Berlin club founded at the turn of the century, the Wandervögel movement grew to encompass many thousands of German youths who rejected the industrialized city in favour of the 'freedom' of hiking the countryside. Although the *Wandervögel* movement was subsumed in other youth movements of the Weimar period, its romantic anti-capitalism provided fertile ground in which early Nazi ideas might grow.

Wannsee Conference. The meeting in the SS RSHA headquarters at Wannsee in January 1942 that formalized the Final Solution (the extermination of the Jewish people) and involved all the government of the Third Reich in its implications. The meeting was chaired by Heydrich and attended by fifteen SS and government officials, including Stuckart, Heinrich Müller, Eichmann and Freisler. It lasted only a few hours, but as a result of it directives were sent to move Jews to the east as part of the 'territorial solution'. No doubt was left that this meant the physical destruction of all Jews, accelerating the process that had already started. The Einsatzgruppen had already been in action for six months and the first extermination camp, at Chelmno, was by then operating.

The conference gave Eichmann the necessary authority for his actions in the various ministries, and thirty copies of the conference record were distributed to them. At no point was killing mentioned. Recipients were expected to understand the meaning of 'final solution' and 'deportation to the east'. But did they? It has been a widely held assumption that the Wannsee Conference set out the Final Solution in the form it ultimately took. But careful reading of the conference document suggests other possibilities. The SS view, represented by Heydrich, seems to be that the vast labour pool, created by the transportation of Jews to the east, should be used as such, in road-building and general construction projects. He realized of course that the death rate would be steep but at this stage he is still discussing labour rather than extermination.

It is only when Heydrich considers those who *survive* the stringent conditions of labour that extermination is to be resorted to: they are to be dealt with accordingly because they, by their survival, 'represent a natural selection . . . a germ cell of a new Jewish development'. Heydrich in other words was resorting to extermination only at the point when it was necessary to prevent the development of a Jewish 'master race'.

This issue within the Final Solution of the primacy of labour or extermination, was to dog the SS – and indeed the Third Reich – until the concentration camp system collapsed; and it seems fair to suggest that it first became apparent in the differing interpretations at Wannsee.

War Dead, Military.   The following is an estimate of military war dead in the war of the Third Reich, 1939–45:

Russians	7,500,000
Germans	3,500,000
Hungarians	410,000
Yugoslavs	410,000
British and Commonwealth	400,000
Italians	330,000
Polish	320,000
Rumanians	300,000
Americans	290,000
French	210,000
Finns	85,000
Belgians	12,000
Dutch	12,000

The total excluding China and Japan exceeds 13 million.

War debts.   ➤Reparations

Warsaw ghetto rising.   The heroic resistance of the Jews in Warsaw to the final SS attempt to clear the ghetto, April/May 1943.

From the time of the German occupation of Warsaw in October 1940, the existing Jewish quarter was surrounded by a wall and divided into three areas: one contained a number of minor industries, the second a large brush factory, and the central district included a number of factories and the Jewish administration.

Before the end of the year, 80,000 Gentile Poles had been moved out of the 'infected area' and were replaced by some 150,000 Jews who had been living in other, not specifically Jewish parts of the city. By the end of 1940, therefore, over 350,000 Jews were now confined in a 3.5-square-mile area of the city, the ghetto had been sealed and its twenty-two entrances closed. Contact with the German authorities was maintained by the *Judenrat*, the twenty-four members of the Jewish Council who maintained order through their own police and organized the labour battalions the Germans demanded. During the first period of the ghetto, from 1940 to summer 1942, it is estimated that 100,000 Jews died of starvation, disease or execution. In July 1942 a six-week sweep of the ghetto was carried out and 300,000 Jews were transported, most to the extermination camp of Treblinka. In March 1943 there were, officially, only 35,000 Jews in the ghetto; but there were in fact at least as many more 'illegal' Jews hiding in the ghetto, those who had escaped from the trains to Treblinka or who had filtered through from other towns.

From the beginning in the ghetto, Jews maintained underground activities, newsletters and an 'Anti-Fascist Block' (which was uncovered and wiped out in 1942). The underground kept in touch with other surviving ghettos in Bialystok, Vilna and Kovno through 'Aryan' friends. The Farband ('Yiddischer Militärischer Farband', the Jewish military union), formed in 1939, had links with the underground Polish 'Home Army', from whom they received arms. In the ghetto the Farband had the reputation of hiding Jews on the run and of catching and executing traitors and spies. In addition they made tunnels linking the three parts of the ghetto and giving access to the main town. A communist 'Jewish Fighting Organization' which also received arms from the London-based 'Home Army' was set up late in 1942.

This was the situation in 1943 when Himmler ordered an end to the Jews of Warsaw and the SS planned to make the city 'Jew-free' by Hitler's birthday, 20 April. They assembled 2,000 Waffen SS, supported by the artillery and sappers from three army divisions, 200 German and 350 Polish police, some Jewish ghetto police and 300 Ukrainian and Latvian SS auxiliaries; in all nearly 3,000 men with another 7,000 in reserve. The Jews were determined to resist. Against the SS, the ghetto was armed with those weapons which had been smuggled in from the Polish 'Home Army' and with whatever could be captured from the Germans once the fighting began.

At 6.00 a.m. on 19 April the Germans moved into the ghetto and their column was met with firing from three sides. They were forced to withdraw, leaving the dead – and their weapons – behind. A second column led by Ukrainians and Latvians was equally repulsed and tanks and armoured vehicles were countered with 'Molotov cocktails'. At the conclusion of the first day's fighting Stroop's SS and auxiliary forces had suffered heavy casualties. The next day the Nazi Governor of Poland, Frank, reported to Berlin that the ghetto resistance was such that heavier forces with aircraft and artillery would be needed. Organized fighting now continued for over twenty days in the ruins of the ghetto, with fires burning in all parts. The Jews, moving from prepared bunker to bunker, forced the Germans to fight across every foot of ground. In a month's fighting some 60,000 Jews perished.

By mid-June the ghetto was overwhelmed, but even in July there were still occasional breakouts by hidden fighting groups. To the end of the year there were reports of fighters appearing from the ruins in search of food, and in June

1944 German police were still suffering sporadic attacks from the ghetto ruins. It is believed that only some 100 Jews survived the ghetto uprising.

Warthegau. The name of the new German province in what had been western Poland, annexed after the successful campaign of September/November 1939.

Weimar. An adjective to suggest the vivacity, excitement and *laissez-faire* cultural conditions which existed, mostly in Berlin, during the 1920s and early 1930s.

Weimar Republic. The name commonly given to the German Republic (1919–33), between the end of WWI and the advent of the Third Reich. In February 1919, after Germany's defeat at the hands of the Allies, a national assembly met in Weimar, a town about 150 miles south-west of Berlin, chosen because the capital was not felt safe in the month after the *Freikorps* had crushed the Spartacists there. The national assembly drew up a new constitution in the Weimar National Theatre.

The new republic came from a revolution which had overthrown the Kaiser but retained the traditional army and civil service and had accepted and signed the detested Versailles Treaty. Although the Weimar Republic (under Chancellors Stresemann and Brüning) saw the pressures of Versailles reduced, a recovery from inflation and some stability in Germany, it was doomed by the hostility of nationalists and both left- and right-wing politicians.

Although the constitution contained many democratic elements, they were for the most part vitiated by Article 48 which placed in the hands of the (admittedly elected) president the power to suspend the citizens' civil rights in a national emergency. It was furthermore the president who defined and declared a national emergency.

Weiszäcker, Freiherr Ernst von (1882–1951). A career diplomat who was German ambassador in Switzerland in 1933–36. In 1937 he became the senior official at the Ministry of Foreign Affairs and was in this post at the time of the Munich agreement. From 1943 to the end of the Third Reich in 1945 he was German ambassador to the Vatican.

In 1949 he was sentenced to five years' imprisonment as a war criminal, but released the next year under an amnesty. In his trial he claimed that he had been a Nazi Party member and had accepted SS rank only for 'decorative' reasons and had in fact supported the resistance to Hitler. His son, who defended him at the trial, became President of the Federal Republic of Germany in 1985.

Wels, Otto (1873–1939). Social Democratic politician. An upholsterer who became a devoted member and finally leader of the SPD. After WWI he sat in the Reichstag as a Social Democratic Deputy, becoming Chairman of the SPD from 1931 until the Party's dissolution in 1933. His great speech of March

1933 rejecting the Nazi Enabling Act made exile inevitable. In Prague until 1938 and then in Paris, he continued to work against Nazism. He died in Paris two weeks after the outbreak of WWII. ▸*Gleichschaltung*

Weltanschauung (World view).   One of Hitler's favourite terms, used with deadening frequency in *Mein Kampf* to elevate any passing opinion or trivial viewpoint into a timeless, and ideologically correct, philosophical proposition.

Werewolves.   An underground army recruited and trained in 1945 for guerrilla warfare against the Allies overrunning Germany. The idea was first proposed in the spring of 1944 when SS *Gruppenführer* Prutzmann assembled volunteers. They had little success in delaying the advances on either Eastern or Western fronts but claimed some small success behind the Allied lines. In March 1945, the American-appointed Mayor of Aachen and, in April, an American divisional commander were shot, possibly as a result of Göbbels' call to Germans to raise up 'werewolves'. But his appeal came too late and succeeded mainly in alarming some of the Allied soldiers into a more suspicious and hostile attitude towards the conquered German civilians.

Wessel, Horst (1907–30).   An SA man killed in a street-fight with communists. The 'Horst Wessel Song' which he wrote became the Nazi marching song and took second place only to the National Anthem ('*Deutschland, Deutschland . . .*'). The tune is said to have been originally a Salvation Army hymn.

> *Die Fahnen hoch, die Reihe dicht geschlossen!*
> *SA marschiert mit ruhig festem Schritt.*
> *Kam'raden, die Rotfront und Reaktion erschossen,*
> *Marschieren im Geist in unsern Reihen mit.*
>
> The flags held high! the ranks stand tight together!
> SA march on, with quiet, firm forward pace.
> Comrades who, though shot by Red Front or Reaction,
> Still march with us, their spirits in our ranks.

The Nazis took their revenge for Horst Wessel. Within a few days of Hitler coming to power in 1933, the supposed killer, Ali Höhler, was murdered by SA men.

Wever, Walter (1890–1936).   Director of infantry training in the *Reichswehr*. A committed Nazi, Wever transferred from the army to the new Luftwaffe in 1936. His work as Chief-of-Staff to the new Nazi air arm was much praised by Göring after his death in an air crash in 1936. He was succeeded by General Albert Kesselring.

Wewelsburg Conference.   A meeting of senior SS leaders called by Himmler early in 1941 at Wewelsburg, the castle where they were supposed to steep themselves in the myths and rituals of a Germanic faith. According to

Bach-Zelewski, who was there with eleven others including Heydrich, Karl Wolff, Berger and Daluege, Himmler prepared them for an invasion of Russia in which they would undertake operations to 'reduce' the Slav population by 30 million.

White Rose. A student resistance movement organized in Munich University under the leadership of Hans and Sophie Scholl. Children of a markedly anti-Hitlerite father, the elder Scholl children were already moving towards an anti-Nazi position before the war. In January 1937 Hans was among a number of young people arrested in Ulm for 'loose talk'. Released after seven weeks in jail, he was warned of the consequences of further 'deviation'. On his return home Hans joined the highly unofficial DJ One Eleven youth group, an organization named after a member who had died mountain climbing on 1 November the previous year. The group was not in open opposition to the Nazi Party but there is no doubt that its ethos was strongly unsympathetic to the regimentation of the new state.

By 1939 the young Scholls, under Hans's leadership, had moved into active opposition, distributing a small anti-Nazi newsletter at the University of Munich where Hans was a medical student. Returning to Munich from France where he had served as a medical orderly, Hans Scholl now began to make contact with other anti-Nazis at Munich University. To his friends Christoph Probst and Alexander Schmorell were now added Karl Muth, the editor of *Hochland*, and Theodor Häcker, a Catholic essayist and philosopher. Hans Scholl's sister, Sophie, was also by now in Munich after a period in National Labour Service. Shortly after Sophie's arrival in Munich, where she was to study philosophy, the Scholls received the text of Bishop Galen of Münster's sermon against the Nazi euthanasia programme. With Schmorell and Probst, Hans now began to print and distribute anti-regime leaflets under the heading *The White Rose*; within weeks, his sisters Sophie and Inge joined the group. The first leaflets asked: 'Is not every decent German today ashamed of his government?' But from the beginning security was insufficiently tight; well-disposed people on the fringes of the Scholls' circle knew of their activities. It was only a matter of time before less well-disposed acquaintances talked to the Gestapo.

Meanwhile the quality of the White Rose leaflets was improving under the influence of Professor Huber, a Catholic conservative opponent of Nazism, who now advised the group. The White Rose leaflet of June 1942 condemned the slaughter of Jews after the Polish campaign and contained perhaps the first news published in Germany of the *Einsatzgruppen* activities on the East Front. By August 1942 Hans Scholl and Schmorell were both serving on that same front. They were appalled at the brutality they saw. Unable to do anything effective, they were reduced to gestures. Scholl ostentatiously shook hands with old Jews in cattle-trucks on railway stations in eastern Poland.

In November 1942 Scholl again returned to Munich to resume his medical studies. In the meantime his father had again been sent to prison for making disparaging remarks about Hitler; and his sister Sophie had collected further information on the previous year's gassing of spastic children.

With Willi Graf, an old friend from the Russian front, Hans and Sophie began a new leaflet campaign with 500 Marks contributed by a Württemberg businessman. By January 1943 they were, however, distributing leaflets on a much wider scale to towns in central Germany. The leaflets were now greatly improved in content: long-term aims were discussed, the establishment of democracy, the restoration of social justice and the decentralization of the *Einheitsstaat* into a federal constitution.

On the morning of 18 February 1943, Hans and Sophie Scholl, having decided to abandon clandestine methods, distributed leaflets in lecture rooms and across the university square. The Gestapo was summoned; Hans and Sophie Scholl made no attempt to escape. They were arrested with others, including Probst. For a few weeks Munich University simmered; collections for retaining lawyers were made; graffiti – '*Ihr Geist lebt weiter*' ('Their spirit lives on') – appeared on walls.

Under interrogation Hans Scholl refused to name collaborators. Gestapo Berlin even complained later that Gestapo Munich had been 'too easy on the students'; yet there are still records (for Sophie) of a seventeen-hour interrogation.

On 22 February 1943 Hans and Sophie Scholl and Probst were brought before the People's Court judge, Roland Freisler. Sophie accused the court of agreeing with all White Rose had written but of being afraid to admit it. The three were taken to Stadelheim prison and were executed in the courtyard there. Following the Nazi practice of imprisoning kinsmen, the other members of the Scholl family, the parents, Inge and Elisabeth, were arrested and placed in *Sippenhaft*. Graf, Schmorell and Huber, along with some 80–100 others, were arrested. After several courtroom attacks on the regime, Huber was sentenced to death, along with Graf and Schmorell.

This ended the most significant revolt of students of the Third Reich against Hitler and the values and policies of Nazism.

***Widerstand* (Opposition).** A broad term for all those, from senior officers to politicians and churchmen, who opposed Hitler from 1933.

Wiedemann, Felix (1891–1970). Adjutant of Hitler's WWI regiment. He joined the Nazi Party in 1934 and became personal adjutant to Hitler until 1938. He was sent to London to inform the Foreign Minister, Halifax, of Hitler's demands on the Sudetenland, and he attended the 1938 Munich conference.

After Crystal Night in 1938 he lost favour but was sent as consul general to San Francisco, USA, until he was expelled in June 1941. He was then German consul in Tientsin, China, until arrested by the Americans in 1945. At Nuremberg he was sentenced to 28 months' imprisonment. Captain Wiedemann wrote memoirs of Hitler in 1964 (*The Man who Wanted to be the Commander*) which are useful evidence of his WWI record.

Wild camps (*Wilde Lager*).   Concentration camps came into being almost immediately on Hitler's assumption of power but members of the SA and local Nazi officials were not prepared to wait for the construction of even the earliest 'authorized' camps like Dachau. They therefore established makeshift or 'wild' camps to hold the thousands of untried, unsentenced prisoners whom they were arresting on the merest suspicion of opposition to the regime. The wild camps were closed down as the SS, under Theodor Eicke, took over responsibility for concentration camp construction and administration.

Wilhelm, Crown Prince (1882–1951).   The eldest son of Kaiser Wilhelm II and heir to the imperial throne. In 1932 he supported Hitler in his bid for the presidency of the Weimar Republic, but it is doubtful if he was ever a committed Nazi.

Wilhelmstrasse.   A Berlin street in which the Reich Chancellery was located. In the Hitler period, the word was widely used as a synonym for German government.

Winterhilfe **(Help for the winter)**.   An enormous charity for the better-off to help their poorer national and racial fellows. Contributions were collected in the streets by uniformed SA men. In spite of the many opportunities for corruption usual in Nazi fund-raising, the needy did actually benefit from *Winterhilfe*: in 1937 about ten million people received parcels or cash. Families were supposed to join in national 'one-pot-meal' days six times a year and to add the savings made from this simple food to their contribution. Ten per cent was deduced from workers' wages during the winter, and Siemens the industrialist gave private concerts at which he conducted the Philharmonic Orchestra himself for the benefit of the charity. Failure to give could bring private threats of violence or public shame.

Wirmer, Joseph (1901–44).   A Berlin lawyer who performed a valuable liaison function between different groups involved in the July Bomb Plot. He was arrested shortly after the failure of the attempt, tried and executed in Fürstenberg prison on 8 September 1944.

Witzleben, Erwin von (1881–1944).   One of Hitler's Field Marshals, hanged after the 1944 Bomb Plot. A regular army officer who progressed to command the 1st Army at the outbreak of war in 1939, he was one of the twelve new Field Marshals promoted after the fall of France. But in 1942, when in command of the German armies in France, he was retired from active service on the grounds that he was not a whole-hearted supporter of Hitler's plans. (This was in fact the case. In 1938, in command of Berlin district, he had been ready to arrest Hitler if the military High Command had decided to act. He was throughout the war in touch with many who were not content with Hitler's rule and would have been the July Bomb Plot conspirators' choice for Commander-in-Chief.)

He was one of the first arrested and tried by Freisler's People's Court. Upon conviction, he was executed by slow strangulation in August 1944.

Wolf, Lore (b. 1899). A communist from the Saar who returned to Germany from Russia. During the Röhm Purge of 1934, her underground group distributed pamphlets, supposed to come from SA men and demanding the 'second revolution' – the programme of the radical Nazis – and distributed smuggled copies of the *Brown Book* (an account of the Nazi terror printed in France in 1934). A Gestapo informer infiltrated her group and she was forced to flee to the Saar. When Hitler occupied the Saar in 1935, she escaped to France, where she remained until arrested in 1940; she was held in German prisons until the end of the war.

Wolff, Karl (b. 1906). SS adjutant to Himmler from 1935 to 1943, and his liaison officer with Hitler from 1939. Throughout the period he was a close confidant of Himmler and shared in the development of the SS and its Teutonic mystique. He had become an honorary SS officer in 1931, one of those invited to join because of aristocratic connections and a suitably Nordic appearance. He was made ADC to von Epp, the governor of Bavaria, in 1933 until he transferred to Himmler's office two years later. It was he who found the masseur, Felix Kersten, who relieved Himmler's constant stomach cramps; and he became part of the close inner circle of the *Reichsführer*.

In 1943 he was promoted to SS General and made military governor of northern Italy and the Third Reich's link with Mussolini in the last stage of the war. But the real power lay with Kesselring, commanding the German armed forces there. Wolff attempted to make peace with the Allies in Italy, making contact with Allen Dulles, the American head of the OSS in Switzerland. Although forbidden by Hitler to negotiate peace in Italy, he went ahead, and a surrender was signed in April 1945, on the day of Hitler's death.

Women in the Third Reich. In general, the economic position of women improved during the first years of the Third Reich; their range of employment widened and their entry to university education increased between 1933 and 1940 – but this was undoubtedly due to economic pressures and in spite of Nazi theories.

The Nazi state specifically excluded women from politics, from the army and from the administration of justice. The original Party programme, the 25 Points, saw women's role in motherhood and the family and the Party, once in power, set out to remove women from the labour market. It was hoped to take 800,000 women out of employment within four years, so, in August 1933, couples were offered loans to set up homes and start families. There were grants for large families and heavier taxation for single men and childless couples. Men, it was planned, would take women's place at work, and the increase in home-building and demand for household goods would create further male employment.

There had been a small girls' section in the Hitler Youth since 1927 and, with the 1936 Law on Hitler Youth, girls from the age of fourteen to twenty-one were also organized into the *Bund Deutscher Mädel*. From 1939, a year's labour service was made compulsory for all women unmarried and under twenty-five; most of this service was farm work. In 1938 there were only 25,000 women in labour service (there were 300,000 men), but by the end of the war 7.5 million girls were thus mobilized, and the early ideals of 'faithfulness and beauty' had faded. Normal service was put at six months in 1941 but, as many girls were enrolled in auxiliary military units, signals, anti-aircraft units or base office-work, labour service became of indefinite length.

In 1932, before the Nazis came to power, there were 18,315 women students at universities; however, entry to university was restricted and did not favour women, and the requirement of a period of labour service before university entrance reduced the number of women students in 1939 to 5,447. The vacancies in universities caused by men being called up for the war and the number of women completing their labour service, however, brought an unprecedented 28,378 in 1944, an unintended result of Third Reich policies.

A few women achieved prominence, notably the film director Leni Riefenstahl and the aviator, Hanna Reitsch. The leader of the Women's Front (a result of the *Gleichschaltung* of a variety of societies), Gertrud Scholtz-Klink, walked a narrow tightrope between her role as a woman and the political nature of her post. There were key secretaries at the top of the Nazi administration; notable among these were Hitler's staff who were in the Bunker at the end of the Third Reich, Gerda Daranowski Christian and Gertrud Hump Junge.

The Nazis made great efforts to gain the women's vote and did this in spite of their outspoken anti-feminism, their violent campaigns against lesbians and even against unmarried women. Their 'children, church and kitchen' attitude seemed to give greater security than the socialist 'equal pay and equal opportunities' policies at a time of severe unemployment. However, by October 1933 the first concentration camp for women was opened at Moringen, into which were despatched thousands of women accused of being communists, socialists, members of rival youth organizations, Jehovah's Witnesses, Jews or others considered racially unfit. But in 1938 Moringen was unable to accommodate the flow of women prisoners, and the Lichtenburg camp in Saxony became the second women's camp, to be followed in May 1939 by the camp at Ravensbrück in Mecklenburg, which gained international notoriety.

Work Book (*Arbeitbuch*). An important personal document required by everyone taking employment.

Introduced by a law of February 1935 and brought into force in June that year. Only those in possession of a Work Book could be employed. The book was an employment record and was required to be given to the employer when a worker was taken on, and returned at the end of employment. The Labour Office kept a central Registry of Work Books and false entries or misuse were subject to severe penalties. In practice the Work Book was an instrument controlling workers and effectively denying them freedom to choose their place of work.

Workers' educational camps (*Arbeitserziehungslager*). Special training and indoctrination camps for prisoners released from concentration camps. After 1939 it became so much less common for prisoners to be released that the educational establishments were discontinued.

Y

Yorck von Wartenburg, Graf Peter (1903–44).   A member of the Kreisau Circle, he was arrested and hanged in 1944, after the 20 July attempt on Hitler's life.

Young Plan.   ➤Reparations

Youth Organizations: Hitler Youth.   The Hitler Youth was the Nazi Party organization for German boys aged between 15 and 18, made compulsory by the Hitler Jugend Law which from December 1936 banned all other youth organizations.

The early twentieth century saw the growth of many European youth movements of which the Boy Scouts is simply the best-known example. In Germany many people devoted to hiking and the outdoor life were known as the *Wandervögel*, the birds of passage. They were inspired largely by a love of the German countryside and a distaste for the ugliness of industrialization; by extension, they tended to be idealistic and anti-capitalist. It was this early example of 'Green' feeling which the Nazis successfully captured and incorporated in their appeal. For younger boys between ten and fourteen years of age the Party set up the *Jungvolk* and for girls the *Jungmädel*. From the age of fourteen, girls joined the *Bund Deutscher Mädel* which included a year of farm or domestic service. A boy entering the *Jungvolk* was known as a 'Pimpf' and had to undergo an initiation test, recalling points of Nazi dogma, reciting the Horst Wessel song, running 50 metres in 12 seconds, joining in two-day cross-country hikes, practising semaphore and learning arms drill. It would be a point of immense pride to advance to the full Hitler Youth, to wear the uniform and carry the special dagger marked 'Blood and Honour'.

Hitler Youth provided a wide range of activities as well as initial military training. The aim was to take adolescents out of their social class and turn them into good Nazis by the age of eighteen; if they were not ready then, compulsory labour service would speed the change and any remaining class consciousness would be dealt with by service in the army. Country boys travelled and were given access to sports and the facilities previously only available in towns. In the same way the *Bund Deutscher Mädel* gave girls access to a wider world than their parents had known.

The Hitler Youth was founded in 1926 as a branch of the SA. In 1931 Baldur von Schirach became leader and two years later, at *Gleichschaltung*, absorbed all other youth groups except the Catholic movement – until it too was banned in 1936. The organization rapidly grew in strength, reaching 3.5

million by the end of 1934. While early membership had been made up of working-class boys, the mass organization became dominated by the sons of the middle class and the university educated.

During the war the Hitler Youth were given a role in air defence work in the cities and many of them enrolled in the 12th SS Panzer Division, commanded by the youngest of the German generals, Kurt Meyer. The division fought in France in 1944 and in Germany in the last months of the war. In the final days in Berlin in 1945, the Hitler Youth, under Artur Axmann, the leader since 1940, were armed to fight to the last.

Youth Resistance to Nazism.   By the nature both of resistance and of the Gestapo state, it is doubtful whether it will ever be possible to know the full scope of German youth's struggle against Nazism. It was certainly extensive: a special youth section was created in the RSHA in Prinz Albrechtstrasse, Berlin. But the most obvious indication of the extent of youth resistance was the establishment of a youth concentration camp at Neuwied. Beyond these facts it is possible to list only a representative few of those who were known to have been convicted for resistance activities: Helmut Hülmut, arrested in Hamburg in 1942; he was charged with listening to the BBC and producing and distributing anti-Nazi leaflets. Hülmut was denounced and executed in October 1942 at the age of seventeen. Jonathan Stark, arrested in 1943 for refusing on religious grounds (he was a Jehovah's Witness) to take the oath to the Führer and to do his military service; Stark was sent to Sachsenhausen, where he continued to speak his mind until he was hanged in 1944. Michael Kitzelman, whose experiences on the Russian front had made him a pacifist, was sentenced to death in the Russian town of Orël in 1942. His diary which survives shows the depth of his anti-Nazi convictions.

Members of youth resistance groups appear to have adopted as a symbol the Edelweiss (from the name of a Catholic group of resisters originally founded in Bavaria). Broken up by Gestapo informers, they re-formed and spread to many other parts of Germany. In Cologne in 1944, twelve members were publicly hanged as an example to other youth; and at one time the Gestapo believed that nearly a quarter of the Hitler Youth members in the Rhineland town of Krefeld belonged to Edelweiss groups.

In Berlin, the Werner Steinbrink movement was broken up in the summer of 1942 and ten of its members executed without record.

The Alfred Schmidt-Sas group are known to have distributed leaflets and put up wall-posters during 1942. Arrested by the Gestapo, four boys under twenty-one were sentenced to death, and one girl was sent to prison for seven years.

Other groups have survived by name alone – *Die Meute* in Leipzig, the *Kittelbach Piraten* in the Ruhr, the *07* group in Munich and the anti-Nazi *Verband* in the foothills of the Alps.

It is certain, however, that the White Rose were the best organized and the most effective of German Youth resistance movements. The Munich Gestapo which arrested members of the group in early 1943 had been watching them for nearly six months. During that time the leaders had made their anti-Nazi views known to many thousands of Munich students and White Rose sympathizers were found (and sentenced to death) as far afield as Hamburg. ►White Rose for a full account of the movement.

It is a harsh judgement on so much heroism and so much young blood shed to say that these resistance movements contributed nothing or next to nothing to the downfall of the Third Reich; but the fact is inescapable. Perhaps, however, the real contribution of the youth resistance is to be found elsewhere, as an inspiration to young Germans who came after and an affirmation that not all Germans (of whatever age) docilely swallowed the seductive propaganda of the Nazi state.

Z

Zahnschirm, Father.   The parish priest who allowed himself to be deceived or persuaded in January 1877 into altering the Dollersheim, Austria, register of births to change Hitler's father's name from Alois Schicklgruber to Alois Hitler.

Zeitzler, Kurt von (1895–1963).   Chief-of-Staff OKH, from September 1942 until after the Bomb Plot in 1944.

Credited by Hitler with repelling the Anglo-Canadian Dieppe Raid in 1942, he was promoted over the heads of more senior officers to replace Halder as Chief-of-Staff. Although the post no longer involved the initiation of operations, Zeitzler at first made serious attempts to dispute Hitler's plans. Realizing the futility, he adopted a novel form of resistance. He reported sick and ceased carrying out his duties. He was dismissed from the army in July 1944 and so survived the war.

Zellenleiter **(cell leader)**.   A Nazi Party official immediately above the *Block-wart* and responsible for the activities of households in a number of city blocks. ►Ranks

Zetkin, Klara (1857–1933).   International socialist and a leader of the German Communist Party. Klara Zetkin had already achieved prominence in Social Democratic politics when the outbreak of the 1914 war offered the choice (as it did to others) of international socialism or 'bourgeois patriotism'. Choosing to oppose what she saw as an imperialist war, she broke with the Social Democrats. In 1915 she was imprisoned for making contact with Russian Bolsheviks in an attempt to organize an anti-war international conference of women.

From 1919 she was a senior member of the German Communist Party and sat in the Reichstag from 1920 to 1933. As rotation president of the Reichstag in 1932, she called for a united front against the rise of Nazi power. It was by then much too late; bound by Comintern policy, the German Communist Party had concentrated its attacks on the wrong enemy, the Social Democrats rather than the Nazi Party. Moscow's *volte face* was ineffective in preventing the final Nazi electoral victory.

Klara Zetkin died in June 1933 and her ashes are buried in the Kremlin wall.

Zossen.   Army command headquarters, located just outside Berlin.

Zossen Putsch.   An outline plan by generals from the Zossen army headquarters near Berlin to overthrow Hitler and the regime in 1939. After the military successes in Poland, many German generals expected a rapid political solution. When it was made clear to them that the Polish campaign was simply the prelude to an offensive in the west, a plot was considered, the object of which was to remove Hitler from power. Precise details are not known but a mixture of guilt and hesitancy on the part of the generals can be assumed; certainly, when Hitler at the beginning of November 1939 berated some generals for their lack of drive and ruthlessness, loyalty and commitment to the state, the Zossen Putsch was abandoned before it began.

Z-Plan. Plan for the development of a German navy, initiated in 1938. Released from the restrictions of Versailles by the Anglo-German Naval Agreement of 1935, Hitler planned a surface fleet which would eventually be in a position to challenge Britain's Royal Navy. In the event, the outbreak of war diverted resources towards military production, and the Kriegsmarine never achieved the dominant position to which it aspired. ➤Raeder, Erich

Zyklon-B. The gas used for the massacres at extermination camps. When killings by shooting or hanging had proved too slow for the mass programmes of the Final Solution, experiments were made with gases. There were trials of 'mobile gas chambers', leaking the carbon monoxide from vehicles into the sealed back of trucks containing prisoners. But this method lacked the production-line efficiency the system demanded. There was some competition among SS advocates of different gassing systems until Rudolf Höss, the Auschwitz commandant, introduced the commercial gas Zyklon-B, which was based on prussic acid. Groups of about 250 victims were brought to the camp and marched to a building marked 'disinfection' outside which they undressed. They were sent in, the doors were closed and one or two opened tins of Zyklon-B dropped in. They might all be killed within a quarter of an hour. After half an hour, a special squad of concentration camp prisoners would drag the bodies out for cremation. At first Höss used pits filled with firewood and soaked with kerosene for burning, but by late 1942 he had received crematoria designed to improve greatly the disposal rate of the bodies.

APPENDIX I

Blitzkrieg, the Campaign in France and the Low Countries

1939

September 3   France with Britain declares war on Germany.

October   Fall Gelb (Operation Yellow), the invasion of France through the Low Countries is planned. The intention had been expressed in *Mein Kampf* in 1925 and in the Hossbach Memorandum in 1937, arguing that Britain and France would stand in the way of German expansion to obtain *Lebensraum* (land needed for the German people) and the only solution was by force.

1940

April   9   Denmark and Norway are overrun by Germany and an Anglo-French force is landed then evacuated from Norway.

May   10   Hitler moves to his forward headquarters, Felsennest (Cliff Nest) at Bad Münstereiffel, about thirty miles from the Belgian frontier, and issues the code-word 'Danzig' which sets Fall Gelb, modified by Manstein, in operation.

Before the Netherlands are attacked, a key frontier bridge is taken by 'Brandenburgers' (small groups of Dutch-speaking and sometimes Dutch-uniformed specialist troops).

Parachute troops are landed near The Hague (Dutch government) and communications are soon in German hands.

'Brandenburgers' dressed as tourists pass into Luxemburg, clearing minefields and roadblocks and keeping bridges intact.

   11   Fort Eben Emael, guarding a bridge on the Belgian border, is taken by German troops landing gliders on top of the caissons. Two Panzer divisions move into Belgium.

   14   Rotterdam is heavily bombed on the fourth day to hasten the Dutch surrender.

Rundstedt's Army Group A moves through southern Belgium, with a Panzer corps under Guderian moving through the Ardennes hills and forests. The French, taken by surprise at armour coming through the Ardennes, wait for them to halt at the River Meuse.

Rommel's 7th Panzer Division crosses the river Meuse. The same day, all of Guderian's Panzers are across and racing through the open country beyond, with Ju87 ('Stuka') dive-bombers clearing opposition before them.

15 The Dutch army surrenders. One of Guderian's divisions is forty miles beyond the river and still advancing west.

17 Belgian capital, Brussels, is taken.

19 French Premier Reynaud appoints Marshal Pétain as Vice-Premier.

20 The German army reaches the Channel, cutting the Allied forces in two. The Commander-in-Chief, von Brauchitsch, wants to round up the trapped Anglo-French and Belgian troops, but Rundstedt decides to halt and regroup his forces; Hitler confirms these orders to give Göring's Luftwaffe the chance to distinguish itself by destroying the Allied armies in the Dunkirk pocket.

27 British start evacuating troops, including French and Belgian, from beaches of Dunkirk to England.
The Belgian King Leopold surrenders.

June 3 Dunkirk evacuation ends; over 300,000 soldiers taken to England, but without their equipment and weapons. Another 200,000 are taken from other ports.

5 The German army resumes its offensive, moving south and west into France. Guderian takes the French defensive 'Maginot' line in the rear and encircles a large part of the remaining French army.

10 Italy declares war and moves troops into southern France.
The French government leaves Paris, first to Tours, then to Bordeaux.

14 Paris is entered by German troops.

22 The French sign an armistice with Hitler at Compiègne.

APPENDIX II

Norwegian Campaign and the Occupation of Denmark

1939

December   Admiral Raeder, commander of the German navy, urges Hitler to seize Norway to make sure that Britain does not block the sea route from northern Norway, used to carry Swedish iron-ore to Germany.

Rosenberg introduces Vidkun Quisling, leader of a Norwegian nationalist party with pro-Nazi views, to Hitler as a possible puppet leader for Norway.

1940

February   The German supply-ship *Altmark*, carrying British prisoners taken in the south Atlantic by the raider *Graf Spee*, is boarded in Norwegian waters by the British.

March   3 Hitler, convinced of his military planning ability after the victory of Poland in 1939, orders an attack on Norway. Denmark is included in the plan. He takes personal charge, issuing orders through Keitel and his OKW rather than planning through the army command, OKH.

April   8 British lay mines off Norway.

9 Denmark is overrun and taken under control.

The German navy sails into Norwegian ports from Oslo to Narvik in the north and lands troops. German naval losses are heavy, with three cruisers sunk and a battleship badly damaged.

In southern Norway German troops are also landed by air. Luftwaffe units take over airfields and gain air superiority over Norway.

14 Anglo-French troops are landed at Narvik and near Trondheim, but are unable to do more than hold some of their landing areas. Norwegian King escapes to Britain and a government in exile is formed; in Norway, Quisling proclaims himself political head of the state council of thirteen Nazi-appointed commissioners. Terboven, *Gauleiter* of Essen, is made Reich Commissioner as the effective ruler.

May   The re-embarkation of Allied troops leaves the Germans in control of southern and central Norway. At Narvik, in the north, 2,000 German Alpine troops are slowly pushed back by 20,000 Allied troops.

June   8 The last British troops are evacuated from Narvik in northern Norway as the Anglo-French military position disintegrates in France.

APPENDIX III

North African Campaigns, 1941–3

Italy's declaration of war in 1940 and her attack from Libya on British-controlled Egypt turned into a disaster. Only when Hitler sent General Rommel with a special force was the situation in North Africa recovered.

1941

January	Hitler issues Führer Directive No. 22 to create a special force.
February	5th Light Division (later renamed 21 Panzer) as the nucleus of an Afrika Korps, under the command of General Erwin Rommel, lands at Tripoli in Libya.
April	With three reinforced Italian army corps and the German 15 Panzer Division, Rommel moves on through Libya towards Egypt, bypassing Tobruk, where the 1st Australian Division holds him off and is left in a state of siege.
June	British counter-attack at Egyptian border fails.
September	Afrika Korps is reinforced by the specially equipped and trained 90th Light Division.
November	British attack towards Tobruk.

1942

January	Rommel retreats and the British 8th Army move into Libya again. Two Australian divisions are moved from Egypt to the Pacific theatre of war to hold Japanese advances, while Rommel receives reinforcements from Germany.
	Rommel attacks and smashes British armour.
February	Rommel again nears Tobruk.
May	Afrika Korps outflanks the British and attacks towards Tobruk, although delayed by Free French outpost at Bir Hacheim.
June	The British retreat into Egypt, losing Tobruk. Rommel is promoted to Field Marshal.
July	The German and Italian armies reach El Alamein, within sixty miles of the Nile Delta. The Afrika Korps now has three divisions with supporting units, and under Rommel are three Italian corps, including élite Italian armoured forces. The British have divisions from South Africa, India, New Zealand and Australia.

September   Rommel's offensive is halted by a strengthened British 8th Army, now commanded by Montgomery.

October   Battle of El Alamein destroys Rommel's Panzers.

November   An Anglo-American force lands in French North Africa in Morocco and Algeria, with little opposition.

German troops now occupy all France.

Rommel is forced into a long retreat, with the Afrika Korps as the effective rearguard, across the desert past Tripoli.

1943

February   Rommel retreats into Tunisia, defeating advance American units at Kasserine Pass, but still pursued by Montgomery.

May   Surrender of 150,000 Afrika Korps and Italian troops to a combined Anglo-American force. Only Rommel and a small number escape.

APPENDIX IV

Italian Campaign

1943

May	German and Italian armies in North Africa surrender at Tunis.
July	Anglo-American forces under the command of General Eisenhower land in Sicily.
	Mussolini is dismissed as Prime Minister of Italy, the king regaining temporary power and Marshal Badoglio forming a government.
August	Sicily is occupied and an Allied military government set up.
September	Allied troops land on mainland, at Messina, Calabria and Salerno, south of Naples.
	Italy surrenders and German troops under Kesselring, already commander in southern Europe, occupy Rome and move south. Rommel is transferred to north-west Europe.
	Mussolini is rescued from imprisonment by a raiding squad under Skorzeny and installed as head of a new government in northern Italy by the Germans. Many disbanded Italian soldiers take to the hills to form partisan units.
October	Italy declares war on Germany.
	Hitler orders a line to be held north of Naples, south of Rome; a winter battle in the hills starts.

1944

January	Generals Eisenhower and Montgomery moved to England to prepare for invasion of France.
	Allies land at Anzio, south of Rome, and the British attack in the centre, particularly at the Abbey of Monte Cassino.
May	Allies break through at Anzio and at Cassino, and advance on Rome.
June	Rome is captured, and the next day the Anglo-Americans land in northern France – D-Day.
	Partisan strength in northern Italy reaches 100,000.

1945

April   Allies start final offensive; partisans take over cities.
Mussolini tries to escape to Switzerland but is captured and shot by partisans.
SS General Wolff negotiates with US agent Dulles in Switzerland, and Kesselring surrenders German forces in Italy.

APPENDIX V

Russian Campaign

Operation 'Barbarossa'. The final code-name of the plan to invade Russia

1939

March	Hitler occupies Czechoslovakia and makes demands on Poland for a settlement of the 'Polish Corridor' and the recognition of German rights in Danzig.
July	Hitler's Foreign Minister, Ribbentrop, starts trade talks between Russia and Germany which include secret talks on improving political relations and spheres of influence.
August	While French and British military missions are in Moscow hoping to make plans for co-operation in the event of war, a Soviet-German non-aggression pact is signed in Moscow by Ribbentrop and Molotov, taking the outside world by surprise. Until then, Nazi Germany and Communist Russia had publicly declared deep hostility for each other.
September	Hitler attacks Poland with a '*Blitzkrieg*' campaign which ends in October. France and Britain at once declare war on Germany, while Russia enters Poland from the east. Germany and Russia partition Poland between them, according to the secret agreement made earlier. The Russians occupy key ports in the Baltic States.
November	Russia attacks Finland, but the invasion only penetrates border areas and is carried out so inefficiently that Germany (and the world) thinks the Russian army of poor quality. But Russia had purged its officer corps in the three years before (on suspicion of political disloyalty) and had not yet completed the training of enough new officers.

1940

March	Finland signs a peace treaty with Russia, giving territory around the Baltic to improve Russian defences.
June	After the fall of France, Hitler is secure in Western Europe. He imminently expects the surrender of Britain which will enable him to turn his attention to the east.

Russia moves into Estonia, Latvia and Lithuania (other than Memel, already occupied by Germany).

August	Russia makes all three Baltic states Soviet Republics. Hitler secretly orders his staff to prepare a plan for the invasion of Russia (to be code-named 'Otto') while making provisional plans for an invasion of Britain.
September	Axis treaty joined by Japan.
October	German invasion of Rumania, seizing the oilfields at Ploesti.
November	Hungary, Rumania and Slovakia (a puppet state taken from Czechoslovakia) sign treaties with Germany.
December	Revised plan of attack on Russia agreed by Hitler and given the new, final code-name 'Barbarossa'.

1941

January Germany continues to make trade and frontier pacts with Russia, to import through Russia essential commodities, such as rubber and petroleum.

March Hitler, pre-empting a suspected Russian move, occupies Bulgaria from his Rumanian base.

To control the Balkans, Hitler persuades Yugoslavia to join the Axis treaty, but Yugoslav army officers opposing the treaty stage a *coup d'état*. Hitler makes his intentions clear to the German army by briefing 250 senior officers on his plan for war against Russia.

April Germany attacks Yugoslavia, and its government surrenders. German troops occupy Greece, brushing aside the small British army.

May Heydrich prepares the SS for its part, instructing the leaders of *Einsatzgruppen* (special task forces) on their work of murdering all Jews, 'Asiatics', communist officials, intellectuals, professionals and gypsies.

June The 'Commissar Order' is issued to the army, under the signature of Hitler's chief of staff, Keitel; Russian army political commissars to be killed on capture. General orders are addressed to all troops to be ruthless against the 'Bolshevik' Russians.

Despite reports from his own intelligence agents and from the British that an attack is imminent, Stalin refuses to believe them. The Russian news agency TASS issues a statement seven days before the invasion: 'To counter absurd rumours, responsible bodies in Moscow judge it necessary to declare that these rumours are sheer propaganda put out by the forces opposed to the USSR and Germany, attempting to spread and intensify the war.'

At 4.15 a.m. East European time on 22 June 1941 Operation 'Barbarossa' is launched.

1941. *From the first attack in June 1941 to the failure at Moscow in December* 1941

June	Operation 'Barbarossa' is ordered. German forces, with Rumanian, Finnish, Hungarian and Slovak troops taking part (Italian and volunteer Spanish troops were to follow), invade Russia from north to south. The Russian command is taken by surprise, in spite of warnings from British intelligence and their own agents in Germany (the *Rote Kapelle*).

The Luftwaffe destroys nearly half the Russian air force in the first attacks, and Lithuania is taken immediately.

The British immediately declare themselves as allies of the Russians.

July   Göring orders Heydrich, the head of SS security (the RSHA), to clear occupied lands of Jews. SS *Einsatzgruppen* follow the armies according to plan.

By the end of the month, Germany has occupied Latvia, the River Dnieper is reached and Smolensk captured. Nearly three-quarters of a million prisoners are taken.

August   The German advance continues. Estonia is occupied and incorporated into a new territory, subject to the Third Reich, 'Ostland'. The British and Russians move into Iran to secure Russia's southern flank and prevent any German link with the Middle East.

September   The Shah is forced to abdicate and two zones of control, Soviet and British, are established in Iran.

German troops take Kiev, having already occupied most of the Ukraine and besieged Leningrad.

October   In the south the Germans take Sevastopol in the Crimea while in the north they begin what is planned to be the final crushing offensive against Moscow. Hitler in Berlin speaks to the German public and describes the extent of his victory: 2.5 million prisoners, 22,000 guns captured, 18,000 tanks knocked out and 14,500 Russian planes destroyed.

November   The offensive is slowed by rain then halted by frost, although German tanks are within twenty miles of Moscow. The intense cold halts the Germans who are not equipped for a winter campaign.

December   To the surprise of the German general staff and the bewilderment of the front-line troops, Russian counter-attacks come through the snow using reserves fresh from training in Siberia and well equipped for the weather. Stalin, gambling that Japan would not attack Russia in the east, moves these troops across Asia to the European theatres.

In the south Rundstedt is forced to evacuate Rostov, which he has just taken. Shocked by news of his first major military setback ever, Hitler dismisses Brauchitsch and takes over his role of Commander-in-Chief. Other army commanders are dismissed, including Rundstedt and Guderian.

At the end of 1941, the Third Reich is still in command of a vast empire, but it has suffered its first check. Now, when Japan attacks Pearl Harbor, Hitler declares war on the USA, an absurd gesture of solidarity with Japan which is to have significant consequences for Germany's struggle against Russia in the coming years.

1942. *The German advance on the southern fronts, to the Caucasus and Stalingrad*

Although the German advances into Russia in 1941 had been halted by the onset of winter and the unexpected Russian counter-attacks, Hitler planned to continue his conquest of Slav land as *Lebensraum* for the Third Reich. The difference was that the difficulties were now more realistically appreciated and Soviet manpower supply was seen to be practically unlimited. Industrially, the Soviet Third Five-Year Plan from 1939 had begun to develop resources beyond the Ural mountains. From 1942 Russian production of munitions, tanks and aircraft increased dramatically; by 1943 they would be producing more tanks and aircraft than Germany. The new Russian tanks were another surprise for the Third Reich, whose Panzers found themselves out-gunned and matched by equal or better armour. Although Russian aircraft design had been backward, the Il-2 'Stormovik', which had been designed as a fighter and had proved inadequate in that role in 1941, was now converted to a successful ground-attack aircraft. During the year American and British aircraft, vehicles and munitions also began to reach the Soviet Union in increasing quantity.

Behind the German lines the Russians had set up partisan groups to harass the enemy. In 1941 these had had little effect and were mostly overrun before they could be effectively armed or organized. During 1942, partisan activity gradually forced the Germans to keep up to 250,000, second-line troops away from the front.

Nevertheless, as the campaigning season of 1942 began, Berlin still held the initiative. Hitler, now Commander-in-Chief, planned to renew his offensive by striking south to the Caucasus, taking Stalingrad as the bridge across the River Volga and clearing the Russian forces from Leningrad and the Baltic.

1942

May   Manstein's army takes the Crimea and besieges Sevastopol, which falls in July. Satisfied with this, Hitler moves Manstein north to tackle the siege of Leningrad.

Von Bock's Army Group South defeats Russian tank forces in the Ukraine and takes Kursk, but when von Bock pauses in his attack on Voronezh, Hitler dismisses him.

July   Hitler moves to his Ukraine headquarters at Vinnitsa (called 'Werewolf') and supervises the 6th Army's advance to the River Volga at Stalingrad.

September   German troops reach the Elbruz mountains in the Caucasus. Hitler had however hoped to reach the oilfields at Baku. He dismisses Field Marshal List for not advancing fast enough.

At 'Werewolf' there are arguments between Hitler and his military advisers who claim that his strategy has stretched out his forces too widely. When General Halder, the chief of the Army general staff, warns that the Russians, with growing strength, could soon counter-attack, he too is dismissed and eventually sent to the concentration camp at Dachau.

Von Paulus's 6th Army takes most of Stalingrad and, with control of the air, seems to be on the way to break through the town to the river. But the Russians hold on, their backs to the river, their artillery supporting them from the other bank.

November   Hitler is in Munich at the annual celebration of the November 1923 Beer Hall Putsch when news comes of a Russian counter-offensive threatening to encircle the 6th Army at Stalingrad. The new chief of the Army general staff, Zeitzler, suggests a withdrawal to the River Don, but Hitler insists that he will not leave the Volga and orders the 6th Army to stand at Stalingrad.

The Russian counter-attacks to the north and south of Stalingrad break through. Von Paulus is surrounded. Hitler sends reinforcements, including Rumanians and Luftwaffe ground forces.

December   Göring says he can supply von Paulus with 700 tons of supplies a day by air. Though he soon reduces the promise to 300, this cannot be done in the Russian winter. Nor can Manstein's relief army reach them.

1942 had ended with defeat for the German army by Montgomery at El Alamein and with an even greater defeat at Stalingrad. The British Prime Minister, Winston Churchill, said at the time: 'This is not the end. It is not even the beginning of the end. But it is perhaps the end of the beginning.'

1943. *The turn of the tide at Stalingrad and Kursk*

1943

January Russian offensive retakes Voronezh on the River Don. A Soviet drive might have cut off the Wehrmacht in the Caucasus, but the retreat of the German Army Group from the south-east is well managed and they elude the Russian net. On the last day of the month von Paulus surrenders at Stalingrad.

February 90,000 Germans become prisoners. Hitler is furious: 'The man should have shot himself just as the old commanders threw themselves on their swords . . . That's the last Field Marshal I shall appoint in this war.' From now on, Hitler gives preference to the Waffen SS over the regular army. Relying on the original six SS divisions as his élite troops, he allows the Waffen SS to take in conscripts and double in size.

    The Russians now retake Kursk although the Germans, hoping to begin a spring offensive, hold Kharkov and Orël to the south. Hitler orders Speer and Guderian to improve the production and design of tanks.

    The successful Soviet Yak-9 fighter plane becomes operational.

April The Jews of the Warsaw ghetto rise and hold off attacks for four weeks; some survivors fight on in the ruins for months. In the Balkans, the Yugoslav partisans grow in strength and increase from 20,000 men at the beginning of the year to nearly 250,000 by the end.

May All Italian and German troops in North Africa surrender to the Allied forces.

July The Russian front-line gives the appearance of a huge and vulnerable bulge, the Kursk Salient. Hitler orders Kluge in the north and Manstein in the south to attack, using a million men and nearly 3,000 tanks. The object is to encircle and destroy the Russian armies and move on to Moscow. The German attacks are held and the Russians, using rockets from aircraft for the first time, break up the German tank attacks and go over to the offensive themselves.

August Orël and Kharkov are recaptured by the Russians, and the German army is in general retreat.

September Bryansk and Smolensk retaken to the north. Germans withdraw to a line in front of the Upper Dnieper.

October Kiev in the centre retaken.

December Stalin claims that the Germans have lost a million men in the last year – a figure four times greater than likely German losses. From now on, Soviet claims for German losses or their own seldom have a basis in fact.

The year 1943 ended badly for the German armies. From the beginning the qualitative improvement in the Red Army was matched by a marked increase in the supply of matériel from beyond the Urals. Tanks, artillery – and particularly rocket artillery – became increasingly available to Soviet commanders, and problems of mobility were largely overcome by the supply of American trucks. The quality of Soviet leadership had also greatly improved during the year as younger commanders gained battle experience and took the places of older men killed, captured or purged during the defeats of 1941–2. On the German side, the year's end saw serious shortages of manpower which could not be disguised by fielding divisions at half-strength. Nor were these shortages fully compensated for by the supply of the new Tiger and Panther tanks to the Panzer divisions; however great the qualitative improvement over earlier German tanks, they were still not arriving at the Panzer divisions in sufficient quantity to maintain formations at last year's fighting strength. Thus while the Red Army was growing, the *Wehrmacht* was shrinking as 1943 came to an end.

The end in 1944 and 1945

1944

January	The Russian offensive to relieve Leningrad succeeds.
	Soviet troops on the centre front reach the 1939 eastern border of Poland.
	Vatutin's left wing converges with Koniev's right wing to surround German forces between the Russians' Kiev and Cherkassy bridgeheads.
February	Elements of six German divisions are caught in the pincer movement, but 3rd and 47th Panzer Corps succeed in a desperate attempt to break through to the trapped Germans. Of the 60,000 German troops in the pocket, 30,000 are extricated. But action on one part of the front now necessarily weakens German forces on another. Nikopol with its valuable manganese-ore mines is abandoned on the 8th, Krivoi Rog is lost before the end of the month.
March	The Russians attack in the Ukraine and surround Minsk. Koniev and Zhukov's forces reach the Carpathians and Germany occupies Hungary.
April	Zhukov's troops reach the entrance to the Tartar Pass but are unable to penetrate it. A strong German counter-attack tempor-

arily stabilizes this section of the front.

May   Russians clear the Crimea and retake Sevastopol. Hitler dismisses Manstein and other senior commanders, to show where he places the blame for Germany's failures.

June   The Allies take Rome, and on 'D-Day' Anglo-American troops land in Normandy, making a second front against the Germans in northern France. Soviets launch their summer offensive, concentrating on the White Russian fronts and advancing 150 miles in one week.

July   Minsk falls. Army Group Centre is virtually destroyed. Total German losses exceed 200,000. Vilna falls. Soviet forces approach East Prussian frontier. Lvov falls to Koniev's army at the month's end.

August   The Polish resistance (the 'Home Army') in Warsaw rises as the Russians approach. But German counter-attacks hold off Russian forces and the Poles are forced to surrender. Russian troops surround fifty-five German divisions on the Baltic coast. Bucharest falls. Rumania and Bulgaria sue for peace.

September   Finland accepts Soviet armistice terms.

October   Malinovsky's forces drive towards Budapest. In East Prussia Soviet spearhead is blunted at Gumbinnen.

November/   Hitler leaves his Rastenburg headquarters for Berlin, abandoning
December   the appearance of being a front-line commander. But his interventions continue to reduce the impact of the German success in stabilizing both the East and West fronts as 1944 comes to an end.

1945

January   Russian army groups, both north and south of Warsaw, break through and take the city, crossing the river Oder within 100 miles of Berlin. They reach the Baltic at Danzig and overrun industrial Silesia, seizing the last possible coal supplies of the Third Reich.

February   The German navy evacuates troops from Baltic ports, Danzig and East Prussia.

April   The German army collapses, leaving only individual units fighting. Vienna is taken by the Russians, and American and Russian troops meet on the river Elbe. Soviet forces enter Berlin.

May   Final battle for Berlin. Hitler commits suicide.

APPENDIX VI

Normandy to the Rhine: defeat in the West

1944

July

A month after the landings, the American, British and Canadian forces have consolidated their D-Day beachheads and linked up. For the loss of 5,000 men killed, 750,000 have now been put ashore. The Americans (to the west, on the Allied right wing) have cleared the peninsula south of Cherbourg; the British, holding the centre, face the city of Caen; and the Canadians on the Allied left bear the heaviest weight of the German Panzer attacks. In the air, the Allies have complete superiority and are able to attack German army ground targets at will. Field Marshal von Rundstedt is dismissed when he expresses pessimism over the battle's outcome.

American 1st Army with over 350,000 men and 1,000 tanks starts its advance south, while British 2nd Army and the Canadian army attack Caen.

Field Marshal Rommel, German commander, is injured in a car crash and replaced by Field Marshal von Kluge. In East Prussia, the Bomb Plot fails, but German command in Paris starts to take over from the Nazis until news of the failure comes through.

Fourteen British and Canadian divisions are holding fourteen German divisions and are engaged in heavy fighting for Caen. General Omar Bradley on the other wing has fifteen US divisions facing a mixture of German units amounting to nine divisions. At the end of the month the Americans move out of the peninsula and reach Brittany, while the Canadians and British take Caen and slowly push the Germans back.

August

By this time the Allies have landed 1,500,000 soldiers, 300,000 vehicles and 1,600,000 tons of stores. The twenty German divisions are now faced by thirty-six Allied divisions, each stronger and more liberally equipped.

The British and Canadians now advance south; US divisions sweep south and turn east at great speed, threatening to surround the German forces.

Von Kluge directs his army to move to the attack in obedience to Hitler's orders and is recalled to Paris to answer for his part in the July Bomb Plot. He kills himself. Hitler replaces him with the general already in the front line, Hausser, and gives command in the west to Field Marshal Model.

The Americans now begin to advance at fifty miles a day. In the south of France, US forces land and move north against little opposition. Aix-en-Provence is taken by US forces. The French II Corps advance on Marseilles. In Paris the French resistance takes over part of the city and within days the Free French 2nd Armoured Division, accompanied by US units, liberates Paris. On the last day of August Patton's 3rd Army reaches the Meuse.

September   General Eisenhower, supreme commander of the Allied forces, takes over from Montgomery as commander of the Allied ground forces and decides to advance on a broad front towards the Rhine. Field Marshal von Rundstedt is given back command in the West. Allied forces now have a complete front from the Channel to Switzerland and move towards the German West Wall (the 'Siegfried' Line). France is almost totally liberated.

October   Montgomery plans to strike through Belgium to Holland rapidly and send parachute troops ahead; the furthest division lands at Arnhem on the Rhine but cannot hold the bridge.

December   Ardennes offensive; Hitler puts all his forces in the west into attack and, taking the Americans by surprise, drives in the direction of Antwerp. Eisenhower gives immediate charge of the US troops north of the German attack to Montgomery to co-ordinate defence; the town of Bastogne is held by an American paratroop division rushed there, and the German attack fails against this resistance, through its shortages of fuel and supplies and Allied air superiority.

1945

January   The Russian offensive in the east causes Hitler to move armoured forces from the west, including Hitler's favourite, Sepp Dietrich, and his 6th SS Panzer Army. German losses in France since D-Day amount to 1,500,000 men, over half being prisoners of war.

February   1st Canadian Army, on the left flank of the Allies, attacks down the west bank of the Rhine, drawing the last German reserves.

March   Americans cross the River Rhine at the unguarded bridge at Remagen. This is followed by other crossings. The British move across north Germany towards Hamburg while the Americans spread across central and southern Germany.

April   American and Russian troops meet at Torgau on the River Elbe. Effective German military resistance to the western Allies collapses.

May   German forces in north-west Europe surrender, followed by the surrender of all German forces.

QUOTATIONS

1923–28

The accused were inspired by the pure spirit of patriotism.

(Judge Neithardt at the trial of Ludendorff, Hitler and others after the Beer Hall Putsch, 1923)

Lüger [the anti-semitic Mayor of Vienna when Hitler lived there] gave great importance to winning over those groups who, when their existence is threatened, tend to fight rather than give in. And he took great care to make use of all the instruments of authority at his disposal and to bring powerful existing institutions over to his side.

(Hitler, on one of the heroes of his youth)

Instead of working to achieve power by a Putsch, we shall have to hold our noses and enter the Reichstag against Catholic and Marxist deputies. If out-voting them takes longer than out-shooting them, at least the result will be guaranteed by their own constitutions . . . Sooner or later we shall have a majority – and after that Germany.

(Hitler in Landsberg prison, in conversation with Kurt Ludeke, 1924)

I shall start again from the beginning.

(Hitler, on release from Landsberg prison, 1924)

It is not the aim of our present-day democracy to form an assemblage of wise men, but rather to collect together a crowd of subservient nonentities, especially as the intelligence of each individual is limited.

(*Mein Kampf*, 1925)

The multitude does not invent majorities, neither organizes nor thinks; it is always only the one man, the individual.

(*Mein Kampf*, 1925)

The world is not for craven-hearted races.

(*Mein Kampf*, 1925)

No sacrifice would have been too great in order to gain England's alliance [in 1914]. It would have meant renunciation of colonies and importance on the sea, and refraining from interference with British industry by our competition.

(*Mein Kampf*, 1925)

If we divide the human race into three categories – founders, maintainers and destroyers of culture – the Aryan stock alone can be considered as representing the first category.

(*Mein Kampf*, 1925)

Now that I realized that the Jews were the leaders of Social Democracy, scales, as it were, began to fall from my eyes. My long mental struggle was over.

(*Mein Kampf*, 1925)

1929–32

We are promoting catastrophic policies, for only catastrophe – that is, the collapse of the liberal system – will clear the way for the new order . . . Every weakening of the system is good, very good for us and our German revolution.

(Gregor Strasser, June 1929)

You ask me what tomorrow will be like and I answer – I don't know except that it will be as different as possible from today.

(Gregor Strasser, 1929)

The good of society before your own good.

(Nazi Party slogan, c. 1930)

We must be ruthless. We must regain our clear conscience as to ruthlessness.

(Hitler speech, 1931)

Herr Chancellor, if the German nation once empowers the National Socialist movement to introduce a constitution other than that which we have today, then you cannot stop it . . . When a constitution proves itself useless for a nation's life, the nation does not die – the constitution is changed.

(Hitler, in an open letter to Chancellor Brüning, December 1931)

[Communism is more than] a mob storming about in the streets of Germany, it is a conception of the world which subjects itself to the entire Asiatic continent.

In my view it is to put the cart before the horse to believe that by business methods Germany's political power can be recovered, instead political power is the condition to improve the economic situation . . . There can be no economic life unless behind the economic life there stands the determined political will of the nation absolutely ready to strike – and to strike hard.

Today we stand at the turning point of Germany's destiny . . . Either we shall succeed in working out a body-politic hard as iron from this conglomeration of parties, associations, unions, and conceptions of the world, from this pride of rank and madness of class, or else Germany will fall into final ruin.

(Hitler, in a speech to leading industrialists, January 1932)

The Bohemian Corporal.

(President Hindenburg's description of Hitler, 1932)

1933–9

No danger at all. We've hired him for our act.

(Von Papen, on Hitler's first becoming Chancellor in January 1933)

We are the result of the distress for which the others were responsible.

(Hitler, in a speech in Munich, February 1933)

Every bullet that is now fired from a political pistol is my bullet. If that is called murder, then I have committed murder, for I have ordered it all.

(Göring, in a speech confirming his orders to the police of February 1933)

It's not my business to do justice; it's my business to annihilate and exterminate, that's all.

(Göring, ibid., February 1933)

[The emergency decrees] 'For the protection of the people and the state' and 'Against betrayal of the German people and treasonous machinations'

(Decrees passed immediately after the Reichstag Fire, February 1933, which, even before the Enabling Law, provided a legal basis for Nazi actions)

What do figures matter now? We're the masters in the Reich and in Prussia.

(Göbbels, in March 1933, after the last Reichstag elections when the Nazis and their allies obtained only 51.9 per cent of the vote)

The stream of revolution released must be guided into the safe channel of evolution.

(Hitler, to Party leaders, July 1933, warning against radicals who wanted their policies against commerce and industry to be followed)

Adolf Hitler is Germany and Germany is Adolf Hitler. He who pledges himself to Hitler pledges himself to Germany.

(Hess, February 1934, in a radio address to all Party, Hitler Youth and labour leaders)

The grey rock must be drowned by the brown tide.

(Röhm, c. 1934) (meaning that the army must be taken over by his SA)

The second revolution.

(The term used by Nazi radicals, hoping for a follow-up to the 1933 takeover)

All revolutions devour their own children.

(Röhm, June 1934, before he was shot)

A second revolution was being prepared, but it was made by us against those who have conjured it up.

(Göring, June 1934, after the Röhm Purge)

I swear by God this holy oath, that I will render unconditional obedience to the Leader of the German Reich, Adolf Hitler, supreme commander of the armed forces and that, as a brave soldier, I will be ready at any time to stake my life for this oath.

(Sworn by all officers and men of the German army from August 1934)

I go the way that Providence dictates with the assurance of a sleepwalker.

(Hitler, in a speech in Munich after the reoccupation of the Rhineland, March 1936)

First: the German army must be ready for action within four years. Second: the German economy must be ready for war within four years.

(Hitler, in a memorandum on the Four-Year Plan, autumn 1936)

For the solution of the German question, only the path of force remains.

(Hitler, reported in the Hossbach Memorandum, November 1937, to a group of generals and ministers, on *Lebensraum* and the war he planned)

If other methods do not succeed, I intend to march into Austria with armed forces in order to restore constitutional conditions there and to prevent further outrages there against the German population. I personally shall command the operation . . . [which] shall proceed without the use of force, with our troops marching in and being welcomed by the people, so all provocations are to be avoided. But if there is any resistance it must be smashed by force of arms with utmost ruthlessness.

(Hitler's Directive No. 1 for the march into Austria, March 1938)

A quarrel in a faraway country between people of whom we know nothing.

(Chamberlain, on the Sudetenland and Czechoslovakia, 1938)

It is the last territorial claim which I have to make in Europe.

(Hitler, on the Sudetenland and Czechoslovakia, 1938)

Peace for our time.

(Chamberlain, on his return from Munich, 1938)

Oh, we can't do that, that's private property. Next you'll be insisting that we bomb the Ruhr region!

(British cabinet minister Sir Kingsley Wood, on hearing of a proposal to fire-bomb the German Black Forest, September 1938)

'Case White' [code-name for the plan of attack on Poland]: The aim will be to destroy Polish military strength . . . Intervention by Russia cannot be expected to be of any use to Poland.

Preparations must be made so that the operation can be carried out at any time from 1 September 1939.

(Hitler's Directive to OKW, his military commanders, April 1939)

Mr Roosevelt! I fully understand that the vastness of your nation and the immense wealth of your country allow you to feel responsible for the history of the whole world and for the history of all nations. I, sir, am placed in a much more modest and smaller sphere.

I once took over a state which was faced with complete ruin . . . I have succeeded in finding useful work for the whole of the seven million unemployed . . . I have brought back to the Reich lands stolen from us in 1919. I have led back to their native country millions of Germans who were torn away and were in misery . . . and, Mr Roosevelt, without spilling blood and without . . . the misery of war.

(Hitler's speech to the Reichstag, April 1939, after an appeal for peace by the American President)

There will be no war with Britain.

(Hitler to Admiral Raeder, commander of the German navy, during 1939)

This means the end of Germany.

(Canaris, Head of Military Intelligence, to Gisevius, on learning that the order to attack Poland had been given, August 1939)

What now?

(Hitler to Ribbentrop, on learning that Britain had declared war, September 1939)

The Jewish-capitalist world will not survive the twentieth century.

(Hitler's New Year Message, 30 December 1939)

1940–45

Mr Churchill ought perhaps for once to believe me when I prophesy that a great empire will be destroyed – an empire which it was never my intention to destroy or even to harm.

(Hitler, speaking to the Reichstag, July 1940)

[Waiting for a German invasion]: Perhaps it will come tonight. Perhaps it will come next week. Perhaps it will never come . . . we shall seek no terms, we shall tolerate no parley, we may show mercy – we shall ask for none.

(Winston Churchill, British Prime Minister, July 1940)

Herr Hitler assures us he is coming. We are waiting anxiously for the German army to attempt the Channel – and so are the fishes.

(Winston Churchill, September 1940)

When people are very curious in Britain and ask, 'Yes, but why doesn't he come?' we reply: 'Calm yourselves! Calm yourselves! He is coming! He is coming!'

(Hitler, speaking at the opening of the eighth Winterhilfe campaign, September 1940)

The German Armed Forces must be prepared to crush Soviet Russia in a quick campaign even before the end of the war against England . . . Preparations . . . are to be begun now . . . and are to be completed by 15 May 1941.

(Hitler, December 1940, Directive No. 21 for 'Barbarossa', the invasion of Russia)

The war against Russia will be such that it cannot be conducted in a chivalrous fashion. This struggle is one of ideologies and racial differences and will have to be conducted with unprecedented, merciless and unrelenting harshness . . . The [Russian] Commissars are the bearers of an ideology directly opposed to National Socialism. Therefore the Commissars will be liquidated.

(Hitler to his senior officers, March 1941)

When National Socialism has ruled long enough it will no longer be possible to conceive a form of life different from ours.

(*Hitler's Table Talk*, July 1941)

In the long run National Socialism and religion will no longer be able to exist together.

(*Hitler's Table Talk*, July 1941)

A New Order for Europe.

(The slogan taken from the report of the meeting between Hitler and Mussolini, August 1941)

Berlin must be the true centre of Europe, a capital that for everybody shall be *the* capital.

(*Hitler's Table Talk*, September 1941)

When I think about it I realise I'm extraordinarily humane.
. . . If they [the Jews] refuse to go voluntarily, I see no other solution but extermination. Why should I look at a Jew through other eyes than if he were a Russian prisoner of war?

(Hitler discusses the Jews. *Hitler's Table Talk*, 23 January 1942; 11 April 1942)

Our guiding principle must be that these people [the Russians] have but one justification for existence – to be of use to us economically.

In the field of public health there is no need whatsoever to extend to the subject races the benefit of our knowledge.

(Hitler discusses the Russians. *Hitler's Table Talk*, 23 January 1942)

I therefore order that from now on all opponents . . . in so-called commando operations . . . are to be exterminated to the last man in battle or while in flight . . . Even should these, on their being discovered, make as if to surrender, all quarter is to be denied on principle.

(Hitler's 'Commando Order', October 1942)

Forbid surrender. The army will hold its position to the last soldier and the last cartridge, and by its heroic endurance will make an unforgettable contribution to the building of the defensive front and the salvation of Western civilization.

(Hitler's telegraph to von Paulus, surrounded with his army in Stalingrad, January 1943)

How easy he has made it for himself! . . . The man should shoot himself as generals used to fall on their swords when they saw that their cause was lost.

(Hitler, speaking at a conference at his HQ, February 1942, after von Paulus had surrendered)

Most of you know what it means when 100 corpses are lying side by side, or 500 or 1,000.

This is a page of glory in our history which has never been written and is never to be written . . . !

(Himmler, on the killing of Jews, in a speech to SS leaders in Poland, October 1943)

My Führer, I congratulate you! Roosevelt is dead. It is written in the stars that the second half of April will be the turning point for us.

(Göbbels, to Hitler, April 1945)

You may safely call me Frau Hitler.

(Eva Braun, to a domestic servant in the Bunker, after her marriage and before her death, April 1945)

It is untrue that I, or anybody else in Germany, wanted war in 1939. It was wanted and provoked exclusively by those international politicians who either came of Jewish stock, or worked for Jewish interests. After all my offers of disarmament, posterity cannot place the responsibility for this war on me.

Before my death, I expel from the Party the former Reich Marshal, Hermann Göring, and withdraw from him all the rights conferred upon him by the Decree of 29 June 1941 and by my Reichstag speech of 1 September 1939. In his place I appoint Grand Admiral Dönitz as Reich President and Supreme Commander of the Armed Forces.

Before my death I expel from the Party and from all his offices the former Reichsführer SS and Reich Minister of the Interior, Heinrich Himmler.

(Hitler's 'Political Testament', April 1945)

FURTHER READING

Bekker, Cajus, *Hitler's Naval War*, Macdonald and Jane's, London, 1974

Bracher, K. D., *The German Dictatorship*, Penguin, London, 1985

Broszat, Martin, *The Hitler State*, Longman, London, 1981

Buel, H. P., *Strength through Joy*, Secker & Warburg, 1973

Bullock, Alan, *Hitler, a Study in Tyranny*, Penguin, London, 1962

Calvocoressi, Peter and Guy Wint, *Total War, Causes and Courses of the Second World War*, Allen Lane, London, 1972

Carr, William, *A History of Germany 1815–1985*, Arnold, London, 1987

Carr, William, *Arms, Autarky and Aggression, 1933–1939*, Arnold, London, 1973

Davies, W. J. K., *German Army Handbook*, Ian Allen, London, 1973

Deighton, Len, *Blitzkrieg*, Cape, London, 1979

Deighton, Len, *Fighter*, Cape, London, 1977

Dornberg, John, *The Putsch that Failed*, Weidenfeld, London, 1982

Elephanten, *Frauen untern Hakenkreuz*, Berlin, 1983

Eyck, Erich, *A History of the Weimar Republic* (2 vols), Harvard, 1962–64

Fest, Joachim, *Hitler*, Weidenfeld, London, 1974

Fischauer, Willi, *Himmler*, Odhams, London, 1953

Gilbert, Martin, *The Final Journey, the Fate of the Jews in Nazi Europe*, Allen & Unwin, London, 1979

Goldhagen, D. J., *Hitler's Willing Executioners*, Little, Brown, 1996

Gross, Leonard, *The Last Jews in Berlin*, Sidgwick & Jackson, London, 1983

Grünberger, Richard, *A Social History of the Third Reich*, Weidenfeld, London, 1971

Hildebrand, K., *Third Reich*, Allen & Unwin, London, 1984

Hoffmann, Peter, *History of the German Resistance*, M.I.T., 1977

Höhne, Heinz, *The Order of the Death's Head*, Secker & Warburg, London, 1969

Irving, David, *The Destruction of Dresden*, Kimber, London, 1963

Irving, David, *The War Path, Hitler's Germany 1933–1945*, Michael Joseph, London, 1978

Jones, J. Sydney, *Hitler in Vienna 1907–13*, London, 1983

Kershaw, I., *Popular Opinion and Political Dissent in the Third Reich, Bavaria 1933–1945*, Clarendon, Oxford, 1983

Kirstein, Lincoln, *Art in the Third Reich*, Magazine of Art, New York, 1945

Laqueur, Walter, *The Terrible Secret*, Weidenfeld, London, 1980

Loftus, John, *The Belarus Secret*, Penguin, London, 1982

Lucas, J., *Commando*, Grafton, London, 1985

Manvell, Roger and Heinrich Fraenkel, *A History of German Cinema*, Dent, London, 1971

Mason, Herbert, *To Kill Hitler, the Attempts on the Life of Adolf Hitler*, Joseph, London, 1979

Middlebrook, Martin, *The Battle of Hamburg*, Allen Lane, London, 1980

Noakes and Pridham, *Nazism 1919–45* (3 vols), University of Exeter, 1983/4/7

Overy, R. J., *The Air War, 1939–1945*, Europa, London, 1980

Overy, R. J., *The Penguin Historical Dictionary of the Third Reich*, Penguin, London, 1996

Reitlinger, Gerald, *The Final Solution*, London, 1953

Sayer, Ian and Douglas Botting, *Nazi Gold*, Granada, London, 1984

Sereny, Gitta, *Albert Speer: His Battle with Truth*, Macmillan, 1995

Shirer, William L., *The Rise and Fall of the Third Reich*, Secker & Warburg, London, 1960

Speer, Albert, *Inside the Third Reich*, Macmillan, London, 1970

Taylor, A. J. P., *The Origins of the Second World War*, Hamish Hamilton, London, 1961

Toland, John, *Adolf Hitler*, Random House, New York, 1976

Trevor-Roper, H. R., *The Last Days of Hitler*, Macmillan, London, 1962

Tusa, Ann and John, *The Nuremberg Trial*, Macmillan, London, 1983

Wheal and Pope, *Dictionary of the Second World War*, Macmillan, London, 1995